Displaying Death
and Animating Life

ANIMAL LIVES

A series edited by Jane C. Desmond, Barbara J. King, and Kim Marra

Displaying Death and Animating Life

Human-Animal Relations in Art,
Science, and Everyday Life

JANE C. DESMOND

The University of Chicago Press   Chicago and London

JANE C. DESMOND is professor of anthropology and gender and women's studies at the University of Illinois at Urbana-Champaign.

The University of Chicago Press, Chicago 60637
The University of Chicago Press, Ltd., London
© 2016 by The University of Chicago
All rights reserved. Published 2016.
Printed in the United States of America

25 24 23 22 21 20 19 18 17 16   1 2 3 4 5

ISBN-13: 978-0-226-14405-4 (cloth)
ISBN-13: 978-0-226-14406-1 (paper)
ISBN-13: 978-0-226-37551-9 (e-book)
DOI: 10.7208/chicago/9780226375519.001.0001

Library of Congress Cataloging-in-Publication Data

Names: Desmond, Jane C., author.
Title: Displaying death and animating life : human-animal relations in art,
    science, and everyday life / Jane C. Desmond.
Other titles: Animal lives (University of Chicago. Press)
Description: Chicago ; London : The University of Chicago Press, 2016. |
    Series: Animal lives
Identifiers: LCCN 2015046019 | ISBN 9780226144054 (cloth : alk. paper) |
    ISBN 9780226144061 (pbk. : alk. paper) | ISBN 9780226375519 (e-book)
Subjects: LCSH: Human-animal relationships. | Human-animal relationships
    in mass media. | Human-animal relationships in art.
Classification: LCC QL85.D485 2016 | DDC 590—dc23 LC record available at
    http://lccn.loc.gov/2015046019

♾ This paper meets the requirements of ANSI/NISO Z39.48-1992
(Permanence of Paper).

Contents

Acknowledgments

It's always such a pleasure to write the acknowledgments section of a book. No book is written alone, whether we recognize the work of so many scholars coming before us or the community of scholars and friends who provide the context for new work and urge us on while providing the invigorating challenge of engaged critique. This book has taken nearly a decade to complete in the midst of other obligations and projects, and I have many individuals and institutions to thank for sustaining me and this set of investigations along the way.

In 1999, when I published *Staging Tourism: Bodies on Display from Waikiki to Sea World*, which compared the "cultural tourism" industry with the "animal tourism" industries in zoos and theme parks, the number of humanities scholars who were taking "human-animal" relations seriously was relatively few. It's been exciting to be in on the ground floor of this emergent scholarly community's explosive growth. Now, colleagues at all career stages and across multiple disciplines feel freer to focus on the human and nonhuman animal interface, and this once neglected and very important aspect of social organization is entering a period of intense development as increasingly, institutional structures like conferences, book series (like the one I am editing at the University of Chicago Press), and curricular changes adjust to this new arena of knowledge production.

My own work was inspired by key scholars in animal studies during this emergent period, many of whom made significant contributions in clearing a space for important, intellectual community building and foundation-setting conversations to happen. I particularly thank Nigel Rothfels, Erica Fudge, Kari Weil, Harriet Ritvo, Ralph Acampora, Susan McHugh, Barbara J. King, Kim Marra, and the many others whose names appear throughout the endnotes of this work.

My superb editor at the University of Chicago Press, Doug Mitchell, has been essential to the development of this project. He maintained a passion for these issues over a long period of time, even as they morphed into totally unanticipated realms. His abiding support, creative mind, and stimulating intellectual engagement deserve special recognition and personal thanks here. Sincere thanks also to trenchant thinkers and generous colleagues Kim Marra and Barbara J. King for joining me in starting a new Animal Lives book series at Chicago, with Doug's support. Working with Doug, Kim, and Barbara has been a terrifically exciting and pleasurable experience that always advances my thinking. Their influence is felt in these pages.

Key institutional structures also helped me move ahead with this work, even in its formative stages. At the University of Iowa, Jay Semel and the Obermann Center for Advanced Studies offered a transformative setting off campus, and support in terms of time released from teaching, for "Articulating the Animal," a faculty working group initiative that I co-convened in 2005–6 with my marvelous colleague Teresa Mangum of the English Department. Meeting every week with a small interdisciplinary group of colleagues (Ed Wasserman, Mary Trachsel, Kim Marra, and Pamela White) invigorated my belief in animal studies and shaped my thinking. An article from an art newspaper that Pam casually dropped on my desk one day gave rise to the final third of this book, about art by animals.

At the University of Illinois at Urbana-Champaign, where I moved in 2007, I was fortunate once again to receive institutional support. A faculty fellowship from the Illinois Program for Research in the Humanities brought my work on this book into the rich interdisciplinary seminar ecology led by IPRH director Diane Harris. The UIUC Center for Advanced Study, and especially associate director Masumi Iriye, were my mainstays for "Knowing Animals: Histories, Strategies, and Futures in Human-Animal Relations," a yearlong, campus-wide initiative I spearheaded in 2010–11. My graduate students in the associated seminar, "Knowing Animals," produced stimulating work that continued to move my thinking forward, and I thank them, especially the artist Maria Lux, and my assistant, Michele Hanks, now Dr. Hanks, for their passionate and challenging engagement with the issues. In addition, the UIUC supported a sabbatical in 2013–14 that enabled me to bring this manuscript to completion.

My colleagues in American Studies at Iowa and in the Departments of Anthropology and of Gender and Women's Studies at Illinois have also been supportive, even when this work was far afield from their own. I especially thank Paul Garber and Rebecca Stumpf of the UIUC Anthropology Department for guiding me in my exploration of primatology. Most recently, colleagues at the University of Illinois College of Veterinary Medicine have become important interlocutors as I continue to think about animals.

At the Oklahoma City Zoo and Botanical Garden, I thank the curatorial staff for granting me access behind the scenes and for welcoming my research so warmly. Scholars Linda Kalof, Georgina Montgomery, Julie Smith, Robert Mitchell, Una Chaudhuri, Jonathan Skinner, Helen Kopnina, Eleanora Shoreman-Ouimet, and others helped bring early versions of chapters to fruition through invitations to contribute to their innovative edited books. Graduate assistants and undergraduates at UIUC and at Iowa dug up important leads. Thanks over the years especially to Nikki Taylor, Sharon Lake, Brian Hallstoos, Danielle Rich, and Lance Larkin.

Audiences along the way—at the International Society for Anthrozoology conferences, at many wonderful animal studies conferences, and at lectures at the Clinton Institute for American Studies at University College, Dublin, the Polish Association for American Studies meetings in Lodz, the Summer School for American Studies at Orientale University in Naples, Italy, and Miami University of Ohio—all provided further stimulation in the form of probing questions. The faculty and graduate student working group at the International Forum for U.S. Studies at UIUC gave very helpful feedback on the mourning chapters.

Longtime friends Lucy Winner, Barbara Streeter, and Mary Bennett may not know how much their constancy means in a long-term project. Thank you for sending stories and clippings about animals, and for supporting my ever-changing passions. My parents, Dr. Alton Desmond and Dorothy Ann Garfield Desmond, provided a model of engagement by welcoming animals into our home and by encouraging risk taking in pursuing the exploration of new realms. One of my formative memories is of Robbie, our rescued robin, hopping down the hall on his daily rounds. Although both parents are gone now, their influence remains: from them I learned early on to see animals as "subjects" in their own right and to question received knowledge.

My deepest thanks go to Virginia Dominguez, an extraordinary scholar and thinker, and one who shares my deep passion for animals and for understanding our human relations with them. She has accompanied me literally and figuratively on this book's journey for nearly a decade, bumping along rutted roads to a country pet cemetery outside Rio, stopping at old bars in Wisconsin so I could take pictures of comedic taxidermy installations, purchasing numerous paintings produced by animal beings like Michael the gorilla, and welcoming into our home felines Mocha and Pumpernickel; parakeets Zsuzsa and Mr. Miklos, Sydney, Pesto, and Blueboy; rabbits Baylor, Chwistopher, Jasmine, and Giorgio; and Mama the dog. Each of these nonhuman animals has been an inspirational part of my life, and I thank them, as I thank my human interlocutors, for challenging my assumptions about what "animals among us" might mean for us, both as scholars and as citizens.

Earlier versions of some of the work in this book appeared as articles or chapters in the following publications. I thank the publishers for the opportunity to draw on them again in this manuscript, and I send huge thanks too to editor (and animal lover) Linda Forman for helping me tame the mix of multiple styles into one seamless whole.

"Postmortem Exhibitions: Taxidermied Animals and Plastinated Corpses in the Theaters of the Dead." *Configurations* 16 (2010): 347–77.

"Can Animals Make 'Art'? Popular and Scientific Discourses about Expressivity and Cognition in Primates." In *Experiencing Animal Minds: An Anthropology of Animal-Human Encounters*, edited by Julie A. Smith and Robert W. Mitchell, 95–110. Copyright © 2012 Columbia University Press. Reprinted with permission of the publisher.

"Animal Deaths and the Written Record of History: The Politics of Pet Obituaries." In *Making Animal Meaning*, edited by Linda Kalof and Georgina M. Montgomery, 99–112. East Lansing: Michigan State University Press, 2011.

"Requiem for Roadkill: Death and Denial on America's Roads." In *Environmental Anthropology: Future Directions*, edited by Helen Kopnina and Eleanor Shoreman-Ouimet, 46–58. New York: Routledge, 2013.

ONE

Introduction: Passionate Encounters with Animals in Everyday Life—Beyond the Mainstream

On a warm June day in 2013, I stood in a Midwestern cattle barn gently sweeping fecal material out of the lower intestinal tract of a bull. My shoes were covered in black rubber boots, something I was glad of as the pile of warm, smelly manure grew at my feet below the bull's tail. Overalls protected my clothes, and my right arm was encased in a clear plastic disposable sleeve running all the way from my hand to my shoulder. The day's activities focused on bull semen collection, and the goal of the scientific study I was observing and taking part in was to determine whether some types of chemical fly protection for the bulls were less detrimental than others in terms how the chemicals affected the bulls' ability to produce viable sperm for the insemination market. As a researcher that day, I was increasingly uncomfortable in my role of participant-observer, but I was committed to finding out more about a realm of human-animal relations I knew next to nothing about and which is a key node in farm-animal economics in the United States.

Another study, beyond the fly-repellent one, was simultaneously being conducted in the barn. This study strove to assess the degree of comfort or discomfort, physical or psychological, of the bulls involved in the semen study.

A cohort of about thirty bulls had been trained to walk into a restraint chute, where stockmen precisely, and not without care, guided their heads into the metal framework that kept them from moving very much. For several weeks, the bulls and the researchers had been participating in this study, in which artificial (electrical) stimulation was applied, via the insertion of a heavy, foot-long, torpedo-shaped "probe" into the bull's cleared-out anal tract, pulsing in gradually increasing intensities of current. Although the pulses could be manually dialed up or down, in most cases a preprogrammed cycling wave of precisely calculated electrical pulses was selected on the machine, designed to bring each bull to a semen-producing sexual climax. I kept wondering who had designed the computer program for a bull's sexual release. On what were they basing their carefully calibrated surges of electricity through what could be regarded as a giant vibrator for a giant bovine? How did they know what the bull "liked"? Responded "positively" to? Was there a precise calculation of pleasure or pain and efficiency?

As I squatted later by the side of a bull, semen-collecting cup on a stick and at the ready below his extended penis to collect the (scientifically and economically valuable) liquid before it squirted uselessly to the floor, I wondered about the scope of such "peculiar intimacies" that had brought economics, scientific research, a cultural studies scholar, and the bulls together during that five-minute cycle. How did I feel about it? How did each bull feel (about) it? Some bulls seemed to enter the chute swiftly, even with (how can we know?) what some stockmen described as a positive anticipation of this ritual, while others struggled in the chute, their massive two thousand pounds pushing against metal constraints in (either) pleasure(?) or a desire for release from a painful stimulation.

The researchers and stockmen were sensitive to the bulls, the latter guiding them with calls and whistles and an occasional light tap on the flank along a winding skein of wooden-walled pathways toward the metal holding chute. They knew each one, even if just by number, and had compiled a history of how the animal had reacted to the procedure in the past. This usually came through as a warning—"Watch out, we know he won't want to stay in the chute" or "Stand back—he tries to kick you." The research in the parallel study was precisely targeted to assess, on scoring matrices, the bull's positive or negative reactions to the semen-gathering process, reading these physical reactions.

During each procedure, one of the researchers recorded the bull's movement in the chute to assess discomfort: Was the bull craning his neck in the headlock, looking toward his tail? Lowing with low-toned groans? Did he show the whites of his eyes, lids pulled back, eyeballs bugging out? Did he fall to his front knees in the chute (a rare but not unknown reaction)? Or did he seem to stand passively, braced in the metal squeeze cage, simply rhythmically clenching his huge rump muscles in response to the throbbing waves of stimulation? These transspecies scoring systems are sign systems that, like a translator at the United Nations juggling different languages, translate human observations of animal kinesthetic and vocal productions into a grid of behaviors that can then be interpreted by humans. Specific motions, responses by the bulls to the actions of those same humans, are then read as physical and emotional indices of pain and fear.

We could say that notions of "welfare" and "science" stood side by side in the barn and were seen by most of the participants as not mutually exclusive but rather as mutually necessary. The researchers' goals were to protect the bulls from annoying and potentially disease-carrying flies (via the fly-repellent chemical embedded in tags worn in their ears like yellow plastic earrings) while minimally affecting sperm production and causing the least physical or emotional harm to each animal. Welfare was adjudicated within this set of parameters because the starting point for this event—that humans stimulate bulls to ejaculate for the insemination industry—was not under consideration; nor, within the scientific communities they were part of, was it up for debate.

For decades, artificial insemination of breeding stock has been the norm in US agriculture, and this requires, of course, collecting semen from bulls. Standing outside this norm, as neither stockman nor breeder nor animal science specialist, seeing the process for the first time as I was, decouples it from an explanatory, and ideologically naturalizing, history of husbandry. It reveals—casts into sharply etched relief—what I refer to above as the "peculiar intimacies" involved—the purposeful, scientifically controlled sexual stimulation of animals by humans for profit and propagation. Outside such breeding contexts, our laws and ethics often define such actions as "interfering," as a crime (even a crime against nature), or sometimes as animal abuse, but in the husbandry context, whether involving highly regarded dog breeders, horse breeders of multimillion-dollar stallion "covers," or the cow insemination necessary to the dairy or beef industries, these actions of stimulation are perfectly acceptable, calling on highly technical skills and training. They are not crimes. (A human parallel might be the detached, highly trained physical touch of MDs during a patient's physical exam in the hospital versus the unwanted physical touch of a stranger during an assault on the street.) This disparity is part of the complex social world of contradictions enfolding humans and animals that Erica Fudge has shown is fundamental to how humans have historically related to animals—marking some as food, some as pets, some for sport, some for hunting, some for experimentation, some as the focus of entire realms of scholarly research, and some for looking at in zoos or displaying dead, stuffed, and mounted on walls of museums.[1]

The bulls fit into the food-animal part of this matrix, and the semen collection into the economic and scientific realms. Our actions at the barn take place largely outside public discourse, within a complicated matrix of histories of animal husbandry, scientific research, farm-animal production, veterinary care, and transspecies bodily knowledge. The ambiguities, contradictions, contraindications, ethical questions, and scientific realms that collide, sometimes with a force echoing that of the power of these massive animals, haunt me. I will never forget the moment when, after scooping fecal matter out of the anal tract of one bull in preparation for the probe insertion and, as instructed, stroking with my enveloped, gloved hand the long, smooth bottom of interior muscle lining that cavity, I felt a rippling wave of those muscles contracting against my hand and forearm, the first indicators of the bull's physical response—a very peculiar intimacy indeed. At that moment, I knew that "animal studies," in terms of a scholarly community, a swell of academic investigations, must find a way to keep the bull and his response—that is, our engagement with animal lives—at the heart of our work. The epistemological and scholarly challenges of doing so are great but impossible not to engage. An "animal studies" without living animals and not, ultimately, in the service of a "better life for animals" is not one I wish to build.[2]

After the research trip to the bull farm, impossible without the generosity of other scholars conducting their own semen-based research, who welcomed me even though my own questions were so different from theirs, I thought deeply about that experience. Writing up my field notes for my files, I circled back again and again to the personal ethical line I felt I had come up against that day—toes hanging over the abyss—as a researcher conducting participant observation. Did I personally cause a particular animal pain by taking part in a procedure that might have frightened him? How would I know? What if I couldn't know?

Origins and Terminology

I do not consider my farm experience, which forms part of a separate plan of future research, any further here, but the moments of clarity about animal studies that it provided resonate throughout this book. While none of the investigations for the chapters that follow have posed similarly pointed ethical questions for me as a researcher conducting participant observation, the sites under consideration in these chapters, from museums to cemeteries, are also embedded in contradictions and offer their own challenges. Their material effects may be much more benign, but this makes these sites no less powerful in shaping and articulating human relations with, attitudes toward, ideas about, and ways of living with animals.

Throughout this book, as was the case during that never-to-be-forgotten physical experience on the bull farm, my analytical focus is not solely on visual or verbal representations of human relations with animals, although those play a large supporting role. My focus rather is on sets of social phenomena, on social practices enacted in time and space at specific locations and based on the intimate performative relations that mutually construct humans and animals through their embodied copresence. Embodied performative enactments are a key node in articulating human-animal relations, and as I repeatedly suggest, they take place in spheres far beyond the more obvious ones we might imagine.

But first, a note on terminology. Throughout this book, I use the terms *humans* and *animals*. I do this to point to the ways that conceptual divisions between human and nonhuman animals are socially constituted, mobilized in discourse, and ever present. At times, I shift to the more unifying *nonhuman animals* to underline our shared evolutionary origins and interdependence.[3] Similarly, I use the term *animal studies*, especially in this introduction, to reference an emergent set of scholarly conversations and research that explores the social, cultural, political, and epistemological relations between and among human and nonhuman animals. Other ways to reference this work include human and animal studies (or HAS), anthrozoology, and the study of human-animal relations.[4]

Composed of a series of case studies, this book is organized into three related units, each of which focuses on the interactions of humans and animals in daily life. By my own choice, these arenas fall outside the most widely distributed relations: food production and pet keeping (although I deal with relations after the death of a pet). Nor do these spheres deal with other highly visible arenas like animals in sport, fashion, transportation, staged performance, wildlife tourism, or the scientific lab. Instead, I examine spheres of daily life that have as yet received relatively little attention: selected museum exhibitions, burial and mourning practices, roadkill, and art by animals. This "ex-centricity," or movement away from the obvious centers, is by design. I believe that it is on the margins, in the less highly codified, that we often see the constitution of relations in process and can best chart change.

Each of the realms I have chosen to investigate in this book focuses on an embodied set of relationships articulated through a series of *en-actments*—viewing, posing, burying, mourning, not mourning, buy-ing, making, and displaying. I thus offer a *performative analysis*—one focused on what people do and what they say about what they do. And while animals cannot articulate their position in a similar way, I strive too to focus on when, where, and how the embodied aspects of ani-mals are brought to the fore—whether in the display of their dead body parts in a museum or in the traces of their scales, or fingers, or even thought processes that are encoded in a piece of "art." This approach unites materiality, the analysis of social processes, and the discursive generation of meaning by explicitly linking visuality, embodiment, display, and the construction of cultural and economic value. It places phenomena within a wider frame of socially generated meanings and asks: what values are being articulated by whom, and with what effects for whom (human or animal), in a certain realm of practice in daily life? In short, I work to understand how what people and animals do matters to both humans and animals.

Each case study in this book, I argue, provides a privileged site of analysis for human-animal relations. Privileged sites are especially dense, fecund, and important, and they reveal nexuses of multiple his-torical, economic, and political relations and social formations.[5] Taken together, they reveal that our lives (and those of so many animals) are significantly constituted in and through our engagements with ani-mals, living or not, and that these arenas are proliferative, radiating from the far more obvious presence of the steak on the dinner plate, the fur coat in the closet, the racehorse at the track, or the story of Babar the Elephant lurking in the bookcase. Even in our burial prac-tices and in our purchase of wall decor, we find powerful and genera-tive circumstances of interaction, and these too deserve our attention and analysis.

Over the course of the book, I move from a consideration of visual display of (largely) nonindividuated animals and humans (through taxidermy and anatomy museum displays) to mourning for animals who are known and individuated (or refusing to mourn, in the case of roadkill, for those who are not) and the marketing of intimacy through the sale of artworks made by animals, some marked merely by the visual trace of their unique bodies pressing paint on paper and others attributed the subjectivity of aesthetic choice making associated with human artists. Along this arc of discussion, I move from the anonymous to the individual and from the material to the subjective.

The eclectic content of the book and its structure reflect its genealogy and, I hope, communicate the passions on which it is constructed. This is not a book built around a single clearly delineated arc of argument, with each chapter adding another sturdy brick to the arch. Instead, it is the result of a continually morphing set of investigations that, developed over multiple years, kept changing in response to new passions. Its structure is organic, with unpredictable but generative relations among multisited parts and a whole that, I hope, cannot fully contain them.

It didn't start out this way. Just when I thought I had a structure locked down, another striking phenomenon would edge its way in and demand attention. For example, a few years ago art historian Pamela White casually dropped on my desk an article from an art publication announcing the sale of very expensive paintings by Congo the chimp at the prestigious Bonham's auction house in London. I read it with interest, my pulse quickening (always a dangerous sign). "*What* is going on here?" I asked myself (a second dangerous sign), and then I put it aside in the "interesting for future" file. It had no place in the book I was imagining. But eventually, that file took on a life of its own and demanded that I acknowledge it, that I let the passions that drove me to amass its contents take over, in the process overturning what had been a tightly imagined set of relations among preselected topics. Entirely new chapters emerged, and pet obituaries, roadkill, and animal art edged their way into this book, which, to accommodate them, had to change dramatically. I retained my earlier concerns about how humans relate to nonhuman animal bodies, but the spheres of investigation expanded exponentially.

Now, while I continue to pursue major themes and arguments, the "productive frictions" among my case studies, just like the lived arenas of action they explore, are complex and unpredictable. They don't neatly line up but instead coexist, jostle, and contravene one another, revealing in their own dynamic relationships the complexities of how these unruly multiple spheres intersect in our lives in unpredictable, productive, and, at times, incommensurate ways. Taken together, the case studies resonate with one another, drawing out our embodied relations and performative practices, and help us better understand some of the messy, contradictory, multisited, and nearly inescapable ways we engage with animals and they with us.

The Structure of the Book

This book has a tripartite structure intended to maximize the resonance of the case studies. I considered other ways of organizing the chapters, embracing the idea of productive frictions and knowing that reading across the grain would produce multiple texts for engaged readers. One option, offered by a very astute reader, was to start with the chapters about the art market for works by animals (which currently make up part 3), and then work backward from those displays to museum displays and finally the covered displays of gravesites. There is a good logic, and a pathos, to this structure. Indeed, some readers may choose to take this path through the book. But I decided ultimately to begin with museum displays, the realm most readers may find most familiar—if only through school field trips to natural history museums and their dioramas of taxidermied animals—and then to proceed to a less common mode of display of dead animals, in pet cemeteries. From this better-known terrain, I wanted to lead readers toward a consideration of an embodied component of human relations with animals that is widespread but less talked about in public discourse: the art market. This drilling down from the familiar to the less well known, and from the undifferentiated to the highly individualized, gives the book its trajectory. Although death, and the display of dead bodies, is a central focus, this is not a book about thanatology. The ultimate arc of the book curves away from the dead to end with the living, moving away from pathos and toward an expansive, provocative realm of the unknown, the communication of animal subjectivity across the species barrier through the artworks of human-language-enabled apes, like Koko.

Part 1 examines exhibits of dead animals and dead humans and contrasts the world of taxidermy with Gunther von Hagens's Body Worlds shows, stunningly popular exhibits of plastinated cadavers—in fact, the most-attended museum exhibitions of all time. I attempt to under-

stand the conditions of possibility of such displays, and the ways that
some people embrace them. "Animals,"[6] I argue, retain their skin but
are stripped of cognitive, affective, and "cultural" dimensions in these
displays, precisely the dimensions emerging in new scientific studies
of animal lives. Humans, by contrast, are stripped of skin and hence
the markers of race, ethnicity, age, and individuality. Through these
processes, both are abstracted: genericized (in the case of animals) or
universalized (in the case of humans). However, one category (the animals) has always already been genericized in the practice of taxidermy,
whereby an individual stands for an entire class of animals; whereas
for humans, history—both personal and collective—which usually attaches to bodies, must be actively excised in the move from the individual to the "universal."

Part 2 continues this focus on dead bodies but turns to the question of mourning and not mourning, ultimately framing it through
the lens of attributed individuation and subjectivity for animals. I examine how people mourn (certain animals) at pet cemeteries, where, as
in the museum exhibits described in part 1, the presence of the animal
body is essential. Even though here the body must not be seen, covered
by an expanse of well-trimmed grass, it nonetheless functions as the
anchor for physical copresence. I explore the creative mobilization and
refashioning of mourning traditions for dead humans when reoriented
toward animal lives, and research how the pet cemetery, as a marginal
space for marginal deaths, is currently being reconfigured as a creative
arena for mourning. I close that discussion with an analysis of a new
trend in the United States, whereby humans are electing to be buried
with their pets (in either human or pet cemeteries), thus articulating
through another embodied practice new contemporary conceptions of
kinship, a kinship based on mutual attribution of subjectivity.

Kinship is recrafted too in the third chapter of part 2, in which I analyze explosive debates over the inclusion of pet obituaries in contemporary newspapers and argue that such notices become assertive political acts. Closing part 2, I ask how Americans manage *not* to mourn
the millions of animals killed on US highways each year ("roadkill"). I
examine the cultural work necessary to forge this forgetting, including
both species categorization and an active refusal to attribute individual
subjectivity, and engage the work of those few artists who are directing
us to remember.

In part 3, I turn to the actions of living animals, analyzing their role
in the surprising transnational market for art *by* animals. Tracking the
importance attached to the physical trace of individual animal bodies,

from turtles to elephants, in this market, I end with a consideration of paintings by nonhuman primates. I examine how these paintings function in the intersecting beliefs about ape cognition held by primatologists and by lay art collectors, and explore implications for notions of animal subjectivity, a theme that runs throughout the book. I argue that in these paintings, the dreams and desires of some primatologists and the lay public merge, and that titled paintings by human-language-enabled apes including "bicultural" celebrities such as Koko the gorilla hint at the transcendent possibility of experiencing and mutually articulating shared worlds. This talismanic transcendence is the source of these animals' economic and symbolic value.

In each of the three parts of the book, I keep a tight focus on shared experiences of embodiment, of physical copresence, and on enactment as a way of articulating relationships in time and space. I analyze these issues in light of the historically constituted conditions that shape interpretation and our generation of meaning and hence a politics of relation while simultaneously offering opportunities for rewriting that meaning.

To do so, I reference research I conducted onsite at major museums, taxidermy conventions and workshops, pet cemeteries, a professional conference for obituary writers, a Las Vegas convention for owners of pet cemeteries, a meeting of primatologists, and a behind-the-scenes visit to a zoo's primate building. I meet Kanzi the bonobo, watch an elephant paint, attend a weeklong training session on how to enrich the lives of animals in confinement, and help prepare animal-made art for auction. To better grasp our relation with dead bodies, I visit and observe in cadaver labs for medical students taught by my colleagues. I assist in animal dissection labs—feeling the surprisingly hard oval of an unlaid egg still nestled inside a dead chicken and watching the huge roiling intestines of horses pour onto the necropsy floor. Along the way, I also conduct formal and informal interviews, and gather and analyze primary and secondary documents, including public discourse from newspapers and magazines, images and text, web discussion group postings, recordings of music played by elephants, and paintings created by "ratistes," their little paint-dipped toes running across the canvas in a rainbow of colors. Not all these research experiences make it into the book, but all inform my thinking.

In identifying and analyzing the diverse phenomena and cultural practices taken up in these chapters, I draw on frameworks and methodologies from multiple disciplines and interdisciplinary conversations that traverse and connect the humanities and social sciences. I conduct ethnographic research and textual and visual analyses, and I immerse myself in scientific, institutional, and creative worlds. My work is in conversation with, and is indebted to, several communities of scholars; chief among them are those associated with anthropology, American studies, animal studies, science and technology studies, cultural studies, gender and ethnic studies, and performance studies. Social history, art history, literary studies, sociology, museum studies, and the study of public culture intersect in the second ring of analyses.

As this list reveals, I am committed to analyzing cultural phenomena through an interdisciplinary approach that unites analyses of cultural politics and cultural practices, epistemologies, and economic and material manifestations of social formations in action. This approach requires both imaginative creativity in tracing under-recognized connections across multiple spheres of social life and restraint in doing so.

An eye to the past, and to the geopolitical frameworks of the present, requires that I take care in defining the scope of claims I make based on my research. I have tried to be careful to delineate a focus on predominantly contemporary and predominantly US-based realms of investigation. I strive to be attentive to the status of the "evidence" I draw from the written, visual, and performative records, or what performance studies scholar Diana Taylor would call the (written) "archive" of history and the embodied (performative) past of the "repertoire" known and continually repurposed in new contexts of meaning making.[7] Finally, I try to uncover the larger implications of my multisited case studies for our understandings of human and animal relations more fully, and for the further development of our field-in-formation. I hope that many of the case studies in this book resonate with readers outside the academy, but in the next section I specifically address the ways this work is situated in relationship to scholarly developments.

As two of my main interlocutory scholarly communities are animal studies and anthropology, I turn to them now and engage those relations in more detail.

Interlocutory Conversations

By "animal studies," I refer to the work of that emergent and rapidly growing group of scholars from the humanities and humanistic social sciences (like literature, history, sociology, cultural geography, and cultural anthropology) who, for the last two decades or so in the United States, Europe, Australia, and New Zealand and increasingly in some other locations, like India and South Africa, have been taking as their research focus aspects of human relations with "animals."[8] This is a multifarious field, sometimes, as I note above, also called "human and animal studies," that takes in everything from the posthumanism of Cary Wolfe and related scholars to a focus on the legal history of statutes codifying "acceptable" and "unacceptable" relations with animals; philosophical debates tracing the history of Continental philosophy in terms of ideas of animals, animality, and the lines dividing (or not) human and nonhuman animals; and works in anthropology, sociology, and art history.[9] While a full accounting of this intellectual topography is not my goal here, readers can find excellent overviews in the work of Kari Weil[10] and Margo DeMello, among others.[11]

Certainly, many scholars in various disciplines have written about human relations with animals before the contemporary juncture; just think of anthropologist Claude Lévi-Strauss's oft-quoted assertion that "animals are good to think."[12] And of course, academics in biology, ecology, physical anthropology, animal science, and veterinary medicine have long taken animals as their locus of research. But now, after twenty years of growth, we have reached critical mass in terms of a cohort of committed academics outside the more conventionally animal-centered disciplines of biology and animal science who have turned their attention to questions involving animals. These scholars in the humanities and humanistic social sciences are now asking: What do animals mean to humans, in certain times and places, and why, and how? How is the category "animal" conceived? Contested? Revised? Mobilized? How has it been used to constitute the limits of the "human"? How have notions of "animality" been deployed in philosophy or shaped the lived experiences of social hierarchies built on concepts of alterity? What are the histories of those conceptions and the politics of their continuing legacies? And how do those understandings, those matrices of meaning, rendered in literary and visual representation or the structure of scientific disciplines, religions, public policies, and philosophies, shape the lives of animals and humans? Most broadly, how do "animals" matter to humans and vice versa?

This growth has not taken place out of the blue. It represents, in part, a continuing extension of the exploration of alterity that formed the engine for a great deal of poststructuralism, and for the rise of "cultural studies" in the academy in Europe and the United States and their areas of intellectual influence, in the 1980s and 1990s. This exploration, in turn, built on the explosive politics of the late 1960s (especially 1968), which championed the rise of the everyday, worked for peace in a time of wars, and strove to overturn the hierarchies that historically placed men over women, "whites" over everyone else, and the hegemony of European colonial powers over many other populations in the world. The notion of the "other" as the limit that constitutes the "self," or the boundaries of community or state, revealed especially in studies based in linguistics and structuralism, became a primary focus of investigation.

Within this context, scholars focused on how hierarchies were embedded in philosophical and political systems, and how such hierarchies, and their material effects, might be undermined and ultimately transformed. Within these analyses of "others," the concept of "the animal" emerged and garnered increasing attention, first perhaps in terms of metaphorical deployments of "animality" in the maintenance of human hierarchies linked to colonialism and "scientific" racism, and later in terms pointing to the lives of "nonhuman animals" themselves.[13]

But the academy is part of, and not apart from, the larger world. And just as the politics of the street of 1968 framed changes in the academy and ultimately led to the "culture wars" over what ideas about whom would be taught and learned in European and US universities, recent shifts in public discourse and in scientific findings about animals have played a role in the emergence of "animal studies." Increasingly, ecological studies place humans and nonhumans in relational positions, fates mutually sealed, and newspapers announce new scientific findings like "Octopuses have consciousness—can plan ahead!" or "Monkeys can do math!" that challenge long-held beliefs.[14] At the ballot box too, citizens debate and sometimes approve proposals for fundamental changes in how animals raised for food in the United States are housed, calling, for instance, for a phasing out of tiny battery cages in commercial egg production; and here and abroad, legal boundaries are being pushed as new laws seek heightened levels of welfare protections for some taxonomic orders of animals like primates and cetaceans.[15] Even the US government has reconsidered its relation with some animals—"retiring" many chimpanzees from research labs and funding their lifetime care at sanctuaries.

This union of the history of academic change, scientific findings, and political challenges to long-standing epistemologies has prepared the fertile ground for the emergence over the last twenty-five years of new scholarship exploring the lives of animals and their lives in relation to humans. There are now, on a few college campuses, moves to institutionalize this emergent community of scholars and their work in "animal studies" as initiatives, programs, or minors.[16] In addition to some academic journals like *Humanimalia* and *Society and Animals*, an increasing number of academic presses, among them Columbia University Press, Penn State University Press, the Johns Hopkins University Press, the University of Chicago Press, and Palgrave Macmillan have now begun to offer special series of books about animals and how they live with, by, and sometimes at the behest of humans. We can anticipate continuing growth and visibility over the coming decades.

I am thrilled by this success and happy to have so many more colleagues than twenty years ago, when I first started writing about animals in the context of tourism and performance.[17] Therefore, it may seem odd to issue caveats based on this surge; but as we approach this new stage of "legitimacy" and instantiation in the academy, I am alert to two unintended consequences of that success, each of which I have attempted, to some degree, to address in this book.

The first caveat concerns interdisciplinarity, and the second the status of "animals" in our emergent animal studies. I express these succinctly in the form of two questions:

1. How can we continue to benefit from the interdisciplinary encounters that used to be a necessity and now must be sought out?
2. How can we keep "real animals," as French theorist Jacques Derrida would term them, at the heart of animal studies, as I believe we should?

Let me take up the question of interdisciplinarity first. My work is situated at multiple intersections with these ongoing discussions, each node of which has passionate interlocutors and some of which are in battle with the others, purposefully or not, for supremacy in the emergent institutionalization of animal studies in the academy. Will our humanistic studies of "animals" (as category, as concept, as historical beings, and as embodied living individuals) turn out to be most aligned with philosophical studies, with literary studies, with social history, with sociology, with anthropology? With freestanding multidisciplinary units?

In the past, say, twenty years ago, the crew of humanists working on animal-related issues was so small that by necessity we had to reach out to other disciplines and beyond the humanities–social sciences–sciences divides that shape and police knowledge production in the academy. I have benefited from this necessity, as I did when sociologists at a 2003 International Society of Anthrozoology conference in Ohio[18] asked for data with statistical information to support the more generalized assertions I was developing in a project on gender and online mourning for animals. Realizing that my cultural studies–based focus on textual analysis hadn't required me to measure, no matter how imperfectly, the cohort about which I was speaking, I went home and redesigned my study to include those critiques. The work was the better for it, more precise, and in that precision generated new questions about male mourning, which I had overlooked in my focus on the female mourners who made up the majority of online posters. I offer this remembrance not as a revelatory story, a transformative moment of a neon light bulb going on over my head, but rather as a material demonstration of the stimulating challenges that cross-disciplinary communities can supply.

The multifaceted aspect of our shared focus—animals and their relations with humans—demands work in all these humanistic and social science disciplines and academic communities, and yet the positive growth of the "field" or "field-in-formation" is, as an unintended consequence of its success, now making it possible not to have to talk across these divides to find colleagues. More and more often, we can find interlocutors right in our home department or at our national discipline-based conferences, like the MLA (Modern Language Association), AAA (American Anthropological Association), or ASA (American Sociological Association) meetings. This is a good thing, but perhaps not good enough.

As individuals, and within disciplines, we are necessarily severely limited in the range of materials and research and analytical tools we can deploy expertly. Can we expect an art historian to be fluent in the disciplinary concerns and analytical frames of, say, international agricultural economics? Can we expect a cultural anthropologist to be a master of the current literatures in biomimetic robotic design? Can we expect animal science scholars to be proficient in literary interpretation? Probably not, although a decent understanding of the key issues, methods, and stakes in another disciplinary formation can be gathered through intensive study and engagement, without claiming expertise. Even as our own cohort grows, it behooves us to remember the earlier necessity of reaching out beyond our home disciplines to find interlocutors lest we inadvertently lose the challenge that such engagements yield.[19]

As we grow in size and scope, it will be to our long-term advantage to seek out and create truly multi- and transdisciplinary arenas, not only within the humanities but also across the humanities and social sciences, and even reaching beyond to the so-called hard sciences. In crafting this set of essays, I have tried to employ multiple methodologies, drawn from both the humanities and the social sciences, and to read and engage with works by scholars situated in many different fields, from museum studies to social history and from cultural anthropology to literary studies, primatology, and medicine. While shaped by the limitations of what one scholar can do, the intention and thrust of this work are to engage the possibilities of multiple disciplines, from visual studies to rhetorical studies, from cultural studies to performance studies, from historical eras to the present—to unite the study of text, practice, history, and social formation.

Embodied Actions, Texts, Performance, and Knowing—a Note on Methods

In the chapters that follow, I focus on how we live, "perform," and "embody" some of our relations to nonhuman animals. In doing so, I have drawn on concepts from cultural anthropology about how communities and epistemologies are generated and how they exert their power in material effects. I have also drawn on cultural studies theories that work across visual and verbal textual representations to the physical experiences that constitute relations. The interrogatory two-step between social practice and the production of meaning, and our abilities to theorize the historically specific epistemological and ideological paradigms through which those meanings might be generated, questioned, and contested (their "conditions of possibility"), is laid bare in these chapters. In each case study, I draw together visual and verbal representations with my observations of what human and nonhuman animals actually do—that is, I take a performative approach.

This is not to posit action or enactment as somehow the transparently "true" rendition of belief. Feminist historian Joan Scott, in her foundational essay "The Evidence of Experience," has eloquently argued that experience is just as socially contextual in its meanings as textual productions like literature.[20] Experience may *serve* as the ground of truth claims or of access to special knowledge granted to only a few in specified contexts, or as the functional grounds of identity claims, but this *functionality* is part of a wider epistemology of social formations. Experience is always not only (somehow simply a value-free mode of) doing, feeling, or saying but also an *interpretation* of the meanings attached by particular individuals, groups, or communities to those doings, or sayings, at particular times and places.

In other words, human experience is never outside history—although—and this is crucial—it may claim to be. Experience is both constitutive of and takes its generation of meanings from history and the historical construction of subjectivity in different times and places. This doesn't diminish the importance of investigating individuals' and communities' claims to knowledge based on their experience; rather, it notes that the *meanings attributed to experience*, and even the cultural frameworks that accord to certain actions, thoughts, and feelings the designation "experience," are always already historical and politically framed as *meaningful*.

Such an approach insists that our analyses of philosophical systems not ignore their place in a historically situated social history of ideas (the very conditions that led Derrida to feel shame when his cat saw him naked) and of actions. As long as we do *not* endeavor to track the connections between ideology, institution, social formations, intellectual history, and the verbal, material, and somatic practices of daily life, we run the risk of theorizing about animals without anchoring our debates in the co-constitutive living worlds of the "human" and "nonhuman."

In this book, I strive to acknowledge the co-constitutive presence of human and nonhuman animal bodies and beings in particular times and places, recognizing the particular political and epistemological legacies that give them meaning. I want to understand how embodied relations are acted out, imagined, and articulated in select realms of passionate engagement between humans and animals. For me, some of these realms, arenas I see as particularly generative, are the social practice and business of taxidermy, mourning for animals, exploring the "art-making" potential of nonhuman animals, and considering the "peculiar intimacies" of human-directed animal sexual reproduction, which I touched on in describing my experience on the bull farm. Like most arenas of social action, these practices are shot through with contradictions. Writing a pet obituary for publication in a newspaper, for example, is for some a solemn act of mourning and for others a silly folly or a deeply offensive equation of human and animal lives, demanding public excoriation.

Unpacking those lived contradictions is part of the work of animal studies scholarship. In the chapters that follow, I find that often the crux of these contradictions depends on whether humans attribute "subjectivity" to the being(s) in question. My focus is not on adjudicating whether some beings have something we call the "capacity for subjectivity" (which some primatologists might call "theory of mind") but on tracking the emergence of this *attribution* in specific realms of daily life and charting the effects of that active attribution of individuality—of a sentient, agential life with a before and an after the current moment—to a nonhuman animal. For example, an unstated but pervasive denial of that subjectivity and individuation is a foundational structure for the von Hagens Animal Inside Out museum exhibit I analyze in part 1, but subjectivity is embraced and foregrounded in the acts of mourning for pets I discuss in part 2. In part 3, which explores the market for art by animals, the role of the individual animal is further underlined, either as bodily trace and talisman or as origin of subjective expression.

"Animals" in "Animal Studies"?

My second anxiety about potential unintended consequences of the exponential growth of animal studies has to do with the relation of our scholarly work to the lives of what Derrida has called "real" animals, as distinct from ideas about animals, in his oft-cited essay "The Animal That Therefore I Am (More to Follow)."[21]

I recognize that for anything called "animal studies," the very meaning of "animals" is and must be up for debate, as it can refer to everything from camels to viruses, manatees to humans, and cyborgs to apes or ants. Debates about the category of "animals"—who and what is and is not included in that concept, when it is used and by whom, and what that use means in terms of epistemologies, cultural practices, or public policy, are essential questions for us.

The mobilization of this act of categorization, of naming a being as "animal," arbitrary and historically generated as it is, has been a crucible through which social hierarchies and their material manifestations have been crafted for centuries. We understand now, and have since at least the rise of structuralism in the 1960s, that these conceptual and linguistic matrices for distinguishing some beings from others are arbitrary, dependent on historically contingent philosophies and cosmologies. The oft-cited example of writer Jorge Luis Borges "thinking otherwise"—in his imagined different species ordering, such as "animals belonging to the emperor and not"—reminds us to hold at arm's length the categories that function in everyday life while simultaneously noting their operations in realms from the grocery store meat counter to the Watch for Deer warning signs on the highways.[22]

New scientific revelations have introduced us to other life-forms too . . . named and categorized as "viruses" or "bacteria," for example, that eat away at the edges of the animal-human divide, as do seemingly never-ending scientific declarations of how what was once seen as a definitive line between animal and human capacities has been under-cut once again ("Reptiles have memories!" "Dog learns 1,000 words!"). Unpredicted mergings of human, animal, and machine into cyborgs or cross-species heart-valve transplantations in which pig hearts are broken to serve the needs of sclerotic humans further smudge arbitrary categorizations.

Part of our work in animal studies is thus necessarily focused on articulating and understanding the operation, and implications, of these challenges to the (historically constituted) category of "animals." We emphasize an analysis of how visual and verbal representations of animals and of the category of animality function, and debate the con-tinuing legacies of European philosophy's epistemological renderings of "the animal."

But as we see substantial growth in these academic areas, and as our intellectual community benefits from them and becomes more robust, a nagging question remains. Like a burr festering under a horse's sad-dle, it is demanding our attention ever more urgently as time goes on: what is the relation of our work to the lives of Derrida's "real" animals?

Put more directly, what is the status of (living, breathing, fart-ing, shedding, growling, purring, screeching, howling, swimming, or crawling) animals in animal studies?

Although this is a question that has arisen over conference coffee breaks and in informal e-mails, we have yet to put it squarely on our national or international agendas. This isn't an easy question to pose, because, as academics in the humanities, we are trained to immedi-ately take apart every assertion to find its gaps, fissures, opposites, and inconsistencies. Thus, a seemingly straightforward query, "What is the status of animals in animal studies?" becomes "What is (or might be, or should be) the 'status' of 'animals' (or those beings designated in some cultural frameworks as belonging to the category of 'animals') in (something emergent in the academy that is getting called) 'animal studies'?"

I believe that our multifaceted investigations must—ultimately—unite considerations of representation and interpretation, of narratol-ogy and action, of epistemology and philosophies, with material con-sequences for embodied beings.

Disciplinary affiliation doesn't determine whether "real" animals emerge in our research, or in our considerations of the long-term ef-fects of research, for representational practices aren't simply separable from other aspects of life. They help constitute those aspects and shape our understandings of them. I am not setting up a dichotomy here between, say, literary studies and history versus anthropology and sociology, or between science and technology studies and the philosophical specialty of applied ethics. Animals, "real" animals, as Derrida calls them, can appear or disappear in any discipline.

To name just a few examples, we can look to the very disparate work of cultural historian Gene Tempest writing about animals on the western front in World War I; anthropologist Alex Blanchette investigating hog farming's gendered relations; theater scholar and performer Kimberley Marra thinking through issues of social class, sexuality, and horseback riding; and literary scholar and theorist Susan McHugh analyzing stories about service dogs and blind detectives.[23] Each of these scholars produces work, whether anchored in literary texts, dusty archival records, or manual labor on a farm, that keeps our sense of (once) living, breathing, sweaty, noisy, moving animals active on the page. This work reflects a commitment on the part of researchers to help us understand and engage animal lives to the extent that our limitations as humans deploying necessarily human-centric analytical frames might allow. As these works do, we need to keep circling back, to keep animals in animal studies, to hone our understanding of the intense, complex, and often indirect relationships between representations, reception, perception, and action in the world as it affects human and animal relations.

Especially important for the articulation of these relations are the practices of everyday life, which I embrace in this book. To some extent, this work is in conversation with a new move in cultural anthropology that calls for "multispecies ethnography." While only part of this book is based on fieldwork, and none of it is based on long-term, months-long community-based immersion, its attention to what people do and what they say about what they do is consonant with the intellectual and ethical focus of ethnography, a methodology long associated with cultural anthropology.

As a discipline, anthropology has a long-standing relation with animals, crossing all four of the traditional US subfields of linguistic anthropology, archaeology, cultural anthropology, and biological anthropology, as Molly Mullin has noted.[24] Whether as totems or taboos, sustenance for much of human prehistory, or, in domesticated form, the basis for much social organization, animals populate anthropology (the study of humans) but rarely serve as the focus of our investigations. In proposing a new emphasis on "multispecies ethnography," S. Eben Kirksey and Stefan Helmreich take the nature-culture divide not only as mutually constitutive but also as a site of productive instability. In a special issue of *Cultural Anthropology*, they bring together several authors who explore human relations with nonhuman beings at ever smaller or larger scales of biological form: viruses, insect swarms, corals, and primate colonies.[25] "Multispecies ethnography," they write, "centers on how a multitude of organisms' livelihoods shape and are spread by political, economic and cultural forces" and on "where encounters between *Homo sapiens* and other beings generate mutual ecologies and coproduced niches."[26]

This work is variegated; some is anchored in science and technology studies, and some in different realms. My studies in this book, to the extent they intersect with this new anthropological work, are most in conversation with those "interspecies ethnographers" like Jake Kosek and Agustín Fuentes, who track from animal bodies and beings to humans, to larger social and political structures, and back again.

Fuentes, a primatologist, investigates human interactions with macaques in Bali, especially conflicts arising between animals and humans at heavily touristed sites.[27] He promotes what he calls a new, "revised primatological practice—an inclusive view that places humans and alloprimates [primates who are not human] in an integrated, shared, ecological, and social space."[28]

"Mutual ecologies," says Fuentes, are dynamic multidimensional spaces "that an organism lives in and creates interactively with multiple other species."[29] For Fuentes, these ecologies involve local and foreign tourists who come to see the macaques as well as religious sites, Balinese experts on the monkeys, tour guides whose income depends on the macaques being there, site managers who wish the troublesome, playful, intrusive monkeys would stay away, and of course the macaques themselves, drawn to the easy food sources of leftover ritual offerings. Drawing on methods associated with cultural anthropology, ethnography, geography, and sociology, his interdisciplinary studies strive to keep "the forces of history, political economy, inter-individual relationships, and culture clearly in view."[30]

Several aspects make this model attractive to me: the emphasis on dynamism, on change and action, on interspecies interaction (even, at times, on collaboration), and on not merely coexistence but mutually crafted behaviors. In addition, moving beyond studies that focus on individual experiences, Fuentes makes us aware of the structural formations, social histories, and political institutions that frame these possibilities. In the chapters that follow, I try to follow suit, often discussing the "conditions of possibility" for a specific phenomenon.

Jake Kosek takes a related stance in his work on the intersection of war, empire, and honeybees, concentrating on the work of the US Defense Advanced Research Project Agency and its funding of insect research.[31] To the uninitiated, this funding stream might seem nonsensical, but the military has multiple interests in insects, including understanding "swarming" as a model for potential future military techniques. This research on military funding could have been conducted solely through archival research and interviews, but it is deeply informed by Kosek's years of working with honeybees as an amateur beekeeper, observing their behaviors, noting consistencies and variations in social organization, and coming to understand how human breeding of bees has resulted not just in a "better bee" but in a bee transformed in many ways from earlier ones, including modifications of the exoskeleton and of social structures in the hive, to make the bee better for human uses. The richness of Kosek's intellectual contribution is enhanced by, and fundamentally indebted to, his understanding not only of US military research policies but also of living honeybees.

Both Kosek and Fuentes offer samples of what I think of as "multiscalar analyses," which start with and recursively double back on the lives of individual or collective animals, and animal colonies or communities, while engaging large issues of political economy. This linking of multiple scales of analysis isn't something that every scholar may want to take up, but it is something that we should, collectively, keep in the foreground of animal studies.

We must not let the figure of the metaphorical animal, the *idea* of the animal or its extended ideological deployment of "animality," be decoupled from living, or once-living, animals. This is an enormously challenging intellectual task. The mutually productive imbrications of representation, ideologies, and material effects are never linear or simply instrumental. Sometimes these lines of connection aren't obvious; they live in recursive, wandering, and surprising tetherings. Often they aren't the immediate focus of some of the questions we choose to investigate. I am certainly not arguing here that we only explore questions that directly focus on living animal beings or that have an immediate positive impact on their lives.

This would lead us to an intellectually bankrupt instrumentality that would severely constrain scholarly research, and even intellectually undercut the project, for it would prescribe where the interface between animal lives and ideologies about animals exists. Probing and extending that interface, even into the realm of the microscopic or the megascale of the swarm, are just as urgent as exploring within known boundaries. Rather, my caution here is different. I call for a long-term question to always motivate us and to haunt us collectively as we go about our work: what difference can our understanding make, and to whom? This is the ultimate intellectual stake of any scholarly work, the big "so what?"

To the extent that all knowledge production is a political act, that it is a set of investigations and resultant assertions based on a constitution of an object of study (itself a political act), in the long—or perhaps long, long—run, what we assert makes a difference in how people perceive their world and hence how they act on it. I suggest that that world we are ultimately perceiving, articulating, engaging, creating, and acting on should, for animal studies, put animal lives at its center.

The interface between the academy and the wider world is a continuous seam. Twenty years ago, this seam, as it concerned human relations with other animals, was populated mainly by biologists and animal science specialists, not literary scholars, sociologists, art historians, and cultural anthropologists. Twenty years from now, my hope is that the foundational questions that "animate" these emergent conversations in the academy about animals—how do we relate to animals and how do they relate to us, how is that very category constituted, why is it so constituted, and with what effect?—will have expanded and created innumerable intellectual niches, latching like corals on to substrate that allows them to infiltrate the concerns of, and even transform, many disciplines. I envision a continuing academic transformation, such that no student can graduate without having thought deeply about animals and our relations with them from a variety of disciplinary perspectives, from the economic to the literary, and from the anthropological to the biological.[32] This growing sophistication of a citizenry can have a long-term transformative effect. It can help us imagine and construct a world in which our relations with animals are less detrimental for them and, not coincidentally, for us as humans who share that world with them.

This is a long view, a distant horizon, and I offer what follows not as a model but rather as a set of explorations. Many of my assertions in this introduction are not ones I began with as I formulated the research for the book. In that sense, this introduction does not simply offer an interpretive frame for the chapters that follow. I share here instead a set of concerns, anxieties, and hopes reached after the long and winding road of exploring phenomena that just wouldn't let go, that surged into a book in which I once thought they had no proper place. Not every chapter focuses on living animals and our relationships with them. Many don't focus on living animals at all. But all will, I hope, help us better understand how so many, and so many unexpected, arenas of everyday life unfold in an embodied concert with animals, in linking their lives with ours.

PART ONE

Theaters of the Dead: Humans and Nonhuman Animals

Postmortem Exhibitions: Taxidermied Animals and Plastinated Corpses in the Theaters of the Dead

It isn't unusual to see dead animal bodies on display. The public display of animal remains in scientific, educational, and decorative formats has a long history and well-established conventions. Most of us have seen the taxidermied deer head on the wall as part of home decor, or the extensive dioramas of natural history museums with their hundreds of "stuffed" animals—a sort of "theater of the dead." In contrast, the display of human remains is tightly controlled and often subject to religious censure. Yet the ongoing Body Worlds exhibitions—public displays of human corpses prepared by anatomist Dr. Gunther von Hagens—have, despite initial religious condemnation by some, become the most visited touring exhibits of all time. How did this happen? What are the conditions of possibility that enabled such an event? How can a comparison of conventions governing the public display of dead human and nonhuman animals reveal our distinctive cultural attributions of subjectivity to each of these categories?

In this chapter, I compare these two phenomena—dead human and dead animal body displays—to find out which aspects of the conventions of taxidermy are carried over into von Hagens's displays and which of these modes of display are different. I suggest that even though both display dead bodies in aesthetically framed ways, the Body Worlds exhibit is not like taxidermy at all but is rather a form of "antitaxidermy." I believe that this distinction, and the conceptual and ideological framework that it activates, is the key to the exhibit's success. Analyzing this framework can illuminate how notions of human specificity, universality, and social differentiation are inscribed in or on the body, surviving even death in ways that are fundamentally different from, and revealing of, those for nonhuman animals. This analysis, in turn, helps illuminate the process of taxidermy as a distinctive mode of human relating with dead animals, one that melds uniqueness with genericism, life with death, and killing with resurrection.

Von Hagens opened his first exhibit of corpses in Japan to great success in 1995 and then moved it to his home country of Germany, to the Museum of Technology and Work in Mannheim, with the stated goal of increasing appreciation for and understanding of anatomy and bodily aesthetics. Protests against the exhibit on religious grounds erupted there, but demand for access was so great that the museum extended its hours, eventually staying open twenty-four hours a day to accommodate the huge crowds. After running in several other European countries such as the United Kingdom, Belgium, and Austria, where it appeared in both art and science museums, the Body Worlds exhibit finally reached the United States.

The show premiered in Los Angeles in 2004, where the press was almost uniformly positive. Since then, a version of Body Worlds—I, II, III, or IV, each featuring different corpses in different poses—has toured to many US cities, including Chicago, New York, Portland, Boston, Phoenix, Dallas, Milwaukee, Salt Lake City, and St. Louis. In this country, it is presented only in science museum settings, not art museums, and always draws huge crowds.[1] It has also been shown successfully in Singapore, Taiwan, Korea, Canada, and many other sites, and has even inspired several imitation exhibits. To date, more than 38 million visitors, an astounding number, have seen the exhibits in Europe, Asia, Africa, and North America.[2]

Von Hagens's human body display, although generating some controversy, is ultimately acceptable to these millions of viewers, I argue, precisely because it functions as a form of antitaxidermy. The skins that are the essence of taxidermic work on animals are absent from the human displays, which present the interiors of the bodies only. In this way, the two forms of preservation and reanimation are diametrically opposed. I suggest here that this difference isn't simply a choice about how to reveal human anatomy—namely, to show the muscles under the skin—but is, in fact, crucial in explaining how such a display of human remains became the most-viewed exhibition in history. The absence of skin facilitates a deindividuation that remains in tension with our understanding of each human body as a unique subject. This anonymity facilitates the "right to look" under the twin supports of discourses on anatomy and art. The antitaxidermy approach in Body Worlds is the key to these operations and the difference between its censure and its celebration. Taxidermy exhibits require none of the compensatory framing, as the attribution of subjectivity to the animals thus publicly displayed was rarely attributed to them during their lifetimes and therefore does not feature in their lives after death.[3]

In the sections that follow, I lay the grounds for this argument by first describing the goals and technical practices associated with taxidermy in the United States, drawing on my readings of taxidermy how-to manuals, information from commercial taxidermy-training schools, attendance at formal taxidermy competitions at the state, national, and international levels, conversations with practitioners, and analyses of historical and contemporary documents. From these sources, I assess the notion of the ideal form in the practice of taxidermy and the material status of the animal on display.

I then contrast this practice of preservation and public display with that used on human bodies in the Body Worlds exhibit, drawing on personal observations of the exhibit in both the United Kingdom and United States as well as on newspaper coverage, visitors' comment books, and other informational materials available from the Body Worlds organization. Throughout these descriptions and analyses, I trace the ontological status of organic material from once-living beings as it is discarded or kept, rearranged, reanimated, and cast as either *objective subject* or *subjective object*. Assessing the role of genericization, individuation, and skin for each type of exhibit leads me to conclude that despite some presumed similarities—after all, both are postmortem exhibits—taxidermy and plastination (explained below) are necessarily antithetical, and that plastination as an exhibit technique is deemed ethically acceptable only and precisely because of this antithetical status.

Taxidermy

The history of taxidermy is generally recorded as a narrative of technological, scientific, and aesthetic progress, with changing techniques of mounting dead animals for display resulting in ever more "realistic" and "lifelike" renditions. While the practice of preserving dead animal bodies has varied widely, both historically and geographically, the techniques we associate today with taxidermy in the United States developed during the nineteenth century. Key to this development was Henry Augustus Ward's founding, in 1862, of his Natural Science Establishment in Rochester, New York (where pioneering taxidermists Carl Akeley and William Hornaday worked), which prepared professional mounts for natural history collections.[4] Taxidermy blossomed as a profession during this period, as museums expanded from being scientific collections for research to civic institutions for public education and demanded growing numbers of mounts for their public displays. But taxidermy never became an exclusively professional endeavor, and amateur or hobbyist taxidermy coexisted with this increased professionalism and continues to do so today.

Often referred to as "stuffed animals," taxidermy specimens were originally skins filled with sawdust and straw and beaten into shape with wooden clubs. Our toys today—stuffed animals—are somewhat analogous, consisting of miniaturized versions of (fake) fur filled with a soft material. But by the mid-nineteenth century, more sophisticated methods of preserving animal specimens had developed. Straw models were covered with clay before the skins were applied, and later, hollow wooden forms were used, followed by hollow plaster-of-paris forms reinforced with wire. The latter style was hailed as a breakthrough—"unlikely ever to be improved upon"—in the early twentieth century.[5]

The development of motion pictures and the increased availability and portability of still cameras during the early twentieth century also contributed to changes in taxidermic aesthetics. Experimenters like Eadweard Muybridge, renowned for his motion-study, still-photo sequences of both humans and animals from the 1870s through the 1890s, helped change scientific knowledge of biomechanical motion.[6] No longer limited to sketches to capture live images to work from, taxidermists placed more emphasis on rendering movement and musculature in greater detail. Museum dioramas, like those in New York's Museum of Natural History, now resituated previously isolated specimens in static taxonomic displays into more dynamic environmental contexts, with implied social relations and temporal dimensions.[7] Part of the power of these displays rested, as Rachel Poliquin has argued, on the oscillation between presentation and representation—that is, the copresence for the viewer of an awareness of the "thing-ness" of the animal remains and the once-living animal they represent.[8] Killing the animal was necessary to obtain the remains, but, Poliquin suggests, this killing was motivated not by brutality but rather by longing for connection within the natural world. This longing—for wonder, beauty, spectacle, order, narrative, allegory, and/or remembrance—depended, Poliquin argues, on what she calls "visceral knowledge": a bodily knowing that occurs in contact with physical things.[9]

The dramatic diorama displays often featured these "physical things" through a presentation of family groups and staged moments of arrested action, protonarratives that implied a moment "before" and one "after" as well. In these stagings, the animals are presumed to "perform" themselves—that is, to render an accurate and authentic vision of their animality. These stagings not only index the "reality" of the animal body, through the presentation of its authentic exterior covering, but also appear to present scientific "truth" in that their posings, postures, and relationships are underwritten by the authority of the museum, its scientific staff, and prevailing beliefs about the organization of human and animal typologies. In turn, the presumed "naturalness" of "nature" could be used to underwrite ideologies of social difference and hierarchy, thus naturalizing relations that were products of historical relations, as Donna Haraway has argued.[10]

Taxidermy techniques remained relatively unchanged from the 1930s until the 1970s, when another technological change—the development of premodeled urethane body forms—strongly influenced the profession. Individual taxidermists no longer needed special sculpting skills to model clay muscles over plaster, but could now fit the skin over a premade form designed by a gifted sculptor or artisan and then mass-produced and distributed by taxidermy-supply companies. The ability to present convincing three-dimensional bodies was now democratized through mass production. As a consequence, the popularity of taxidermy not merely as a profession but as a hobby grew during this period, when practically anybody "could mount a pheasant that looked exactly right."[11] In 1972, the National Taxidermy Association was founded to disseminate the latest techniques to amateur enthusiasts and to improve the image of the taxidermist from that of the bloodstained basement hobbyist to the professional artist or craftsman.[12] The profession has continued to grow since the 1970s, and today taxidermy is displayed in museums, in sporting-goods emporiums like Cabella's, in home trophy rooms, and even in art galleries, stores, and restaurants as decor.[13]

In taxidermy manuals from the 1840s to the present, each of these technological developments is celebrated as yet another step on the road to realism, and the ultimate goal of the art has remained to create as lifelike an image as possible. Even as the criteria for realism have shifted historically, this overarching goal hasn't wavered. The only recognizable variations during this span came during the Victorian period and again during the 1930s and 1940s. During the latter period, comic scenes and humorous hybrids became popular among amateurs: rabbits playing poker and chipmunks dressed in tuxedoes joined jackalopes (jackrabbit bodies with antelope horns) in home installations and barroom decor.[14] And even in these humorous pieces, the "realism" of the animal body—its skin and the re-created three-dimensionality— is crucial to the humor that results from the incommensurability between the body (a rabbit) and the action (playing poker).

That these products were necessarily and intentionally comedic highlights the fear that underlies taxidermy: the fear of specimens failing to appear lifelike enough. Unintentionally "bad" taxidermy is either grotesque or laughable; a poorly rendered fiction is lifeless, pointing to the fact of death and failed resurrection. It references the act of killing, the unspeakable ground that cannot be enunciated without deconstructing the foundational fiction of taxidermy's equation.[15]

Besides these comic pieces, a second arena of antirealism, or antinaturalism, can be found in the contemporary arts world, where visual, conceptual, and installation artists, like Annette Messager and Mark Dion and Damian Hirst, are increasingly integrating taxidermy into their work. For example, the work of the group Rogue Taxidermists uses taxidermic techniques in the service of critical commentary and creative innovation. Their work features precisely those things forbidden in professional taxidermy competitions: blood and guts and creatures created out of multispecies parts—the body of a cat adorned with the wings of a bird, or a raven eviscerating a squirrel, with entrails trailing from its beak. The unexpected horror or intriguing polysemy associated with these bodies on display is directed toward an art world and its participants. These pieces foreground the work of representational praxis through an explicit rejection of conventions of naturalism and, through this self-reflexive rhetorical structure, address a narrower, more elite viewing public. This type of powerful work is generally excluded from professional taxidermy competitions, natural history museums, and other commercial settings, where conventions of realism obtain. Although recently it has generated a significant amount of commentary by cultural studies and art history scholars, building on Steve Baker's concept of "botched" taxidermy,[16] this approach remains a tiny part of the contemporary production of taxidermic works;

as taxidermy "out of place" or disassociated from standardized criteria for realism, it is not the focus of my discussions here.[17]

The illusion of realism in taxidermy, as I have argued elsewhere, depends on a fundamentally ironic epistemological structure:[18] death is the absolute and always indispensable prerequisite to the process of creating lifelikeness. For the fiction of realism to work, though, this fact (the necessary killing that precedes the fictional resurrection) must be so masked that it doesn't interrupt the viewing pleasure. The relationship between viewer and object is fundamentally theatrical. This is clearest, of course, for the natural history museumgoer, who peers into a lighted proscenium-like diorama whose theatrical subjects cannot return the spectator's gaze. But the theatricality exceeds this literal parallel; it extends also, I suggest, to the looking relations in a trophy room or at a sporting-goods store's taxidermy display.

The "as-if-ness" of the looking relations, the invitation to imagine as alive that which patently is not, creates for a moment an imaginary relationship of "being there"—for instance, in front of a living, about-to-charge bear. The ideal viewer completes the imaginary act of resurrection that taxidermy invites; the depicted moment is like an excerpt from a play, a fictional (yet naturalistic and naturalized) narrative based in and on dominant tropes of human-animal relations. This fictional act of resurrection is also part of taxidermy's appeal to its practitioners. One young taxidermist at the Iowa state competitions remarked to me that what he really enjoys about it is "taking a *dead, bloody* bird with shattered leg bones, breaking it down, and building it back up to something beautiful."[19]

To avoid calling attention to the required killing that precedes the taxidermic state, all marks of the cause of death such as bullet holes and arrow incisions must be hidden through meticulous stitching of the hide. With the cause of death excised from the visual equation, so also is the presence of the human who precipitated it. The resulting museum dioramas seem to restore the Edenic state before or outside human presence. In the mounting of hunting trophies, like the deer head on the wall as home decor, the equation is of course slightly different; in this environment, although the lifelikeness of the animal is still required, the very presence of its body serves as mute and silenced testament to the power and prowess of the hunter, indirectly invoking both the cause and the moment of death. The more magnificent the animal, the more lifelike its pose, the greater, supposedly, is the power that reduced it from living being to lifelike rendering of itself.

Paired with these structuring ironies of realism is another that materially parallels the conceptual and perceptual moves just described. To be presented as "lifelike" and whole, the animal body must first be totally disarticulated and then reconstructed. With a turkey, for example, it is not just a matter of draping a skin of feathers over a polyurethane form; the original head must be cut off and replaced with one that has been hand painted and freeze-dried, and the tail must be detached so that the feathers may be spread into a glorious fan shape and stuck on again with pins sunk into the foam form; the wings are shaped with wire, the feet detached (for reattachment later in the desired strutting position), and the organs and entrails totally eviscerated and, along with the skeleton, discarded. Only the skin is left intact.[20]

For as the word *taxidermy* tells us, the dermis (or skin) is all-important. This outer covering is the only component of a taxidermic specimen that cannot be fake; glass eyes and plastic tongues, noses, and even feet are acceptable and easily available from taxidermy-supply companies. But the actual skin, with its covering of fur, hair, or feathers, is the absolute prerequisite for taxidermy. An animal rendition without the skin is not taxidermy; it is, instead, termed a "re-creation" in taxidermy competitions and is by far a marginal category. The skin defines the animal and demands of the taxidermist a commitment to its particularity and uniqueness, for professional standards require that the body mold always be tailored to fit the specific skin, not the other way around.[21] The skin provides an outer, touchable "realness" to the eye and hand; it authenticates the mount, which vacillates in status among trophy, ideal, and specimen and makes it at once unique (*this* deer) and representative (*a* deer).

The outer condition of the skin is very important, and tacit conventions require a clean, well-groomed animal. Obviously, no traces of blood from the killing can remain, but even more, no mount is ever shown with muddy hide, flyspecked ear, spots of mange, or tatty feathers. As I overheard one taxidermist remark upon seeing a scruffy white turkey in a viewing pen at a taxidermy convention: "Try mounting one that looks like that and entering it in a competition!"[22] Taxidermists use many techniques to groom the animal: shampoo degreases fur, hair dryers fluff feathers, and careful combing guides hairs into place, replacing the animal's own grooming techniques with human ones now applied cross-species.[23]

As these techniques demonstrate, each individual mount becomes, if not a representative of an "ideal type" (tiger, duck, deer, et cetera), at least an idealized version of an individual. Like a teenager dressed for the prom, each animal is presented at its best—a denaturalized vision of nature, with all its mud, tangled feathers, and ratty fur. While bestowing an award at the 2005 Iowa state taxidermy competition in Des Moines, one judge commented that the winning specimen "looks nice—better than he did alive."[24] But even allowing for individual variation, there are limits. No animal can appear sickly, starved, disabled, maimed, or decrepit. If not an outstanding specimen (for instance, for predators, large, well-muscled, and vigorous), it must be at least "average," and the range of polyurethane forms available for purchase reflects this size variety. While old, crippled animals are unwelcome (marking one of the limits to realism), there seems to be no age limit on the young. Taxidermic compositions often include juveniles, even tiny, newly born specimens: a duck with her fuzzy ducklings or a mouse with her tiny, hairless, pink babies all "sleeping" in a pile. In these cases especially, the awareness of the killing that had to occur for the scene to be staged must be kept at bay, or the "ooohhh" factor—the sighing over the cuteness of the babies and the endorsement of protective motherhood that it recalls—cannot be sustained.

The other part of the word, *taxi*, is important also. In biology, *taxis* refers to the movement of an organism in a particular direction, and in surgery it refers to manipulation without cutting.[25] Taxidermists I have spoken with commonly use *taxi* as a verb—they taxi the skin into place over an adhesive-covered body form, adjusting it this way and that for a perfect fit. All these uses call our attention to the way in which "lifelike" is code for "capable of motion." Animals, like humans, can move of their own volition, and the lifelike pose, while itself necessarily static, must read as arrested motion or potential motion. Taxidermy-training workshops stress that the outer realism of the skin and "correct" shape of the form must combine with a credible rendering of biomechanics. The expert taxidermist will calculate the effect of a curving neck on a leap and will shorten the stride to maintain a believable sense of momentum. Each part of the body will be visually and kinesthetically balanced against the others. The final construction of habitat—using real or fake rocks, hillocks, grasses—must complete the illusion so that the points of impact of hoof on terrain are perfectly matched to the body's balance.[26]

This creation of the illusion of movement is a form of choreography of the dead to simulate life. The expert taxidermist must design each body position by cutting, gluing, reassembling, and then sculpting ready-made polyurethane forms—which come in only a limited repertoire of postures and poses for each species—into the particular movement desired. I observed master taxidermist Jason Snowberger at the 2005 World Taxidermy Championships demonstrating techniques for this redesign of body and pose. Taking a chainsaw to a precast foam form of a bighorn sheep, Snowberger sliced the torso into three vertical sections. Fanning the sections like an accordion, he repositioned the parts to depict the animal twisting to its left. Using Bondo (an expanding foam), he filled in the cracks and held the parts together with huge drywall screws to let the form dry. Next, a back leg was sliced off and rotated in an imagined arc of movement until the correct stopping point was reached. It also was then reattached, and the foam area between the back tendon and calf muscle was carefully thinned out with a knife. Tendons thin out when they are stretched, so when the ankle was extended as if to push off for a jump, stretching the tendon, the corresponding space had to be hollowed out on the form. This level of detail in craftsmanship, combined with biomechanical knowledge and the ability to choreograph convincing movement, is prerequisite to achieving the goal of lifelike renditions. (As we shall see below, the Body Worlds exhibit's displays of motion aren't biomechanically sound, precisely because they are intended to reveal exposed muscles rather than create the illusion of bodily integrity that taxidermy emphasizes in its whole-body mounts.)

Through this choreography, the taxidermist can stage physical relationships to imply psychological ones. For example, in a multianimal setting, the widened eyes and shrinking pose of a frightened ram will contrast with the extended leap and open-mouthed, flared-nostriled snarl of an attacking wolf, whose gaze is riveted on its prey. According to master taxidermist Marcus Zimmerman, these details, such as the widening of the nasal passage on the wolf, are important to what he terms the "story you are trying to tell."[27]

Selected moments of heightened emotional tension are among the most popular representations, revealing "stories"—such as the dramatic moment of encounter between predator and prey, and the maternal relationship of a female caring for her babies—that parallel some of the most popular subjects of nature films. Matings, however, are excised from the repertoire of possible choreographies. While it may be permissible viewing in two-dimensional film documentaries, the three-dimensional presentation and memorialization of the moment of coitus is apparently tacitly forbidden, for I have never seen such a representation in either instruction manuals, taxidermy publications, or public displays. Realism, as a concept with a politics and an aesthetics though never a "fact," has definite ideological limits, as these absences reveal.

Taxidermy presents specimens performing specific behaviors from a limited repertoire of approved activities. The representation of these behaviors (leaping, eating, fighting) not only displays that which is valued but also animates the figure—it gives it something to do. For instance, few animals are posed sleeping. Even small fish seem to have active, exciting lives: nowadays, mounts often depict a fish diving through reeds, navigating acrylic currents, or attacking a frog. While dioramas and multianimal displays represent relationships and ecological context, the primary goal remains to show the (dermis of) the body itself, not to reveal extensive documentation about behaviors. When such information is added, as in museum settings, it is usually via written text.

This representation of activity and interaction, including predation, allows taxidermic scenes to do what zoos cannot: make activity visible on demand and without risk (the price of life has already been paid) to the animal, the audience, or the institution that owns it. Zoo designs have grappled with the problem of what to show and thus what people can see: many animals spend a great deal of their time sleeping, which isn't kinesthetically intriguing, and mixed-species habitats cannot include those predators and prey who would normally live within the same ecosystem.[28] Taxidermic scenes extract, value, and validate key experiences of animal life and freeze them forever for our contemplation, a privileged form of vision usually unavailable in the wild. We gain a sense of physical closeness and, through it, perhaps a notion of psychological connection made possible only because the animal is dead. Its death, and the domination implied, is the price of our pleasure in physical proximity and the imagined connection that such closeness indexes. But even though this moment is preserved or created, it is the palpable, three-dimensional, bodily presence that dominates, emphasizing spectacle over narration. The more invisible the technologies that make this preservation and presentation possible, the more spectacular the spectacle.

The World Taxidermy Championships

The current professional standards of realism, authenticity, and morally appropriate relations to a natural world are assertively articulated and discussed at the World Taxidermy Championships, held every two years since 1983. Part competition, part continuing-education seminars, these events attract the most highly regarded professional taxidermists in the world and those who would learn from them. I attended the 2005 championship, held in Springfield, Illinois, during three days in March. Since its inception, although the parameters of the competition have remained the same, the roster of participants has continued to grow, approaching five hundred entrants in May of 2015, when the competition was held in Springfield, Missouri.[29] Analyzing the competitive categories and their criteria, the judging practice, the presence and absence of certain types of taxidermy, and the winning entries gives a striking picture of the field as it defines itself. The winners and judges assert a strong authority in the field; their techniques and compositions are featured in taxidermy magazines, showcased at sporting-goods stores, and imitated by less-skilled practitioners.

Highly regulated, the World Taxidermy Championships feature multiple divisions (master, professional, novice, youth) and are open to everyone. To emphasize skill over reputation, each entry is submitted anonymously, the entrant's name being revealed only after awards have been given. Each division has its own subcategories and judging criteria; for example, the masters' division—the most competitive and most rigorously judged—offers sixteen world titles, broken into categories such as medium-small mammals, large mammals, whitetail deer heads, medium-small game heads, large game heads, game birds, nongame birds, turkeys, warm-water fish, cold-water fish, and reptiles, amphibians, and others.[30] Within each category are several subcategories. For example, the turkey competition has four subcategories, each judged separately: strutting, open wings, standing, and turkeys in a group. The whitetail deer heads compete in four listed subcategories based on hide and mouth: long/thick hair with open mouth, long/thick hair with closed mouth, short/thin hair with open mouth, and short/thin hair with closed mouth. This degree of elaboration reveals both the standardization of the field and the notion that each species represents its own specific technical and artistic challenges. While it is hard to imagine that a lowly mouse could beat out a charging bear for the coveted Best in Show award, it is technically possible, given a theoretical equality accorded to all animals in all categories.

The rules for entry in the competition prohibit contravening accepted taxidermy methods or exhibiting items displaying what is termed "poor taste." The latter comprise nonrealistic portrayals or "novelty mounts," like the poker-playing rabbits popular during the 1940s or hybrid bodies, as well as domestic dogs and cats and animals in traps.[31] The simple rubric of "taste" thus reveals the conceptual margins of what is valued: realism in dermis, choreography, and habitat are required. The domestic realm is forbidden; taxidermy, whether of a tiger or a tarantula, should reference the "wild," and the act of killing must be absent from the representations. When killing is allowed, it must be the result of one animal acting on another (for instance, a fox posed with a rabbit in its mouth is permissible and even common), but not of a human killing an animal or being killed.[32] The one arena of exception to the categorical exclusion of the domestic and the domesticated is the barnyard, as the occasional duckling might be shown. Pets are unequivocally excluded, despite highly successful freeze-drying techniques available for pet preservation that are hawked by vendors at some of these shows.[33]

The judging is meticulous, with each judge carefully examining and evaluating multiple aspects of every mount: the positioning of the ears, the craftsmanship of the invisible sewing of the hide, the realism of the pose. Novices and masters alike are judged, though in different categories, and numerical scores are assigned, with the highest scorers in each category awarded blue ribbons. Each entrant receives written score sheets with marks for different aspects of the work: nose, eyes, habitat, and so on.[34] Judges inspect each mount in intimate detail, grading the invisible as well as the visible aspects of the craftsmanship. They peer into nostrils with tiny flashlights, looking for premade septa, which lower a score. Nictitating membranes of the eyes are inspected carefully for placement; tear-duct depth is analyzed: too little and the eye doesn't look functional, too much and it looks exaggerated. Even the pores on the nose are important. Judges comment on the "stippling" on deer noses, for example, and entrants must achieve just the right depth and closeness of these small indentations on the black surface to make even the nose "come alive." The obsessive level of detail borders on fetishism—a fetishism of currently accepted criteria of realism in representation, right down to the pores on the nose.

About two-thirds of the judging criteria are concerned with craftsmanship and mechanical soundness (no wobbly mounts are allowed) and with anatomical accuracy.[35] The final third concern artistic merit. The criteria for the highly regarded Carl Akeley Award, which "best represents that taxidermy is indeed a valid form of wildlife art," spell out what this means. Winning entries should demonstrate an extremely high skill level while portraying the subject "with taste and dignity" and anatomical accuracy. But in addition, "the entry itself should be a work of art, and as such be a three-dimensional, artistic composition which could be judged alone for visual balance, color coordination, line, shape, form and artistic appeal." Moreover, the rendering must be original, not a copy of someone else's idea. It should tell a story so that the composition reinforces the concept behind the objects, thus successfully rendering the artist's intent.[36]

In 2005, the entry awarded the most points demonstrated these criteria. The "Judges Choice: Best of Show" and "Best in the World Small Mammal" winner was "Whitetail Fawn" by Tommy Hall. In this piece, a tiny fawn, its dappled, dun-colored fur soft as velvet, balances on too-long legs. It has turned quickly to spy a sinuous, green garter snake. Dainty grasses and ferns embrace delicate hooves, and a tucked tail and pricked-up ears indicate attention on the brink of concern. A full twist in the neck animates the pose, and the forward momentum of the high hips is barely checked by the pull-up of a front leg. With not a hair out of place, the fawn radiates youthful health combined with worldly inexperience.

Discourses of success, as the Akeley criteria demonstrate, hover between discussions of artistic merit and technical skill or craft, and these two discourses validate the taxidermic practice. The 2015 Best in Show winner featured two ring-necked pheasants locked together in an embrace of aerial combat. Talons grasping, feathers splayed, their jewel-toned bodies expertly supported by fine wires, they appeared to tumble freely through the air, suspended forever in a heightened moment of a life-and-death narrative. While biomechanical and behavioral accuracy is valued, few educational claims are made (they surface when taxidermy is displayed in a museum context). Within the field, it is this challenge of melding craft and artistry that dominates and that seems to appeal to the mostly male, mostly middle-aged, and mostly white, rural or small-town, middle- to lower-middle-class participants. Taxidermy may be one of the few forms of artistic expression deemed appropriate among this group of men.[37] There is some evidence, though, that the demographics of highly skilled practitioners are changing. In the last fifteen years or so, increasing numbers of women and of urban dwellers are entering the world competitions.[38]

Taxidermy does not draw protests, and in my fieldwork I have heard no one involved in the practice speak of the need to defend it. Some spoken and journalistic references to PETA (People for the Ethical Treatment of Animals) and animal-welfare organizations like the Humane Society of the United States acknowledge that these groups do not support the hunting that is the basis of so much taxidermy.[39] The 2005 championships I attended, with their displays of hundreds of dead animals, drew only positive media coverage, and this trend has continued to the present.[40] Hundreds of participants and spectators crowded the 2005 exhibition gallery after the judging was completed, and documented what they saw with photographs. Careful inspection and fulsome appreciation marked the audience's behavior. Throughout the event, the status of the animals themselves was secondary. While the startling size of a bull moose might draw comments and the roly-poly antics of a raccoon's pose generate smiles, the animals here weren't noteworthy for their individuality, even though good taxidermy demands faithfulness to the original map of the body—the skin; rather, each individual became a specimen of its type (for instance, a short-haired, open-mouthed deer) and a tribute to the skill of its animator, the taxidermist, or evidence of his or her incompetence. In a room crowded with animals, the animals themselves—as once-living, once-sentient individual beings—almost disappeared.

The roles of individuation and genericization in taxidermy differ from those in the human anatomical exhibits of von Hagens, partly because of the wider ideological matrix imparting differential value to the lives of humans and animals. A comparison of the two display techniques reveals these ontologies in action as well as their limits. For taxidermists working in the realistic mode, an anatomically correct and "honest" rendering of a specific animal is crucial, which is underscored by their reliance on photographs and measurements of just-killed animals as guides.[41] The ethics of professional taxidermy require that the taxidermist not "cheat" by stretching the skin over too large a polyurethane frame to make it look more ferocious;[42] nor is it in "good taste" to mix body parts from different species, except in purposefully humorous mounts. The blood, guts, and gore of the kill and the evisceration must be completely removed from the picture.

But despite this emphasis on the uniqueness of each individual body as the map for the taxidermist working on that mount, there is little sense of that creature's individuation. The individual animal (*the* deer) slips into the generic category (*a* deer), while the taxidermist seeks to represent an ideal (a *good* deer specimen). With the remains rendered available to our eyes and even to our touch, we come face to face with an individual mount that represents an entire category of being, which we might otherwise never come close to.

Taxidermy facilitates, heightens, and frames our acts of looking, but it doesn't generate a "right to look." The right to look is already a given, because the intimacy of looking at animals isn't regarded as intrusive to the animal, dead or alive. The situation is quite different with the display of human remains. There, the function of individuation and the intimacy of looking are structured differently and based on a notion that the "specimens" are (or were) the same as the viewers. The sense of a contemporary, shared human community and anatomical sameness means that this right to look and ideas of reanimation have to be carefully handled to be ethically acceptable within specific cultural contexts.[43]

Displaying Dead Humans: Discourses of "Art" and "Anatomy"

As the preceding discussion of taxidermy makes clear, it isn't unusual to see dead animals. Even outside museums, sporting-goods stores, art galleries, and family-room trophy displays, we often encounter them. Driving down the road, especially in rural areas, roadkill—the corpses of raccoons, opossums, deer, rabbits—lie bloated by the side of the road, rotting where they landed after being struck by a car. And of course, the most obvious place we see them is in the meat department of any grocery store or in a butcher shop, where, depending on cultural convention, the whole duck or rabbit may be hung upside down in the front window or its dismembered parts packaged in sanitary cellophane and placed in refrigerated display cases. It is only in the special case of pets, whose status lies in between property and family member, or of celebrities like Keiko the whale that we are reflective about animal death. But mostly, we regard it passively, unremarked upon and unremarkable.

In contrast, it is very unusual to see dead humans. Only in times of extreme social upheaval, such as war, might corpses lie on the side of a road. And only within the tight strictures of mourning conventions might some corpses be displayed in full view (in an open casket) in a funeral parlor or venerated in a church, as is the custom with the display of saints' bodies or their partial remnants in reliquaries in some parts of Europe. Otherwise, for most populations in the contemporary United States at least, viewing the dead is usually limited to family and friends in addition to the staffs of hospitals, nursing homes, funeral homes, and morgues, sites that are either private or with limited access dependent on professional expertise. At other times when the living and the dead are present together, such as at a funeral, the dead are covered, hidden from view by a casket and by the earth, grass, and flowers of a cemetery plot.

What happens when this privateness goes public, when the public display of dead bodies, usually reserved for animals, is accorded to humans? There have been some precedents for this—apart from times of war or terror—both in the display of entire bodies and, more commonly, in the display of body parts. The United States has a long history of the—increasingly contested—museological display of Native American skeletons.[44] In other instances we see the sacred display of scapulae, or bones, of saints in churches and ossuaries like the massive catacombs in Paris, built in 1810 to solve the problem of overflowing cemeteries. This remarkable underground burial site, which I visited in 2001, houses tens of thousands of skeleton pieces, neatly stacked in decorative patterns that you can now stroll past on 1.6 kilometers of pathways. Moreover, anatomical museums to this day still display the odd, the grotesque, and the poignant. Visitors to the National Museum of Health and Medicine in Washington, DC, can gaze on severed ele-phantine legs, an esophagus with dentures still lodged in it, and thigh-bones shattered by a still-embedded bullet. Much rarer are the displays of long-embalmed entire corpses, such as Vladimir Lenin's. Thanks to the development of a secret embalming technique, Lenin still lies in state in his own tomb in Moscow's Red Square, more than ninety years after his death in 1924. When I visited in 2001, his pale, flac-cid body, dressed in a dark-blue suit and covered with a blanket rising to his chest, seemed to float on its bed under dim, milky light in his mausoleum.[45]

Although Lenin had his own team of on-call embalmers to attend to the upkeep of his corpse (a luxury curtailed by budget cuts in 1991), oc-casionally the unfamous also get the super-embalming treatment, such as Charles Henry "Speedy" Atkins. Speedy, an African American man embalmed using a secret technique developed by funeral home direc-tor A. Z. Hamock, resided in a closet for sixty-six years after his death, occasionally being brought out for tourists, until he was finally buried as a celebrity in 1994.[46]

Body Worlds: The Anatomical Exhibition of Real Human Bodies

But Lenin and Speedy Atkins are obviously exceptions that prove the rule. Even though successful long-term preservation techniques exist, displaying preserved dead humans in public is a nearly unthinkable aberration of convention. I suggest here that to avoid censure, a spe-cial set of circumstances must be brought to bear on any contemporary public exhibit of human bodies, and that these include an active invo-cation of powerful legitimizing discourses on art and anatomy as well as a display strategy that replaces individualism with universalism, ac-complished through an antitaxidermic preservation strategy.

Gunther von Hagens has contravened the conventions prohibiting full-body display of the ordinary dead and done so in a big way. His ongoing controversial display of human corpses and assorted human body parts in his Korperwelten, or Body Worlds: The Anatomical Exhibition of Real Human Bodies, exhibit has attracted more than 27 million visitors since its opening in Japan in 1995,[47] making it one of the most popular touring exhibitions in history.[48] After Japan, where it drew 2.8 million visitors, the show toured to Germany, Austria, Switzerland, Belgium, the United Kingdom, and South Korea. I saw this show in London in October 2002 and never actually thought it would make it into the United States because of its potential to incite religious protests, but it did. It finally opened in July 2004 at the California Science Center in Los Angeles, where in its first three weeks, 35,000 visitors paid $12 each to see the exhibit.[49] Newspaper reviews described audiences as being of "all ages and all races," and the exhibit continues to be widely and wildly popular throughout the United States, drawing only mild criticism.[50] US visitor rates pale in comparison with those in Japan, however, where more than 400,000 people saw the exhibit in its first two months.[51]

Before I describe the exhibit, I must summarize the technical process that makes it all possible: *plastination*. Originally developed by von Hagens and embraced by medical schools as an anatomy teaching tool, plastination replaces bodily fluids (which constitute roughly 65% of human body weight) with acetone through diffusion. The natural fluids are drained from the body, and a vacuum technology impregnates the body's cells with the acetone in a pressure chamber. Unlike formaldehyde preparations of cadavers, which leave the bodily material a dull, waterlogged gray with little sense of life, the plastinated bodies retain a muscular tautness and emerge with a pinkish tint to the muscles and organs, almost as if the tissue were still living though somehow hardened and dry.

Depending on the plastic used, "specimens" (von Hagens's term) can be rigid or pliable. The silicone-infused body must then be formed into a predesigned pose. Using fine needles and pieces of Styrofoam, the dissector positions each organ, tendon, and muscle for maximum visual access before the specimen hardens into its final shape—muscles, sliced from their attachments, are arranged to fan out from the bone; a brain is propped up so it emerges from its skull; a cavity in the torso swings open like a drawer to reveal the organs packed inside. This is a highly technical, expensive form of handicraft produced by experts, with each whole-body specimen requiring up to fifteen hundred hours, usually over eight to twelve months, to prepare. The average cost is

$35,000 to $45,000 per body.[52] Because the fluids that cause decomposition are removed, von Hagens estimates that these clean, dry, rigid, and antiseptic specimens could last a hundred years.

The Body Worlds I exhibit consists of several body parts and twenty-five full-body plastinated specimens, or "plastinates."[53] When I first saw the show in London, it was at a makeshift art-gallery space. The visitor encountered the body parts first—organs, a skeleton, cross sections of a lung—before ascending stairs to a second, larger room, where full-body plastinates were presented. Each body had its own area, set off by a decorative architectural arch though directly exposed to the viewer, with no casement intervening. Potted plants were interspersed to soften the stark white-painted brick walls of this former warehouse turned artsy hi-tech gallery space. Whatever the venue, the specimens' accompanying text is minimal, simply giving the title of each plastinate as if it were an art piece: "The Runner," "The Chess Player," "The Fencer," "The Pole Vaulter," "The Ballerina," with bodies positioned accordingly and with occasional props. "The Chess Player," for example, sits bent over a Lucite table while pondering a chessboard; his back is splayed open so that we can see the various layers of muscles, all the way down to the spine.

Another section of the exhibit features more body parts, these in pairs that give a didactic "healthy living" message, showing the difference between cancerous and healthy tissue—a smoker's lung and a nonsmoker's, for instance. The wall of this section is decorated with blowups of medieval and Renaissance anatomy prints and dissection illustrations, thereby anchoring the exhibit in the past's melding of art and anatomy and consequently claiming the legitimizing power of historical antecedents. The final section, set off from the earlier displays so that parents can divert their children if necessary, contains exhibits of developing fetuses at different stages and one of only two female bodies on display: a full body of a reclining pregnant woman, torso split open from chest to belly to reveal a seven-month-old fetus.

One of the most interesting aspects of this entire exhibit is the broader sense not of a taboo being broken but of the ontological status of the "exhibit" itself—the precise opposite of the taxidermic processes analyzed above. In taxidermy, the skin is all that is kept (perhaps along with hooves and antlers); the bones, muscles, brain, soft tissue, eyes, and entrails are all discarded and replaced by an armature or foam form. Above all, the perfect-fit draping of the skin or fur over the form is crucial. Motion is implied through the placement of limbs, lift of the neck, flaring of nostrils, and so on. The goal is to convince the

45

viewer that the specimen is as lifelike as possible—that it could, with the magical jolt of a "code blue," be sparked back to life and continue its leap right out the door.

Von Hagens's display is dramatically different. In the vast majority of cases, the skin—all that is left in taxidermy—is completely missing,[54] and of course along with it goes markers of skin color and thus the potential for racialized interpretations by lay audiences. These bodies, their faces stripped away, are literally genericized at the same time that they are explicitly unique (for instance, a real body, a real person who chose to donate her or his body—no mixing of body parts from one person to another to make a third). The plastination process itself also literally strips away distinctiveness by stripping away fleshiness—not just skin but fat and soft tissue as well; no bulging paunches or sagging chins, wrinkled necks, or saddlebag hips here. Age becomes relatively indeterminate; all bodies appear lean and muscular, though some are more muscular than others, and clean, nearly machinelike in their demonstration of the body's efficient design, showing all that is necessary and nothing that isn't.

The tension between the uniqueness of each real person or body (person's body) and the stripping away of nearly all identity markers except those of sexual difference—that is, the markers of the history of that individual's life—is one of the foundational structures of the show. It both galvanizes and facilitates our viewing pleasures. The realness is the lure, and the anonymity gives us the right to view another human being's three-dimensional body in a way that we can usually indulge in only during intimate moments, pornographic shows, or medical situations. Yet here, such a peering at bones, muscles, and orifices is condoned, among strangers, in public. This unique opportunity depends on the *authenticity* of the bodies and the viewing permission granted through the forum of an exhibit.

Although occasionally a bit of lip or hair or skin remains on a full-body plastinated specimen, all other social information—including name, occupation, place of residence, religion, age, nationality, moral or political views, and past activities—is erased or left to the visitor's imagination. How dramatically different it would have been to have each body posed next to a photo of the deceased. How much more noticeable might have been the tension between specific individual and generic specimen, a tension significantly more muted in taxidermy because of the "wild" animal's status as always already more generic than individual.

At the root of the Body Worlds exhibit's appeal and its controversial nature is the issue of authenticity. The grand attraction of the show is that these are real bodies, not anatomical models. The exhibit's sub-title—The Anatomical Exhibition of Real Human Bodies—underlines this fact and advertises it to potential visitors. But the realness of these bodies is severely attenuated; rather, it is the physical material that is real, the muscles, the bones, the tendons. Their composition, however, has been altered in both senses of the word: the biological composition had watery substances like blood, fat, and viscous fluids that were re-placed with clear, dry, firm though pliable plastinate, thus robbing the biological material of smell, wetness, and "ability" to decay. The "yuck" factor is completely gone.

We aren't confronted with the messy organicism of death, with its leaking bodily fluids, sloughing skin, and sunken eyes. In a sense, the process of death is erased, because death normally leads to the pu-trefaction of organic matter, to decay, to loss of bodily integrity and shape, to *dehumanization*. In this sense, plastination is similar to taxi-dermy's evisceration. However, these corpses are *rehumanized* when they come to stand for universal structures of human bodies—the ana-tomical complexity of organs, bones, tendons, and muscles in complex relation. These bodies are like ours; these bodies are "us" in a way that animals' are rarely recognized to be.

In another sense, the bodily composition is severely disturbed or distorted in the name of greater clarity. Compact muscles are pulled apart, orifices are pried open, cavities are emptied and the organs they once cradled now held out to the side for better viewing, as in the case of the "exploded" figures; these are pulled apart vertically like an accor-dion and stretched upward ten feet, like giants towering above us. Ac-tion is staged but without the muscularity of movement that would be necessary to produce it. (For example, "The Runner," posed midstride, would fall down, because his muscles aren't attached to the bone.)

With Body Worlds, realism lies not in the biomechanical dyna-mism of the pose or in the presentation of a narrative moment among a group of subjects, as it does in taxidermy, although everyday actions such as playing soccer or skateboarding may be referenced, and occa-sionally, two corpses are posed together, as in one display of a skating pair. Instead, the realism, or authenticity, advertised in the very name of the show resides primarily in the remnants of the bodily material, not in the bodily depictions. This may be a key factor in the exhibit's success in terms of audience numbers and satisfaction. It may also be a key factor in the show's ability to successfully overcome censure on the religious grounds that it is contravening the dignity of the dead—or even, in Europe, charters of human rights that would extend ethical protection beyond the end of life. Human corpses with their skin on, posed as if engaged in everyday activities and relating to other human corpses in a stop-action diorama, as taxidermied animals often are, might ultimately be too lifelike for their exhibit to be successful; such dead statues might seem macabre and exploitative, whereas the plastinates, posed to reveal the muscles in action, seem still to have an educative goal to demonstrate the (generic, universal) body's functionality.

Von Hagens has consistently claimed that his purpose is educational, to democratize knowledge once limited to the elite cadre of the medical profession. He refuses to call himself an artist, yet he also claims that the artistic posing of the full-body corpses helps set people at ease, drawing them in. Some displays clearly go beyond the staging needed to reveal a specific internal body structure and reach for the self-consciously aesthetic. For example, "The Fencer" is divided into three lengthwise segments joined at the knee and is lunging with his foil; the pregnant woman, in a display that several viewers decry in comment books as bad taste, lounges odalisque-like, propped up on one elbow, with slightly parted rouged lips.

In these instances, as in the arrested-motion poses of taxidermy, narrative is invoked—a sense of a moment before the one we see and therefore, perhaps, of an after. But this narrativization and sense of mobilization are much weaker than in taxidermy, where they are crucial to the manufacture of lifelikeness. In the Body Worlds exhibit, lifelikeness is not really welcome—it's too disturbing, too macabre. Even in the few instances in which arrested motion is displayed, the persons are so disembodied because of the subtraction of bodily substance and the absence of skin that we can barely imagine these bodies as persons situated in time.

The single exception in the Body Worlds I exhibit is the lounging pregnant woman. A few small areas of her skin, like the aureoles around the nipples, her ears, and her lips (erogenous areas), remain intact. The rouging of the lips is particularly unsettling, an act that signals sexual allure, underlined by the figure's pose. Against this sexualizing, we are confronted with the conceptual violence of slicing the belly away to reveal the fetus, the presence of which forces us to grapple with the individuality of motherhood (each child is unique). The insufficient genericization of this "person (mother)/specimen," and the oscillation between those two categories in our perception, is profoundly disturbing.

Seeing the nearly fully developed fetus completely exposed to our view heightens this disturbance. The fetus is the only body in the entire exhibition retaining all its skin.[55] As such, despite its status as dead "fetus" and not dead "child," it has the greatest sense of subjectivity of any of the specimens, and this is the source of our distress. This plastinate has since been removed from the exhibit after drawing protests. Human "taxidermy"—that is, the display of human bodies with their skins on in "lifelike" poses—although technically feasible, would probably be an impossible, unacceptable exhibit, even if buttressed by the strongest invocations of the discourses of art and anatomy.[56]

Other clues point to the blurring of the artistic and scientific discourses framing this exhibit and enabling its legitimization.[57] Body Worlds has appeared in both science museums and art galleries.[58] The poses themselves, as noted above, sometimes mimic old anatomy illustrations. The exhibit has been reviewed in professional art journals, medical journals like the British *Lancet*, and newspapers and magazines, in both the news and the arts and entertainment sections. Finally, with his distinctive black hat and vest, von Hagens himself seems to affect the fashion of fellow German artist Joseph Beuys. By implicitly aligning himself with artists and asserting his medical authority as a physician, von Hagens manages to simultaneously invoke the legitimizing discourses of both art and anatomy.

Both of these discourses, art and science, and the institutional settings that sustain them work to preserve a right to free speech against religious protests. While we might often consider these discourses to be opposed, von Hagens has successfully mobilized both as ethical guarantors, albeit, in his words, with "art in the service of science." Art takes a backseat to science, and the artistry of posing the plastinates is not, ultimately, to make an artistic statement. The plastinates do not function as a sort of installation art, as we find in the work of some artists like Damien Hirst, who use animal bodies; instead, the artistry of each pose, designed to convey something other than a standing manikin, is intended to draw the viewer's eye with complexity and a pleasing visual form of arrested movement—to invite us to linger and to inspect.[59]

"The Ballerina," for example, depicts a woman not simply standing up, immobile, on two legs with arms at her sides but rather in a balletic pose, on pointe on her left leg, her bony foot encased in a pink satin ballet slipper, her right leg swooping high up behind her and her spine cantilevered forward, arms flying gracefully out behind. The front of her chest is cut away, draped down toward the floor, revealing the positions of the organs inside as she moves. Technically, the entire "mount" is attached to the floor only through the toes of the left foot, the rest of the body balancing unsupported in space. But no imaginary code blue could jolt this corpse back to life, as the body is disarticulated, muscle detached from bone.

As regards each individual person, a plastinate stands at once for uniqueness and specificity—the individual body and the person it was part of—and as a generic specimen of human anatomical structure. With no age, no fat, no race, no social class, no nationality attributed, an idealization through universalization simultaneously invokes the work of art (a sort of fictionalized "portrait" that stands for more than itself) and of anatomy (an individual becomes a specimen of its kind) for "all people," to the extent that we all share a basic anatomical makeup. When the balance tips too far toward the individual specimen, as with the pregnant woman with her belly split open, the exhibit fails and invites censure.

Both of these processes—human idealization and a genericization that exceeds the individual—are distancing ones, and this combination of alterity and similarity is central to the legitimizing of the display as well as to its appeal. Its corpses are both *like* us (in that we have the same basic anatomical makeup but with a full range of anatomical variation) and *unlike* us (in that each full-body plastinate was once an individual living human who was distinct from ourselves, hence an "other"). This combination of perceptual and conceptual nearness and farness creates the conditions for attentive, respectful contemplation, which dominated the audience behavior I observed both in London in 2002 and in Chicago in 2007.

For the exhibit to succeed, in terms of both audience satisfaction (which, judging from the audience comment books I've seen, is quite high, and often references a sense of awe) and escaping debilitating censure, the antitaxidermy approach is absolutely necessary. For humans, unlike animals, a taxidermic retention of the skin would turn a universalized specimen not only into a unique body but also into a specific human. It would also invite us to contemplate the intimacies of touch, the coldness of the dead skin now and the warmth of the individual in life. This surface, as Ron Broglio reminds us, drawing on Mary Louise Pratt's formulation, is a "contact zone." It both separates and invites melding. And while we may desire to touch the soft fur of a taxidermied tiger, we can hardly imagine that the tiger would have sensuously touched us back. If we were to reach our hand out to a skin-bearing plastinate and imagine the skin-to-skin touch of human intimacy, however, the repellent coldness of death would disrupt any tactile pleasure we might have.[60]

This skinless approach is also necessary to the pleasures of audiences caught up in finding correspondences between their own individual yet similar bodies ("Oh, *that's* the rotator cuff I tore" or "I thought my stomach was lower down!") and wondering aloud at the complexity of human (their own) below-the-skin anatomical structures—structures most of us rarely get to view. Seeing human interiors, rather than the exteriors we are used to seeing, evokes a sense of wonder and curiosity in most viewers I observed and is reflected in viewer comments on the exhibit: "It shows the wonders of God because only He can create something so awesome"; "This is the most interesting activity I've ever taken part in"; and, as one young girl (Donna, age 11) put it, "I love to learn about the parts inside of me."[61]

Skin Deep

In von Hagens's exhibit, we see, despite the controversy it has generated, a successful formula for displaying dead human bodies. Genericization, combined with a sense of uniqueness and idealization and cloaked in sustaining discourses of art and anatomy, makes it acceptable—in this case, at least—to view dead humans on public display. What makes this approach so striking is that any display of taxidermied humans remains inconceivable in current social practices and would probably be, to most people, a profoundly offensive idea. Von Hagens's plastinates could never be displayed with their skins on.

The display of taxidermied animals, however, easily hovers between art and craft, the specimens always already sufficiently genericized and desubjectified because of the status of animals in our place and time. We can allow, and apparently even endorse and take pleasure in, their reanimation, because their deaths (as the necessary precursor of that reanimation) are not yet deemed too high a price for our pleasure.

As this comparison of taxidermy and plastination exhibits, exhibition techniques, and public responses makes clear, the realms of humans and animals remain clearly delineated even in those situations, like these two types of public displays, that might at first glance seem to be blurring the boundary between them, because the Body Worlds displays are not taxidermy. In fact, I argue here that they must be *antitaxidermy* to be both accepted and so stunningly popular. In addition, they rely heavily on an explicit activation of the discourses of both art and science (anatomy) to guarantee their moral acceptability. The power of these discourses, activated by the careful placement of medieval and Renaissance anatomical drawings, by locating the exhibition in major art and science museums, by the accompanying educational materials, and by reviews in elite art and science journals, combines with the antitaxidermy technique to facilitate Body Worlds' acceptance by most people and its celebration by many in the multiple sites around the world that have hosted the exhibition.

I have argued here, however, that all the power of art and anatomy discourses wouldn't be enough to legitimize Body Worlds if its techniques actually duplicated those practiced on animals. Human bodies with their skins on, with their histories of age, racialization, and even social class dermatologically mapped, would, I assert, be unacceptable under any conditions. Not only would skin individualize the corpses rather than genericize them, but it would also veer too close to the display techniques deemed appropriate for animals and would demote human to animal and thus to object, not subject. Instead, the von Hagens exhibit retains the sense of individuality and subjectivity accorded to humans through an emphasis on informed consent: the permission granted by each individual to display him- or herself after death. The exhibit keeps that individuation in tension with a universalizing salute to humanness. The human subjects become universalized, as all markers of individual life (aside from sex) are literally stripped away with the skin, the fat, and the viscera. These exfoliated individuals stand in, then, for each of us, demonstrating the "wonder" of the human body and, consequently, the wonder that is human—universal, not generic. And above all, *human—not animal.*

THREE

Inside "Animal" and Outside "Culture": The Limits to "Sameness" and Rhetorics of Salvation in von Hagens's Animal Inside Out Body Worlds Exhibition

Riding up the very steep escalator from the entryway in the Museum of Science and Industry (MSI) in Chicago in August 2013, I pass a large banner advertising the special exhibit Animal Inside Out, which is having its US premiere here. The *Chicago Tribune* has dubbed this expensive exhibit (an additional $12 beyond the normal $18 entrance fee) "an eye-popping spectacle from start to finish" and "a sort of alternate-universe zoo,"[1] and my expectations rise with the steep climb of the escalator. After several globe-touring Body Worlds: The Anatomical Exhibition of Real Bodies shows, Gunther von Hagens has now turned his full attention to nonhuman animals, who previously played a very minor role in his work. Dissected and processed through his patented "plastination technique,"[2] in which polymers replace bodily liquids and skin is stripped away to reveal the anatomy underneath, these posed, dry, rigid, and odorless full-scale corpses of nonhuman animals (nearly one hundred of them) will populate both of the MSI's spaces for temporary exhibits. Promoted as a major event, the exhibit includes displays of full-body plastinates of ostriches, a camel, a giraffe, and many smaller beings, along with vitrine-encased specimens of polymer-infused hearts, lungs, and reproductive tracts and even some plastic-infused, filigreed systems of blood vessels resembling red crocheted animal forms.

My ticket scanned at the top of the escalator, I walk past installations about physics, weather, and trains until I spy the face of a twelve-foot-tall skinless giraffe looking down on me from over a curtained wall . . . this must be it. Yet another ticket taker checks my ticket for timed entry and finally lets me enter the coveted, hushed exhibit space, with its boutique-style lighting and gray carpeting.

If the Body Worlds human plastinates gain part of their draw from the fact that dead and living humans rarely mingle except under exceptional circumstances (funerals, wars), the allure of the Animal Inside Out show is somewhat different, for we *do* often see dead animals. They make an appearance on our plates most nights of the week, or they lie, guts strewn, along the roadside as we pass by in our cars, or they greet us in taxidermied form, as a hunting trophy hung on a neighbor's wall over the fireplace or as denizens of dioramas in natural history museums.

As Georgina Bishop, exhibition developer at the Natural History Museum in London (where the exhibit toured immediately before its Chicago dates) put it, "Usually you see our specimens as skeletons, [as] stuffed animals or preserved in alcohol." However, now visitors will "see animals close up in a whole new way and in the most amazing detail as they get under the skin of some of nature's most incredible creatures."[3] Unlike the cut of meat on our plate, muscle sliced from an animal limb and reaching us as a cooked fragment, full bodies greet us here, in all their complexity and impressive size. Full-bodied ostriches, giraffes, giant squid, rabbits, and even a camel, along with numerous animal body parts, will engage us in their plastinated forms.[4]

As Bishop notes, these animals aren't taxidermied. Rather, they are shown without their skins, a strategy that I suggested in chapter 2 was key to the extraordinary popularity and acceptance of von Hagens's earlier human-plastinate Body World exhibits. Here the stakes and function are different, though. As we have seen in my discussion of conventional taxidermy competitions in that earlier chapter, the individuating and social-context-referencing function of human skin, with its semiotic map of age, health status, racial or ethnic attribution, and so on, doesn't obtain for nonhuman animals.

Already deemed generic, with few exceptions, and already deemed outside history, animals with their skins on do not threaten to cross the ideological border between "specimen" and "individual" that must be kept at bay in von Hagens's human shows through the activated mantle of scientism that makes such exhibits ethically acceptable to so many. With their skins off, animals (when not in the category of "pets" or "celebrities") are no less individuated than they were in skin-on (or skin-only) taxidermied form. What they lose are some of the species-specific semiotics by which we usually identify them—the mane of a lion, the feathers of a bird.

In this Animal Inside Out exhibit (note the singular referent that seeks to cover *all* animals),[5] the skin removal is merely the necessary step to reveal the musculoskeletal design similarity that is the basis of the show. Like Honoré Fragonard's dried animal specimens in late-eighteenth-century Europe, the plastinated animals become evidence for the biomechanical and physiological functional similarity between humans and nonhuman animals.[6]

But after the extraordinary success of previous human-centric Body Worlds shows,[7] why put on an animal-focused exhibit at all? What is at stake? Aren't the stakes much lower, the learning curve less steep, and the allure less forbidden?

In this chapter, I analyze the exhibit in terms of the argument it presents and its potential effects on viewers, and I ask exactly what is different between displays featuring human cadavers and those featuring dead animal bodies.[8] I argue that just as the human Body Worlds exhibits were, the animal exhibit is built on a series of omissions that construct its ultimate argument, but that these omissions differ from those that were essential to the human shows. Additionally, the materialization of this newest exhibit takes place under a set of specific conditions of possibility, and those conditions are different for the human and the animal exhibits.

Scientism, Similarity, and Temporality

Ultimately, in both the human and the animal cases, a discursive biologism and facticity prevail, anchored to material objects that function as "evidence" and setting the stage for an ethical argument built on a radical social decontextualization, a basis on which that argument depends and that it simultaneously challenges. But the overarching argument in the human exhibits is different than in the animal exhibit. This difference ultimately reinscribes the line between human and nonhuman animal, even while the Animal Inside Out exhibit seems devoted to stressing and delineating comparisons based on (physiological and structural) similarity, not difference.

In the human Body Worlds exhibits, similarity (among humans) is also the key organizing trope, and we are left with the sense that "we're all the same under the skin." In the animal exhibit, we take away the idea that animals and humans, although not always alike, are more alike than different "under the skin," based on a calculus of physical and physiological structure and function. In the case of the human Body Worlds shows, I argued that the displays depend on the erasure of individual and collective social histories that cadavers with their skin on would help reveal—in terms of racial categorization, age, health status, and concomitant political power.

While we could say that the human Body Worlds exhibits draw heavily on the "medical gaze" posited by Michel Foucault, the actual copresence of cadavers works against this. Foucault suggested that after the French Revolution, the professionalization of medicine included a shift in *episteme*, or defining conceptions, of how medicine constituted its objects of knowledge and also modes of knowing.[9] Tied to the development of clinical medicine, an increasing rationalization of knowledge began to separate the person ("patient") from a narration of his or her life or illness, resulting in a greater emphasis on disease itself as the object of knowledge and on vision, rather than earlier techniques of touch (palpation) and hearing (auscultation), to diagnose. Such a shift both required and produced a new set of discourses that continue to shape both medicine and popular discourse about knowledge and about the body as something ultimately knowable.

This is part of a larger scientism, or the elevation of science as a dominant mode of understanding the world, that pervades a great deal of European-derived thought and politics to this day, in everything from social science to decisions about what makes the headlines in a local newspaper. We can reasonably expect that at least to some extent, audiences for the Body Worlds shows, at least in most of their venues, and for the Animal Inside Out exhibit are caught in this hegemonic matrix of meaning production, as it is a central component of public education and public discourse. The full weight of this scientism is brought to bear through the location of these exhibits when they appear (as they have in the United States) in institutions called "science museums."

As I discussed in the preceding chapter, our attachment to implied life narratives, and their resultant historicity and social specificity, is at odds with this elicitation of distanciation in the gaze, and this tension undergirds our encounter with the human plastinates in Body Worlds. So rare is the copresence of living and dead humans, outside of war, that the social power of the cadaver is considerable. The plastinated cadaver is composed from the physical remains of a human who, by personal choice, donated her or his body for use in the exhibit and who was thus always already an individual with a life history, situated in social formations. It requires that the full weight of the medical gaze be activated, through discursive framing of the exhibit and the decor of the exhibition room, to enable individuals to adopt the offered "scientific" point of view.

For most viewers, at most times, this tension is manageable. At moments, as with the plastinated pregnant woman on display with her exposed fetus that I discussed in chapter 2, this positioning is abandoned by some audience members, who erupt in protest as the socially significant personhood of that particular plastinate intrudes into the exhibit.

For the animals exhibit, a related erasure occurs, but it is not the erasure of individuality and its relation to a larger human community and the attendant structures of social categorization. Rather, it is the erasure of community *among* a species, of individual life histories, of cognitive and emotional realms of animal life, and of relations *between* species that must take place.

The resulting generic "specimenization"—a fixture of museumification in which parts are called on to stand in for wholes[10]—functions slightly differently than in earlier Body Worlds displays. In those shows, individual human cadavers were posed in action (and sometimes in relation to one another, as in a duo of ice-skating cadavers) and were named in terms of that action. "The Runner" showed a male figure posed in a running posture, with flayed muscles exposed. "The Chess Player" was bent over a chessboard, his exposed vertebrae curved forward in a pose of concentration. "The Ballerina" cadaver was posed balanced on one foot that was encased in a toe shoe, with her other leg in the air and her arms lifted gracefully.

The choices to pose, name, and even add accessories like the ballet shoe help underscore the tension in the exhibit design between plastinated cadaver as "sample," or "exemplar," and as individual subject engaged in intentional activity. Humans, the exhibit implies, are smart (they play chess), are athletic (they run), and have artistic sensibilities (they dance). Whether or not "The Chess Player" is posed using the body of a human who actually played chess, this choice of pose displays human activity as purposeful, varied, and socially valued, and is exhibited within an implied time frame of before and after . . . we want to know if the chess player won his game or how long he has been playing chess.

Thus, human plastinates may not be individualized, but they are temporalized. They presumably existed in a time that had a before and an after of the implied moment frozen in the plastination pose (for instance, a lifted hand about to move a chess piece) and thus are implicitly embedded in history, which demands the passage of time and the construction of a narrative. History also militates against genericization, because it allows for the possibility of change over time. Chess and ballet are examples of learned skills acquired over years of practice. However, by not providing individual biographies of those who donated their bodies, the creators have more freedom to genericize an individual while simultaneously courting the sense of individuality tied to human subjectivity. And as these examples illustrate, Body Worlds' gender stereotyping steps in for the absence of a reported history, providing a social context of sorts. A female plastinate is caught up in the "graceful" (stereotypically feminized) balletic pose, while the chess player, male, appears to focus his mind on the next move in the interrupted chess game, and the male runner exhibits implied physical prowess and strength.[11]

Our engagements with the full-body animal plastinates are substantially different. The structuring motif of the show, its argument and conceptual base, is that of comparative anatomy, arguing that our human physical selves, in terms of the anatomy of our bodily design—the arrangement of our muscles and ligaments, the physiology of lungs and hearts—are very similar to those in the nonhuman animal realm.[12] We see this right from the start of the exhibit, when a film drawing likenesses between human and nonhuman animals stops us at the entryway and effectively frames our perceptions of the displays to follow.

The potential danger of such an assertion of similarity in terms of what it might imply for our relations with and obligations to nonhuman animals (If they are so like us, should we eat them? Experiment on them?) is severely attenuated. It is confined to a single arena of relation: that of salvation. We are, at the end of the exhibit, exhorted to change our human collective behaviors so that the rest of the beings on the planet can also survive.[13] The trappings of scientism, including the opening comparative video and the presence of exhibit guides clad in lab coats help situate us in this distanced way—as sympathetic observers and influential, knowledgeable actors and subjects—connected by similarity but not threatened by sameness.

Structure of the Animal Inside Out Exhibit

Entering gallery 1, we come face to face with a large video screen, which literally stops us in our tracks and blocks further viewing of the space. On it, split into two sides, like a rolling diptych of paired images, a video is set to play continuously. On one side of the screen, we see human images, on the other animals. Parallelism unfolds on a film loop, setting the theme for our engagement. We see, for example, a human male drinking a bottle of water on the left-hand screen, while on the right an elephant, facing in the same direction, pours water into its giant mouth through its trunk. A man of African descent in a camel-colored sweater sits at a table and blinks, sinking down to sleep with his arms crossed on the table; on the paired screen, a brown, tan, and white tiger blinks and lies down to snooze. A human of European descent holds a baby; this image is juxtaposed with a shot of an ape holding an infant. This imagery implies a universality among humans; it also implies that human and nonhuman animals perform parallel fundamental behaviors of drinking, sleeping, and parenting and so are more alike than different.

Thus, from the very moment of entry to this exhibit, we are presented with its defining frame: human and nonhuman animals are more alike than different. We will see this played out body system by body system, from lungs to blood circulation, as the exhibit shows how living beings, for the most part, use oxygen, depend on muscles for movement, transform food into energy via digestive systems, and ultimately use brains and nervous systems to engage their environments successfully.

The exhibit consists of a variety of animal parts displayed in plastic vitrines and carefully labeled by species ("gills, Mackerel fish"; "lung, Asian elephant"), punctuated by several large full-body plastinated animals. Most of these full-body poses are static, with no implied relationality, no visual or textual references to time, place, or behavioral context. The giraffe who welcomes us at the entry to gallery 2 is awesome in its vertical latitude, but it just stands there, limbs frozen, posed as if doing nothing. An ostrich plastinate is shown lifting a running leg, but the rest of the body doesn't surge forward, as it would in conventional contemporary taxidermy. Also, there isn't the slightest hint of environmental context—not even a few blades of fake savannah grasses. What kind of topography must the bird cover that makes those long legs a benefit? Who or what is the animal running from? How fast can she run? How much faster than us?

There are two exceptions to this static pattern out of the many plastinates in the exhibit. At the very end of gallery 1, we encounter the largest animal yet: a plastinated bull. This "specimen" is massive, certainly a ton even with all fat stripped away, its huge reddish plastinated muscles posed straining in a lunging position. The overall effect is of power and arrested movement, with a turning bovine head and large horns angled toward us as if in midstride. A bit more nostril flaring and we might even imagine ourselves as part of the crazy cohort that "runs with the bulls" in Pamplona, Spain, just out of reach of the arrested thrust of the head. And yet, while "lifelikeness" is not the goal of this skin-stripped antitaxidermic display, it is not totally absent in that this pose, with its kinesthetic charge of massive weight in motion, heightens our appreciation of the bull's power in a way that a static pose of plastinated muscles could not.

The implied movement not only serves as a sign of previous life (after all, dead beings cannot move) but also references an imagined kinesthesia that unites body and movement in space to read as "power," even "danger." The species' capacity and potential for dangerous relations with humans are thus subtly underlined, even while the specimen itself is obviously dead, and the display doesn't pretend to capture a moment before death, as do so many taxidermy displays of leaping animals. Here power is tamed, reduced to a pose, held in midmove for our idealized contemplation of the (stereotypically powerful maleness of the) "bull body."

The second exception, a female camel posed with her calf, and thus implying a familial or social relationship (and a stereotypical maternal identification), has this relationship undercut by her sliced physique. Split into three parts to better reveal the digestive system, with clumps of half-digested grass still lodged in the gut, the camel's bodily integrity is destroyed in a more fundamental way than it would be by the simple stripping of fur and skin and fat, making her substantial presence more akin to the body-part specimens in vitrines, despite its size and bulk. A dissected body or excised body part cannot have integrity, cannot have attributed subjectivity, and cannot be imagined as a living being responding successfully to the other beings and the geography of its environmental context. Such a biological fragment is a "nonsubject" and certainly cannot organize to change the world, which is the ultimate invitation or exhortation that this exhibit extends to us as viewers.

Humans, the exhibit asserts, with its closing video "countdown" of the top ten endangered species and their projected time to extinction, are the only beings capable of working to return other animals from the brink of extinction. This projected extinction is largely attributed to human practices that negatively affect our shared physical environment and deprive other species of their oxygen, nutrients, habitat, and social structures necessary for successful reproduction and, ultimately, survival. A wall text at the very end of the exhibit lists actions we can take to "save" endangered species, and exhorts us to "reduce carbon pollution" and "urge your government officials to enact strong legislation to protect" them.

Therefore, like von Hagens's human Body Worlds exhibits, Animal Inside Out makes an argument and invites us to change our behavior in relation to it. In previous Body Worlds, the explicit part of this message was addressed to the individual—a plea to adopt healthier lifestyles, like stopping smoking—accompanied by the contrasting displays of a healthy and a diseased human lung. But its larger message asserted that we are all the same under the skin, and its universalizing stance could, at least theoretically, be seen as implicitly endorsing substantial social change (arguing against racism, ethnic cleansing, and gender disenfranchisement) even while writing out the social history that led to the current inequities of social formations and gendered stereotypes.[14] Animal Inside Out, similarly, has a radical potential, but just as in the human Body Worlds shows, it is rarely activated, as I discuss below.

In the animal exhibit, the argument for recognizing similarity falls far short of calling for a fundamental overhaul in our relations with nonhuman animals. Indeed, by the end of the exhibit, our only relation with animals seems to be to save them, as there is no mention at all of the many uses to which animals are put by humans: food; fur; leather; assistants such as guide dogs; the extension of human capabilities (for instance, bomb-sniffing dogs); stand-ins for humans in some laboratory research; and icon, symbol, and metaphor in so much European-derived philosophy and storytelling, from Descartes to Lassie.

Nor is there any implied relationship among individuals of a single species (with the exception of the camel calf and mother and two reindeer posed running side by side) or between species. For example, we see no staged scenes of predation, although some of the specimens in life were the predators of others on display.

To set up this similarity argument, the exhibit takes us through body systems, one by one, comparing nonhuman animal bodies to each other and to humans. "Every Breath You Take," an unacknowledged quote from an old song by the rock band the Police, focuses on the processing of oxygen, and the "Big Hearted Creatures" segment implies, through the double entendre of its name, a social generosity (big hearted), but focuses instead specifically, and only, on the comparative size of hearts from different species. We see the human heart in comparison with other four-valve mammalian hearts, like that of a reindeer, a pig, a bull, and a giraffe, the latter absolutely gargantuan in comparison, roughly twenty-four inches long and eighteen inches across! "This is awesome," says a seven-year-old girl to her grandfather, looking at the hearts under plastic vitrines.[15]

Remarkably, and as more evidence of our similarity across species lines, a related wall text informs us that whether a heart is that of a mouse or an elephant, apparently all animals are programmed for the same absolute number of heartbeats in a lifetime—roughly a billion. Life-span differences make up for speed in an exponential calculus: "a tiny shrew animal, whose heart races at 1,000 beats a minute, lives for just four years, while the slow beating heart of an elephant can throb up to 70 years."

Related concepts and examples of physical structure and function dominate the rest of the exhibit, organized around additional topics like respiration, digestion, and muscles across a huge range of beings: exhibits include full-body plastinates or body parts from bulls, dogs, reindeer, octopi, rats, cats, giant squid, lions, camels, snakes, chickens, carp, rabbits, horses, sheep, pigs, frogs, scallops, ducks, and humans; mammals, reptiles, amphibians, birds, and fish are all present.

We learn that all these animals depend on oxygen, circulate it through their systems through lungs or gills, imbibe nutrients, extract them through digestive systems, deposit the leftovers through excretory systems, and use the food and oxygen in the building of muscle and cartilage or bone. Although animals move, sense, reproduce, and die in species-specific ways, their lives are presented as fundamentally similar overall, despite huge variations in size, looks, physiology, and habitat. Dramatic variances in capabilities—whether physical or mental—are rarely noted. The ostrich wall text, for example, notes the exaggerated size of the bird and its neck length but nothing about the extraordinarily fast speeds it can run overland. There is no mention of the geospatial abilities of birds like homing pigeons or of the abilities of some canine breeds, like bloodhounds, to distinguish minute particles of scent, far exceeding our human abilities to know the world by smell. Even more important, beyond these special physiological capacities, issues of sentience, sociality, and cognition are ignored—a key structuring absence in the exhibit, as I argue above.

Similarity vanishes at the crest of ethical responsibility because other species aren't seen as ethically responsible or irresponsible. *This, above all*, is apparently what sets humans apart from nonhuman animals, not the number of firing neurons or the capacity for self-reflection. Discussions of cognitive ability, life cycles, and social structures, all areas of vast differentiation among animal populations and between human and nonhuman animals, are eschewed in favor of asserting structural similarity.

But before this similarity can be deeply contemplated, the exhibit organizers stress the ethical sourcing of the material on display. In a large wall text immediately to our left as we enter the darkened space, we are informed of "Our Ethical Stance." The text reassures the visitor that no animals were killed for this exhibit; rather, the bodies are donated by zoos, breeders, and other institutions after death. This is crucial because, unlike the Body Worlds human shows, in which the deceased on display have (we are assured) chosen during their lifetimes to donate their bodies expressly for the purpose of inclusion in the exhibitions, in this case the animals are incapable of assent, and so humans must consent on their behalf.

What is interesting here is that given the billions of animals slaughtered for meat, this notion of killing on purpose (for display and education) is such a central concern that it must be addressed right away. We might ask, what's one more dead chicken or piglet? One of the exhibit facilitators noted that she often has to reassure patrons, especially children, that the animals weren't killed on purpose for the display, saying that many people apparently fail to read the entryway notice or simply want reassurance as they go through the exhibit, encountering multiple animal bodies. How many of these same people then go down to the cafeteria to have a hamburger? Is death in the service of education regarded implicitly as less ethical than causing death in the service of physical sustenance? (Or of laboratory research? Or for trauma-surgery training in the military?) This "ethical stance" assertion, and audience members' need for reassurance as they go through the exhibit, implies that the direct confrontation with a dead animal body—specifically to *contemplate* that body—brings home the potential role of humans in causing death in ways that slaughter for the food industry, hidden from consumer vision, or the learned obliviousness of most drivers to road-kill on the side of the tarmac, does not.

The Audience

These questions bring us to the issue of audience and reception. The organization of an exhibit may address an anticipated audience with a certain rhetorical structure, but audiences bring their own preparations and interpretive frameworks to the experience.[16] Meaning is generated in the politicized and polysemic encounter between these rhetorics and interpretations. In the section that follows, I describe what I saw of audience engagement with the exhibit, and I propose that one of the primary interpretive frameworks for that encounter is the high school biology lab.

When I was on-site at the MSI for two days in August of 2013, observing patrons at the exhibit, I noted a public of many apparent ethnic backgrounds and ages in attendance, indicating the exhibit's wide appeal. Ages ranged from about five years old to late sixties. People often came in pairs, same-sex friends or couples and opposite-sex couples (I am extrapolating here from the patrons' intimacy of physical contact and body positioning during the traverse through the show), and also in multigenerational units—children, parents, and grandparents, and parents and children. I heard languages other than English, including Spanish and a Slavic language, and noted people of apparently different ethnic and racial backgrounds, although without self-identification, these demographic observations are only impressions.

I assume, given the cost, and the fact that I wasn't there on public-school field-trip days, that these socially diverse viewers represent patrons from the middle- to upper-middle-class and above, as this exhibit costs substantially extra on top of the regular museum admission. For a group of four, say, two adults and two children, the additional cost exceeds $40. Sharpened attention may be the result of this value-conscious commodification, especially since timed-entry tickets further heighten the sense of limited access to something very special. It also means that those in the space actively chose to be there and didn't just wander in to take a look in between visiting other unrelated museum exhibits. They were ready to engage, and they did.

The audience activity was impressive in terms of the amount of interaction both within groups and with the texts.[17] People consistently (*actually*) read the wall text and the tented labels in the vitrines. Either they felt so uninformed that they sought authoritative guidance, or they were truly interested. The organizers seem to have hit the "sweet spot" here in terms of how much people will read.[18]

Parents directed their children's attention ("See, this is your trachea!" said one European American woman to her five-year-old son in a seemingly overenthusiastic moment of parental education), and children in turn called to their chaperoning adults ("That looks like a baby cat!"). Partners collaborated on interpretation ("Did you see how big a pig's lungs are?" said a grandmother to her husband while they escorted their grandchildren). And even strangers occasionally exchanged observations, creating momentary community over the exhibit. "I thought that was a diseased lung." "So did I!"

This engaged sense of community differs somewhat from the reverential mode I noted for the audiences of the human Body Worlds. There was engagement there too, as I discussed in the previous chapter, but the copresence of dead and alive humans put a formalized hush over everything. In Animal Inside Out, the decor includes none of the medieval and Renaissance pictorial references to the history of anatomy and dissection that the human Body Worlds had, but no such authoritative imprimatur of the history of science is really needed to justify the dissection of dead animal bodies. The exhibit visitors seem eager to engage with the material, and they come ready to do so, prepared by their previous experiences, unlike the visitors to the human Body Worlds exhibits. In fact, taking apart animal bodies is something that most teens and adults in attendance would have experienced firsthand if they took public high school biology classes in the United States. This experience, I suggest, is one of the primary tropes implicitly framing the encounter.[19] It provides an interpretive frame, but the museum promises a better experience.

The full exhibit title, Animal Inside Out: The Beauty of the Beast, provides a clue to the show's attraction. We see the insides of animals and they are beautiful, not ugly or repulsive, as might be the case in a dissection lab in high school, with its stink of formaldehyde, or even elsewhere in our everyday lives, as in the unavoidable sight on a highway of guts pouring out of the squished body of a squirrel, or blood streaming from the nose and mouth of a dead deer.

I suggest that for visitors, this personal and collective history (trained in high school to examine and dissect dead animals from a "scientific" point of view) forms the ground for the exhibit's interpretation, and militates against any of the more radical interpretive possibilities that assertions of similarity between human and nonhuman bodies might promote. Although exact statistics are impossible to come by for the entire nation, at least one study estimates that 75%–80% of US students dissect at least one animal in their high school career.[20]

Although I propose that the biology lab provides a training ground for how to *perform* science—lab coated, eye protected, scalpel holding, and stoically ignoring viscerality in favor of an emotionally distanced "objective" calculation and analysis—not all students succeed in (or desire to succeed in) taking up this offered performative role of "the scientist." Recent research suggests that some students in biology labs experience substantial "interference" in what I am terming this "performative script" because of their own bodily reactions of disgust and distaste.[21]

Rather than embracing a distanced scientistic "objective" gaze when they are instructed, for example, to cut through a calf's eyeball to observe its optical structures, students instead comment on the squishiness of the orb, the smell, the "yuck" factor, and their own embarrassment in dealing with bodily functions. Acknowledging students' engagement with the body being studied and their own sense of embodiment is necessary to enhance our understanding of what the actual process of engagement with the Animal Inside Out exhibit might entail.

So, if most visitors come to the exhibit with a memory of an embodied distaste for dissection, a ghostly stink of formaldehyde in their nostrils, and the haptic memory of squishy eyeballs, how does the animal exhibit succeed?

The exhibit's participation in the authoritative discourse on science learning is unmistakable both from the science museum setting and from the rhetorics of the display design, a point I made in relation to the human Body Worlds. This helps to move Animal Inside Out from the potentially disturbing performative practice of the lab to the less challenging learned facticity of a (nonstinking, nonsquishy) textbook encounter—yet, extraordinarily, a textbook of the "real." The excising of the smell and touch and viscosity (what I have called the "yuck factor") through the plastination process crucially differentiates the biology class lab and animal exhibit still further. Exhibit-goers' encounters are reduced to a single sense—vision—as in the human Body Worlds exhibits. But for the most part, visitors to those exhibits brought with them little experience with human dead bodies, whereas here, thanks to US biology education, most of the visitors arrive with a viscerally distinctive set of memories about animal anatomy and dissection.

Just as biology teachers guide students' mastery over not only the anatomical material but also the visceral reactions they have, so too do the authoritative matrix of the science museum and its docents, clad in blue lab coats and circulating in the exhibit to engage visitors and answer questions. One docent I saw, a twenty-something European American male, approached a child and pulled a preserved cow's eye from his pocket. "See," he said, "we use fake eyes in the exhibit, because real eyes look dead, and this is an exhibit about life."[22]

A Vision of Science as Subtraction

Subtraction—of tissue, of fat, of social context, of history, of death—is part of the specimenization process. It literalizes the notion that less is more when it comes to scientific education.[23]

That clarity of ("scientific") understanding supposedly depends on a pristine encounter with a reductionist sense of complexity, even in the service of extolling the complexity of the wider biological system as a network of vessels, tissues, nerve fibers, organs, connective tissues, bones, cartilage, muscles, tendons, ligaments, capillaries, and fluids. In the von Hagens examples, whether of humans or of nonhuman animals, we never see a rendition of this complexity in its interactive and contextually situated fullness, as if that fullness is not only unavailable to the scientific gaze and the reductive specimenization that must accompany it but might even contravene it as well.

The subtitle of the exhibit (The Beauty in the Beast) is an invitation to awe and contemplation, and also a play on the title of "Beauty and the Beast," a fairy tale featuring cross-species romance and even hints at sexual taboos. The subtitle includes the term *beast* to separate mindful humans from mindless brutes, and also to overturn it by saying the "beast" is beautiful and, ultimately, more like than unlike us. At this juncture of similarity and difference, von Hagens firmly comes down on the side of similarity. While the responsibility of humans toward animals ("Stop extinction!") is the ultimate takeaway, it's possible to push beyond this liberal notion of caretaking to a greater, more radical assertion of ethical obligation. *If*, we might ask, human and nonhuman animals are so much alike in form and function, do we have greater ethical obligations toward nonhuman animals than is currently recognized?

"Saving" seems to be the only ethical imperative embedded in the exhibit's narrative: as depicted in its closing video, humans are largely responsible for the destruction of habitat and populations that has led to the "top ten" list of endangered species; therefore, it is up to us to modify our behaviors to reverse this trend and to do so because, after all, under the skin, we are more alike than different from nonhuman animals. Even the lowly scallop might be seen in this narrative as our distantly connected "kin"—an animal dependent on oxygen and the processing of nutrients.

The unstated implications of this assertion of similarity over difference, based on a romping rejection of hierarchy of species arranged in terms of human capacities, *could* be radical. If the viewer takes seriously von Hagens's assertion that a human and a scallop share fundamental ways of surviving in the world (we all need oxygen), and that the similarity is not only extant but socially meaningful (In what ways am I like a scallop? How does that matter?), then the power of the exhibit might be to urge us to see ourselves as part of a biome, a shared, relational biological livingness on the earth. This philosophical worldview could potentially lead to a more complex acknowledgment of a co-constitutive relationality that (within such a proposed epistemology) undergirds the possibility of being, drives ecological activism, and helps us regard histories as subject to change in the future.

This is a lot to accomplish in the face of dominant—in the United States, implicitly Christian-derived—ideologies of "dominion," humans' God-given right to (benevolent?) dominance over all else.[24] I suggest that von Hagens's call to salvation is a rhetorical way to manage that conundrum of post-Darwinism without relying on an explicitly Christian-formatted frame for interpreting our relations with animals. "Similarity" gives rise not to disruptive ideological reorganization, with its attendant material and political changes, but to a discourse of salvation, retaining human dominance through an unstated ideology of dominion while transforming it, unchallenged, into a specific mode of ethical obligation.

But in the end, despite its more radical potential, von Hagens's Animal Inside Out is ultimately a conservative exhibit. It does not provoke us to challenging thought, as it immediately provides the easy way out at the end of the exhibit, a sort of "here you go" answer to our "so what?" as we depart. There we are exhorted to *take action* to reduce species endangerment after viewing the "top ten" countdown video of animal species at risk. "Eat sustainable seafood" is one example of concrete actions suggested in the savior narrative.

Some visitors came to a different conclusion: eat NO seafood or any other "animal."

At least one writer in the public comment book asserted that after seeing the exhibit, she had to become, right then and there, a vegetarian. Anecdotal reports from an exhibit guide, of discussions overheard as patrons exited the exhibit, echo this assertion, with some visitors saying, "Well, I can't go eat lunch now!" Presumably, that lunch menu would have included the bodies of some of the species just seen, like chickens. For these visitors, a more radical reading of "similarity" was taken from the exhibit and rendered into action, at least in the immediate future—for lunch. At least temporarily, a "what's for lunch?" became a "who's for lunch?"—an unsustainable locution.

Yet with very few exceptions, we have no "whos" in this exhibit. One exception emerges in the text recounting the story of finding the giant squid, whose bisected halves reach toward each other from across the room with six-foot-long tentacles, offering a striking opening to the exhibit, right after the diptych-style video in gallery 1. Other than this story—that researchers discovered the squid washed up on a beach and donated it to von Hagens—we know little of the lives of the animals whose bodies we encounter whole or in part in this exhibit. Nor are we well prepared to supply imaginatively (rightly or inaccurately) a sense of specific lived experience based on a shared mode of being in the world, as was the case in the human Body Worlds, even if that exhibit militated against this in its moves toward universalism.

But this absence of life stories could have been creatively contravened by the exhibit through a radically different structure, one that might have increased the impact of the conservation message at the end.

Imagine if each specimen (for instance, a lung) or whole-body plastinate, like those of the two ostriches on display, were accompanied by a provenance (a history of ownership of a commodity), as in an art museum to authenticate the origin of a painting, or like a police unit's documentation of chain of custody for authenticating a piece of evidence. (I use the commodity-driven term *provenance* on purpose, rather than a more idealistic *life history*, about which we are likely to know little until the animal came into human contact, and then only from the human point of view.)

This approach would constitute the "display" as a something that we might call not just a thing but a "being-thing," an ungainly neologism that insists on the history of a being jammed up against the presentation of that former self as a "thing." Where was this animal born? How long did it live? Under what conditions? Was it famous? Who cared when it (he or she) died? How did it die? How did it come to be donated to the plastination exhibit? Why? By whom? Did this being have a name, an age, a sex (in the case of the body segments)? Such a pronounced attempt at history building, at individuation, would counter the easy genericization of animals.[25]

I heard one animal history, in informal conversation with a docent, but it isn't reported anywhere in the exhibit. The camel on display, sliced into three segments from the head to the thorax to better show the interiors, came to von Hagens after she had to be euthanized because of an inoperable broken leg. At the time, no one knew she was pregnant, and the corpse was shipped to China to be plastinated by a team working there. The baby camel began to coagulate, and upon its discovery, technicians weren't sure they could salvage the body. Ultimately, the fetus turned out to be fully formed, ready for birth, and the technicians were able to plastinate its body so that viewers of the display of mother and calf never would suspect that the calf had not been born but only "delivered" through plastination. This type of backstory provides an individual life history, and it adds a poignancy to the display as we contemplate the fact that the mother never saw the calf; only humans are able to see her offspring on display.[26]

In addition, key dimensions of living—such as cognition, emotions, and capacities for sociality—dimensions that we assume humans have, even if they aren't indirectly referenced in the Body Worlds exhibit—are nowhere referenced for the animal artifacts on display.[27]

Notably, these are precisely the dimensions of animal lives that not only lend individuation but also currently generate intense discussion by biologists, ethologists, cognitive specialists, and animal ethicists. Recent books explore notions of self-consciousness in various animal species like elephants and apes, whether animals mourn the death of their own, whether apes have something called "culture" that indicates ways of living learned by one generation from another and not instinctually known—a social history.[28]

In a world where scientific studies probe the abilities of parrots to understand conceptual categories and human language, and legal arguments are made to recognize the "personhood" of certain categories of animals, these issues aren't something to be ignored. Or rather, explicitly ignoring such debates constitutes a strategic move, one taken by this exhibit and hence by the science museums that host it.

It is this systematic omission that posts the limit to the "we are more alike than different" argument of Animal Inside Out. This is the limit that makes the exhibit *safe* for most viewers, and doesn't radically challenge dominant views of human-animal relations, although it urges us toward a relationship of stewardship rather than exploitation. Notions of our human superiority, supposedly at the apex of animal creation, are never challenged despite the promotion of a parallelism between human and animal biological structures. Is this reassuring message a cause of, or even a requirement for, the exhibit's success?

For despite the emergence of new scientific research on these issues, broaching *those* realms of similarity brings an element of danger to such an exhibit, one that could require us to change not only our conceptions of nonhuman animals but also our obligations to them if, in fact, "we are all the same under the skin."

In part 1 of this book, I have focused on the display of dead animal and human bodies in predominantly public settings: science museums, art museums, taxidermy competitions, and even home wall decor. In each of these cases, the physical remains of the dead being displayed, whether human or nonhuman animal, are absolutely crucial to how that display generates its meanings and is encountered by its publics, be they museumgoers or guests in the home of a hunter who has a taxidermied deer head on the living room wall.

In the next section of the book, part 2, I continue to track the presence and absence of bodily material remains, but with a focus on mourning. Specifically, I focus on the practices of mourning for pets, and the contestatory politics of doing so. But I also consider those multitudes of instances when we choose not to mourn, and investigate why and how that is so. Mourning is a measure of relationship, and articulating it in the public sphere is a political act, one that argues for the social value of some relationships over others. When those relationships cross the species divide, the politics and practices become complex and contestatory, as we shall see in the next four chapters.

1. Old-style taxidermy techniques involving plaster-of-paris forms under animal skins, on display in the University of Iowa anthropology building, McBride Hall. Photo by Steve Moon, used with permission.

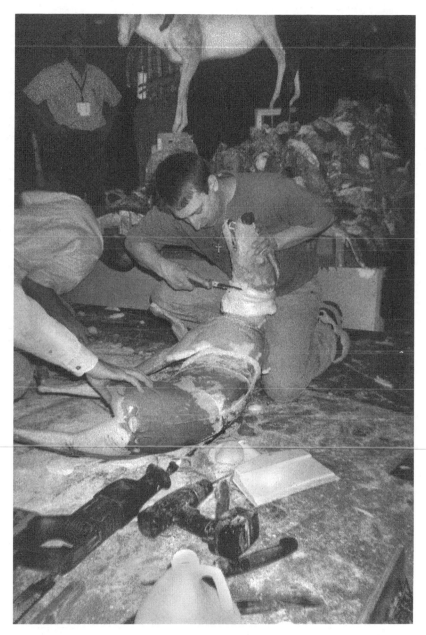

2. Master taxidermist Jason Snowberger demonstrates form alteration techniques at the 2005 World Taxidermy Championships "Super Seminar" in Springfield, Illinois. Photo by the author.

3. Best in show at the 2005 World Taxidermy Championships in Springfield, Illinois, is this "Whitetail Faun" mount by taxidermist Tommy Hall. Photo by the author.

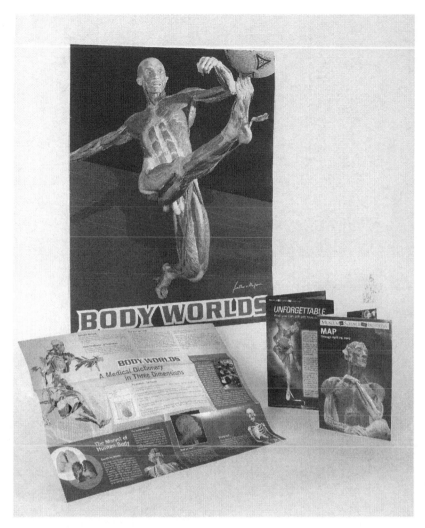

4. Souvenir memorabilia from Chicago (2007) and London (2002) Body Worlds shows gives a sense of the human displays. Personal photography in the exhibits was forbidden, and publicity photos weren't made available for this publication. Photo by Will Arnold, used with permission.

5. Trisected camel display at Gunter von Hagens's Body Worlds: Animal Inside Out exhibit at the Franklin Institute, Philadelphia, 2014. Photo by Darryl Moran, used with permission.

6. A plastinated bull at the Franklin Institute presentation of Gunter von Hagens's Body Worlds: Animal Inside Out exhibit, Philadelphia, 2014. Photo by Darryl W. Moran, used with permission.

7. A towering plastinated giraffe at Gunter von Hagens's Body Worlds: Animal Inside Out exhibit, Philadelphia, 2014. Photo by Darryl W. Moran, used with permission.

PART TWO

Mourning and the Unmourned

FOUR

On the Margins of Death: Pet Cemeteries and Mourning Practices

In late July of 2002, our parakeet, Sydney Desmond Tutu Fluff, died of an untreatable bacterial infection. After struggling for several months, Sydney suddenly took a sharp turn for the worse. One morning he couldn't stand, and within hours this vibrant, sky-blue, twenty-two-gram songster lay still in our hands. What to do next, and how to do it? I was not alone in my quandary of what to do about my pet.

With most US households now including at least one pet, the issue of what to do when the animal dies affects many people, and the expanding industry of pet cemeteries is responding to that need. In this chapter and the paired one that follows, I examine US pet cemeteries, focusing on how people mourn in those settings. The first of these two chapters explores the performative dimensions of mourning—what people do—and the material culture associated with the cemeteries—the tombstones, decor, and landscaping. The second chapter goes into more depth about notions of grievability and animal subjectivity, changing notions of familial kinship, species-specific geographies of death in the cemetery, and how burial practices are changing to reveal emergent conceptions of cross-species kinship.

Most of my research has focused on the contemporary United States, where hundreds of pet cemeteries are formally incorporated as businesses, but this phenomenon is not limited to one part of the world.[1] There are pet cemeteries in many other countries too, and I have visited some in France, Brazil, and Japan. Those facilities deserve their own investigations.[2] Based on my US research, I argue that pet cemeteries are ritual sites of public display and public practice that vary significantly from human ones while outwardly maintaining some of the same trappings: for instance, burial plot, headstone, eulogies, and even satin pillows in the casket.[3] They invite and demand, I suggest, creative, improvisatory cultural practices enabled in large part by their marginality, a theme I develop in this chapter.

Through my research, drawing on newspaper accounts, legal cases, interviews with cemetery personnel, discussions with mourners, analysis of marketing materials, and on-site visits to some of the best-known pet cemeteries, it has become apparent to me that pet cemeteries and pet mourning practices provide a kind of "junior death" experience. Minimized in importance in comparison with human cemeteries, even the largest, oldest, and most beautiful pet cemeteries lack the broad public recognition of dignity that most people grant to human cemeteries. The physical geography of pet cemeteries—their location and layout—and their prohibitions against the comingling of human and animal dead circumscribe a secondary, somewhat liminal status.

Crucially, pet cemeteries are for *pets*, not for animals more generally. I address the history of pet keeping in the United States and the categorical distinctions among pets and other animals more fully in the next chapter. For now, I note only that pet cemeteries are extremely circumscribed in those species they welcome. They do not memorialize the deaths of the billions of animals produced for food; of "wild" animals; of animals regarded as pests, like termites; of animals such as burros kept primarily for their ability to work for humans; or of animals kept for entertainment or research purposes, such as residents of laboratories or zoos. There may be occasional exceptions to these categorizations, notable primarily because of their category crossing, as when a rat, often seen as an urban pest to be eliminated, crosses into the category of beloved pet and is provided with food, medical care, and human affection. A rat buried in a pet cemetery is a "pet." A rat poisoned by urban pest control is "vermin."[4]

This social status of the pet as in between that of the non-pet animal and that of a human results in a flexible arena of meaning making.[5] In pet cemeteries, some of the conventions associated with human burials in the twentieth- and twenty-first-century United States, like funeral services, are often dispensed with; other conventions, such as maintaining a generally somber and formal demeanor in the cemetery itself, may be contravened. In other words, pet burial practices are both similar to and different from those for humans, in terms of both omissions of certain practices and inclusions of others.

My research reveals that in the United States, mourning practices in pet cemeteries allow for a more improvisational, personalized, even exuberant memorialization than is typical in human cemeteries. This is evidenced through individually handcrafted grave markers: decorations like statues, dolls, toys, whirligigs, poems, photographs, and even negative "epitaphs" ("Mean, Rotten Dog—We Will Miss You!") that would be deemed inappropriate in human cemeteries.[6] In addition, through their public programs, some of the large cemeteries, like Hartsdale in New York State, turn themselves into informal community centers, bringing together loosely knit, usually invisible publics—those who mourn for animals. Although data on who buries their pet and how are scant, my observations, and anecdotal evidence so far, suggest that men and women of all classes, ethnic and racial affiliations, religions, ages, and regions of the United States use pet cemeteries today.

Antecedents

Contemporary US pet cemeteries have their antecedents in the Victorian period in the United States and Europe, but there are many much older cases of formal animal burial practices worldwide, some dating back thousands of years. One of the earlier sites is in Palestine, dating from about twelve thousand years ago, where excavation of a stone-covered tomb revealed the remains of a woman posed with her hand resting on the neck of a puppy. As Susan McHugh notes in her cultural history of the dog, similar discoveries at sites in China, Iraq, Chile, and elsewhere indicate the geographic reach of such practices in ancient times.[7] But dogs weren't the only animals interred in prehistory. In Egypt, there is evidence of the mummification not only of dogs but also of cats, monkeys, and birds dating to as early as 1,000 BCE. While some of these animals were interred in people's tombs, parcels of land along the Nile were set aside specifically for animals. Greeks and Romans also honored animal dead during the pre-Christian era. Alexander the Great (356–323 BCE) supposedly led a formal funeral procession for his hound Peritas, erected a large stone monument honoring the dog, and ordered a yearly celebration in the animal's memory.

The global history of animal burials is extensive and far exceeds the scope of this chapter, which focuses specifically on the contemporary period, and especially on US practices. But it is important to note that burying animals is not a new phenomenon, and that such a practice almost always connotes social value.[8] Since most animals aren't buried, the act of interment can be assumed to mark the importance, symbolic or individual, of that animal and her/his relationship to an individual or a community.

In the ancient past, animals may have been buried because they were totems or symbols, or part of ritual sacrifices or other ceremonies tied to specific cosmologies of time and place. Viking burial practices included burying a horse with a horseman, which may have been intended to provide the human with transportation to the afterlife.[9]

But even so long ago, we must allow for the ambiguities of relationships and for the probability that some of the buried animals were valued not only for their material, symbolic, or cosmological value but also in more affective ways. Barbara J. King recounts the evocative case of a burial found in the village of Çatalhöyük in Turkey, dating back to around eight thousand to nine thousand years ago.[10] In this community, sheep and goats were raised for meat, and burying such animals was an extremely uncommon act. Yet excavations by archaeologists Nerissa Russell and B. S. During revealed a man and a lamb interred together in what was, for that community, the traditional burial place—a pit dug beneath the floor of a residence.

We will never know why that particular individual human and animal were so entwined in death. Russell suggested that the lamb, a domesticated animal, had been brought into the household in an ambiguous manner, not quite kin yet part of the household in a way the outdoor flocks were not. King cautions that with little further evidence, all we can know for sure is that this lamb meant a great deal to the person buried with it. This example, though so distant in time and place from my research here, points toward some of the key issues that will unfold in this chapter around the following question: how do our acts of burial and mourning for animals articulate changing social relations and political frameworks of value?

To approach this question, we can look to more recent history, to the Victorian era of the latter half of the nineteenth century, which saw a blossoming of pet ownership and burial needs in parts of Europe. The poor often resorted to placing dead animals in a sack weighted with stones and throwing them in a river. (Three thousand such animals were removed from the Seine in 1899 alone.) The wealthy could bury pets on their estates. But others sneaked into municipal parks after dark to bury their pets illegally, making the parks into unsanctioned pet cemeteries. Some even slipped into human cemeteries and buried their pets there under the cover of darkness, secretly fouling the line between human and animal geographies of death.

As animal aid societies developed in the latter half of the nineteenth century, so too did formal burial sites for pets, with the best-known predecessor of the contemporary pet cemetery being Le Cimitière des Chiens in the Parisian suburb of Asnières, founded in 1899 by Madame Maguerite Durand. Although the French name translates to "the Dogs' Cemetery," in fact, dogs, cats, monkeys, rabbits, parrots, lions, and horses are buried there.[11] In an unusual public exhibition move, and one that would be nearly inconceivable today in a human cemetery, the Cimitière des Chiens supported itself by charging admission to tourists and selling souvenir postcards. In the late 1950s, sunny Sunday afternoons could attract upwards of six hundred visitors. Without more information, I can only speculate about what those visitors, most of whom presumably didn't have a pet buried there, came to see—a beautiful park, the grave of movie-star German shepherd Rin Tin Tin, a spectacle of ornate statuary, like the life-size stone statues of Marquise and Tony, the beloved dogs of one Princess Lobanof, or simply the curiosity of a cemetery dedicated to animals.

The cemetery continues to be used today and to expand. When I visited it several years ago, it offered a calming, serene hiatus from the bustle of the surrounding town and a physical testimony to the thousands of humans who loved their animals and chose to memorialize them in individual graves with unique inscriptions and designs. That this cemetery not only continues to exist and is sustained despite a century of demographic and real estate changes in what is now not so much a separate town as a suburb of Paris, dynamic home to new immigrant communities, asserts the importance of pets to any who would doubt it.

During the Victorian era—the latter half of the nineteenth century—when La Cimitière des Chiens was founded, wealthy pet owners engaged in commemorative acts for dead animals that closely paralleled those for humans. Elaborate monuments, including marble doghouses and animal sculptures, adorned many animal graves, and some people conducted formal graveside services for their pets, reading Bible excerpts and dressing in black mourning clothes. Famous pets even lay in state for viewing by mourners, like the Philadelphia canine thespian Zip, who received his public lying in a velvet robe in a walnut casket. Some people commemorated their pets in photographs taken after death, the animal posed as if sleeping on a pillow, following the custom of the time of portraying dead children. Special lockets or rings provided a hiding place for a lock of fur, and some pets were stuffed and set on the mantle, next to portraits of deceased human members of the family.[12] Other pets were memorialized in poetic eulogies, like that published by the writer Thomas Hardy in his poem "Last Words to a Dumb Friend," in which he declared, "Pet was never mourned as you," recalling his buried cat—"Your small mound beneath the tree."[13]

Contemporary Practices

Today's animal mourning practices are rarely so elaborate, and even more restrained actions are only marginally socially acceptable. Although pet ownership in the United States is booming, with well over half of all households having at least one pet, only a small percentage, perhaps 2%, of deceased pets—mostly dogs and cats—are being buried in pet cemeteries.[14] The rest are cremated individually, their ashes kept in urns at home as a remembrance, or are cremated en masse by veterinarians or animal shelters, dumped in landfills, sent to rendering plants, left for dead on the highway, or buried, often illegally but without penalty, in backyards.

Mass graves, which for humans are associated with genocide or the extremity of war, are a common option for pets, and are usually associated with landfills, where, for example, a veterinarian may dispose of the dead animal if the owner wishes. When a cemetery option is chosen, it is absolutely essential that the actual body of the pet, and that body only, be interred in the chosen spot, or in the case of cremation, that the identifiable ashes be returned to the owners.[15] Recent court cases have shown both the transgression of this expectation for pet remains and the outrage those transgressions cause.

The importance of the grave holding the specific remains of the beloved animal, and no other, is underlined by a 1991 court case that brought federal and state charges against the Long Island Pet Cemetery in Middle Island, Long Island, New York. The cemetery was charged with having cast, since 1984, more than two hundred thousand pet bodies into a pit instead of cremating or burying them in specified graves as the pet owners desired. Rather than the individual cremations that had been requested, mass cremations had taken place, and generalized "ashes" were doled out to mourning owners awaiting the remains of their pet.[16] The case gained visibility when singer La Toya Jackson attended the disinterment of one of the graves to see if her pet's body was there, only to find that it was empty and that the pet, Ruffian, had never been buried there.[17]

In a later court case in the state of New York, Terence McGlashan was found guilty of fraud and ordered to pay $25,000 in damages to animal welfare organizations for dumping thousands of pet carcasses into open burial pits on a local farm after having been paid by those pets' owners to provide cremation services.[18] While cases of human cemetery fraud along similar lines of nonperformance of promised burial services are not unheard of, the mind-numbing scale of bodies involved in these infractions with animals, along with the minimal fines imposed, is a measure of animals' lower, more "disposable" status. A continuing lack of regulation for pet cemeteries and pet crematories (the latter an industry generating more than $3 billion in yearly revenue) reflects this second-class status, and makes abuses more likely than in the human funeral industry.[19]

In these instances, the outrage is at the absence of presence—the fact that the presumed hidden presence of the body buried in a grave is a fraud. Had this never come to light, the mourning process for Ruffian's owner probably could have continued apace; but the absence of the presumed presence deauthorized that process, making it, like the pet cemetery involved, fraudulent. The hidden display of the unique dead body is essential. With cremation, the specific ashes of the specific pet are required, whether or not we could ever detect a difference between the ashes of your dog or the ashes of mine.[20] In this way, the sacrosanct aura attributed to bodily remains in these practices is very similar for both humans and animals. Here notions of individuality and authenticity combine with the "museum effect" of the really real as a talisman that transports us across time and space (in this case, across the "barrier of death" to continued contact with the "departed").

Although fraud continues, such swindles are not representative of an industry that has recently become increasingly professionalized.[21] Today in the United States, I estimate that there are over six hundred formally recognized pet cemeteries, nearly double the number in existence when the Association of Pet Cemeteries was founded in 1971.[22] Some of the most famous have names like Bide-a-Wee (where Richard Nixon's dog Checkers is buried) and Bubbling Well and offer elaborate landscaped grounds.[23] Bubbling Well Pet Memorial Park in Napa, California, overlooks a country club and includes "duck ponds, fountains, waterfalls, a mini-zoo with a llama and an emu, Japanese gardens, and statuary from around the world." Special areas of the grounds include a "Garden for Mighty Midgets" (for miniature dogs), a "Garden of Honors" (for guide dogs and other heroic animals), a "Kitty Corner" for cats, and special sections for turtles, snakes, and birds.[24] For those who do not choose an individual burial, a registry provides the name and human companion's name for each animal cremated or given a "country burial" (deposited in a mass grave off-site). The registry is located at the center of the grounds and is adorned with flowers, so that even those choosing this cheaper method also have a specific site and sight on which to focus their grief, despite the absence of unique physical remains.

Some of these large cemeteries offer clients nearly all the accoutrements that human burials can have: a viewing of the body, a variety of caskets or crematorium urns to choose from, gravestones, and floral arrangements for decoration.[25] Special liturgies for animals are available, and gravestones often have crosses or Stars of David engraved on them.[26] Some burials even attract a large number of mourners. At the Bubbling Well cemetery in California, I spoke to director Dan Harberts, who recalled that one family, of Samoan origin, gathered thirty relatives to attend the burial of a pet. Others mourn in private, as did the man who came to Bubbling Well alone every night for three months, sitting in the dark by his newly buried pet's grave until ten o'clock.[27]

Although burial of a pet in a pet cemetery is clearly a luxury in the sense that it isn't required either by law or by convention, the evidence I have amassed so far suggests that clients come from a variety of socioeconomic realms and age groups, from young families with children to senior citizens. (Senior citizens were the most prominent group in the 1970s, suggests Dan Harberts of Bubbling Well, but this has changed.)[28] The costs can range from under $100 for cremation to $1,000 for a more elaborate affair.[29] For those who desire the more expensive options, interest-free long-term payment plans are sometimes available, making these options available to almost anyone with some disposable income if the burial is a priority for that individual. As Harberts says, "It's a nonmoney issue."[30]

Some cemeteries, like the Key Underwood Coon Dog Memorial Graveyard, are less official and more communal in their attraction of patrons. The Coon Dog Graveyard, in a piney woods in northwest Alabama, is the resting place for more than 170 "coon dogs"—shorthand for a type of American-bred hunting dog known for treeing raccoons and other small prey—and for coon dogs only.[31] It was founded in 1937, when Key Underwood buried his beloved dog Trooper at the site in a cotton sack and marked the grave with a rock on which he had chiseled a cross, Trooper's name, and the dates of his birth and death. Every Labor Day, mourners and friends gather to eat barbecue at the cemetery and to swap hunting stories, and they hold a "liars contest," in which they tell tall tales of hunting prowess. Under the dappled sunlight amid the pine trees, individual graves bear the names of dog and owner and display a full range of individuality and styles, from the formal to the informal, the professionally made to the homemade—including headstones of chiseled granite and incised sheet metal, and simple wooden hand-painted crosses—bearing canine names like Red, Rusty, Champ, and Flop.[32] Some mourners even drive from far beyond state lines to bury their dogs there, organizing funeral services complete with eulogies, caskets, prayers, black-hatted mourners, and guest-book signings, as was the case in 2008, when Raynor Frost of Pennsylvania came down to Alabama to bury his seven-year-old championship hunting dog The Merch.[33] Such formal burials in an informal, non-commercial site create a community of mourners and celebrate a specific type of human and animal bond—that of hunting dog and hunting human.

Variations in Contemporary Mourning for Humans as "Available Discourse"

Social practices of cemetery commemoration and mourning may be different indeed for humans and for animals, even though the physical presence of the bodies or cremated remains of the deceased is usually required in both instances as the anchor of meaning for the place and event. It is hard to imagine a barbeque and "liars contest" being held each year at a human cemetery. However, the range of social events held at human cemeteries may be wider than is generally acknowledged, and may differ significantly among ethnic communities and religious groups—a point that must remain speculative until further research investigates specific practices among various ethnically and religiously identified communities. Traditional Irish Catholic wakes can combine sorrow and gaiety, although they are generally not held at the cemetery itself. And in a study of contemporary Mexican American cemetery practices in San Antonio, Texas, Lynn Gosnell and Suzanne Gott emphasize that for some Mexican American working-class communities, crafting an ongoing relationship with the dead "focuses on the ephemeral objects that appear, disappear, and return throughout the calendar year . . . evidence of a dynamic and artful communication process based within family and community."[34] In their study, bold colors, the repurposing of mass-produced objects, and the direct address to the dead ("A Kiss for You," proclaimed a bobbing, lip-shaped helium balloon) along with the incorporation of handmade items and attentive individualism in grave decoration all point to communicative aspects that appear, with individual distinctiveness, in pet cemeteries too.

While I don't wish to draw any direct lines of influence between this particular San Antonio community's mourning practices for their human dead and the more dispersed pet cemetery mourning practices that I am discussing here, the focus in that community on crafting an ongoing, individualized, creative, and *public* relationship between mourners and the deceased exhibits some key hallmarks that are emerging in pet cemeteries.

What these parallels imply is that in many pet cemeteries and for many mourners from many different ethnic, religious, or regional communities, pets elicit an exuberant public expressivity that *may or may not* be deemed acceptable in their home communities' mode of commemorating dead humans. What we find in pet cemeteries—handmade headstones, remembrances in the form of poems and confessions left at the grave, grave-topping toys and objects—more often echoes the handmade and homemade creativity associated in an earlier century with rural and poor communities—with "folk art"—than it does the quiet restraint and uniform gravesites of the now-popular style of human "memorial park."[35] The cemetery-design movement of the latter half of the twentieth century in the United States has led to acres of close-clipped grass and flat tombstones that interrupt neither the mechanized mower nor the eye of the visitor with (apparently) inconvenient reminders of individuality.[36]

At pet cemeteries, however, this uniformity is rejected, and many graves are decorated with personal objects. The leaving of objects of everyday use, historically associated in some communities with the journey of the dead into an afterlife, seems to have broadened here beyond that particular symbolic import to a more generalized indication of tribute.[37] Such objects serve as personal remembrances associated with the one who leaves the object or as indexical invocations of the now-dead, present but unseen body. This connection to the once-living body that touched or used that material object provides a sort of DNA trace of physical presence and a reminder of the bodily action once associated with the item, a reminder that implicitly evokes memories of the deceased as moving—not still—and alive—not dead.

This evocation of life is especially vivid when toys or objects like water bowls used by the deceased pet are left at the grave.[38] The conceptual linkage of pet with family position of child—indicated by the leaving of toys—may also, for some, loosen the bounds of emotive expression. As Gosnell and Gott note, grave decoration is a communicative practice directed both toward the deceased and toward the living, no matter the specific forms it takes.[39] A toy can evoke not only joyful play associated with a pet, referencing human actions, but also memories of the physical actions of the animal who once used the toy, the talismanic and the indexical combined.

Thus, if a wider range of social practices may be deemed "appropriate" at a pet cemetery than at many human ones in the United States, so too is a wider range of sentimental expression in the design and decoration of grave markers and grave sites—that is, the material culture of mourning. This growing flexibility and creativity aren't due solely to hybrid expressivities regarding burial crossing the physical lines of ethnic communities, like the instances discussed by Gosnell and Gott, or to the influence of social media like Facebook, Instagram, and other forms of easy electronic dissemination that can circulate visual images of grave decoration practices far beyond their locality or community.[40] These changes should also be seen in a wider context of shifting practices in public mourning and the lessening of the power of formal institutions, like churches, in controlling expressions of mourning.

Increasingly, as Erica Doss tells us, various groups in the United States are asserting their "right" to be incorporated into the national fabric of memory by having a memorial to their past erected, whether this consists of a roadside memorial with a Christian cross for a traffic accident victim or a memorial in a town square commemorating victims of past injustices, like that erected in Duluth, Minnesota, in 2008 marking the site where three African American men (Elias Clayton, Elmer Jackson, and Isaac McGhie) were lynched in 1920. Doss offers a very useful formulation of what she calls "monument mania," or an accelerating, urgent, even frenzied effort during the past few decades in this nation to erect monuments, and especially memorials, to articulate public expressions of "affect," or public feeling.[41]

In part, Doss attributes this effort to an expanding notion of rights to public recognition of groups within a populace growing increasingly diverse every decade. But along with that, she sees an expansion in notions of what a commemoration itself can be, now encompassing touring material manifestations, like the Names Project Foundation AIDS Memorial Quilt, and immaterial memorial sites, like hundreds of online tributes to victims of national disasters like the 9/11 terrorist attacks and Hurricane Katrina in New Orleans.[42]

I suggest that material mourning practices at pet cemeteries are drawing from an "available discourse" of dramatic, affective response to death that has become widely reproduced by the media reporting on temporary and immediate mourning at sites of unexpected human death and disaster, like terrorist attacks, car accidents, violent historical incidents, and school shootings. While the growth in pet cemeteries may not approach the "mania" that Doss articulates, it does clearly assert the right to grieve publicly by a segment of the population, pet lovers, who often lack legitimacy in the public sphere.

Public mourning is a political practice. As Doss notes of the contemporary mania for public memorials, it is "shaped by individual impulses and factional grievances, by special interest claims for esteem and recognition, and by efforts to symbolize and enshrine the particular issues and aspirations of diverse and often stratified publics."[43] Specifically, Doss is discussing a passion for public art/memorials, but I suggest here that the material manifestation of mourning, in whatever public form and for whatever form of life, is a political act of claiming importance. It claims importance for the deceased (a "grievable life"— a concept I discuss in the following chapter) and also of the community that asserts its right to publicly grieve. It is the publicness of the grief that is most important, for it claims a right to historical representation.[44] It says, "We are here, and this loss is important to us." In this case, the "us" at a pet cemetery is not a national, ethnic, gender-specific, generational, or social-class "us." It is all these dimensions of social formations articulated in reference to the valuation of a nonhuman animal companion life.[45]

In lacking the legitimizing functions of long-standing social rituals, people mourning for pets draw creatively from a variety of old and new practices and symbolic materializations to produce new forms of mourning. These forms go beyond conventional human cemetery and human mourning templates (a grave site, a gravestone) to encompass the more improvisatory and more dramatically assertive markers of loss that appear in temporary memorials to human victims of unexpected, often violent, death, especially to the "innocent." Pets, I suggest, generally assume the status of the "innocent" dead because, even though in most cases they aren't seen as victims (as human victims of violent crime or terrorism are), they are seen as innocent of human motives and of political maneuvering.

At pet cemeteries, the leaving of original poems, the references to intimate memories, and the depositing of material objects from daily life, like pet toys, all implicitly refer more to the spontaneous mourning practices associated with the deaths of public celebrities like Princess Diana, or the shocking loss of life in the Columbine High School shootings, or the fall of the Twin Towers in New York City in 2001 than they do to the formalized and restrained memorial tablets and carefully arranged flowers prescribed by so many contemporary US human cemeteries. These types of spontaneous memorials, while not new, have become more common in European and US contexts in the last couple of decades and thus more broadly known.[46] The expressive presence, aesthetic style, and practices associated with each of these tragedies' memorials were widely circulated by the mass media, providing a visual and performative archive of mourning practices encountered by millions.

The intimate and improvisatory nature of mourning artifacts at pet cemeteries recalls these temporary memorials, which often consist of bouquets still in their cellophane wrappers, teddy bears as signs of the innocent, baseball caps worn by the mourners and inscribed with their sentiments, toys, candles, handwritten poems, and so on. These mementos serve as a bridge between the tragic event and the mourners' homage to the event, referencing the feelings of the public while serving as offerings to memory. As Doss notes about the material culture of grief, its meaning "rests in how things evoke memories, sustain thoughts, constitute political conditions, and conjure states of being."[47] Things also evoke not only memories but also feelings, and provide a focus for actions (placing, touching, kissing, lighting candles, et cetera), activating "physical, intimate, performative" gestures[48] engaged with these "semantically dense" objects.[49] Pet toys like the squeaky little red fire hydrant or the well-thrown tennis ball are powerful examples of such "semantically dense" objects.

Another growing public practice, spontaneous mourning, is found in the roadside memorials, or *descansos*, literally "resting places," for car accident victims. Like the celebrity death or the mass-killing memorials mentioned above, these too form part of a contemporary public visual archive and performative repertory of grieving, an "available discourse" for pet mourners to draw on in their own improvisatory practices at pet cemeteries.[50] Erected on roadsides, close to the site of a fatal car accident, this type of memorial to a human death often includes a cross, the name of the deceased, flowers or adornments, photographs, personal articles, and season-specific decorative refurbishment at holiday times. The *descanso* asserts the intense grief of those who mourn a sudden tragic loss at a specific site and memorialize not the final resting place of an individual's remains but the site of the last moment of his or her life.[51]

Once most common in the American Southwest, an outgrowth of Catholic Hispanic mourning, these roadside memorials are now seen throughout the United States. They can be erected by family or friends, without formal permission from any business or public entity, thus asserting both the freedom of individuals to bypass the power of corporate, state, and religious institutions and a right to public recognition of their grief. However, their increasing presence has drawn growing controversy. Do they distract drivers? Warn of dangerous roads? Contravene the public separation of religion and the state on state-financed roads? While police often let these markers stay, their persistence can generate legal wrangling between the grieving and departments of transportation.[52] Yet many grieving families defy state regulations prohibiting or limiting the style of roadside memorial that individuals can place. Continuing to tend personal memorials in the face of legal restriction is an assertive act of grieving. It proclaims the right to grieve in a nondominant way and calls on the wider public—hailing every passing driver—to recognize that grief and its mode of commemoration as worthy of respect.[53]

The increase in informal memorials, from roadside tributes to those spontaneously erected at sites of national tragedy, and even the controversies surrounding them, provides widely circulating information, a sort of "available discourse" of mourning through material culture practices. This available discourse can be mobilized, by various individuals and groups, to transpose meaning from one context (human death) to another (animal death). Those humans who mourn beings falling outside the realms of fully recognized legitimacy, such as pets, can find inspiration in other types of nonconventional and not fully legitimized types of public mourning. The creativity of these sites and their powerful, even defiant, claims of a right to grieve publicly are often echoed in pet cemeteries where, even if the "cemetery" designation seems conventional, the subject mourned is always somewhat suspect from the point of view of non–pet lovers.

What People Actually Do: The Improvisatory and the Intimate

After death, as in life, pets seem to elicit "play" and creativity in their owners and a lessening of adult self-censure of amateurishness. For instance, the pets of military personnel are interred in the Presidio Pet Cemetery in San Francisco, and grave markers there are done in the black-stencil print style used to personalize duffle bags in the armed services. Unlike most human cemeteries and many official pet cemeteries, the Presidio keeps no written records of who is buried where or who did the burying (it is a "dig your own" cemetery), adding to the ad hoc air and the sense of emotion-driven improvisation around these animal bodies.[54]

Visiting the cemetery, I found that less-than-flattering, but heartfelt, inscriptions—which would never be found in human cemeteries—are publicly displayed: "Our Knuckle Headed-Parakeet to Paradise," states one wooden marker, and "Puddin' Dandridge, Mean thing, rotten Cat, but loved and missed by us all," reads another. Hand-drawn signs of fish and Siamese cats, a hand-carved wooden crown (for Regina the dog), and elaborate fenced rectangles, like that for Molly, "our Collie," signify the realm of the amateur. Molly's grave site includes a pink-and-purple painted marker displaying a peace symbol, a heart, and a smiley face; an enclosure with geraniums, daisies, and a tiny American flag; an extended poem, "Ode to Molly," including lines like "We ran, we played together, sometimes taking a bath . . ."; and a now-faded color photograph in a clear plastic frame of a man, woman, and collie. Such intimate recollections as bathing together would not be displayed at a human grave.

A similar sense of the improvisatory also reigns at Bubbling Well, where all the graves are carefully recorded and marked. Unlike their counterparts at most US human cemeteries, the grave markers are highly individualized creations. Many include black-and-white photos embossed on porcelain shields, sometimes featuring both the pet and the "owner," giving the public a visual rendering of a bond now severed, symbolized by the grave. Some mourners decorate their pets' graves for each changing season, just as they might decorate their own homes—a pumpkin theme for fall, and a Christmas theme for winter. This practice parallels somewhat the human one of placing flowers and flags on Memorial Day, but is taken much further in its expression of individuality.

Another way the graves are individualized is through adding hand-crafted structures and standing objects. One grave at Bubbling Well Pet Memorial Park has a "headstone" made out of welded copper tubing and, when I visited, was adorned with orange-and-white ghost figures (presumably because Halloween was approaching) along with a stuffed yellow doll figure perched on top. Another grave featuring a standard flat plaque in the ground was accompanied by a three-foot-tall Snoopy whirligig on a post, and several wooden angels and a butterfly were stuck among the flowers planted around it. The grave site resembled a fanciful garden, with whimsical garden ornaments complementing the flowers.

By contrast, exuberant and unique human memorials can cause controversy and ultimately can be taken down, judged "inappropriate" even if the trend in human gravestone design these days is toward personalizing the granite with carved images of things the deceased enjoyed, like a bottle of beer, a pickup truck, a sports car, or a bag of golf clubs.[55] A striking example of this type of policing of taste was reported on CNN in 2013, with the headline "Cemetery Denies Sponge-Bob Monuments for Slain Army Sergeant." Sergeant Kimberly Walker, who survived two tours of Iraq, retuned home to Cincinnati only to be murdered there. Her distraught family ordered two unusual headstones for her grave (the second one reserved for future use for her twin sister, Kara, so they could ultimately rest side by side). The Spring Grove Cemetery in Cincinnati approved the family's plans for the monuments, and two six-foot-tall, seven-thousand-pound statues of the cartoon character SpongeBob SquarePants were commissioned. One wears a US Army cap to honor Kimberly, and the other was carved with her sister Kara's US Navy specialist cap.

The $26,000 giant SpongeBobs, like the TV cartoon character, feature pockmarked sponge heads, with faces sporting a two-toothed grin and big bugged-out eyes, atop skinny legs encased in tiny breeches. The only details distinguishing the statues from the cartoon original are the military caps perched on their blocky heads. Kimberly loved the SpongeBob character so much that each year she had a SpongeBob birthday party, and she decorated her home with SpongeBob curtains. The family strove to salute her passions in the face of murder. Yet despite Spring Grove's original approval, the massive cartoon monuments proved to be too much for the dignity of the cemetery, which ordered them removed just one day after installation.[56] I wouldn't be surprised if a giant SpongeBob existed somewhere in some pet cemetery as a grave marker. This type of playful celebration is welcome in such settings.

Other mourning objects are more touching than celebratory. Pet graves often include mementos—those things the pet used or loved— like a water dish or a squeaky toy. These little homemade memorials, like offerings to the dead in many societies, remain undisturbed by strangers and are oddly touching in their indexical invocation of the once-living pet and her or his embodied actions. A human parallel might be leaving a baby's shoe atop a child's grave or a favorite mug or pipe on an adult's. For humans, these talismans are often thought too intimate for public display, but that intimacy is not deemed obscene or unseemly in the case of animals. Cemeteries allow for the public display of private grief, and pet cemeteries, less bound by convention, have the freedom of the marginalized to exceed convention and to embrace excess without penalty precisely because of their status as marginal.

Long poems written by the pet's owner are popular, and allow for a fuller expression of feeling than the short inscriptions more typical of human graves. Jean Roden left this poem on her cat Samantha's grave at Bubbling Well, a poem that evokes the cat's daily life activities:

For my darling Grayfoots—
Endless paths of velvet for your precious silver paws
Endless fields of flowers for your eyes to survey
Endless breezes blowing intriguing scents your way
Endless sunbeams warming your fur while you pause,
Endless my grief
Endless my love.

A pithier but no less effective inscription marks the plaque for Rosebud (1967–78): "She sang, She snored, She licked, She loved." Both of these poetic expressions describe the animal's world and situate her as an active subject in that world.

Other inscriptions ask for forgiveness or look forward to the time when human and animal will be reunited after death. Sam, an Irish setter, received this memorial inscription: "He gave his heart and asked for nothing. One day I will be with you. Together in Life, together in Death. Please Forgive the wrong I've done Little Brother of my heart." Signed: "Owner: Jerry L. Friedman." While the expression of desire for union in an afterlife is common in many human cemeteries, confessions of "having wronged" the deceased are rare. Again, this disparity reflects the naked expression of intimate, possibly ambivalent, emotion that, by convention, is allowed in pet cemeteries but would be discouraged in lasting form (even if permissible at a graveside service) in a human cemetery.[57]

Processing Loss, Grieving (for) Subjects, and Physical Copresence with the Dead

Some of these sentiments may seem extreme. We can hypothesize that they are a complex mix of negative and positive emotions expressed because, as marginal social spaces, pet cemeteries aren't subject to the same long-standing protocols or social scrutiny applied to most human cemeteries. We might also see them as reflecting the difficulty of coming to terms with a kind of loss that, in the United States, is socially unsanctioned, relatively speaking.[58] Unsanctioned loss may be harder than sanctioned loss to integrate into our lives after the loved one's death, more likely to evoke the lingering melancholy described by Freud.

Expressing the anguish of loss through actions at the pet cemetery such as grave decoration occurs at a somewhat protected, semipublic site, free from the eyes of non–pet lovers. Although, technically, anyone can enter a pet cemetery, no matter how they feel about pets, those who do tend toward a certain type. The pet cemetery, de facto, draws a crowd of similarly minded people and thus becomes a semipublic realm. However, outside that realm and its implied community, daily interactions with friends, family, or coworkers can tend to discount the impact of a pet's death. The physical cemetery, very often so important for the mourning of human dead, can take on an even more charged aura when it is the *only* guaranteed "safe space" for mourning that some grieving pet owners have.[59]

In a careful study of mourning behaviors in human cemeteries, scholar Philip Bachelor, of the Australasian Cemeteries and Crematoria Association, writes about the importance of the physical cemetery as a site of memorialization that mourners can visit to help focus their mourning processes.[60] On the basis of a study of three thousand mourners at several different Australian cemeteries, he finds that despite the cultural, religious, and generational variations in attitudes toward death and mourning practices, the physical site of a cemetery (or mausoleum holding the body or cremated remains of an individual) is extremely important for millions of people. Frequency of visits to the cemetery correlates with the closeness of the relationship with the deceased and with the recency of the loss, declining over time. We have no comparable research for pet cemetery mourners, but it is reasonable to expect that, as is the case with our mourning for humans, seeking copresence with the remains of the dead can be of great importance across many social and demographic divides.[61]

Cemeteries provide not only a place for the dignified and presumably eternal disposition of bodily remains but also a place for mourners to feel and performatively express sadness, grief, and sorrow and to seek solace and peace. It is important that they do so in a site that formally legitimizes their grief, protects them from the immediate demands of daily life, and places them, immediately or at least in principle, in the presence of other mourners. Bachelor puts it this way: "For many mourners, cemeteries are venues of important social support and assistance towards grief mitigation through mutual sharing of personal bereavement experiences with other visitors."[62] This is especially true, he notes, for those sharing a cultural or ethnic affiliation in a specific area or type of cemetery.[63] While Bachelor didn't have "pet lovers" in mind, surely they can be seen as forming a community based on a subcultural affiliation. The importance of access to support by engaging with others in a sacralized space—the pet cemetery—becomes apparent. It is fostered too by pet cemeteries' sponsorship of events like pet-loss support groups and nonsectarian "blessings of the animals" services that bring pet lovers together.[64] We can imagine how the relative *lack* of such sites for pet owners/guardians can inhibit not only the public expression of mourning but also the emotional transitions that enable the mourner to cope with the loss and integrate it into her or his ongoing life.

Although grieving for pets is, overall, becoming somewhat more acceptable in the United States than it was more than fifty years ago, as evidenced by the production of pet-loss condolence cards, for example, this endorsement varies from family to family, between genders (with more women than men regarding the pet as "part of the family"), and from community to community.[65] While slowly growing, the public validation of grieving for pets remains very limited. For one thing, few would imagine that they could request "compassionate leave" from work to attend the funeral of a pet. Therefore, the pet cemetery becomes even more important for the cultural and personal work of legitimizing grief and for helping the mourner see her- or himself as part of a much larger, if widely dispersed, community. (Online mourning sites expand this sense of community even further, and their popularity, I suggest, correlates with the lack of physical cemetery sites and with the delegitimization of grief that that lack indexes. Cybersites, however, never offer the publicly validated copresence of mourner and pet remains that is such a powerful anchor for cemetery grieving.)[66]

The pet cemetery thus becomes a highly charged site of remembrance and legitimation because it is *the one* absolutely safe physical place to freely express grief for a deceased animal companion. This dimension interacts with the improvisatory freedom of marginality, discussed above, to render pet cemeteries uniquely exuberant in their modes of display. At times, this expressivity borders on compulsion. The lone man that Harberts told me about, who came to Bubbling Well night after night, perhaps seeking solace, redemption, or comprehension of the physical finality of the loss of his companion, shows just how hard this process of grieving can be for some individuals when the wider society refuses to sanction their loss and only the pet cemetery provides the literal ground on which to safely express grief.

Bachelor notes that extreme behaviors, like daily visitation over long periods of time, can indicate what he terms "unresolved grief issues."[67] Is it any wonder that socially delegitimized mourning can result in actions that appear to some as obsessive, excessive, and idiosyncratic? Frederick Wiseman's 1978 documentary film *Gates of Heaven* provides portraits of just these types of grieving animal lovers, including some at Bubbling Well; its point of view teeters on the edge of sympathy and ridicule for their "excessive" longing.[68]

"Excessive" or not, taking the actions of grieving pet lovers seriously helps us better theorize intersecting notions of human and animal subjectivities, as I discuss in the introduction to this book. As theorist Kari Weil puts it, reflecting on her own decision to have her horse Peanut cremated: "Mourning means attesting to a life. We are not only autobiographical animals; we are biographical animals who seek to acknowledge those whose lives have been entangled with ours . . . I wanted such a testament to my horse's life."[69] For those who bury their pets in pet cemeteries, there is no doubt that those animals are subjects with lives of their own, intertwined with human ones. They are, without a doubt, "grievable" lives—a concept I engage in detail in the next chapter, along with shifting conceptions of cross-species kinship and new burial practices that literally materialize those concepts.

FIVE

Grievable Lives and New Kinships: Pet Cemeteries and the Changing Geographies of Death

In the opening years of the nineteenth century, the British Romantic William Wordsworth wrote a poem about the death of his dog. It begins like this:

Lie here, without a record of thy worth,
Beneath a covering of the common earth!
It is not from unwillingness to praise,
Or want of love, that here no Stone we raise;
More thou deserv'st; but this man gives to man,
Brother to brother, this is all we can.[1]

Despite his grief, the poet acknowledged that his era's respected modes of mourning did not allow for the erection of tombstones for companion animals. Those markers of individuality and respect, of recognized grief and its historical longevity, were reserved for humans—"this man gives to man." This was to change soon after Wordsworth's lifetime, especially as the Victorian era of the latter half of the nineteenth century unfolded, and change continues today with innovations in animal burials that articulate the shifting politics of value and human-animal relationships that cemeteries craft in stone.

In the preceding chapter, I discussed pet cemeteries, arguing that we should regard them as sites of improvisatory, creative acts of mourning that draw on available ritual forms and social and political discourses, yet reconfigure them to chart new territories of public behavior. I suggested that this improvisation and creativity are both required and enabled by the marginalized status of those cemeteries and of the type of grief that they materialize. In this chapter, I delve deeper into the underlying beliefs enabling and constraining that expressive realm in the contemporary United States. Focusing especially on concepts of grievability and the politics of burial practices and burial real estate, I argue that cemeteries, usually thought of as conservative, perpetual spaces, are emerging as a frontline battlefield in the war over changing notions of cross-species kinship and familial configurations. Today, I suggest, instead of merely writing historical and political change in the granite of tombstones, we are also writing it in the upturned earth of graves. By examining a recrafting of a secular-sacred space at the end of a shovel, we find a new politics of value articulated through the geographies of death and burial that occasionally even crosses the species line dividing humans and nonhumans.

Who or What Is a "Pet," and What Does That Mean?

At the core of these mourning practices lies the status of nonhuman animals designated as "pets."[2] Within the United States, and elsewhere, the status of the "pet" has varied considerably over time in terms of the obligations that designation is presumed to demand of the human "owner" or "guardian." Pet keeping is, as cultural historian Katherine C. Grier reminds us, "an integral part of the history of everyday life in the United States. It is connected to changing ideas about human nature, emotional life, individual responsibility, and our society's responsibility to all kinds of dependent others, including people."[3] Varying municipal and state statutes also constitute a matrix of what is deemed acceptable and unacceptable in terms of caring for a pet, institutionalizing parameters of the relationship according to community belief.[4]

Grier traces the evolution of pet keeping as a social practice, especially one that widened in appeal during the 1800s with the rise of an urban middle class with disposable income.[5] Her focus is a shifting political economy of human-animal relations acted out in a specific realm, for pets occupy a realm distinct from animals in the "wild" and from animals domesticated for food. Pets exist within a sphere of human influence and care, and their contributions to humans are measured more in affective terms than in monetary ones. Although a dog may provide safety for a family or its farm animals, protecting them from human or animal predators, or may assist in hunting or in pest control in a barn, expanding into the affective realm, the category of "pet" exceeds those working relationships, and pet keeping can serve simultaneously as a marker of social capital.[6]

A history of those historical changes exceeds the scope of this chapter, but Grier provides a striking and beautifully researched outline of how, during the nineteenth century, pet keeping was seen as validating behaviors of caring and kindness as part of being "well-bred," as encapsulating appropriate behaviors for males and females, and as consistent with appropriate attitudes toward children and other vulnerable populations. Representations of human-pet relations in stories and visual arts positioned the pet as child, as family member (with "family" constituted as a social unit under the benevolent leadership of a patriarch), as sentient being with emotions, and as friend.[7] Ultimately, in England and the United States, changing attitudes toward animals resulted in the founding of welfare organizations like the American Society for the Prevention of Cruelty to Animals in 1866.[8] This development coincided roughly with a rise in attention to pet burials, the expansion of mourning practices like burials and eulogies, and even practices of postmortem photography of pets, similar to memorial photographs of dead children.[9]

Since the nineteenth century, pet keeping has continued to expand in the United States to the point that as of 2015–16, according to the American Pet Products Association, an estimated 65% of US households own a pet, equating to about 79.7 million homes. Of these, 54.4 million households own one or more dogs, while 42.9% have one or more cats.[10] Fish and birds, followed by small animals, reptiles, and, finally, horses (about 2.5 million households) round out the pet-keeping landscape. We can see an overall upward trend in the last twenty-five to thirty years, with the American Pet Products Association reporting a more than 10% increase in pet ownership since 1988, the first year it began keeping records.[11]

Pet keeping supports a substantial industry in the United States, through expenditures on veterinary care, pet food, pet toys, supplies like bedding and cages, and so on. In 2012, the most recent year for which figures are available, pet owners spent approximately $53.33 billion on these needs and services in this nation alone, a figure larger than the total gross domestic product of many nations, such as Ghana, Panama, and Jordan.[12] To the extent that money indexes importance and care, there is no doubt that pet keeping is an important social practice. But the significance of this monetary measure should not be oversimplified. It tells us little about the specifics of human-animal relationships and of the detailed parameters of what pet keeping involves beyond the monetary commitment.

Pet keeping remains a socially variable practice in terms of both actions and meanings, so we must proceed with caution when discussing it to avoid overgeneralization. There are differences across ethnic communities, between urban and rural communities, and probably, at least in terms of attitudes toward animals, between men and women as well. The provision of care, including veterinary health care, the physical integration of the animal into the human abode and activities, and the conceptions of the durability of that bond vary substantially. And, unlike other familial relations, constructed both by convention and by law, these bonds or legal responsibilities are not always seen as lifelong. While very few parents might be willing to send their children away when they change houses, it is not unusual for pet owners to try to find a new home for their pet if their new apartment complex prohibits pet ownership.

Not only does most of the US population live in households with pets but surveys also reveal that a majority of pet owners consider the pet "a part of the family."[13] The actual meaning of this conception and assertion can be revealed only through investigation across multiple demographic denominators. Age, region, ethnic background, religious affiliation, economic status and social class, educational background, gender, family size, and so on may all shape how a particular family in the contemporary United States will understand its relationship with and obligations to its pet.

Christina Risley-Curtiss and colleagues emphasize that although the cohort of subjects in their study (middle-class women of color from the social work field) attributed specific ideas about appropriate human-pet relationships to their ethnic communities, these subjects also noted that they themselves did not always enact those beliefs. A more effective intersectional framework revealed that beliefs were shaped not only by dominant ideas *within* an ethnic community but also by the women's individual life experiences with animals, encounters with what the researchers termed dominant European American middle-class notions of appropriate human-pet relations as depicted in the media, and the influences of peers in ad hoc communities, such as among work colleagues. Nor was it appropriate to assume that differences in treatment of a pet (for instance, a dog not allowed inside the house versus one that sleeps on the owner's bed) indicated differing levels of attachment and care. Such differences could merely enact a convention of species-spatial division deemed appropriate within a specific community, class, or generation.[14]

In addition, these respondents stressed, even when members of various ethnic communities agree that "the pet is a member of the family," that assessment may be based on differing criteria: it may recognize an emotional integration into the family unit, or that an animal is working to contribute to the welfare of the family as a whole, for instance, as ranch dogs do. This research reminds us of how a multitude of social factors can play a role in such perceptions, just as, the researchers note, an individual human's specific relationship with a unique animal can be transformative of his or her notions of what a human-animal bond is.[15] The complexity of this terrain echoes what Bubbling Well Pet Memorial Park director Dan Harberts noted when he said that for his demographically diverse clientele, money alone isn't the true bottom line in the choice to bury a pet in a cemetery. Conceptions of pet subjectivity and the complex and variable notions of familial frameworks that include both humans and animals seem to play a larger role.

Changing Notions of Subjectivity for Animals

Recently, news reports have focused on scientific "evidence" for the notion of subjectivity in animals, with widely circulating pieces like "Dogs Are People Too," which appeared in the *New York Times*, promoting a neurophysiological model that draws parallels between humans and animals in terms of the function of the brain's caudate region.[16]

While pet lovers may welcome these changing recognitions of animal cognition, they aren't waiting for the legal system or scientific researchers to catch up with what they are already assured of: the individuality and subjectivity of unique nonhuman animals. This is always already ritually recognized in mourning practices. In their performance, funerals for pets point to the valuation of the deceased as an individual being, worthy of mourning, even articulating the specifics of her/his life as a dog or cat. Grave markers delineate individual burials and chronicle names and dates of life, announcing the uniqueness accorded a grievable life. These grave markers, prohibited in Wordsworth's time, now record a social history and politics written in stone, one that increasingly accords individuated subjectivity to pets and places them in culturally specific familial matrices.

In studying gravestones in the oldest US pet cemetery, Hartsdale Pet Cemetery in Hartsdale, New York, anthropologist Stanley Brandes charts some significant changes over time. During the post–World War II period, pets began to be distinguished by sex and personality on the carved stones that adorned their graves. Earlier, more generic, designations of "My Pet" became Cha Cha Girl and Candy Man. Names like Lucas, Max, and Chelsea implied the animal's male or female sex, and inscriptions were also more likely to reveal the species of the pet. Over time, Brandes argues, we see a trend toward conferring a more distinctive and well-rounded identity on the animal. In addition, after World War II, we see more memorial photographs included on gravestones. These photos further particularize the deceased, whereas previously, the animal may only have been represented by something like a generic dog sculpture or engraving adorning the tombstone.[17] Brandes attributes these changes to a conceptual shift that more and more firmly positions the animal as a part of the family, as kin, or, for some, as "substitute" children.

Increasingly, the pet is also accorded more explicit religious and ethnic identities through its linkage with the mourning family unit. This is revealed in the post-1980s trend Brandes identifies at Hartsdale Pet Cemetery of including religious markers on the pet's memorial, such as Stars of David or Christian crosses, along with inscriptions such as "In God's Care." Even affectionate names can reference ethnicity, as is the case with a monument to Tiger Levine, which includes Tiger's Yiddishized nickname, Tigalah, in parentheses. The addition of family surnames on gravestones further situates the pet in a family unit with distinctive national or ethnic origins. Mourning practices and the material traces they leave can also index social identities and tie them to the animal. At Hartsdale, the Jewish custom of placing small stones on a monument to show that someone has visited the grave is often followed, and some graves have *yahrzeit* candles—designed to burn for eight days, marking the intense mourning that follows a Jewish human burial—as well.[18]

Overall, Brandes argues, if we read the inscription practices recorded at Hartsdale Pet Cemetery as a historical document, we can see that "since the 1980s, and with growing intensity to the present day, gravestones reveal a fuller picture of the animals beneath the monuments. . . . The deceased have names and surnames, kinship affiliations, religious and ethnic identity, immortal souls, and even personal and emotional features that parallel those of human children."[19] We are a long way from the Wordsworth opening poem here, with its denial of a gravestone to his dog. Contemporary practices reveal not only an intense sense of animals as unique, individual, social subjects but also an increasing incorporation of them into a relational familial model based on nonbiological kinship. There is no doubt that for the mourners, these are "grievable lives."

Grievable Lives

As a consideration of the geographies of cemeteries reveals, not all grievable lives are created equal, nor do they belong to the same categories—the calculus of burial real estate makes this clear. But before considering the landscape politics of burial as iterations of value, we can engage briefly with Judith Butler's concept of a "grievable life," adapting it to animals. In her book *Frames of War: When Is Life Grievable?* Butler explores, as Larry S. McGrath puts it, how modern warfare represents certain lives as more or less worthy of grief: "through what frames (she asks) are lives registered as recognizable, warranting solidarity or protection, and whose loss spurs mourning."[20] Or, to quote Butler directly, "An ungrievable life is one that cannot be mourned because it has never lived, that is, it has never counted as a life at all."[21] Still in the context of discussing how war constitutes and is also based on notions of whose lives really count, she goes on to assert that "the differential distribution of public grieving is a political issue of enormous significance."[22] "Affective responses," she notes, "are highly regulated by regimes of power and sometimes subject to explicit censorship."[23] These passages unite crucial issues of politics, affect, and public legitimation. As we will see, Butler's statements are extremely relevant to the consideration of grieving for animals as well.

While Butler's ruminations focus on war-zone values, and on human lives, we can reorient this fundamental question to read more broadly.[24] The ultimate question is what (who) constitutes a grievable (nonhuman animal) life, for and by whom, and under what conditions? This formulation enables us to calculate specific acts of mourning like burial, crafting obituaries, and so on in the contexts of the sets of beliefs that render those actions not only meaningful to individuals but also ultimately accessible to many communities—that is, public. Outside such frames of reference, such acts can appear merely comical, as if they inadvertently exchanged the site of a grievable life with that of an ungrievable one, of a death not accorded social value, which casts any actions marked as grieving that death as nonsensical, idiosyncratic, or inappropriately pathetic. (We will see these counteractions emerge in my discussion of controversies surrounding newspaper publication of pet obituaries in the next chapter.)

Butler concentrates on divisions between ontology (beingness) and epistemology (systems of knowledge or belief), emphasizing that while "bios," or life, may exist for some in the realm of ontology, its meaning is always socially ascribed. This is true. Within a social system of belief and institutions, our ability to be recognized as a "subject" is historically and culturally contingent. Such designations of subjectivity are, as Butler notes, relationally constructed. A "not me" helps construct the "me and mine" category of social meaning. While she occasionally skates on the ridge of divisions articulating notions of a human animal and a nonhuman one, Butler's concerns lie elsewhere. However, for my concerns, her broaching the question of what constitutes a "grievable life," and under what conditions, with what effects, and for whom, is right on target.

James Stanescu extends Butler's considerations directly to the issue of mourning for animals, through a discussion of philosopher Giorgio Agamben's concept of "bare life," suggesting that by reframing life as "precarious" we can put human and nonhuman animals together in the same category—both sharing an ontological dependency on reproducing the necessary conditions for continued life, a necessity, Butler suggests, that gives rise to sociality. If this sense of the social unites the human and the nonhuman animal as co-constitutive in a fundamental sameness—the precarity of their lives—rather than in a continually reinscribed line of difference—the human-animal divide—then both can come under the sign of mourning. Stanescu underlines the political power of mourning, which "has the possibility of introducing a community, a social reality of those who also mourn the passing of that life."[25] The political activation of this type of community can be based on bringing out of the shadows and into the public sphere a political claim on the value of the life when that value is dismissed by others. The work of US AIDS activists in the 1980s provides one such example, as when the activist group ACT UP staged political funerals, "all dedicated to making private grief into public grief."[26] Doing so carries risks, including the risk of being castigated as nonnormative. Pet lovers find their attachments (and thus themselves) dismissed or denigrated as eccentric, sentimental, odd, even crazy. This is a mode of dismissal that rests on illegibility—the incomprehensibility of a set of actions within a matrix of social acceptability that restricts grieving to humans for humans. As Stanescu puts it, "Social unintelligibility is . . . a failure of recognition by others, a failure to code as reality what you know reality to be. It is an erasure of existence, an erasure of sense, and an erasure of relations. To have your grief for one you care about rendered unintelligible does not invite simple ridicule; it invites melancholia and madness."[27]

Where my approach differs fundamentally from Butler's and Stanescu's is in its emphasis not only on understanding the rhetorical structure of social categories and the political power they articulate but also on investigating the embodied practices in processes that articulate belief in relation to dominant, marginal, or emergent sets of beliefs. If we examine what people actually *do* as well as what they say, and what they say they believe, we will find a more complex arena of sociality informed by and informing social practice. This is where an ethnographic approach meeting a rhetorical analytical approach, combined with an investigation into institutional structures, can provide the most revealing portrait of a process in emergence.[28]

I suggest therefore that our understanding of shifting relations between human and nonhuman animals in the contemporary United States should take into consideration and foreground for analysis *how* people mourn for *which* animals.[29] The act of mourning *constitutes and asserts as grievable* the presence of a once-living individual, one belonging to any number of historically constituted categories, whether "animal," "species," or "being." This means that what/who is grievable for one individual may not be grievable for another: do you simply flush a dead goldfish down the toilet without further ado, or do you bury it in your backyard and decorate a grave with its name? As leading fish veterinarian and researcher Dr. Mark Mitchell of the University of Illinois at Urbana-Champaign reminds his veterinary students in training clinics, the measure of a client's attachment to an animal does not depend on the category of the animal.[30] Fish owners can become very emotionally attached to fish, even if we can't imagine the fish having an emotional life of great attachment to those humans! Affect does not depend on socially validated conceptions of mutuality. And, we might add, neither does the concept of grievability. Any life can be grieved by an individual mourner, but not every life will be granted what I am terming "political grievability," or the social validation of that grief as meaningful by a wider community.

Pets, as noted earlier in this chapter, are a special "in-between" case—in between human family members and food and "wild" animals. Few people formally grieve for the billions of animals slaughtered in the United States alone to feed humans each year. And there are no cemeteries for those cows "saved" from slaughter. Nor do we find substantial renditions of mourning for "wild" animals who die, say, from old age or are killed by poachers. Yet contestations over grievability continue to chip away at these categories. Recently, the activist animal protection organization PETA (People for the Ethical Treatment of Animals) has filed petitions to put up road signs mourning hundreds of turkeys killed on their way to slaughter in a truck accident in Utah.[31] For many, these animals too—the wild, those raised for food, those killed in accidents, and, as I discuss in a subsequent chapter, even roadkill—constitute "grievable lives," living beings identified as worthy of recognition. But so far, PETA's political efforts haven't substantially enlarged the public category of grievable lives for animals.

Only the category of "pet" is consistently granted a limited grievability (and, even then, not by all pet "owners"). This result combines the apparently necessary individuation, marked by naming and cohabitation with human owners, along with the acceptance of responsibility by those humans for the "precarity" of the animal's life (to apply Butler's term to living beings that cannot survive alone without support from and interaction with other living beings).[32]

Very occasionally, a non-pet animal will fulfill these requirements and garner a public of mourners. The Galapagos giant tortoise "Lonesome George," the last of his subspecies, is one example. He already had a large public when he died. Millions had made the pilgrimage to see this two-hundred-pound centenarian, and his death in 2012, an extinction, made international news. Since 1971, he had been in captivity at an Ecuadorean research station in the Galapagos, and scientists worked valiantly but without success to find him a mate so the subspecies could survive—hence the nickname "Lonesome."

Moved by his death, composer Adam Cole eulogized him in song, offering a "musical memorial for the face of extinction," which he played on National Public Radio.[33] In this case, Lonesome George had attained the status of individual and celebrity, bathed in a pathos of impending loss and irreplaceability, tied not only to human care but also, as a most precarious life, to human ignorance that ultimately led to extinction. His value as the last of his kind was laminated onto his value as an individual, symbol and presence made one; and for that reason, he acceded to the category of a politically grievable life, with a grieving public. While rare, such incidents outside the realm of pet keeping do happen.

Ultimately, a politically grievable life is one that someone, or a community of someones, attaches social value to. Without that social valuation (say, in situations where the only human-ascribed value is one of financial return, as when animals are bred for food), grief remains unarticulated and is certainly unvalidated by others. It is this latter attribute, the proclamation of grief and *a claim on others* to recognize a loss as meaningful, that constitutes the social meaning of grieving for animals. Public acts of proclaiming grief can be contestatory, as my discussion of animal obituaries in newspapers (in chapter 6) will reveal. They demand (though do not always receive) recognition of the legitimacy of a relation as both legible and "worthy" in a broader social sphere. Institutional support follows those categories and communities who successfully make this claim on a wider public.[34]

Let's take a flight of fancy and imagine that half a century from now, perhaps, a substantial shift has occurred in the public acknowledgment of human-animal relationships, allowing for legally constituting "pets" as members of a family. Colloquially, this phrase of familial incorporation is widespread in the United States today, but it is more a metaphor than a structural assertion. What if this metaphor were to become institutional and legal reality? This would result in changes in family law, in property law, in employment contracts that might then recognize "bereavement leave" upon the death of a pet, and so on. Right now, such imaginings might seem not only pie-in-the-sky speculation but also even silly (that is, beyond the realm of reasonable consideration). But taking a longer view, we can see that the category of the "grievable life," as Butler argues, changes over time, since it isn't an ontologically static category but a socially constituted one.

Pets are my focus in this chapter, but pets aren't the only beings in this category of the "potentially ungrievable," even outside the wartime focus of Butler's book. It is helpful to think of pets' status as part of a wider, more complex landscape of beings without fully ascribed "humanity" or "personhood." The ascription of social value to a life can influence not only how that life unfolds but also how the end of that life is recognized or ignored. The dead are ascribed social value that echoes the value socially ascribed to their living selves.

Lisa Marie Cacho, in discussing the devaluation of the lives of some young men of color, such as young un- or underemployed Latinos whose practices of sociality are termed "deviant" and whose lives are considered "nonspectacular," suggests that "deviant" lives give way to "devalued deaths," especially when those deaths are violent, and linked to drinking and driving.[35] While official death notices seem to withhold empathy in these cases, emphasizing the "illicit" cause of the deaths, Cacho notes that the communities of youth who embraced the dead individuals in life create improvisatory shrines and mementos, including roadside memorials and caps and T-shirts, embracing the deaths and articulating the loss they feel.[36] Thus, young men killed in a car crash assumed to be their own fault are deemed worthy of mourning by their friends, even if the wider community blames them for their own deaths and withholds the presumed valuation of a grievable life. Expanding from this observation, I suggest that "grievability" emerges in subaltern communities as an articulation of social value against the withholding of value by dominant communities and ideologies. For my purposes, the transgenerational, transethnic, transregional, and transclass population of pet lovers emerges as a Gramscian "bloc" or politically active community asserting the value of a life and its right to public recognition and mourning.

There are other situations in which an uncertain status of social life comes into play to shape grieving. Think for a moment of women who suffer miscarriages. Medical professionals are trained to be aware of the crushing sense of loss that can accompany a miscarriage, whether early or late in a pregnancy, or of a stillbirth.[37] Often these losses aren't fully acknowledged, because we don't have a socially accepted category in the United States for the "almost born." Friends, relatives, and employers may all be uncertain about what protocol applies in this situation. They must improvise. Do you send condolence cards? Do you offer prayers for the "deceased"? Can someone be deceased without having been born? How do you mourn for a child who never made it into the world or who was never held and named? And yet, parents-to-be often do. Although the miscarried being never achieved personhood, described as living on her/his own outside the womb, we could argue that such a situation demands a more complex understanding of "grievable death," even though full life here was not attained and so death seems a misnomer.[38]

Animals certainly fall into a different category, because they can never, whether dead or alive, become part of that realm of human personhood for which the miscarried fetus was destined. Nor can they claim the social status of young men who, while outside a mainstream of social acceptance, still form part of a human community that values them. Even so, these animal lives become grievable either through human affective attachment (that is, a human cares) or through a spiritual or ethical belief that the nonhuman animal's life is necessarily the life of a unique individual, valuable in its own right, a subject interpellated into discourse, and hence the subject of a life worthy of grieving. I am suggesting here not only that the status of the "ungrievable" is open to contestation, as Cacho argues, but also that this category and its contestability can usefully be seen to potentially span the species divide between human and nonhuman animals as well. Such an assertion does not suggest that the human and nonhuman lives under discussion are "equal" in social value, only that together they can share in categorically specific denials of social valuation.

Among the belief systems and public rhetorics shaping this discursive landscape, those associated with contemporary religion are particularly powerful in providing frames both through which and, as we shall see, against which individuals craft their relationships with their pets not only during but also after life.

What Religions Say

Religions vary widely in their beliefs about the appropriate relationships between nonhuman and human animals. Roman Catholic doctrine, for example, differentiates between mortal souls, attributed to animals, and immortal souls, attributed to humans. According to Catholic readings of the Bible, God grants humans "dominion" over animals, placing them in a superior yet responsible relationship to nonhumans.[39]

Other religions urge members to consider the suffering of animals and to work against it. For instance, the Unitarian Universalists call for "respect for the interdependent web of existence of which humanity is a part" and strive to "increase our proportion of plant-based food" so as to minimize the pain and suffering of animals.[40] Given the complexity of the religious landscape in the contemporary United States, which far exceeds the Christian-focused examples above, and the fact that in practice, individuals and families often choose to disagree with formal religious doctrines,[41] it's hard to generalize accurately about the relationship between religion and pet mourning.

However, even without extensive ethnographic research, it's safe to say that the impact of religion on mourning for animals is certainly one of the key templates through which individuals generate meaning, and that for some at least, this remains a contested area. As an example, let me take areas of contestation within Catholicism as currently practiced in the United States. A 2011 statement in *Today's Catholic News* noted that it is "absolutely unacceptable" for humans to have the ashes of their pet buried with them. "Cremation is already a sensitive allowance in the life of the Church, and we must carefully safeguard the dignity of Christian, human burial, as well as the theological reality of the resurrection of the body. We would not permit the bodies of pets to be placed in a casket with a human body—all the more would we not permit the indiscernible mixing of ashes."[42] Clearly, this statement wouldn't be needed if the practice, which I discuss later in this chapter, weren't either ongoing or under consideration by some Catholics.

In other developments, announced plans for a pet columbarium to be placed in the San Francisco shrine of St. Francis of Assisi roused vigorous debate among Catholics. The Knights of St. Francis, who serve as volunteer guards at the shrine, argued that pet funerals are against Catholic teachings, since animals are incapable of sin; moreover, animals don't go to heaven or hell, and thus cannot be saved. They also asserted that the money could be better spent, for example, in serving the homeless. After a year of protests, plans for the columbarium were discarded in 2014, even though the San Francisco police had stated an interest in placing the remains of working horses and dogs in a special "honor hall" there reserved for service animals.

Facebook posts discussing the debate reveal the intense emotional investment aroused. Posts were colloquial in tone and assertive in strategy, with some employing humor to make their point. The language of religious piety was decidedly absent. Victoria Bennington wrote, "Animals are not capable of sin? Ya'll have NOT met my cat!" Stephanie Romanello wrote, "Pssshhh, my pets are going to heaven. Are religious people really this bored that THIS is the kind of battle we want to fight? . . . I've buried, cremated, and had little pet funerals for my pets for years . . . those who don't like it can buzz off and mind their own business. Unbelievable . . . See you in heaven with all my cats."[43]

Similar comments dismissing the Catholic Church's delineation of animals as lacking immortal souls and its placement of restrictions on appropriate modes of mourning for animals appeared in relation to a query I posted in January 2014 on the Catholic Answers Forum, under its "Family Life" thread. This thread quickly drew a number of responses, with the majority arguing that of course they will mourn their pets, because they love them. "Love is love," stated a member going by the name "Modern Revert."

The question of Catholic teachings seemed moot among my respondents, except for one poster, who stated, "Animals have material souls. When they're dead they're dead." Several posters asserted that they looked forward to seeing their dead pets in heaven. Others argued that pets can be gifts from God, and still others noted that the grief for pets can be as great as for a human. Several told of burying their pets in their yard. Religion emerges in these discussions as an available template for improvising how to mourn rather than as a doctrinal proscription that must be followed.[44]

Still other religious sources offer templates for funeral services for pets. The Reverend Robert Stiefel of Portsmouth, New Hampshire, offers a guide on his website for "A Service of Grieving and Thanksgiving" for pets or other animals, including suggested Bible readings from the books of Genesis, Revelation, Matthew, and Mark. The prayer of committal sanctifies the moment of burial: "Most merciful God, we return to you ('N' . . . name here), a creature of your own making and your gift into our lives."[45]

As these representative examples reveal, no matter what the doctrine of some religions may say about appropriate human-animal relations, some humans will mourn individual animals through extensive rituals they create themselves, even if their religion situates animals in a category decidedly "below" humans or outside the concept of "immortal souls." I call these acts "unauthorized mourning." They are part of a wider set of practices—some socially and institutionally sanctioned by various communities, and some not—that surround human grieving for animals and human disposal of animal remains.

This "unsanctioned" set of practices can include asking (successfully, according to one of my informants working in the human funeral industry) your funeral director to secretly put the ashes of the family cat into the casket with Grandmother or arranging for a Catholic funeral mass to be said for a beloved dog by simply disguising the dog's name to sound more human when making the request, so that the officiating priest never knows the departed is canine.[46] A common unsanctioned practice includes burying animals in the homeowner's backyard when the legality of such interments is unclear.[47]

Given that laws governing the disposal of animal remains aren't national or even statewide but vary by municipality, it is very difficult to make accurate generalizations about the legality of backyard burials.[48] Anecdotal evidence suggests, though, that for homeowners who have one, a backyard is often the final resting place of the family pet, with the legality of burial there being determined by local ordinances. These interments are hard to track except by personal story, since they don't attract a public, nor are they enshrined in the public record via the newspaper or city records. While working on this chapter, though, I have heard from many, many individuals who recount burying their small pets in the backyard, often using a shoebox for a casket and offering a few prayerlike remarks over the grave, whether the burial is for a goldfish or a poodle.

This informality is another mark of the unregulated arena of pet burial that *both requires and allows creative, improvisatory responses* to the animal's death. Whereas burying a pet in your backyard may in some cases be prohibited by municipal regulation, those regulations are often not known or simply ignored. By contrast, burying your spouse in your yard isn't viewed as a viable option and would be subject to legal censure, as a recent case in Alabama proved. Jim Davis buried his wife, Patsy, in their front yard, according to her last wishes, and a legal firefight ensued, ultimately resulting in the removal of her body.[49]

A backyard pet burial is also virtually cost free if the homeowner already owns the land, which may be one reason why the number of animals interred in pet cemeteries is still such a small percentage of all pet burials in the United States. And, since many pets are cremated after death, through arrangements by either a veterinarian or a crematory service, and many of those will be disposed of at the crematory without their ashes being returned to the family, we have a further decrease in the percentage of bodies receiving cemetery burials. Add to this the number of families who do have a pet cremated but then scatter the ashes in the backyard or keep them at home in an urn, perhaps so the ashes can come with the family if they move, and formal cemetery interment of bodies or cremains is reduced still further. Therefore, the low percentage of pets currently accorded formal burials in formal pet cemeteries doesn't accurately reflect the number of pets receiving carefully crafted afterlife disposal of their remains—or the number intensively mourned.

Pet Cemeteries as a Growth Industry

Despite the prevalence of cremations and backyard burials, the number of pet cemeteries in the United States continues to grow, especially because many funeral professionals are expanding their businesses or developing alternative businesses to take care of the pets of their clients. This expansion is often driven by consumer request as the number of pet owners who regard their pet as a familial "subject" worthy of mourning increases; and it is, I suggest, a harbinger of future change.[50] Right now, many pet owners have cremation as a viable choice only through their veterinarian, but this could change in the future as the number of local cemeteries for burying pets or columbaria for cremated pet remains keeps rising.[51]

In my discussions with members of the International Association of Pet Cemetery and Crematory members, it became clear to me that many funeral directors were getting into the pet business because their clients saw them as the appropriate resource to help with their grief.[52] "You buried my mother, and now I want you to bury my dog," is roughly how one funeral director put it to me, recounting a conversation with a client.

Since they regard themselves as being in the "death care" business, human funeral directors aren't merely legally licensed body disposal experts but also professionals who guide a family through formal rituals that can ease their grief, like planning burials and celebration-of-life ceremonies, choosing a casket or urn, designating a stone or monument, supervising interment, helping place death notices, setting up online "guest books" for condolences, and so on. Nowadays, many of these services are also available at pet cemeteries, including an option to view the body to say goodbye and provide interment and funerals. These pet-loss needs are increasingly recognized in the death-care industry for humans, with reports on pet-loss needs appearing in human funeral industry publications like *Mortuary Management*.[53]

In the last decade, the number of *human* funeral homes extending their offerings to serve pet loss has increased, and this trend is recognized among funeral directors as a wave of the future. "It's a growing trend and it's a logical growth from what we as funeral directors do," said Bob Biggins, owner of Magoun-Biggins Funeral Home in Rockland, Massachusetts, and a past president of the National Funeral Directors Association. His business began offering pet services in 2006. "We deal with people when they are facing loss. Anyone that owns a pet knows when a pet dies, it's traumatic. They become part of our families." And it can be good for business: co-owner Bill McQueen says, "What people are willing to spend on their pets is growing astronomically. Pets are more and more considered like another member of the family. Why not give people the opportunity to have their pet treated with the same dignity and care and trust at the time of death?"[54]

Sometimes services are limited to cremation and transport to a local pet cemetery, if available, and sometimes they include advice on how to design a pet memorial service. The Lensing Funeral Home in Iowa City, Iowa, for instance, began offering a "Faithful Companions Pet Remembrance Service" in 2008; it celebrates a pet's life through "balloon releasing, a gathering for Visitation for Friends and Family or a Traditional Memorial Service." Online tributes to pets are also sometimes part of the services offered, just as they are for humans.[55] Like these pet ceremonies, pet cemeteries are thus built to support the attribution of value, the recognition of emotional loss, and the public expression of affect, in the form of texts and objects, related to the death of nonhuman animals. Each being interred in these cemeteries is, at least in theory, accorded a "grievable life" by someone if not everyone.

But the categorization of lives as *more or less* grievable rears its head here too, for even *within* a pet cemetery we sometimes find, at the sight of stone inscriptions or in conversation, the arched eyebrow of disbelief over the grave of a goldfish or rat—nonhuman animals historically ranked very low in the United States on the hierarchy of animal cognition or affective affiliation, far below a dog or cat. Even pet-loving animal cemetery devotees can succumb to an implicit hierarchy of life-value based on the perceived cognitive abilities of the deceased being and its social importance in the cultural matrix of the human mourner. For example, celebrity dogs, like television and movie star Rin Tin Tin, interred in the Cimitière des Chiens outside Paris, are generally accorded more grandiose burial sites than are nonmammals known only to their human guardians. The goldfish buried in the Presidio Pet Cemetery in California is commemorated with a grave marker adorned by a simple, childlike, hand-drawn picture of a fish.

And some animals don't fit easily into the "pet" definition, making their disposition subject to competing categorical and legal claims that can be devastating for their owners. For example, horses, though often very expensive to care for and highly valued, don't reside inside the family home like many pet species, and they also perform "work," even if that work is to provide humans with the pleasure of riding them. Their size is also problematic when it comes to burial. In Iowa in 2012, the Department of Natural Resources fined a Tipton pet cemetery, Pet Memories, ten thousand dollars for burying horses for grieving owners. The dead horses were not "pets," argued the DNR, but should be categorized as "solid waste" and taken to a landfill so they wouldn't pose a threat to groundwater when they decomposed. Cemetery owner Steve Johnson argued that the horses aren't "waste," which is "unwanted material," but rather pets whose owners want them buried with dignity in a cemetery, not dumped in a landfill.[56] This case reveals that even within the "pet" category there is great variation not only in species but also in the cultural and legal value attached to those species.

The hierarchy of life-value is both maintained and sometimes challenged not only within pet cemeteries but also across the dividing line of contemporary American human-nonhuman burials. The species division that typically physically separates human and animal burials in US cemeteries is becoming more porous and is under attack.

Geographies of Death

The dividing line between human and nonhuman animals is usually maintained in the physical geography of cemeteries. This inscription of social differentiation echoes that historically found in many US cemeteries for humans, where a physical separation of individuals of different races, ethnicities, and religions was enforced, just as they might have been in life.[57] "Even in death, we fear the stranger," notes historian Marilyn Yalom.[58] Keeping "others" out simultaneously reinforces a sense of community identity, solidarity, and self-value among those allowed in, enhancing a sense of group identity among the living.[59]

Historically, religion is one of the primary social frameworks in cemeteries for humans that cause division, but all extant US pet cemeteries that I am aware of are secular—not affiliated with a specific religious institution.[60] (This isn't the case in other countries. Japan has Buddhist cemeteries specifically for pets and pets only, including one I visited in 2002 in Yokohama that features traditional Buddhist grave markers as well as niches for individual pets enclosing offerings and photographs of the pet.)[61] However, in the United States, the historical growth in the number of secular human burial places, whether private or municipal, seems also to have coincided with the rapid rise in the number of pet cemeteries. In these cases, burial, mourning, and "sacred" space need not be tied to a specific church or religious denomination, although signifying markers of various religions, like crosses or Stars of David, are sometimes used. Instead, religious practices constitute one of the most available templates for publics to draw on in addressing new circumstances of pet burial, but this template is often then generalized, translated from the religious to what we might term the "secularly sacred" and reworked for the mourning of a pet.

In a nation as complex ethnically, linguistically, religiously, and culturally as the contemporary United States, it is important to keep in mind the multiple modes of mourning and funerary conventions, over time and across regional locations, and even within the same religious denomination. Therefore, the religious templates that are drawn on to yield this "secularly sacred" pet mourning can also be extremely varied. We would find, for example, differences between Mormon, Zuni, and Navajo human burial practices in New Mexico, as Keith Cunningham had in his regional study.[62] Variable conventions include whether individuals are buried by themselves or in family plots, the directional orientation of the graves, how women are named on markers and buried in relation to male members of a community, and so on.

Social formations and valuations are enacted in the disposition of human remains as surely as they are in the social formations governing behavior and opportunity in living communities.[63] Pet burials don't simply duplicate these conventions, but they can be seen as sites of negotiation between human burial conventions (for specific time periods, places, and communities) and nonhuman animal options—shaped not only by secular and religious belief but also by law, finances, and the availability of professional services for pet owners. But for all these variations, one line remains strongly drawn: the separation of human and nonhuman animal remains in cemeteries, underlining the difference in social status in life.

Keeping Human and Nonhuman Species Separate: What's at Stake?

Pet cemeteries are not only secular but also for the most part separate from human cemeteries. If they are located on the same land, they are—almost without exception—physically separated in space, with the pet cemetery subdivision forming a smaller component of the cemetery's overall geography. This is the case in Memory Gardens in Iowa City, Iowa, where our cats, Pumpernickel and Mocha, are buried along with Sydney, the parakeet whose death opened the preceding chapter. That pet cemetery physically adjoins the human cemetery but is located across a bridge and a brook from it, right next to a housing subdivision—the least desirable real estate in the place. It comprises approximately one-twentieth of the area of the whole cemetery. Not everyone who buries a pet is satisfied with this sort of "apartheid" of animal and human burials.[64]

A newly developing burial trend recognizes the emotional bonds between humans and pets, redefines "family" to cross species lines, and reconfigures the geographic ghettoization of pets in the cemetery world. Although we have tantalizing hints of much earlier, even prehistoric, burial practices that may indicate a linking of human and animal in a conception of "kin," as I noted in the previous chapter, the evidence is inconclusive.[65] For the beginnings of contemporary interment practices that rearticulate familial formations, we can look back to the late twentieth century. This trend may have started in England, where, for example, twenty years ago, a newly built cemetery in Devon began offering a chance for animals and people to be buried side by side. The cost was approximately US$400 per human occupant and $40–$160 for the pet's plot; burial of the first pet, and any subsequent tiny pets like birds, was free.[66] Similarly, the Penwith Pet Cemetery and Memorial Gardens in West Cornwall buries humans and their animals side by side in family plots. Although the site started out as a pet cemetery and crematorium, its popularity as a "green burial" site for humans and animals together is growing at an accelerated pace. Some families even hold funeral ceremonies for their pets there, attended by both humans and animals.[67]

A similar trend has been gaining momentum in the United States. The case of a man in Iowa was covered by a newspaper in 2002, indicating that this practice was still regarded as so unusual as to be newsworthy. Jim Crovetti, a retired hospital worker, was cremated in July of that year and buried at his request in the Loving Rest Pet Cemetery in Warren County. His ashes are interred next to those of his dog Lady (but in a separate urn). Crovetti and Lady served as a volunteer anti-drug dog-and-handler team that aided law enforcement, and their plot is part of the cemetery's "Wall of Service" section for service animals. Crovetti's wife, Nancy, wholly supports the unusual burial and plans to be buried in Loving Rest herself along with the ashes of her dog, Kahlua. She and her dog will share a headstone. "I want our headstone next to Jim's and Lady's," she says. "I guess some people do think it is odd, but those animals were a big part of our lives."[68]

These individual cemeteries and individual family stories index a larger phenomenon. In September of 2013, the entire state of New York underwent a legislative change when a new law was passed allowing pet cemeteries there to accept the cremated remains of pet owners who wish to be buried alongside their pets.[69] The regulation is the result of a two-year dispute, during which the state refused to allow the 117-year-old Hartsdale Pet Cemetery in Westchester County, the oldest pet cemetery in the United States, to bury the cremated ashes of former New York City police officer Thomas Ryan beside his three Maltese dogs. Ryan's wife, Bunny, was already buried in the plot, but officials refused permission, even though Hartsdale estimates that about 700 cremated humans are already buried among its more than 110,000 pet graves— an increasingly common phenomenon since the cemetery began offering cremations for animals in the 1980s.

Once the state took notice of this informal arrangement, however, it became a legal issue. That it had been going on for some time is testament to the improvisatory nature of mourning for animals that I have discussed throughout this chapter.[70] Sometimes these creative solutions are extralegal or merely involve arenas in which no legal guidelines exist. Sometimes they actively contravene legal limitations, but without penalty (as with some backyard pet burials). But in this case, the legal adjudication carved out new ground statewide, clearly articulating the shifting configurations of "family" by allowing the mixing of species in the same burial ground.[71] Given the size and population of New York State, this type of ruling could have a domino effect on other states in the future. However, despite these changes and the smudging of species boundaries, note that travel across those boundaries only seems to be one-way.

So far, it appears that people can be buried in pet cemeteries, but pets can't be buried in people cemeteries. The boundary around "the human" remains sacrosanct as far as dead bodies are concerned. While people can sometimes migrate across the geographic boundaries of death, choosing, as some might see it, a sort of self-imposed "slumming" after they die, this is definitely a one-way migration, as animals cannot enter the human realm.[72] Even the possibility of using the same crematory, at different times, for humans and for animals causes some to blanch at the thought of potential categorical pollution. A Nevada bill allowing pet cremations to be done by a wider variety of sites has created fear that an incinerator intended for human cremation could be used for pet corpses. "I don't know about you, but I wouldn't want to take grandma to a place and wonder if she's being cremated in the same place as Fluffy," said Dennis Mastny, owner of Craig Road Pet Cemetery in Clark Country, Las Vegas. Mastny may have ulterior business motives for his statement, but Clark County Commissioner Tom Collins is more graphic in his disdain "at the idea of being 'burned up' in an oven 'where there'd be cat hairs and claws.'"[73]

But even this attitude may be changing, as a recent article in the *Philadelphia Inquirer* demonstrated in reporting on people wanting to be buried with their pets. The mixing of human and pet cremains in pet cemeteries is one thing—easier, because human cremains *are* the "final disposition," and "the family can do whatever they want with those cremated remains," explained Debra Bjorling, owner of Hamilton Pet Meadow Memorial Park and Crematory in Hamilton, New Jersey.[74] But formally being buried together? Only a few places in the country can arrange that.

Such a place is Hillcrest Memorial Park in Hermitage, Pennsylvania, one of the very few cemeteries where burying humans and nonhuman animals together, without cremation, is legal. Hillcrest started out as a people cemetery; then in 2007, it added a pet cemetery and finally, a third segment, the Hillcrest Memorial Park People and Pet Gardens. To accommodate this expansion, "the city adjusted the definition of a cemetery to a place for the burial of humans and/or pets," said Tom Flynn, Hillcrest president and devoted dog owner. 'The light just went off in my head. This is really where we feel the market is."[75] As the facility's website states, "Hillcrest Memorial Park People and Pet Gardens is a unique place where you and your pet can be memorialized together . . . where you and your pets can rest in peaceful tranquility." The familial framework undergirds it all. "Our mission is to provide a full-spectrum of service and support to pet parents and their families in the care of their departed pets as would be provided to any member of a human family."[76]

To enable the burial of humans with their pets in the People and Pet Gardens section, grave dimensions are enlarged, with these special plots measuring three feet by ten feet: room for two pets and one person. If the pets die first, their bodies go under the grave marker, but if the human dies first, there is still room for the burial of two pets in the earth above the human body.[77] In the more than eight years Hillcrest has offered this service, Flynn estimates that he has served about seven hundred families in this way.[78] With burials in general on the decline in the United States because of a rise in cremations, this service provides a new revenue stream (plots cost between $800 and $1,000 each) while also offering a new burial option for humans and their pets. Maybe giving owners the option of being together with their pets for eternity will lead to more pets being buried, rather than cremated, as is the vast majority at this point.

Many human cemeteries are too old to have their codicils changed to accommodate pets, even if owners wanted to be buried with them, but new cemeteries have greater freedom if local ordinances are flexible. One growth area is "green cemeteries," where bodies are interred without embalming, vaults, or caskets in order to hasten their return to the earth. Already popular in England, the environmentally friendly movement is spreading to the United States, and Pennsylvania's first "green" cemetery, Penn Forest Natural Burial Park in Verona, near Pittsburgh, is offering a new "people with pets" burial option as well.[79]

The increasing number of people who choose to be buried with their pets may signal a rising tide of change in the social standing of animals, and in our scientific and legal debates about how similar to and different from us they are. As transspecies organ transplants and changing conceptions of animal intelligence continue to blur the human-animal boundary, it's conceivable that sometime in the imaginable future, some cemeteries will no longer need to have the modifier *pet* in their name.[80] Instead, the migration across the species barrier may go both ways, and the term *cemetery* will refer only to a place for all beings deemed worthy of burial and mourning—all "subjects" who are grievable lives, intertwined.

We shouldn't expect, however, that such fundamental challenges to categorical distinctions will go unchallenged. As my next chapter reveals in a case study of a related frontier—newspaper obituaries for pets—and the vicious firestorm it elicited, smudging the boundaries between human and nonhuman animals in public discourse and symbolic practices is a dangerous proposition, one fraught with high emotion and serious pushback by those fearing a denigration of "the human" through an elevation of "the animal."

SIX

Animal Deaths and the Written Record of History: The Inflammatory Politics of Pet Obituaries in Newspapers

Twelve years ago, a black Labrador retriever named Bear broke the species barrier by making it into the obituary pages of my local newspaper. He was the first animal ever so commemorated in that paper (the *Iowa City Press-Citizen*). Bear died quietly in his sleep on the morning of April 14, 2003, at thirteen years of age. But if his passing was peaceable, the period after his death was not. His obituary became the cause of bitter debate in our community. Why would a simple notice in a local newspaper generate such a firestorm of emotion? What is at stake?

In this chapter, I analyze contemporary US debates over publishing pet obituaries in newspapers. I suggest that these obituaries raise multiple issues about the "appropriate" objects of mourning, the "right" to mourn publicly, and the ways that such public mourning both legitimates social relationships and writes individual lives and relationships into history. As I did in the two preceding chapters on mourning for pets in pet cemeteries, I here seek to uncover the answers to several interrelated questions about this obituary phenomenon: What forms do the obits and reactions to them take? What is at stake in this social practice, and for whom? How is a newspaper remembrance different from a cemetery commemoration? What are the social and political conditions of the emergence of this phenomenon? What might be its implications for the future? I examine how death notices for animals stretch the obituary form and push the limits of writing lives into the social record. Finally, I ask, what phenomena of social value are being contested in debates over the practice? I argue that pet obituaries are seen as dangerous by some precisely because they are a political act signaling the need for far-reaching ethical change.

A Pet as a "Part of the Family"

To begin to explore these issues, let me return to the obituary for Bear. His obituary was placed next to that for Ms. Georgi Addis, which incensed Ms. Addis's sister-in-law, Sue Dayton. She found the inclusion of the dog's obituary on the same page as Ms. Addis's "distasteful and disrespectful to Georgi and [her] family" and, in a letter to the editor, called on the paper to issue an apology to every family involved with the obits printed that day. Ensuing letters to the editor argued pro and con.[1]

A similar debate erupted right around the same time in Philadelphia, when the *Philadelphia Daily News* printed an obituary in March of 2005 for Winnie, a nine-year-old terrier known for her "feisty and fearless" nature. That obit ignited national discussion in columns in the *Washington Post* and in *MediaWeek*, where writer Lewis Grossberger termed it a "grotesque phenomenon."[2]

These contemporary contestations over the public newspaper memorialization of pets chart both the shifting status of the "pet," in terms of family and kinship relations, and the changing practices in obituary writing as authority moves from the funeral director to the family in the era of paid obituaries.

It appears that the concept of a pet as a "part of the family" is being taken more literally today than in the past, a phenomenon I examined in the preceding chapters on pet cemeteries, mourning practices, and the changing geographies of burial that bring together human and animal dead from the same social unit or "family." Reviewing a few statistics can remind us of the scale of this issue. The American Pet Products Association reports that in 2015, approximately 65% of US households owned at least one pet. A related poll based on a random sample of one thousand pet owners, taken by the Associated Press in

2009, reveals that 50% of all pet owners surveyed regarded their pet as a *full* member of the family (with a low of 43% of married males and a high of 66% of unmarried females).[3] These respondents agreed with the statement "My pet is just as much a part of the family as any other person in the household." A further 36% also regarded the pet as part of the family, "but not as much as the people in the household." Such polls are certainly not conclusive and actually tell us little about exactly what the notion of "full family member" means;[4] however, they suggest a substantial commitment to and emotional investment in the animal.

Pet obituaries articulate an extended notion of kinship obligations and recognition by publicly acknowledging this bond with nonhuman animals. In this way, they are similar to the new burial options I discussed in the preceding chapter whereby human and nonhuman animal remains are buried in the same place. Such contiguity materializes arguments about familial inclusiveness and transspecies valuation and rewrites conventional burial practices to reflect shifting understandings of social kinship that can cross species lines.

Pet obituaries, which publicly commemorate a life and make that life part of the historical record, provide a test case of this shifting positioning of the "pet" in relation to human companions.[5] In recent decades in the United States, obituary conventions have also been challenged by increasing acceptance of same-sex partners, but pets push the boundary of acceptable kinship further. As they do for humans, pet obituaries assign value to a life, define its highlights, extol socially validated accomplishments, articulate important social relations in the deceased's life, and serve as models for living.[6]

History of Obituaries

Like so many other social conventions that we take for granted, the US obituary, as a genre of writing and publication, has changed over time. Once reserved primarily for wealthy and powerful white men, public recordings of life and death have gradually expanded to encompass a much wider range of the population.[7] While major newspapers like the *New York Times* still feature obits of famous people, local papers print death notices or obituaries of just about anyone. In this sense, death has become democratized. As historian of English-language obituaries Nigel Stark puts it, "It is through the obituary, above all other forms of journalism, that an insight is obtained of what it was like to be a citizen of a particular community at a particular time, for it offers a sustained, often dramatic reflection, of prevailing mores."[8] Thus, the modern obituary form still reflects the contours of social hierarchy while expanding the notion of whose death is worthy of public notice.

For example, recent research has found that in the same paper, women continue to receive significantly fewer obits and, even when included, to have shorter obits than men.[9] European Americans continue to receive longer and more complex obits than African Americans.[10] Some of these differences may be attributed to continuing racialized and gendered differentials in social power, prestige, and professional accomplishment, but they also attest to the obit's function as a measure of presumed social worth.

In the past, the death of an animal was deemed newsworthy if it fit into one of two categories: animals of the famous or famous animals. For example, Igloo, Admiral Richard Byrd's dog, a "polar hero" himself, received an obit in the *New York Times* in 1931.[11] Titled "Igloo, Byrd's Dog, Polar Hero, Is Dead," the piece featured a picture of Igloo, a white-and-black fox terrier, posing with Admiral Byrd, alongside a long discussion of key points in his life, including the moment when he and Byrd circled the North Pole in a plane and "he became the most famous dog in the world." Considerable space is given over to describing his personality, and note is taken that "his courage and daring exceeded his [small] physique."[12] Simple funeral rites, the story related, were scheduled at the Pine Ridge animal cemetery in Dedham, Massachusetts. Although a news article, the piece includes the hallmarks of the obituary style, noting age, place, and cause of death, life accomplishments, and grieving survivors, along with funeral plans. A later report on the funeral pictured Byrd, his son, and the pallbearers, which included Master Sergeant Victor H. Czegka, a member of the South Pole expedition, who carried the small white casket to the grave where Byrd had placed a spray of white roses.[13]

More recently, in 2002, Marjan, the one-eyed lion in the Kabul Zoo who became a symbol of war-torn Afghanistan, received attention in the *Chicago Tribune* in an article titled "Kabul Zoo's Shell-Shocked Lion Dies." Opening with a description of the "people from all walks of life who came . . . to the battle-scarred Kabul Zoo to pay homage," the article notes the lion's physical ailments, the work of the veterinarians, and the past horrors of his captive life, including being starved, bombed, and beaten. His role as an international symbol of the need to rebuild both the nation and the zoo was emphasized, as were details of his burial.[14] Notably, this appreciation, like that for Igloo, appeared in the news pages, not the obituary section, but it still detailed the life, accomplishments, and personality of an individual animal.

The democratization of obituaries has only recently expanded to encompass the ordinary pets of ordinary people. The national move to charge a fee to print obituaries has been key in enabling this shift. By 2002, paid obituaries had become the national norm, although some papers were still making the transition.[15] A paid obit, written by the family and not by the newspaper staff, ensures that the notice gets in the paper in a timely manner; it also allows a family to customize the notice by spending extra money to include photos, symbols, and memorial information. This publicity doesn't come cheap. While most newspapers continue to publish death notices for free if they consist of only a few lines, longer obits can cost more than $10 a line, with an extra fee for a photo.[16] For example, even a decade ago, a ten-inch obituary with a photo cost $634.14 in the *Dallas Morning News*.[17] "Cash, not cache," appears to be the new criterion in filling obituary space.[18]

Some journalists worry that home-written obits aren't subject to fact-checking and cannot be considered official records. More important, perhaps, they allow touchy social issues to invade a paper. For instance, editors no longer get to decide whether a gay partner should be included among the deceased's survivors, or whether an unborn child who died at twenty-five weeks' gestation should have an obituary, or whether unsavory sentiments could be included. A media critic worries, "Should the angry, long-abused sons of a hard-drinking father be allowed to include that 'dad was a mean drunk' in their copy?"[19] In a very few cases, obituaries even cross the line from the solemnity and facticity historically required of newspaper staff writers into the realm of humorous celebratory satire. As the *New York Daily News* reported on May 6, 2013, Antonia Larroux, who died at age sixty-eight in April of that year, received a tongue-in-cheek obituary that was only supposed to appear in the print and online editions of her local Bay St. Louis, Mississippi, paper. Somehow, however, it went viral and was posted on the *New York Times* website in its entirety, attracting nearly two hundred commentaries, including some from people who had never met her. Written by her two grown children, the obituary saluted her wicked sense of humor, declaring that Antonia, Waffle House Restaurant lover and former librarian, had left behind not only her children and grandchildren but also several overdue library books and recounting her supposed long battle with rickets, scurvy, and feline leukemia. "Tell them the check is in the mail," she supposedly instructed from her deathbed concerning the library fines.[20]

This satirical obituary was so unusual that it made the national news, indicating that the constraints of the form are both alive and well and that, thanks to the paid-obituary format, nonjournalists can write obituaries that take full advantage of increasing flexibility. All the pet obituaries I have found were paid obits. People mourning the loss of loved ones, including pets, are capitalizing on the declining authority of newspaper editors by shifting the boundaries of the includable.

It's hard to track exactly how widespread the pet obit phenomenon is, since the notices aren't indexed. However, it is clear that the practice, though still in its infancy, has spread throughout the United States. Pet and human obits can appear side by side in a paper, by chance or by policy, sometimes even by subterfuge.

Papers that publish pet obits are diverse in size and geographic range. Among them are small community papers like the Bremerton, Washington, *Sun*, a daily with a circulation of thirty-three thousand, and the smaller weekly *Jamestown News* in North Carolina.[21] But the phenomenon is not limited to newspapers with tiny circulations. Most recently, the *San Antonio Express News*, the newspaper with the fourth-largest circulation in Texas, made pet obits available. Earlier, the *Anchorage Daily News* published the obituary of Carl, also known as Mr. Handsome, the dog of the former governor of Alaska, in its regular obit section in August 1999. A newspaper spokesman called this "an unfortunate mistake," saying the *Daily News*'s policy was to run pet obits anywhere but the human obits page.[22]

Another "mistake" occurred in the 1990s, when the obituary editor of the *Durham (North Carolina) Morning Herald* received a mysterious phone call from a local funeral director. He wanted a death notice (a two-inch announcement) put in the obituary section the next day, and identified the deceased by a human first name and his own last name. He refused to give an age but noted when the death occurred. The dead "person" turned out to be a dog, as the newspaper found out the next day when a local citizen, who knew the pet's family, called to express his outrage that a dog was listed on the obits page with the humans. The editor was furious about being tricked, but the example shows how savvy people can work the system—the individual placing the notice was a funeral director, after all—to stretch its limits, improvising a space for pet mourning when no official one exists.[23]

Like Mr. Handsome in Alaska, Axel, a police dog, also got special treatment because he himself was special. In 2001, the *News Tribune* of Tacoma, Washington, published his obituary, complete with a photo of him posing with his police partner, Officer Stephen Shepard, that was captioned "Tracking Bad Guys in Heaven." He was praised for his courage in apprehending 220 felons and for improving the safety of Tacoma's citizens.[24] The obituary was printed in the regular obits page right next to the obit for Mr. Earl Criss, a man whose list of survivors included "his beloved dog, Maggie." This single page thus demonstrates two moments of disruption of "traditional" obituary practices, both in its inclusion of an animal obituary among human ones and in listing a pet among a deceased person's grieving family members, exemplifying the expanding notion of the family across species.

Public Contestation

These examples might have remained isolated local incidents rather than indicators of a national phenomenon contesting social boundaries and shifting human-animal relations had the *Philadelphia Daily News* not announced in 2002 that it would start printing pet obituaries (actually, pet death remembrances to be published once a month in a special section in the classifieds titled "A Fond Farewell to Our Beloved Pet").[25] The Associated Press picked up the story, and a media blitz exploded. As the *American Journalism Review* reports, "CBS News called, as did NBC's 'Today' show. Local TV and radio in Philadelphia reported it; 'Imus in the Morning' talked about it; Canadian public radio ran a story; Robert Siegel of NPR's 'All Things Considered' covered it and CNN's 'Talk–Back Live' devoted two discussion segments to it."[26] Bob Levey's "Washington" column in the *Washington Post* newspaper called the *Daily News* decision the "Latest in Questionable Taste,"[27] and Lewis Grossberger skewered the idea in his scathing satirical column in *MediaWeek* titled "Spot Dead! City Mourns."[28]

The alarmist hyperbole caricatures the obits, with Levey saying the implications "are too awful to contemplate. We will soon be buried in a tidal wave of mawkish cuteness. Dogs, cats, hamsters, ponies, iguanas and macaws will take over the obit page, crowding out your poor Uncle Oscar who was not so photogenic as Skippy the distinguished cocker spaniel, who suddenly took ill after ingesting an excessive amount of dead squirrel and antifreeze, having, unfortunately, slipped his chain." Or, he declaims, "we will be informed that former canine officer Blitz, who expired at his retirement kennel in Florida, was a graduate of the Centurion Attack-Dog Academy, where he was voted Most Likely to Seize a Fleeing Perpetrator by the Throat." Or, we will "note that funeral services for Edwin the late, beloved, goldfish, probably father of entire schools of descendants, will be held tomorrow in the toilet of his bereaved owners."[29]

Beneath the venomous humor, several real issues as well as clear moral judgments emerge. First, for Levey, mourning animal death can only be a mockery of the valor and dignity of human lives. The hierarchy of value is clear, and to challenge it is to descend into the realm of the ridiculous, or worse, the embarrassment of "bad taste," here feminized as excessively mawkish and emotional.[30]

And second, just what would a "proper" animal obituary consist of anyway? Obits are a literary genre—they report birth, parents, education, marriage, divorce, children, grandchildren, work, hobbies, membership in fraternal, religious, or service organizations, and moral or personality traits. So how must the genre change to accommodate animals? What ideals of "petness" do we underline in their obits? Should there be an emphasis on "immanent" personality traits (loyalty, generosity) or on accomplishments (won best in show or saved a child from drowning)? How do we list survivors? Do we include other animals? The form is straining under these challenges, and examples have varied from short appreciations of the "we will miss you, brave dog" type to long, wrenching cries of loss that detail the owner/guardian's anguish.

These obits are thus situated between the brevity of a tombstone epitaph and the lengthy outpouring we can find in eulogies for pets on major websites like Petloss.com. Creative improvisations like those I discussed in the context of pet cemetery practices—including the leaving of personal poems relating intimate memories or articulating grieving senses of failure—may occur in death notices. But these emotional outpourings are constrained too, hemmed in by the formality of the newspaper obituary convention. This formality, even in its more elastic form in the era of paid obituaries and even when that form is stretched to accommodate new species and new relationships, remains formulaic. However, the formalism of the formulaic can also be disruptive.

Columnist Betty Cuniberti of the *St. Louis Post-Dispatch* (quoted in Levey's column) fears the embarrassment of bad taste, in part because of the potential for refilling the obituary form with novel animal material. Discussing the printing of pet obits among human ones, she says, "I'm trying to imagine a sorrowful son opening our newspaper to look for his mother's obituary and finding her picture next to one of a hamster." Even worse, Levey summarizes, would be "the issue of the hamster's many survivors." Cuniberti imagines there would be 427 hamster children and grandchildren, "including 154 named Fluffy."[31]

The choice of the hamster, easier to satirize than a golden retriever or the cat who has been with a family for twenty years, tries to reduce the pet obit issue to a dismissible absurdity. Its premise is based not only on the differential attribution of value to human and animal life but also on gradations of value among animal species. (Similar comparisons of value emerge in one of the CNN segments devoted to discussing pet obits.)[32]

Ultimately, what is at stake for some is the "insult" to human life that public records of pet death threaten. A parallel form implies a parallel value—a distasteful concept for some, abhorrent for others, and the source of outrage at Bear's obituary.

This type of media outcry didn't occur when observance of pet death was confined to online virtual cemeteries or to online memorial pages or to physical pet cemeteries. Despite their large scale, those modes of pet commemoration have not attracted such venomous resistance, I suggest, because their "public" consists solely of like-minded individuals. My analysis of five hundred memorials posted online indicates that most appear to have been written by women who loved their pets. These memorials, posted on sites like Petloss.com, which houses more than fifty thousand obituaries for individual animals, constitute a sort of "private-public" sphere. The public for these sites must seek them out on the web and thus most likely consists of those who value what those sites enable: a public legitimation of loss, the elicitation of sympathy and understanding, and contact with a community of people going through the same experience. (While it's possible that "trolls" could enter a site and denigrate its users, I haven't seen this happen.)

Such legitimation of loss, and of the object of the loss as appropriate for mourning, is often unavailable in other realms of daily life. For instance, a pet's death is not seen as a legitimate reason to stay home from work. And a common response to someone announcing the death of his or her cat might be "Oh, too bad. Are you getting another one?"[33] Like a broken toaster, the pet can supposedly be replaced by another in the same commodity category, in this case feline. Online memorials work against this genericization by mourning a particular feline and legitimate both the grief and the griever, who becomes cast in the role of "survivor," not merely of "owner," and thus is acknowledged as worthy of emotional caretaking by other posters to the site.[34]

As I discussed in the preceding two chapters, pet cemeteries also combine the public and the private, but in such a way that anchors mourning in the copresence of the dead animal body (or cremated remains) with her/his human mourners. The resultant sacralization of cemetery space, attenuated perhaps in pet cemeteries because of the lessened respect for those buried there, nonetheless makes that place distinct from online mourning sites and from obituaries. Like online sites, the pet cemetery's public space is de facto a semiprivate space but in this case a sacralized one, further restricting the public for it. These cemeteries, which must be physically sought out and not just happened upon, are most likely to attract like-minded individuals who themselves are there to mourn or who, caring about animals, are exploring the cemetery as a monument to human bonds with pets. Mourners in those spaces are substantially shielded from the outside world as their grief is enfranchised.

Newspaper obituaries are fundamentally different. They are part of the historical community record for anyone to see. They don't have to be sought out specifically but rather land on our table in the news pages, flopping open by the bacon and eggs, inserting themselves into every household. Thus potentially engaging readers of all persuasions, they are seen by many not as an appropriate extension of the obituary form but rather as an explicit challenge to it, a desecration or defrauding of the form.

Pet obits also assert the legitimacy of a pet's family-member status and implicitly legitimate mourning for that familial loss. In doing so, they challenge the constitution of the "family," a concept already under stress from shifting configurations that range from single-parent households to gay families. The decision in October 2002 by the *New York Times* to include gay civil ceremonies in its marriage announcement pages exemplifies this tension. It underlines the centrality of the public record as legitimizer and similarly redefines kinship.

In the last decade, as legal recognition of same-sex marriage increased, culminating in the Supreme Court ruling in 2015 that marriage is a right guaranteed to all by the Constitution, newspapers large and small have had to reconcile their role as public record with that of recorder of community values.[35] Changing conceptions of pets as family members, combined with ever-increasing democratization not only of who gets an obituary but also of who gets to write it and what its content can say, now offer, or require, the contemplation of a similar new frontier. The most common solution so far has been for newspapers to put pet obits as paid announcements in special sections of the classified ads. This is the move that my local paper announced after receiving letters to the editor decrying the inclusion of Bear the dog's obituary in the regular (human) obits section.

This solution manages the tension between animal as subject and animal as object by granting an obit but grouping its subject with property. Even so, this in-between status drives a wedge into the convention of obits—implicitly rendering an ordinary animal's death and life, its subjectivity, worthy of public acknowledgment by writing its individual life into the historical record.

Despite these very public debates and the resistance of some newspapers, people still persist in writing obituaries for their animals and trying to publish them in the obituary pages. One of the most recent examples I have come across is from the Santa Barbara, California, *Independent*, a substantial weekly running about one hundred pages per issue. On October 30, 2008, it ran an obituary for Cyrus the cat, "May 1998–August 2008," which featured a photo, as did the three other (human) obituaries it ran that week. Unlike most obits, however, this one gave the names of its authors, Vivian Olsen and Viola Freeman, who saluted the ten-year-old, long-haired orange tabby with "big eyes, a hairless tail, and golden fur" who was "so intelligent and sweet."[36] I didn't find any follow-up complaints in the paper, so it may be that weeklies, perhaps seen more as community services than regular "hard" news publications, might offer a more welcoming venue for unconventional obits.

When I discussed these issues with obituary writers at the 2008 meeting of the International Association of Obituarists outside Albuquerque, New Mexico, strong opinions emerged. For some, the issue is moot. Kay Powell, award-winning obituary writer on the staff of the *Atlanta Journal Constitution*, feels that obituaries for animals is oxymoronic. By definition, she says, an obituary is a life story about a person. This opinion comes from the writer who penned and published an obituary for the planet Pluto when it was demoted from major celestial body to the new, less prestigious category of "dwarf planet" by the International Astronomical Union in 2006. Pluto's "survivors" were listed as Jupiter, Mars, Earth, Mercury, Neptune, Uranus, Saturn, and Venus. But in that instance, although the piece follows the regular obituary form, noting the deceased's influence on Walt Disney, composer Gustav Holst, and astrologers, it wasn't a "real" obituary. It was done tongue in cheek, sharing in the general sniggering in the popular press that accompanied the poor planet's demotion. When it comes to real obituaries for nonhuman creatures rather than planetary matter, Powell is adamant: "Obits are for people. Pets are animals. Period."[37] For others, the problem of parallelism emerges . . . a parallel form seems to imply a parallel value, and that's just not acceptable or even conceivable to some. It also offers particular challenges for writing.

Challenges of Writing a Nonhuman Animal's Life

As discussions with obituary writers made clear to me, an obituary is not a story about a death; it is a story about a life. If the inscription on a tombstone is the shortest life story of all, then the obituary comes in second, followed by the expansive forms of memoir and biography. And life stories in obituary form have a certain format. Obituary writer and journalist Marilyn Johnson describes it this way: "There is . . . a template for the obituary that almost every newspaper publication follows. Writers have absorbed it and readers come to expect it, almost as if an invisible metronome accompanied its unfolding."[38] The required pieces of the template include the "bad news" (he died) and the "death sentence" (why and how), followed by paragraphs of anecdote, often describing a unique turning point in the subject's life, and ending (at least, if the paper is British) on a note of elegant, literary irony.[39] The point is to announce the death and emphasize the life story. This is where a particular challenge arises in accommodating the obituary form to encompass animals.

What, after all, can we say about the life story of a dog? The unknown (to humans) interiority of a dog's perception of the world, of his or her actual daily experience, presents a boundary. We can't know the significance of things in the world, and of relationships, actions, and events, from the dog's point of view by interviewing family members and friends or reading commentary left behind by the individual, as we might for a human . . . because the species difference means that the world is a different world for the dog than it is for the human. That difference means that those markers used by obit writers to craft the life story won't work. This untranslatability contributes to the writers' biting humor. That the pet does not, and cannot, fit our categories of social contribution and social worth makes the dog's life seem insignificant and lacking when measured by these human standards.

To understand this challenge to or incompatibility with the conventional obituary form, we can examine the tips offered in a document meant to help grieving families prepare a death notice for a human: "Honoring Your Loved One in Print," provided by the *News-Gazette* of Champaign, Illinois. This booklet states that "through a personalized obituary, you can share thoughts about your loved one by writing about the personality, the relationships, the accomplishments, the interests, and the associations that made up the tapestry of his or her life."[40] Its "checklist for creating an obituary" suggests including facts like full name and age; time and place of death; birth date; parents' names; marriage date and name of spouse; survivors, including names of children, siblings, and parents; information about funeral services; and aspects of life history, including occupation, memberships, interests, activities, and accomplishments.[41]

For animals, many of these facts are unknown (who are the "parents"?) or considered unimportant unless the animal was a "purebred," like an AKC (American Kennel Club)-registered dog. Other categories, like work record, are irrelevant unless the dog was a "working dog," like a service dog specially trained to assist the disabled. Still others, such as "activities," appear ludicrous in human terms . . . does your parakeet like to look at himself in the mirror? Sing along with music on the radio?

Below is my attempt to engage the challenge of the human obit form when transferred to animals. In this unpublished obituary I wrote for my pet rabbit Baylor, not only are the categorical distinctions of valuation a challenge to the form, but so also are the sensorial differences in how nonhuman animals experience the world. They have a fundamentally different way of being in the world. They literally see the world differently, knowing it through smell, and they have a different sense of acting physically on the world. How do we know what the highlights of this life are for individual members of those animal-kinds?

AN OBITUARY FOR "BAYLOR WABBIT"

Baylor Wabbit, senior gentleman and shyly gracious fellow, died on Memorial Day weekend, 2008, at the University of Illinois Veterinary College, after what appeared to be a sudden stroke. Excellent emergency care was provided by the small-animal vets, but Baylor's age, at eight and a half, rather advanced for a rabbit, worked against him.

Baylor was born in Iowa and spent his first several years there with a human companion before a brief stint in the Iowa City Animal Care Center, where we found him available for adoption. His silvery coat and dark chocolate-colored eyes, paws, and long floppy ears gave him a sophisticated look that stood out from the crowd there and caught our eye. Baylor trained us in rabbit care, especially regarding the necessity of fresh vegetables—above all, carrots with their leafy tops still attached. These were ideally followed by something sweet, like yogurt drops or a piece of fully ripe banana. The drops were (apparently) so good that—when we combined them with a special Morse code of taps and entreaties—they could even tempt him back into his wire house as he traded footloose freedom for tasty treats.

Baylor established his supremacy in the home at once, and when Mama the dog joined our household soon after his arrival, he stood his ground and did not back away from a sniffing investigation, earning him instant respect from our curious canine. Later he was joined by a second house rabbit, a white floppy-eared boy named Christopher, who brought out Baylor's playful side and stimulated him to hop, dig, and leap around the kitchen, where their homes (big wire pens on wheels) took up most of the space. For these two, each was the other's most important companion, although Baylor needed to keep his distance to establish his superiority in the rabbit ranking. Despite this, they often spent the night sleeping one by the other, separated only by the widely spaced metal mesh of a cage as one or the other, on the outside, had roaming rights that day.

Baylor spent five years with us, most in Iowa City, but the last few months in Champaign, Illinois, after a smooth move to a new house that brought him the pleasures of a dedicated rabbit room, with a window for fresh breezes, lots of room for cardboard boxes to deconstruct, and a glass door through which to keep an eye on the workings of the household.

Strong, quiet, gentle, soft, and opinionated, "Mr. B" was a big presence in a small body.

Social Worth and Social Obligation:
Why Pet Obituaries Are Dangerous

Beyond the challenge of translating the obituary form from human to animal life is the issue of social value—of social worth—which speaks to an even more fundamental dividing line. We can certainly imagine human situations in which social contribution by such measurements is also minimal: babies, drug addicts, murderers, deeply mentally disabled persons, and, even more broadly, those whose life contributions revolve around a very small circle, such as family. Do these situations offer us any clues?

A child who dies in infancy after a severe illness may have deeply touched the lives of her family circle and even of the medical professionals who treated her. Perhaps a church or other organization was also involved in caring for her, praying for her, raising money for her medical bills, assisting the family, and so on. If so, the reverberations of this individual's life are already wider than those of most domestic pets, moving outward beyond the immediate family unit. But this status, if we can use that word here, is due less to anything the small child herself might have "accomplished" than to her status as a child at the center of widening circles of attachment and care.

Few would imply that such a life is unworthy of an obituary, or that the story of that life would somehow be offensive to others whose lives by more conventional measures of accomplishment were listed on the same page. Being a "public figure" can catapult an animal, and thus its death, into the newsworthy category; but social measure of public contribution is not necessary for the death of an individual person to merit an obituary—perhaps not a news obit but at least a family's paid death notice. However, it is precisely these latter forms that are deemed by some to be so offensive when applied to animals.

Social worth becomes a useful measure for understanding attitudes toward obituaries when we apply it not to the individual but to the category. Humans are granted an intrinsic social worth merely by being born into that category of being, whereas animals may earn this membership through notoriety or heroism. And in most cases, this possibility is extended only to pets, not to nonindividuated animals denoted as "wild" or as "food."

The real threat posed by obits for animals is that they drive a wedge into the epistemological boundary between the "worthy" and the "not worthy." By pointing to and contesting that boundary by publicly proclaiming a parallelism between the human and nonhuman animals, obits raise the specter of shifts in social practices that the attribution of such value portends, including a radical reorganization of food, sports, some scientific research, and so on. It's no wonder that the categorical threat—the threat to supposedly distinct conceptual categories, and hence distinct moral obligations to humans and animals—which an animal obit represents has been so strongly resisted through the twin techniques of denigration and moral outrage.

Writing animal lives into the historical record through newspaper obituaries offers the potential for a fundamental challenge to the status of animals, and it helps legitimize the constitution of the multispecies "family" as a social unit. By definition, an obituary asserts, in no uncertain terms, the subjectivity of individual animals and the fact that they are regarded, at least by some, as grievable lives. In making this assertion, it is similar to the pet cemetery. But obituaries are more public than pet cemeteries, addressing an undifferentiated audience through the newspaper. And they offer the opportunity to expound on the details of a life. The obituary form details an individual animal's impact on other humans and animals in the world, and makes that life and that impact part of social history, underwriting this notion of a new social history through the legitimizing function of the press as public record.

By contesting denials of value, animal obituaries thus simultaneously assert the value of animal lives and the rights of those grieving humans who, by writing the obituaries, would proclaim it. This is why they have elicited such vehement responses. The implications of such political moves are far-reaching, but their effects remain to be seen; they are part of a wider context rearticulating human understandings of animal subjectivity across multiple realms. But what *is* evident is that this phenomenon, the crafting of animal obituaries to write ordinary individual animal lives into history, is a profoundly political act.

SEVEN

Requiem for Roadkill: Death, Denial, and Mourning on America's Roads

The deer lying on its side; the raccoon on its back, grotesquely bloated as if about to burst; the flattened gray-black wing feathers of a starling, eerily fluttering in the breeze on a highway, all that is left of a buzzard's meal; or the small hand-like paws and surprising red entrails of a common gray squirrel too unfortunate to make it to the other side of the road. These are some of the everyday images that catch our eyes, or that our glance evades, as we hurtle along highways and glide through housing subdivisions cocooned in our cars.

In this chapter, I examine one of the relatively unexamined sites of human-animal encounters: roadkill, that is, the destruction of "wild" animals by automobiles. How can something so ubiquitous be so absent from public discourse? What are the numerous rhetorical strategies and ideologies necessary to render invisible this enormous amount of animal carnage? What might it take to move these roadkilled bodies from the status of the "unmourned" to the "mourned"? Drawing on ecological studies, anecdotal evidence, ecological writings, roadkill food sites, artists' renderings, and popular publications, I suggest that the status of roadkilled animals, and of human relations to those animals, is undergoing a shift. No longer simply the remains of unavoidable, "accidental" killing, the animals whose corpses litter the side of the road are beginning to be accorded subjectivity. As scholars, we may be able to hasten this shift and through our analyses point the way toward a less deadly and less unacknowledged highway toll.

Roadkill is the material result of a social phenomenon. It is a massive calculus in carcasses but has received very little attention as yet by anthropologists, sociologists, or cultural studies scholars.[1] The few studies I am aware of are by Alexandra Koelle, Mike Michael, Dennis Soron, David Lulka, and, in an art context, Susan McHugh and Steve Baker, Helen Molesworth, and Julia Schlosser (in German).[2] These works probe the cultural meanings associated with roadkill, at times suggesting new frameworks, like Mike Michael's notion of intersecting human and animal mobilities. My goal is to accelerate this critical attention and enlarge it to eventually include a fuller analytical spectrum of roadkill as animal corpse, as metaphor, as comic image, as art material, and above all as a stimulus to mourning—a punctum of death, to use Roland Barthes's term—and ultimately a goad toward change, a shift toward a recognition of this type of animal mortality.

In contrast to those animals at the center of the immediately preceding chapters about pet cemeteries, pet obituaries, and their resultant controversies, roadkilled animals are rarely granted the individuation of subjectivity that pets receive. As "wild," not domesticated, animals, they are unnamed and do not live intimately with us in our homes. They coexist beside us, relatively unacknowledged and rarely even seen, until those moments of impact when our lives literally collide. Their deaths are rarely mourned, for such mourning would mean granting value in a way that could challenge ubiquitous categories of value. It would mean shifting our categorization from the generic animal who happened to cross the road at the wrong time to the individuated animal being whose life intersected with ours. This is a major refocusing, but if we look carefully enough, there are some signs that this shift is beginning.

To date, most academic work on roadkill has emerged from environmental studies of road safety and ecology, including the construction of "ecopassages," or safe pathways (underground corridors or overhead bridges) for the passage of wildlife across roadways.[3] I suggest that with this shift in building considerations, the status of the animal changes from that of necessary collateral damage sacrificed to the needs of human technomobility to that of a subject in need of human assistance.[4]

A second recent shift in the conceptual status of roadkill is related to the growing "ethical eating" movement. Dead animals on the road make a transition from "trash" to "food" in these contexts. "Ethical eaters" are now promoting information about how to gather, and safely prepare for human consumption, animal carcasses found by the side of the road. These individuals place a moral value on not letting the animal's death be for nothing. Instead, the lost life is purposely transformed into sustenance for another species, humans.[5]

Ultimately, I want to point to the shifting human-nonhuman animal relations in this arena to illuminate what I am terming a "contradictory ethics of care and dismissal." In what follows, I focus on the situation in the contemporary United States, and caution that we shouldn't assume that the situation is necessarily the same elsewhere. I sketch some of the parameters of the concept of roadkill, the material reality of that death, and the questions it raises for us as scholars, artists, and individuals traveling on the roads.

What Is Roadkill?

First, let me explore the implicit parameters of the term. What is "roadkill"? Generally, as the term is deployed in the United States, it refers to animals killed by cars on the road and who are not owned and are not domestic, food-production animals. Raccoons, opossums, snakes, squirrels, rabbits, badgers, turtles, birds, and deer are some of the most common victims. Occasionally, pet animals are killed by cars and left by the side of the road, but this isn't the prime referent of *roadkill*. Insects squished on the tarmac or crushed against the car's windshield aren't generally included in the referent. Therefore, *roadkill* references an implicit species and size range.

It is impossible to quantify the tonnage of animal corpses attributable to roadkills in the United States. States and municipalities generally do not keep records of these deaths, although some, like New Hampshire, map the sites of animal-car collisions as a safety measure.[6] As Richard T. Forman and colleagues observe, "Systematic record keeping of wildlife mortality on U.S. roads is nonexistent for any species."[7] Wildlife biologist Jim Sipes suggests that "an estimated *one million* vertebrates—amphibians, reptiles, birds, and mammals—are killed on [US] roads and highways *each day*."[8] The toll is breathtaking, but the isolation of the incidents masks the totality of the phenomenon. This is part of the reason that roadkill and roadkilling remain submerged in public discourse.[9]

Generally, *roadkill* is a generic plural referent. The species of animal is not indicated, and there are no common linguistic clarifications—for example, "big roadkill," or "good roadkill," or "annoying roadkill," or "dangerous roadkill"—although all these implications can be found in everyday usage. For example, deer are big animals often hit by cars, and their deaths are problematic in the sense that a car's impact with such a large being can not only kill the deer but also cause extensive damage to the automobile and can potentially severely injure or kill its occupants.

Roadkill or roadkilling is generally seen as a category of human-caused animal death for which responsibility is not attached. The general presumption is not that the driver of the car intended to kill the animal—this isn't about hunting with a car instead of a shotgun—but rather that the death was unavoidable because of the conventions of highway travel (high speeds, night and day driving, placing human above animal life if evasive maneuvers would be dangerous, et cetera). The notion of an "unavoidable" event coupled with the "I would have avoided it if I safely could have" rationale result in a legal and ethical understanding that does not attach blame to the driver of a vehicle that causes the death of an animal. The road is presumptively the province of the car and driver. The animal, in contrast, is an unfortunate and largely unknowing interloper who crosses into human territory with sometimes-disastrous consequences. A few ecological studies are now reframing the road as a shared space used by both humans and animals,[10] but this notion has not moved into dominant public discourse. Share the Road signs, when addressed to automobile drivers, undoubtedly refer to sharing with bicycles or motorcycles, not animals. Watch for Deer is the closest we get in highway-speak to acknowledging shared access with animals.

Roadkill, and *roadkilling*, my coinage to invoke not just the outcome but the action itself, is ultimately attributed to an animal's being in the wrong place at the wrong time, not to driver negligence or malfeasance. In other words, the animal is presumed to be unwittingly responsible for his or her own death. In most cases, unless the impact causes a car accident and police are called, the driver is unknown and simply drives on.[11]

The closest we have in terms of a human parallel is the concept of involuntary manslaughter, or "hit and run," in which anonymity is emphasized but responsibility still attaches. But we have no parallel linguistic term when animal victims are involved—"involuntary fauna-slaughter," for instance—since the very conception of responsibility attaching to the killing does not obtain. This lack of a name for the act is indicative of the difference in conceptual, moral, and practical attributions of meaning and responsibility that such animal deaths occasion, or rather, don't.

This is not to say that some "road killers" don't regret causing the death of an animal, and/or that some may not even stop the car and see if the animal survives and could be helped, especially if that animal is not "wild" but perhaps a person's pet to which (presumably) emotional value attaches. Other drivers, however, may develop personal rituals of mourning as they whiz by the carcasses they see on the road, whispering while driving, "I'm sorry."[12] This acknowledgment of death may be more widespread than we imagine. In a discussion with students in a colleague's large Animals and Society class at my university in 2011, to which I gave a guest lecture, I was able to gather some suggestive data on this point. Out of 159 undergraduate students, 86% reported (on a simple survey) that they sometimes acknowledged an animal they saw dead on the road by commenting on it then or later or even by some other behavior, such as saying a prayer.[13] Apparently, the innumerable deaths of animals on the highways aren't going unacknowledged, even though that acknowledgment remains largely private (perhaps because of fear of ridicule?).

Occasionally, very occasionally, a creative writer or poet draws our attention to the dead by the side of the road, rendering them worthy of public contemplation. In the late 1960s and early 1970s, Pulitzer Prize–winning US poet Gary Snyder wrote about animal death, hunting, killing, and eating, and about encountering roadkilled animals, as part of his wider commitment to ecological writing. He urged us, with foresight and subtlety, to attend to the ways we engage with animals. Many of these works were gathered in his collection of writings called *Turtle Island*, which includes the poem "The Dead by the Side of the Road." In it, he asks:

> How did a great Red-Tailed Hawk
> come to lie—all stiff and dry—
> on the shoulder of
> Interstate 5?[14]

How, indeed? A question rarely asked, and even more rarely answered in the artistic realm. As the poem unfolds, Snyder catalogues a range of roadkilling encounters at the complex nexus of human and nonhuman animal lives in transit: logging trucks hitting fawns;

a skunk with a tire-crushed head, its pelt taken away for tanning by someone who passed by—the happenstance of opportunity; a doe who finally collapsed by the side of a road, shot by incompetent hunters incapable of delivering the neat coup de gras, its carcass later scavenged by stew-makers on the lookout for free meat (and why not, since the deed was already done?). "Pray to their spirits," Snyder says of the dead animals. "Ask them to bless us . . . (with their) night-shining eyes. . . . The dead by the side of the road."[15]

A cross-species intimacy of vision and bodies emerges here with the "night-shining eyes" of the animals, their reflective retinas lit up in the headlight's beam. Hurtling through the dark highway's tunnel of night, the car as an instrument of sudden death doesn't discriminate—a glinting eye, a screech of brakes, a sudden jerking turn, a sickening thud announcing the impact. They, the too suddenly visible, end up as the dead by the side of the road—hawk, deer, skunk. But, accident aside, says Snyder, this death by our modern machines should not go unremarked. "Pray to their spirits, Ask them to bless us," he intones, linking these deaths by our modern machines to notions of ancient hunter-hunted rituals.

But much more often, I'd suggest, no such poetic remembrance of ritual, intended to sanctify killing of animals by humans, emerges as we whiz along the highway. Even if we were to accept the human kill- ing of animals for food as a necessity (and not all of us do), the implied nobility of Snyder's life exchange—yours for mine, with thanks for and recognition of your (animal) subjectivity in my (human) gun sight— bears little relation to the highway slaughter, mostly inadvertent and leaving ungathered the bodies of millions of animals on US highways each year. Snyder is ambiguous in his mourning of these dead, link- ing them instead to a potential spiritual absolution. In contrast, Barry Lopez, an equally powerful writer, is unabashed in his mourning.

Lopez is one of the very few authors I've found to publicly express emotions about animal deaths on the roads. His 1998 piece "Apolo- gia" ruminates on the roadkilled animals he encounters while driving across the United States. He stops his car and gently, though they are already dead, carries the splattered remains of raccoons to the road's edge. He lays them in the grass in a sort of quasi burial, a simple act of mourning—a technique, he says, of "awareness." Here is his wrenching rendering of one of these acts, performed after he fails to swerve fast enough to avoid hitting a young sage sparrow in Idaho. Getting out of the car, he crosses to the just-dead body:

I rest the walloped bird in my right hand, my left thumb pressed to its chest. I feel for the wail of the heart. Its eyes glisten like rain on crystal. Nothing but warmth. I shut the tiny eyelids and lay it beside a clump of bunchgrass. Beyond a barbed-wire fence, the overgrazed range is littered with cow flops. The road curves away to the south. I nod before I go, a ridiculous gesture, out of simple grief.[16]

This momentary pressure of fingers to feathered breast, of human skin to bird's eyelids—intimate acts impossible when the bird was alive, for it surely would have taken flight at the approach of a human—emphasize the specialness of death, its disruption of expected human and animal relations. But the conventions of our roadkilling contravene this specialness of the passage from the living to the dead, for they usually call for no such recognition or intimacy; indeed, they call for nothing at all except learned obliviousness or an active turning away from these often gruesome and grotesque spectacles of death, what Carolyn Duckworth calls "dark spots and small lumps" on the highway.[17]

Barry Lopez's writings are unique and his actions so unconventional that we might think that such unabashed mourning for roadkilled animals hardly ever takes place. We would be wrong, however. As scholars like Barbara J. King have noted, evidence suggests that the category of feeling that we label "mourning," and the actions that articulate it, can no longer be attributed solely to humans. More and more evidence is mounting that highly social animals like chimpanzees and elephants respond to the death of a member of their group with reactions that we would term "mourning" if we observed them in humans . . . gently touching the dead, staying with them, gathering together around the body, exhibiting a depressed appetite and activity level, and even visiting the homes (locations) where those left behind may be grieving.[18] Anecdotally too, thousands of pet owners would probably agree that their surviving pets seem to be "depressed" ("mourning"?) after another pet or person in the home dies, disrupting the social relations of that minicommunity. Is their "grief" our "grief"? We can't be sure of what animals know, feel, or fear, as anthropologist King notes, yet we do know that both humans and animals respond to severed bonds. As she says, "Grief blooms because two animals bond . . . because of a heart's certainty that another's presence is as necessary as air."[19]

With some imagination, then, we can assume that many of the road-killed animals we see flattened into furry spots on the road are being "mourned," "missed," or, at the very least if even those concepts can be dismissed as too anthropocentric, "waited for" by other animals. Perhaps the dead rabbit, distinctive ears still visible in the flattened carcass by the side of the road, but now never coming "home," was the bonded-for-life partner of another rabbit, the latter safe now in the once-shared burrow. Bonded rabbits, we know, maintain their closeness for years and, domesticated or wild, spend hours nestled side by side, an intimacy roadkilling forever interrupts. How long will the surviving member of the pair wait for his or her companion's return? Without simply dismissing such ideas as "anthropomorphic," we should bring to bear all that is currently known about nonhuman animals (the science of ethology is relevant here) and the social communities they form, to ask not only what roadkill means for humans but also what impact it might have on animals, beyond the obvious decrease in numbers. First, though, we have to move from seeing roadkill as collateral damage to viewing roadkilled animals as grievable lives.

Roadkill in the Visual Arts

In addition to writers like Gary Snyder and Barry Lopez, some visual artists are exploring the realm of mourning for these "dark spots and small lumps." Although their work is not widely circulated in public discourse, these experiments creatively point the way to a deeper engagement and challenge us to follow. In the next section, I discuss the work of three artists, Brian D. Collier, Craig Stecyk, and Steve Baker, each of whom takes a distinctive approach to bringing roadkill into public discourse.[20]

US-based artist Brian D. Collier engages the visual rhetorics of human roadside memorials to point to animal deaths. By the side of the road, close to the carcass of a roadkilled animal, Collier erects a memorial consisting of an acrylic-framed photograph of a living representative of that type of animal, installed on a concrete base and accompanied by assorted plastic flowers. These small roadside memorials echo and cross-reference the roadside shrines erected in some parts of the country to mark the spot where a human loved one was killed in a traffic accident, which I discussed in chapter 4. In those cases, the shrine does not replace burial and memorialization elsewhere, but it does move the death into the public domain, demanding recognition that *this* death happened *here*. Often, a smiling, full-color photo of the deceased beams out from the shrine, an individual addressing us as individuals as if to say: I died here. This fleeting introduction, a split-second engagement as we drive by, creates the possibility of a connection between the person in the photo and the viewer . . . and in this momentary linkage we can feel the specter of possibility. An implicit hailing into this narrative situates us, drivers passing the spot where this death occurred, as potential victims or potential killers. Our own mortality and our own responsibility in driving a potentially lethal machine are evoked in that moment.

Similar shrines for roadkilled animals could clutter the road with the marking of accumulated deaths, too numerous to count as we go whizzing by. Imagine shrines like those produced by Collier, to squirrels, snakes, birds, raccoons. Rather than the single dead sparrow or deer that we see dead by the side of the road or squished into the tarmac, these roadside memorials to roadkilled animals would mark an ever-increasing litany of deaths. Collier's shrine, placed to acknowledge the death of a rock dove, or a common pigeon, marks this bird as an individual and its death as worthy of commemoration. Other works in his series recognize the deaths of other types of animals, such as opossums, squirrels, raccoons, rabbits, deer, skunks, and crows. Each commemoration insists that this too was a grievable life.

In each case, Collier makes a standardized placard containing an image of the type of animal killed, adorned with plastic flowers. The flowers immediately invoke the funereal act of mourning. The placards, bland, black-and-white photos against a sky-blue background, not only genericize the type of animal by presenting a picture of a living specimen in contrast to the often mangled carcass nearby but also translate its drubbed, damaged, and dislocated parts so that we can be sure of its species. This is what this body used to look like, say these shrines, forcing us to see the disfigurement and dismemberment for what they are, implicitly reassembling this flattened organic matter so that our minds may reconstruct it into the three-dimensional shape of its recently breathing, living incarnation.

Still, this memorialization of an individual animal remains dependent on generic visuals—recording a tension between individuation and the subjectivity it implies, and our generic categorizations of wildlife as "types." The rock dove commemorated by Collier, whatever the particular age, or sex, or life experiences (who knows where he or she flew, or what he or she saw right before the deadly impact with a car?), exists in tension with the generic category of "bird" or "pigeon" that encompasses almost all our relations with and perceptions of avian wildlife.

More than two decades before Collier, West Coast artist Craig Stecyk

III combined the genres of sculpture and performance art to erect temporary memorials to roadkilled animals. In 1983, he produced a "series of site-specific sculptural installations called *Road Rash* that incorporated the bodies of animals who had been killed by automobiles."[21] Unlike Collier's low-tech materials, Stecyk used bronze, an expensive metal associated with commemorative busts and memorials, to literally add value to the deaths of roadkilled animals. A 1989 exhibit catalogue essay by Bolton T. Colburn describes this process and the interlocutory relationship it forges with place, road, and danger: "After taking a photograph to document the animal's position, he [Stecyk] picked it up from the roadway, skinned it, and still working on the site, cast the guts in bronze. Finally, he sewed the skin back over the casting. The bronzed animal was then epoxied to the surface of the road in the original position of the find."[22] Working from a studio setup rigged on the bed of his pickup truck, Stecyk cruised roads until he found roadkill he wanted to memorialize and then set to work, casting in metal from the dead body on-site, using his truck as a temporary foundry.[23] Capped in his protective eye-shading hood, pouring sparking molten bronze in the middle of the road, he interrupted the normal traffic flow in a quasi-ritual act.[24]

The resulting sculpture was installed (glued to the road or road edge) where the dead body had lain, inserting the memorial directly into the paths of oncoming cars and thus following the originary killing trajectory. The bronze "body," re-covered in the original skin, recalls, as Julia Schlosser notes, Steve Baker's idea of "'botched taxidermy,' in which the body of the animal is 'present in all its awkward, pressing thingness.'"[25] Inside the insistent thingness of these installations, however, were not the deteriorating guts of the roadkilled animal we might expect when we pass by on the road or the antiseptic plastic of the taxidermist's foundation but rather the gleaming husk of bronze, secretly placing commodity value amid seeming detritus.

Few of us seek out roadkill, but this is precisely what Stecyk had to do to launch his commemoration, since the nature of roadkilling—an unexpected event at an unpredictable site—means that it is usually encountered by happenstance, underlining the arbitrary nature of the death. Stecyk cruised for roadkill, ironically reproducing the driving-death nexus that defines roadkilling. Schlosser notes the irony of placing a memorial on a roadway where it, in turn, could constitute a distraction and cause a motorist to crash.[26]

Eventually, Stecyk decided to remove his pieces because of their potential to cause accidents. Since they were epoxied in place on the road and made out of metal, they weren't easily squished into the pavement, unlike their dead referents. As Schlosser puts it, "The animals themselves are momentarily elevated as a result of the artist's attentions, but ultimately the monuments are as fleeting as the lives of the animals."[27]

Whereas Collier erects temporary memorials by the side of the road, Stecyk works in long-lasting materials but places them in tenuous positions that cannot be sustained. In both cases, the artists grapple with the material-immaterial nexus of living matter as the stimulus for their art of memorialization or recognition. Roadkilled bodies are either cleared away for safety's sake by state or local authorities or eventually pecked to oblivion by carrion eaters, ground into the asphalt by repeated tire drubbings, or washed down a storm drain in a mass of fur and tendons. The road remains a site of traversing, not a site of stopping to recognize. The incommensurability of static, site-specific memorials to death caused by motion reminds us of the absolute extent to which the automobile rules US roadways.

The only other "in situ" memorials I am aware of are not by artists but by the animal advocacy organization People for the Ethical Treatment of Animals (PETA). For several years now, PETA has been attempting to call attention to the deaths of farm animals in highway wrecks. This effort mobilizes a different definition of *roadkill*, since that term usually refers to nondomesticated animals. In PETA's campaign, the animals in question were bound for slaughter but met their planned death in an unplanned way—on the road and not in the slaughterhouse. The clear referent for the PETA effort is the roadside memorial, or *descanso*; but rather than the improvised memorials of crosses and flowers erected by loved ones, it is the regularized, state-sanctioned sign that some states offer in their stead that PETA seeks to erect to memorialize animals, not humans.

As mentioned in chapter 5, the only successful campaign to erect a memorial to farm animals has been in Wisconsin, near the city of Madison, where no municipal ordinances prevent the placing of such signs. There, a PETA-sponsored blue metal sign with black print says, "In memory of the cows who were crushed to death in a truck accident at this spot en route to slaughter. Try vegan." Like the artworks discussed above, the sign marks the exact spot of death and explicitly commits it and the lives lost there to memory—it is an act of memorialization. At the same time, it evokes the image of crushed bodies ground into the tarmac by truck tires—our image of roadkilled animals. The word choice too—"crushed to death"—brings a sense of action, of *roadkilling* as a verb, to our minds and our imaginations in an

all-too-visceral image, connecting it to the wild-animal roadkill referent. Similar PETA campaigns in Virginia, Georgia, and Illinois have
been rejected by those states. A request in Utah to memorialize seven
hundred turkeys that died in a crash in April of 2014 was denied by the
Utah Department of Transportation.[28]

This road-based initiative is important for its attempted revaluing of
farmed animals, inviting us to mourn those slated for death and thus
turning their normally "ungrieved" lives into grievable ones. However,
it lacks the arresting visual power of artistic work like that of Collier
and Stecyk, and doesn't address the loss of wild animal life usually
referenced as roadkill. With the work of artist/theorist Steve Baker, art
about roadkill moves from the road to the gallery, widening its potential audience.

Collier's and Stecyk's in situ installations mark the dead animal
body and the site of the creature's demise, and clearly reference the memorializing function of the gravestone (in Collier's case) or the bronze
marker (for Stecyk). By contrast, the photographs by UK artist/scholar/
theorist Steve Baker are more open ended in their engagement with
roadkill and its representation. They are two-dimensional works, not
three-dimensional site-specific installations, and are shown not on the
roadside but in an art gallery, safe from swipes by passing tires. One
of a very few gallery artists engaging with roadkill as a topic and as a
subject of their work, Baker recently completed the series he began in
2009, *Norfolk Roadkill, Mainly*, which he discusses in a pithy, scalpel-
sharp dialogue with animal studies and literary studies scholar Susan
McHugh.[29]

For this series, Baker produced a series of large-scale color-photo diptychs of roadkill(ed) animal bodies in the city of Norwich, England.
Each pair includes a close-up of a dead animal and a locationally relevant (non-roadkill) image, such as a segment of a mural or an architectural detail referencing Norwich's medieval past. Unlike the work
of Collier and Stecyk, these works aren't site-specific commemorations
or memorializations of specific dead animals, even though they depict
such bodies. Rather, they command and enable our contemplation of
roadkilled death more generally by bringing it into the orbit of art historical visual conventions and sites of active looking and display, like
an art gallery.

The diptychs implicitly pair the death of a pictured animal with its
wider social and geographic location, pointing to this death here and
now, but connecting it implicitly with the long reach of history. As
Schlosser eloquently puts it, "These diptychs emphasize the ephem-

eral nature of the animals' bodies—which have fragmented, becoming more and more illegible as they are slowly kneaded into the surface of the street—by uniting them with crumbling, centuries old stonework . . . [so that] these panels speak of illegibility, abstraction and negation."[30]

For example, one of the diptychs (untitled) pairs two vertically stacked, large-format photographs, both cropped to a similar scale and both with sand-colored backgrounds, using the frame of formalism to help contain the challenging content. In the top image, we see the dead, partially dismembered body of what appears to be a squirrel. Its gray-furred body is placed upside down in the frame, a still-fluffy white belly exposed, tiny arms flung up above the head as if in surrender, a red gash at the bottom of the face, almost like an open mouth. At the top of the image, the bodily integrity of the animal begins to disintegrate: pink guts start to fall out in the coils of intestines, the right leg is splayed out and scraped to the bone like a chef-prepared drumstick, and the left leg is flattened and bent in an unnatural ninety-degree angle against the tawny, sandy substrate. The hues are delicate: no big pooling of aggressively red blood, just the pink, white, brown, and tan shapes against the tan background.

The paired image below echoes the same muted hues. Umber brushstrokes outline a human shoulder and arm, touches of muted red call attention to the design of an arch, a barely sketched visage, and centrally, the delicate gesture of an upturned hand, fingers opened as if to receive the animal body suspended in the panel above. The flat aesthetics of European medieval painting echo the flattened body of the roadkilled animal above, and both are pasted into the muted sand color of their respective backgrounds. Both also highlight expressive arms and open digits—hands or tiny claws evoking the fragility of touch. The tension in the formal aesthetics of parallel design features in the historical diptych format, and in a dramatic subject matter—contemporary death—reveals the artistic challenge Baker has tackled. He must simultaneously point to the presence of death and avoid gratuitously spectacularizing its potential to evoke sentimentality.

As Baker states, "In many cases the 'look' of these splayed animal bodies is both terrible *and* magnificent."[31] How to avoid aestheticizing what he calls the "unexpected beauty of some of those dead and sometimes mutilated bodies"?[32] As McHugh notes, these bodies aren't simply objects to be fetishized in themselves but mark the intersection of multiple vectors: travel, food for scavengers, decomposition forces, and so on. This is where the supposed facticity of the photographic medium, its evidentiary effect, can work against sentimentality, drawing the viewer into pondering the "how," or the historical events and forces that converged at the moment of the photograph. In some images, the body is so mangled or decomposed that the species is no longer even recognizable. Baker resists telling us what it is, even if he knows, so as not to foreclose the possibilities of the viewer's experience of the image. He asserts, "In figuring it, picturing it, as a previously living thing, it would be a distraction to invite viewers to indulge their likely sympathies for some species over others."[33]

One of the strongest impulses behind this series is to present the normally overlooked or unpresentable and to call our attention to it through artistic means. Can art solicit emotive reactions to roadkill without being didactic? Can it make us look when we want to look away? I might state it this way: can artistic engagements with roadkill engage the aesthetic without anesthetizing the ethical? These are some of the provocative questions that artistic engagement raises for Baker and McHugh. Baker places his striking photographic images in an artistic setting, immersing a gallery-going population in a social issue usually left far outside gallery walls.

For artist Brian Collier, though, such open-ended engagement in an explicitly artistic context is not the goal. His approach, like that of the earlier bronzed works by Craig Stecyk, is more interventionist and site-specific, literally intervening in the road and our travel of it. By presenting us with memorials placed roadside next to the carcass of a dead animal, Collier invites us to ponder the carnage, the species involved, the exact location of death, the cause of death, and our own future implication as motorists in killing other animals on a road. Mourning is directly referenced and invited through the memorial form, even though it may be rejected by some viewers of this work as preposterous, an invocation to mourn for the unmournable—the category of the "not worthy of mourning" or, to reference my discussion of Judith Butler's formulation (in chapter 5), a being beyond the pale of a "grievable life."

Whereas Baker's images engage us and succeed (as McHugh says) in "shepherding attention" far from the road itself, displayed on the gallery wall,[34] Collier's and Stecyk's works interrupt our physical passing, hailing us from the road, risking ridicule on the odd chance that some passengers streaking down the road might ask, "What if?" What if the violent deaths of these roadkilled animals were given meaning through mourning? What might that change?

Surely these artistic commentaries on roadkilled animals evoke multiple responses among those who see them, whether along Illinois highways in the case of Brian Collier, on California back roads for Stecyk, or in British art galleries where Baker's prints have been shown. But we do not yet know how these responses to an artist's work shape a potential driver's response to the material remains of animals encountered while hurtling along the road. Here the interface between art and everyday action and between art perception and public discourse remains unknown.

From Absence to Presence, from Denial to Acknowledgment

Only additional ethnographic research will reveal the complexity of people's responses to roadkill in situ and to its invocation in art and/or public discourse. To my knowledge, little research has been initiated into people's feelings and actions when encountering and dealing with roadkill. But legally, and in terms of dominant public discourse, no response is required of citizens, and no public opprobrium ensues that I am aware of to lack of response, although it might come into play in isolated circumstances, as when onlookers notice the impact and feel the driver could have safely avoided it. (At this point, I have only a little anecdotal evidence to show that some drivers not only don't avoid the animal but drive straight for it.)[35]

What are the cultural, legal, and ethical conditions of possibility for this situation, which renders the deaths of what must surely be millions of animals a year a sort of "collateral damage" necessary to the conduct of the nation's business on the roads? And what cultural presence does this tonnage of animal bodies and strewn guts have in contemporary discourse? Where is an acknowledgment of its presence as a phenomenon to be found? Is it in legal codification? Discourse on food? Ethnic and regional humor? Its metaphorization in daily speech?

Roadkill as metaphor appears to have, by far, the largest presence in daily discourse. As Michele Hanks found, in assisting me in preliminary research for this chapter, the vast majority of references to roadkill on the Internet—an imperfect but suggestive measure—have nothing to do with real animals but instead deal with someone or some idea that has suddenly lost viability. Out-of-favor politicians, financier Bernie Madoff's victims, and movies that fail to bring in big profits are all referred to as "roadkill."

But aside from the information superhighway, real roadkill has a geopolitics. While animals can be killed on roads and streets anywhere, from the most rural to the most urban of locations, roadkill generally is more prevalent where the confluence of cars and wild animals is great-est—in rural areas and some suburban settings. The particular associa-tion of roadkill with rural life is revealed in the subgenre of roadkill jokes and cookbooks, like the 1980s series (still in print) put out by B. R. "Buck" Peterson that includes *The Original Road Kill Cookbook, The International Roadkill Cookbook*, and the *Roadkill U.S.A. Coloring and Ac-tivity Book* (the latter presumably could be paired with a child's road-kill Halloween costume sporting tire tracks across the belly and sold in 2011 at Meijer's grocery stores in my city of Champaign, Illinois).

Unlike the "ethical eating" movement, which promotes the use of roadkilled animal flesh as a good source of protein and takes the po-sition that a life should not go to waste, the humorous roadkill jokes and cookbooks focus on stereotypical "hillbilly" life, referring to poor, rural, Anglo American residents of the Appalachian Mountains who presumably must scrounge for any useful meat they can get and thus have recipes for cooking roadkilled opossum or squirrel, minor gamey meats, out of necessity. Author Peterson is the leading contributor to this genre. Tongue in cheek, these books nonetheless reference poverty and desperation, and denigrate so-called hillbilly populations as a mar-keting tool.

The blurb on the back of Peterson's *Original Road Kill Cookbook* from *Playboy* magazine (note the male target of the audience) describes the book as "the perfect put-on to leave in plain sight the next time seri-ous foodies stop by to check out your culinary skills."[36] Rejecting the presumably upper-middle-class (effete?) "foodies," this book thumbs its nose at urban aficionados, asserts the comedy of tarmac cuisine, and is dedicated to "Budweiser bums." One of the first recipes in the book is for "Windshield Wabbit," roadkilled rabbit to be transformed with a little barbeque sauce into "Barbequed Bugs Bunny," also, by the way, providing fur adornments for one's lady friend. These joking publica-tions not only depend for their humor on a denigration of Appalachian poverty and uses of found meat but also dismiss the value of the road-killed animal's life, turning it into a cartoon character (Bugs Bunny). This genre of roadkill "humor," however, is of minor significance.

My larger questions here are about the cultural work necessary to so successfully banish the tonnage of roadkill carcasses from daily conver-sation, from legal debate, and from ethical responsibility. How is it that something so ubiquitous can be simultaneously so absent from public consideration?

The simplest answer is that roadkilled animal lives have little value for most US population(s), as these animals have no owners, lack monetary or emotional value, aren't pets or livestock, and don't have the charismatic following that megafauna like elephants and lions in zoos do. This calculus of devaluation clears the way for such carnage to be ignored in public discourse and legal venues, to be out of mind while insistently in sight.[37]

In their collection *Killing Animals*, the British Animal Studies Group makes a similar point about the vast majority of animal killing: billions of animals are routinely killed out of sight in slaughterhouses for meat, and as Claire Palmer argues, millions more die invisibly every day via euthanasia of unwanted pets in animal shelters.[38] And these are just some of the arenas of intentional killing; animals are also killed in some scientific experiments, for clothing materials, and for recreational hunting and display. The scope of these killings is "stupefying," the Animal Studies Group says, and "reflects human power over animals at its most extreme and yet its most commonplace."[39]

To this list of out-of-sight slaughter we can add the technically not out of sight but surely out-of-mind commonplace slaughter that occurs on our highways. While only a relatively small proportion of this killing would be dubbed "intentional"—the driver who swerves not to avoid an animal in the road but to strike it—the larger structure of human mobility technologies has largely cast roadkilling as "collateral damage," that is, as "acceptable" if not actively intentional.

As wide as the range of practices involving the killing of animals is, there is a similarly wide range of meanings ascribed to such practices, asserts the Animal Studies Group: "Killing an animal is rarely simply a matter of animal death. It is surrounded by a host of attitudes, ideas, perceptions, and assumptions,"[40] historically shaped and articulated. Researching attitudes toward and phenomena surrounding animal killing should take high priority but has yet to do so, the group argues.

With respect to roadkill specifically, the lack of acknowledgment of the material fact, and the lack of urgency in addressing it in the humanities and social sciences, is enabled by many things. First, we encounter individual dead animals not as part of collectivities but as individuals ourselves, simply riding along in our cars. The roadkilled animals I see in a week are a tiny faction of the unknown total number killed on the roads during that time. Thus, the cumulative scale of roadkilled death is ungraspable and unreported. Even government bodies lack reliable national estimates, and achieving them is a low priority. The unreported scale of roadkilling helps make its ubiquity invisible.

Second, there is no public discourse on these killings as a "phenomenon," which could draw attention to the true scale of the problem. Unless something is named a social problem, it's hard to generate institutional response and further public discussion. (We see the emergence of social phenomena in naming practices like "the war on drugs.") And finally, a third component is an impulse that we might call "looking and looking away," related to the loss of corporeal integrity of the dead animal on the highway. We all see roadkilled animals, but our tendency is to look away because of the nature of the death and its gruesome results. In other words, constituent aspects of roadkilling itself can make it hard to bring to public consciousness.

In his discussion of the use of dead animals in art, Steve Baker draws on the writings of Elaine Scarry, whose assessment of pain, torture, the body, and language in her book *The Body in Pain* is relevant here. While Scarry is primarily concerned with how pain interrupts the power of language, Baker draws on her analysis to consider its visual effect, specifically her observation that "the human mind, confronted by the open body itself (whether human or animal) does not have the option of failing to perceive its reality that rushes unstoppably across his eyes and into his mind, yet the mind so flees from what it sees that it will . . . (assign) that attribute to something else."[41] Scarry points to the opened body's power to draw our gaze while simultaneously repelling it, pushing it and our thoughts elsewhere. In the case of roadkill, that "elsewhere" can be an averting of the eyes, a discourse of unavoidable collateral damage, acceptance of a sad but presumed necessary loss of life when animals wander onto the tarmac, being in the wrong place at the wrong time.[42]

The "opened" body, the disruption of bodily integrity through violence that breaches the body wall to reveal the normally unseen interior, diminishes the subject of that body while simultaneously calling attention to the loss of that subjectivity. Breaching that integrity results in bodily pain and in extreme cases to cessation of life. In most cases, our views of roadkilling are not of the moment of impact and pain. Rather, we see the results—the dead animal's carcass either shunted off to the side of the roadway or subject to innumerable compactions as vehicle after vehicle runs over it. When the carcass retains its integrity—like the dead bird, hit in the head by a moving car as it swooped across the road and now lying still but without signs of trauma by the roadside—our response may be a brief sadness: "Ohh . . ." When the carcass remains in the middle of the traffic flow, however, and is purposefully or unavoidably run over again and again by cars, the disintegration of its bodily integrity, aided by scavenging animals and rain and snow, leads to its complete unrecognizability—those dark spots on the road—or, in the splaying out of organs, tissues, and bones, to its reduction to "thingness." In either case, the result is the effacement of "the subject" (an entity accorded subjectivity and agency), the physical integrity so egregiously breached as to be ground into mere undeterminable matter on the road.

In between this state of identifiable bodily integrity and unidentifiable dark stain is the state of dismemberment, in which the telling shape of rabbit ears, or the furry squirrel tail, or the feathered wing continue to mark the kind of animal, drawing our attention if not to the individual squirrel, rabbit, or hawk, now dead, then at least to a species marker that we recognize and can apply a name to. With the loss of even this naming capacity, the once-individual animal, first moved into species example (a rabbit), moves further into the undifferentiated category of organic matter, on its way to total dissolution and eventual disappearance.

During these stages of bodily breaching and disintegration, our response can shift from "ohh . . ." to "ewww . . . ," as we are impelled first to look at that which is so rarely exposed (red intestines) and then to look away at that marker of violent transgression of bodily integrity, as Scarry describes. The roadside monuments and the visual representations discussed above can help draw our gaze back to that scene, providing time for contemplation of the fact that "this was once a unique life." In so doing, they work against dominant conceptions of "wildlife" that do not recognize individual subjectivity but rather move immediately to the "categorical" designation—a squirrel, a hawk, a snake, not that squirrel, that hawk, that snake. If we continue to look away, as drivers, as citizens, and as scholars, we can't reconceptualize roadkilled animals, and the "everyday wild," as grievable lives. To do so requires our granting subjectivity to individual "wild" animals rather than enclosing them in their generic referents. This "ensubjectification" process requires our attribution, as both a philosophical and a political act of will, of a notion of individuated life to each being beyond our home. This means acknowledging the individuality of members of the "everyday wild" in the same way so many of us welcome a pet into our home as a "member of the family." It means activating our imaginative capacities to envision lives of meaning among animals very different from us and about whom we know little—the life lived by the now-bloated squirrel by the side of the road, by the drubbed rabbit, flattened beyond recognition but for the telltale ears. It also means taking seriously the enormous barriers to doing so and the resulting challenges to normative everyday life that such an acknowledgment may require. How to proceed?

Street-side shrines to roadkilled animals and photographs of road-kill in art galleries may be tiny acts of recognition, but they point to the possibility of greater emotional cognizance of animal carnage on highways, and foster this sense of attributed subjectivity. We cannot assess their impact, however, without knowing how people already feel about roadkill. We currently lack any extensive ethnographic data on how people from various communities respond as they encounter dead animals on the road, when they cause the deaths of animals on the road, what they do with and to the carcasses, and whether they alter their driving in view of these deaths. Do they then narrativize these events and weave them into their recounting of daily lives so that they become part of everyday discourse, subject to discussion, validation, or critique by others? Do they ignore them altogether, placing the acts outside discourse, or recognition, and certainly outside the historical record? No postings on Facebook? Tweets? Luckily, scholars like Stephen Vrla are starting to take up this challenge with new sociological research.[43] By taking roadkill seriously as a phenomenon of scholarly and ethnographic investigation, we can contribute to changing the phenomenon from ubiquitous and unmarked to markedly ubiquitous and hence worthy of public discourse, and ultimately of public action. We can begin to turn the category of the ungrievable into the grievable, granting subjectivity and individuation to these lost wild lives. In doing so, we shift slightly the perception of "collateral damage" so that the smudge by the side of the road is not merely "something" from which to avert our eyes but a marker of "someone," a grievable life lost.

8. A turn-of-the-twentieth-century postcard depicting the Cimitière des Chiens pet cemetery in Asnières, France, outside Paris, features the elegant porticos of the entrance, which indicate the importance of the site and those buried there during the Victorian era. Postcard found by the author in an antique postcard shop in Paris, collection of the author.

9. Cimitière des Chiens, Asnières, outside Paris: pets' gravestones designed to resemble doghouses, embracing the specifics of animal lives. Photo by the author.

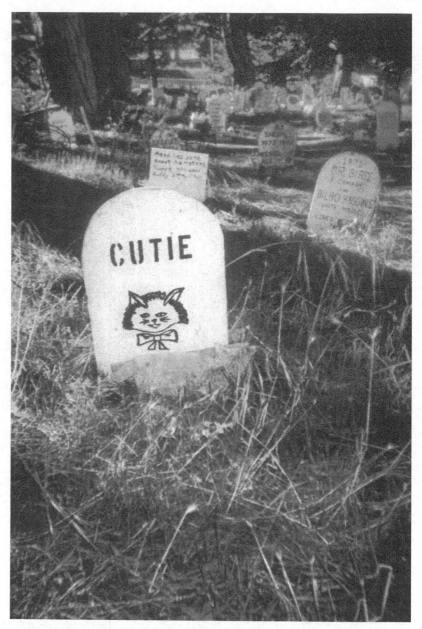

10. Presidio Pet Cemetery, outside San Francisco: a handmade decorated grave marker for "Cutie" the cat. Photo by the author.

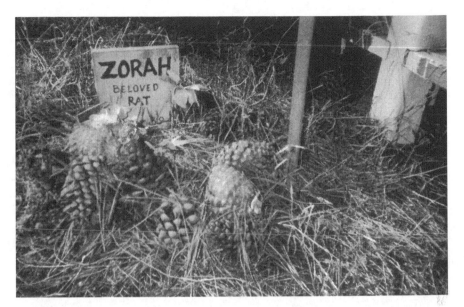

11. Presidio Pet Cemetery, outside San Francisco: A decorated gravesite for a beloved pet rat, "Zorah." Photo by the author.

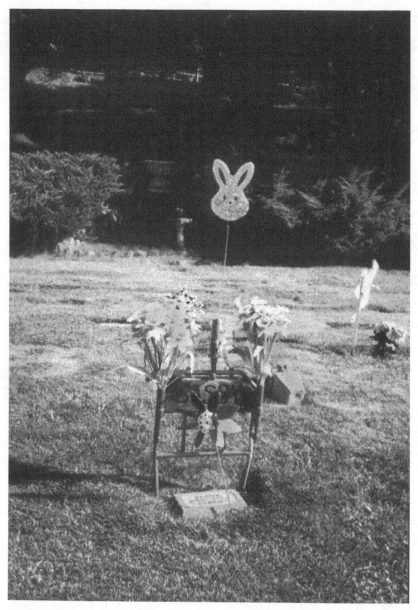

12. Bubbling Well Pet Memorial Park, Napa, California: "Sassy" grave marker adorned with bunny decoration shows the improvisatory creativity available to and utilized by human mourners for pets at this cemetery. Photo by the author.

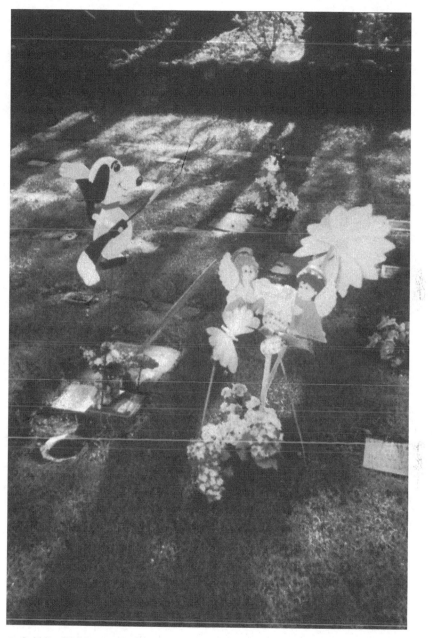

13. Bubbling Well Pet Memorial Park, Napa, California: "Snoopy" decorations reflect the improvisatory and playful celebration of animals' lives in pet cemeteries. Photo by the author.

Bear, 13

Bear was known widely in the Iowa City community for his gentle humor and his tendency to nap on the streets.

An inveterate lover of humankind, and particularly of the ladies, he was at h o m e wherever there was an out-stretched hand, and cherished t h o s e

Bear

most whose offerings were most dependable.

Bear passed in his sleep on the morning of April 14, at 13 years of age.

14. An obituary for "Bear," a black Labrador retriever, age thirteen. Source: *Iowa City (IA) Press-Citizen*, April 15, 2003. Collection of the author.

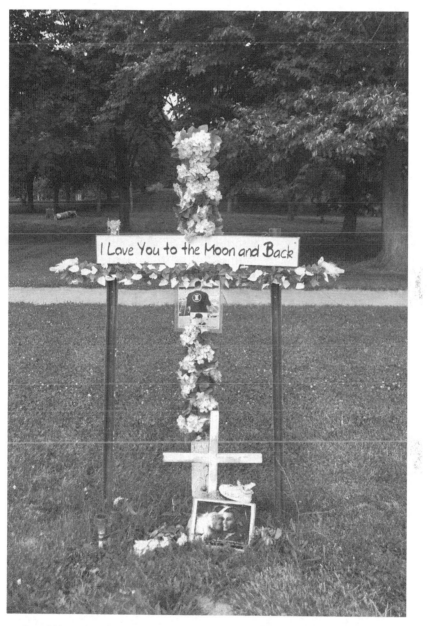

15. A roadside memorial on Duncan Avenue in Champaign, Illinois, 2015, marking the death of a pedestrian, Jonathan Ryan McDougal. Photo by Maria Lux, used with permission.

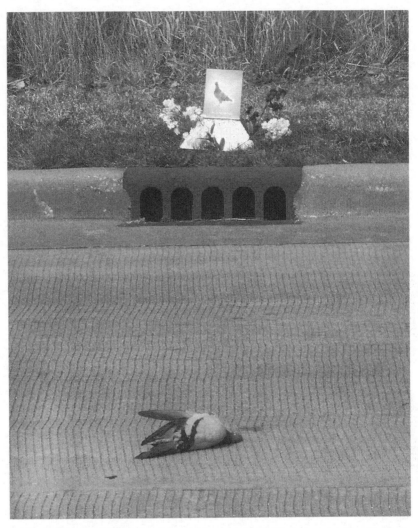

16. Brian D. Collier, "Roadkill Shrine, Rock Pigeon 3.17.06," 2006. Concrete, gold paint, acrylic framed photograph, plastic flowers, rock pigeon (deceased). Photographed in situ by Brian D. Collier, used with permission.

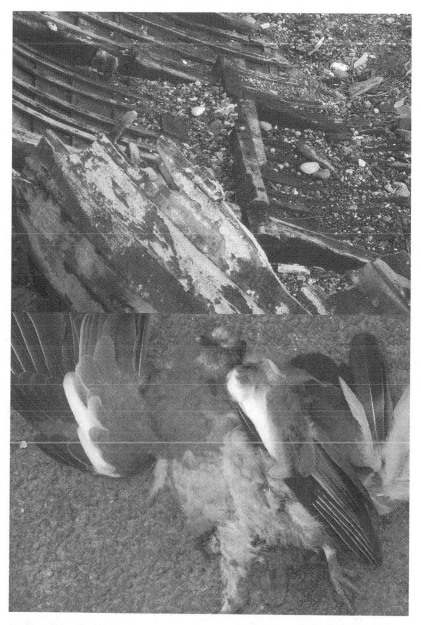

17. Steve Baker, *Untitled* (2012), from the series *Norfolk Roadkill, Mainly*. Courtesy of the artist.

PART THREE

Animating Life: Cognition, Expressivity, and the Art Market

"Art" by Animals, Part 1: The Transnational Market for Art by (Nonprimate) Animals

One evening in April of 2011, I was sitting at a dinner table in a hotel ballroom, attending a fund-raiser for a local wild-life medical clinic. The event was sponsored by the veterinary medical college at my university. At least a hundred people were there, each having purchased a ticket, which included a chance to see resident wildlife up close—mainly, raptors like hawks and kestrels who served as educational ambassadors after their injuries, though healed, made it impossible for them to be successfully released back into the wild. An auction of donated items and experiences (a visit to a tiger sanctuary, ten bottles of wine) was about to begin.

The clinking of forks on china subsided, and an expectant hush drew over the room as one of the main auction items was carried up to the stage. It was a beautiful, professionally framed painting, two feet tall and three feet long, its white canvas covered with dots of purple, gold, and teal in light tones. The swift strokes of the artist had flown over the surface, leaving an impression of motion captured in the refractive properties of raindrops. It was the prize of the night.

The bidding started low, at around a hundred dollars, and then began to catch fire. Somewhere behind me, not visible from my seat, an auctioneer kept shouting out, "Yup! Yup!" each shout followed by a higher number as someone bid anew.

I'd thought about bidding on the painting—it was my favorite of all the auction items, its colors delicate but strong, their travel across the surface even, even pointillistic. But the bids soon rose beyond my limit. Still, the battle went on, pumped up by the encouragement of the auctioneer (a charismatic veterinarian who surely must have worked in the auction business in a previous career): "Imagine how this will look on your wall!" "Think about the animals and all the good your money will do them!" "One of a kind, ladies and gentlemen, one of a kind!"

Gradually, the field of bidders thinned. A lot of people had wanted this piece, but only two were willing to go the distance. The price kept climbing. It topped out at several hundred dollars, and finally the auctioneer's gavel dropped. "Sold to the bidder at table number three!" That was MY table, and as I twisted around to see who in the world had been making those bids, I was shocked to find my partner, grinning triumphantly. The painting, by Odin the Red-Tailed Hawk, was coming home with us! Jealous "oohs" and "aahs" floated across the room as another painting was brought up for sale. That painting, by a different bird, was nice, but it was smaller than the first one, the marks were less assertive, and the composition was less beautifully balanced in its mix of colors and shapes. The bidding for it never reached the same frenzied pace of the bidding for Odin's artwork. In fact, that painting outsold nearly everything else at the auction, including a week in Paris at a donor's pied-à-terre! Why?

This snapshot of desire, money, and artwork captures several of the components that drive the expansive and expanding market for "art" by animals; "artists" include elephants, dolphins, apes, seals, horses, dogs, cats, and birds. The transnational market spans the United States and several other countries, and is anchored in local nodes of production and sale. However, it draws in international auction houses as well as online sites like eBay, and media reports of such sales span the globe, from Britain to India, the United States, and beyond.

In this chapter and the paired one that follows, I investigate this "art by animals" phenomenon as a counterpoint to the first two-thirds of the book, which focused on the display of dead bodies and the tensions that emerge in social practices meant to attribute subjectivity to only some of those bodies as a prerequisite for mourning. In those chapters, on taxidermy and human plastination, pet cemeteries, pet obituaries, and roadkill and roadkilling, my focus was on the materiality of the (primarily nonhuman animal) body and the ways that that materiality anchors or disrupts social meaning: in scientific discourse that simultaneously objectifies the body while touting a value-free search for knowledge untied to cultural or historical specificity; in the tensions between bodily remains and mourning practices when the mourned is an animal, not a human; and so on.

Humans can be and have been constructed historically (and differentially) as both objects and subjects of knowledge, as sites of investigation and producers of new knowledge through those investigations. Nonhuman animal bodies are more likely to be thrust, physically, discursively, and epistemologically, into the "object" category, as museum displays like Animal Inside Out demonstrate. But other registers of belief and of practice contravene this denotation as object, although only partially, only with respect to specific animals or specific species, and only in specific times and places. In the aesthetic realm, some animals do indeed emerge poised on the cusp of being recognized as subjects producing objects.

In this chapter and the next, I examine the traces of these *living* animal bodies, activated and captivated in the transnational market for "art" by animals. Here the materiality of the animal being is still paramount, as I discuss in relation to items that get designated as "artworks" when they record the physical trace, static or moving, of a specific animal body: an imprint of fish scales pressed onto paper, the strafing lines left by claws on canvas, or a sinuous curve of paint drawn out by a side-winding snake—the trace of animal movement across a surface, an actual event, captured in the rearranged remnants of pigment.

Physical Trace as Subjective "Evidence"

In the aesthetic realm, we see not only the importance of the physical trace left, intentionally or not, by a living nonhuman animal but also the ways in which, for some specific categories of animals, that trace can serve as both (scientific and popular) evidence of and a utopian desire for the external revelation of a complex interior subjectivity. But first, to understand this phenomenon, we have to excavate the contemporary complex of institutions and relations that bring it into being.

Art production by nonhuman animals sits at, and reveals, a unique, complicated nexus of concepts and of communities who otherwise would not be engaged with one another: conservationists, (human) artists, gallery owners, comparative psychologists, primatologists, zookeepers, animal enrichment technicians, news reporters, the animals themselves, and the lay public. Each forms a node in the generation of meaning surrounding the phenomenon. I suggest that art making and the market it engenders form a particularly revealing intersection of ideas, desires, practices, and interests that illuminate some of our defining beliefs about human-animal relations.

These beliefs are both broadly general and widespread (in other words, that humans are and are not "animals"), and specific to historical moments, places, and publics—a tension I plan to keep in view throughout this discussion. In this chapter and the paired one that follows, I argue that the concepts of "art" and "artist" are mobilized in the European-influenced world with reference to animals both to emphasize their difference from human subjects (a painting by a snake is not a Rembrandt, although it might resemble a Klee) and to assert their similarity, as is the case with unique primate individuals like Koko, Kanzi, Michael, Chantek, and other human-language-enabled apes who live in a "bispecies, bicultural" environment.

When I refer to "artwork" by animals here, I usually mean a drawing or painting made with crayons, chalk, or paints on a flat surface like paper or canvas, although some experiments are under way to develop sculpting opportunities for animals.[1] It's also possible to buy recordings of "music" by animals, such as those by the Thai elephant orchestra sponsored by New York City–based artists Komar and Melamid. Paintings, however, are the dominant works in this art market.

I explore this new market phenomenon, map its range and scale, probe the reasons for its expansion, and assess what's at stake for the multiple communities involved: the animals, their caretakers, the buyers, the promoters, and the scientists and news reporters who also engage with the phenomenon. Why has such a market emerged, why now, and what difference does it make to whom? What longer-term cultural effects might be in play?

To research this phenomenon, I draw on records of sales and sales promotions; participant observation at zoos and clinics; interviews with zookeepers and (human) art makers; analysis of online discussion boards, website images, and textual presentation; newspaper reports; and scientific articles by animal cognition experts. On the basis of these sources, I argue that "art" by animals is not merely an oddity of local significance but rather should be seen as a dynamic, growing field of commerce and scientific investigation that spans multiple countries across the globe. The motivations of producers, sellers, and buyers for engaging such artwork diverge considerably from those of the scientific community, however, except when the category is art by primates.

The range of practices and products associated with this phenomenon can best be understood as a continuum arranged along an ascending hierarchy assigned to animal species, with those most like humans

placed on the "high" end of the scale and receiving the most attention as well as commanding the highest prices for their work. Along
this continuum of "art"—ranging from the squiggly smudges made
by snakes to brush-painted, self-titled pictures by (human-)language-
enabled apes—mark making, intention, knowledge of visual conventions, and active choice are the main components parsed by scientist
and purchaser alike. The more likely the linkage between mark making
and active aesthetic choice in that mark making, the greater the value
attributed by both scientist and layperson, and the greater the amount
of money attached to the resultant object.

"Art" is a historically and culturally specific concept, and I use it
here in the senses it has accrued in Europe and in Europe's spheres of
influence since, roughly, the Renaissance. Among the hallmarks of this
conceptual category are its denotation of something separated from
"craft," or the skillful production of items with practical use, and its
association with a single producer, or "artist," who creates something
"original" and expressive of his or her interior emotions, ideas, passions, and visions.[2]

In my consideration of art by primates, I highlight the activation of
these hallmarks, but they are lacking among other species whose works
should, I believe, be seen as "art," with a knowing embrace of the distanciation, or "wink," that the quotation marks imply. However, in all
cases, the final artwork—usually a flat piece of paper covered with paint
marks—bears the physical trace of an action by a nonhuman animal,
and this embodied trace is the key to how these items accrue value in the
social and economic spheres. Among these markers of valuation are the
sense of intimacy and authenticity that attaches to the physical traces of
a specific animal's body and the extent to which these marks are taken
as evidence of aesthetic choice by the animal producing the work.

In the next chapter, I focus specifically on art made by nonhuman
primates, analyzing not only the market for such works but also the
role they may play for lay purchasers and for animal cognition experts
in assessing primate intelligence and the linkage of primate actions and
abilities to human evolution. I point too to the crucial lack of cultural
and historical contextualization that can attend these evolutionary assertions and ask, instead, what difference does or might it make for
primates' perceived status when the artist is an ape? Is this art making
a potential contestation of humanism?

But for now, let me return to the realm of art making by nonprimate
animals, as I begin to sketch the contours of the transnational market
for animal art, starting with the unexpected work of one Tony Blair.

Accidental "Art"?

For many of us, the name Tony Blair conjures up an image of the energetic, boyish-looking former prime minister of the United Kingdom (1997–2007). But there is another Tony Blair to be reckoned with in Britain, and this one is an artist—or perhaps the more accurate term is "ratiste," for Tony Blair is the name of a chocolate-brown rat. His works consist of modifications of "found objects," such as an avocado (craftily chewed to sculptural perfection, exposing the spheroid center of the pit) and a four-leaf clover (gnawed to the point of provoking its titular question, "Am I Still Lucky?"). Tony, now deceased, was owned by artist Helena Seget, who runs an art studio and mounted an exhibit of his works there. But his fame is widespread, thanks to the Internet. "Tony has gained international attention since Ms. Seget posted Tony's work on the Saatchi gallery's website. When his work went up against others in an online competition, he received 500 votes," wrote *Telegraph* reporter Megan Levy in 2008, indicating that members of the art-loving public were engaging with his works.[3] The cross between tongue-in-cheek and avant-gardist realms of the art world evoked in his creations gave Tony Blair a boost in his bid for celebrity, orchestrated by his artist-owner.

But Tony Blair is not alone as an artist among the Rodentia, as evidenced by the promotion of the "ratistes" associated with ScamperArt productions. The gobsmacking appeal of their work comes from its being done by *rats*. It's hard to imagine a type of being farther from the realm of the artist (although on the Scamperats website, the ratistes look very cute in their tiny French berets). Perhaps a sea slug or spider would be less includable under the rubric? But as mammals go, rats don't have a large fan base. Instead, they're often the target of mass extermination and, at least in Europe and the United States, are regarded as sources of disease and associated with filth and poverty. But in their anthropomorphized promotions of rat-produced artworks, the ScamperArt folks link visual art, wordplay, neoteny, or childlikeness, and ratness to produce a genre of "cuteness"—a culturally specific category of appreciation. The presumed silliness of the association of art making and rat being produces this recuperative cuteness, complete with little berets and the play on American presumptions of French pretension with the term *ratistes*.

The ultimate goal in producing these artworks and selling them is to benefit rats, as the Scamperats website indicates: "We donate a part of every sale to the Rattie Ratz Rescue Service. This organization is dedicated to the rescue, rehabilitation and re-homing of our domestic rat-friends, and other small animals. Even better, become a loving foster or adoption home for our needy cousins!" Sales at rat lovers' events, like the Northern California Rat Community's Annual Holiday Pot Luck Costume Party (the rats dress up, not the people), or local public events, like the 2006 San Jose Art and Wine Festival, provide a way to link to a potential public of buyers.[4]

But none of us believes, despite the pictures on the promotional website, that the rats are daubing paint onto canvases with tiny brushes, carefully considering the placement of each color. This, despite the website's assurance that "history is replete with diminutive artists of great stature. Painters such as Toulouse-Ratrec, Pablo Ratcasso, and Thomas Hart Raton challenged their contemporaries, and left lasting marks on the art-world." And "vibrant colors and free-form shapes define the abstracts lovingly created by these 'ratistes' as they SCAMPER about!"[5] No. We know that the rats simply run across the canvas with their paint-dipped feet, leaving colorful traces behind that track their rapid little steps.

The results, bright nontoxic colors on white prestretched canvases, bear the marks of well-defined little sharp-toed feet and long curving arcs of dragging tails. My own (eighteen-by-twenty-four-inch) painting arrived well packaged in bubble wrap and featured a dramatic linear swoop of teal across the diagonal (a quick run with a dipped tail?), punctuated by fire-engine-red footprints rhythmically marching across the upper right quadrant—clear evidence of a ratiste on his or her way somewhere beyond the confines of the canvas.

These are works by what we might call "unwitting artists," not contemplative ones. A whole category of "art" is produced by such beings, including my beautiful Odin the Red-Tailed Hawk painting, which was created by the bird's toes and wing tips carrying drips and drabs of color across a white expanse of paper. Where an animal's body leaves an identifiable mark—the multi-toed imprint of a rat foot, for example—we see the artwork as the evidentiary result of animal presence, animal movement through space for a purpose other than leaving that mark. The "art" is a byproduct of animal movement, not the purposeful result. The resultant entry of the objects so produced into the art world depends on their nomination to be so included. That nomination is made by humans, like rat lover Helena Seget, who promotes the "works" of Tony Blair for their sculptural properties.

This "accidental art" is not new. As Thierry Lenain notes, the famous Japanese painter Hokusai bested his opponent in an 1806 painting contest by drawing a rolling blue line on a long horizontal scroll and then topping it with the paint-dipped footprints left by a hen that he had encouraged to walk across the paper. For Hokusai's audiences, the visual references of the curving blue line and russet triangular shapes were clear—burnished autumn leaves floating on water, as the painting's title bears out: *Maple Leaves Floating on the Matsuta River*.[6] But in this case, Hokusai, known for his creative, nonconformist stances, was just using the hen as a living, moving paintbrush, a figurative extension of his own arm, and activating a visual genre of referential symbols—curvilinear waves and point-tipped leaves—well known to his audiences. The actions of the hen, and the hen herself, were hardly the focal point. No profiles of the hen as "artiste" were produced. But even here, the animal inserts herself into art history, for the exact pattern of her steps, their rhythmic spread, the quality of contact with the ground—firm or tentative, quick or slow—all influence the final product, the paint recording bodily movement and directional intent of that long-ago, unique, individual hen, whose strut across the scroll remains tangibly imprinted.

A few contemporary artists use this approach, that of the unwitting animal artist, somewhat differently, to interrogate human-animal relations and to produce artworks that are collaboratively generated. These creations are dependent on both the work of the human artist and the physical engagement, whether through sliding or biting, of a living animal interacting with a shared object or surface. For example, the avant-garde duo Olly and Suzi, based in the United Kingdom, have traveled to extreme environments like Antarctica and the Amazon basin, placing themselves as much as possible in animals' worlds to achieve this collaboration. They've even courted danger, the extent of which is etched in the teeth marks of a shark's bite on submerged fiberboard or the slither-slide marking of an anaconda on a canvas in the wild.

Ron Broglio, writing about these events, argues that the sheer physicality of animals refuses to be easily consumed and repurposed by human artists for their own expressive ends. Instead, Broglio suggests, the resulting artworks render an alternative economy of relations to animals, one in which the animals leave their marks by "biting back."[7] While Olly and Suzi emphasize shared cross-species surfaces, the mark making of the animals also leads us toward an imagining of intent, and direct action. Steve Baker states that the artists see their concerns as articulating the immediacy, specificity, and "intense unfamiliarity" of each encounter with an animal.[8]

The artworks described above are quite different from the ones I discuss here. Most especially, the art in these two chapters is produced under conditions of captivity, and the intended audience is not an elite with high cultural capital, attuned to the avant-garde artworld. A much wider range of the public purchases the works I discuss, from wealthy collectors to those more middlebrow patrons seeking unique home decor and claiming to know nothing about art. The human presence in the production of these animal-made artworks is (with just a few exceptions) not the focus of the event of art making or the final product.[9] And yet, art-made-with-animals and art-made-by-animals coexist in a wider matrix of visual representation, ideas about animals, ideas about art, and structures of commerce.

For the vast majority of the artworks that I discuss in this chapter, a unique animal leaves its anatomical and kinesthetic trace on something that is then conceptualized and sold as "art," but with a wink that acknowledges that the "painting" animal has goals other than artistic expression. This intent, expressivity, and knowledge of aesthetic conventions—or the lack thereof—comprise a key issue that emerges only in paintings by primates, and I consider it in the next chapter. I've been arguing that nowadays, art production by animals is not just an isolated event but part of a larger phenomenon uniting visual product with commerce. Just how does it work?

Like most sectors of the art market, the animal art market operates on a principle of rarity. Only a few members of a few species have produced "artworks." Among the painters: Tillamook Cheddar, a fox terrier in New York City; Gambi and Premja, two Lithuanian dolphins; several elephants in Thailand; and Cholla the horse, Rosie the rhinoceros, Koko the gorilla, Alexander the orangutan. To apply pigment, some of these artists rub canvas with their lips; others scratch with their claws, or hold a paintbrush with their trunk or clenched between their teeth. Artworks by these artists are offered for sale on Koko's website, in Thailand at an elephant sanctuary, in Brooklyn at the store Tillie Ltd., at the Sea Museum Dolphinarium in Klaipeda, Lithuania, through major art auction houses like Christie's in New York, at zoos, and on eBay auction sites.

The Scope of the Phenomenon

It's difficult to gather reliable evidence about how many animals currently paint in the United States, Europe, Southeast Asia, and Japan (the four geographic areas I am aware of with press reports of contemporary painting animals). Most of these instances stem from an individual trainer's, owner's, artist's, or zookeeper's initiative, as was the case with ratiste Tony Blair. However, anecdotal evidence is plentiful and can be gleaned from web links to sanctuaries, local press reports, articles on enrichment practices for captive animals in zoos and research facilities, oral reports from keepers and primatologists, and discussions on web forums among zookeepers and zoo scholars and aficionados, such as the Zoo Keeper's discussion list of the Association of Zoos and Aquariums.

While I cannot confidently estimate the total number of animals painting in the United States today, it's clear that the phenomenon is widespread and growing. By one estimate, about thirty elephants were painting in US zoos in the year 2000.[10] Art making by a variety of animal species is taking place today at sites like the Oklahoma City Zoo and Botanical Garden, the Indianapolis Zoo, the Virginia Zoological Park, the Great Ape Trust in Des Moines, the M. D. Anderson Cancer Center Department of Veterinary Medicine and Surgery in Houston, the Woodland Park Zoo in Seattle, the Milwaukee Zoo, Jungle Friends Monkey Sanctuary in Florida, Chimp Haven in Louisiana, and the Wildlife Medical Clinic at the University of Illinois in Champaign-Urbana, to name just a few.

Paintings by animals clearly aren't anything new, and some earlier celebrity animal "artists" have developed their own following. Ruby, an Asian elephant born in Thailand in 1974 and a longtime resident of the Phoenix Zoo, started painting as an enrichment exercise in 1987, to give her something stimulating to do. She followed in the (large) footsteps of Carol, an elephant kept at the San Diego Zoo, who had painted in the 1960s. Ruby continued painting when she wanted to up until her death in 1998, and her abstract creations with sweeping brushstrokes are estimated to have raised up to $100,000 a year for the zoo.[11] Her most expensive painting sold for $25,000.[12]

Obviously, even though several of these painters are elephants, we can't assume that these works sell for "peanuts." Nonetheless, the full dimensions of the market for art by animals are hard to ascertain.

Economic Dimensions of the Art Market

The Association of Zoos and Aquariums, which offers accreditation to leading zoos on the basis of their meeting criteria in management and animal care, does not keep any statistics on art by animals, nor does any other official body. A few sales by celebrities like Ruby garner widespread publicity as a result of media coverage of major auction houses. However, most paintings are sold more modestly, and figures on the majority of sales of animal artworks are hard to come by. Occasionally, a newspaper article that brings discussion of art by animals into the public sphere and also offers conceptual frameworks for interpreting it provides a peek into the economics of the deal. It's important to frame an understanding of the prices these works command within the overall concept of "philanthropy"—here democratized, putting it in reach of many zoo visitors—because the proceeds from most sales of paintings go toward the support of zoos; in some cases, such as the Oklahoma City Zoo and Botanical Garden, these funds go directly to the unit whose animals had produced the artwork.

In 2007, the Hampton Roads, Virginia, newspaper the *Virginian-Pilot* printed a feature on animal art produced at several sites in the state: the Virginia Zoological Park in Norfolk, the Virginia Living Museum in Newport News, and the Virginia Aquarium in Virginia Beach.[13] We can take this set of sites to exemplify how the market works in zoo and sanctuary gift shops around the country. One of the stars profiled in the piece is Munchkin, a South African black-footed penguin at the Virginia Aquarium who's about the size of a duck. Her art offerings are created as a byproduct of her web-footed jaunts across white paper, her feet dipped in nontoxic purple paint by her keepers. Although only about half her footprints make it onto the paper, it's enough for her keepers to cheer, and Munchkin, apparently enjoying the task, waddles quickly across the floor, shaking her head in what is taken to be a sign of contentment. Mounted and framed, such "Penguin Prints" go for $50–$70 in the aquarium gift shop.

Seals also sell at the Virginia Aquarium. They're trained to touch preloaded paintbrushes to canvas, leaving sweeping swaths of colorful paint, and their works fetch higher prices than penguin art. Framed as "Seal Signatures," the creations cost from $90 to $180 in the gift shop; images are also printed onto T-shirts and mugs. Visitors really like these items: in sales of Seal Signatures alone, the aquarium rang up about $15,000 in less than two years, from the fall of 2005 to the summer of 2007. At the nearby Norfolk Zoo, a fund-raiser in April of 2007 raised about $5,000 from art made by the zoo's elephants. These sums may not seem huge, but for a nonprofit organization, every thousand dollars makes a difference. The overall impact of the sales can be considerable.

And, still focusing on this one region and time period in Virginia, even more fund-raising art by animals surfaces. In August of 2007, Prince George Art and Frame hosted "the first mid-Atlantic showing of art by elephants in Thailand, Cambodia, and Indonesia."[14] Proceeds benefited the Asian Elephant Art and Conservation Project based in Thailand and headed by human artists Komar and Melamid. Two hundred art and elephant lovers showed up to peruse twenty-five paintings priced from $450 to $600 each.

This selection from just a two-year period in a single region of southeastern Virginia indicates that art making by captive animals is being sold in a variety of venues, including not only animal-oriented organizations like zoos but also art-oriented venues like galleries. These sales bring in a significant, if not huge, amount of money for nonprofit animal-related institutions, and their market, as demonstrated by the sale of the Thai elephant paintings, is both local and transnational.[15]

We know from these types of reports that art by animals is being produced and presented for sale all across the United States and in some other countries as well. But how do people actually perceive these artifacts? Why do they buy them? Do they distinguish between the species of producer and the final product? What sorts of aesthetic judgments are involved in purchasing the art? How do purchasers integrate these unique items into their domestic lives and their relations with others?

It's not easy to find answers to these questions, since gift shops at zoos and galleries are unlikely to release information about who their clients are and what they have purchased. However, an online discussion list of zoo aficionados provides a glimpse of how, in their own words, people who buy these paintings value them.

Judging from comments on the ZooBeat discussion list—an English-language forum for those passionate about zoos and conservation—many purchasers echo the taxonomy of intellect that I mention above, which places turtles at the bottom, elephants and cetaceans toward the top, and nonhuman primates at the pinnacle. Somewhere between turtles and dolphins lie cats, dogs, and horses.[16]

One of the very active forum regulars, "Patrick" from Melbourne, Australia, puts it this way:

I think it looses its punch when you start talking dogs and turtles. People probably like to think that the animals somehow not only know what they are doing and have a self-awareness that they are in control, but also make decisions based on their own artistic esthetics.

Now, regardless of whether or not this is true, I expect people like to think it is and thus the whole concept is somewhat undermined when you start offering art by species that are not generally considered by the public as being "hyper-intelligent".

ask anyone what the smartest animals are and they will no doubt mention the great apes as well as elephants and dolphins. maybe if your lucky, a monkey or parrot.

but a turtle? now that's pushing it . . .[17]

This post is followed by a quip from the list moderator, "ZooYouth-Ben" from Adelaide, Australia, who writes, "Dip a turtle in paint and get it to walk across a canvas, turtle painting done!"

A newer member of the forum, "Jo" from Adelaide, who works with animals as a researcher, asserts, "I think people buy it [art by animals] because it is a tangible connection to an animal they may never see up close. Also, it is a unique piece of art, because the number of animals doing it is far less than humans. the raising money for conservation/direct benefit to that animal also is a factor."

A commentator from Auckland, New Zealand, "NZ Jeremy," shares in some of these rationales when he writes about his desire to buy a painting by an elephant or chimpanzee at the Auckland Zoo as a present for a friend, but found them too expensive (ranging in price from AU$300 for the chimp art to AU$700 for the elephant paintings). "Why did I almost buy that one for mi lady . . . ?" he asks. "Well because we both love the zoo and the animals . . . having the painting on the wall would not only be aesthetically pleasing but would also remind us of our favourite place and, let's? face it, when friends came over, [would allow us] to say, "guess who painted that!"

But he goes on to refine the motivation more precisely: "Personally I wouldn't buy a painting that's proceeds were not going to conservation and that wasn't done by an animal that could not (potentially) recognize that it represents something, i.e. as likely Elephants, Great Apes and some Cetacens can."

A final comment in this string of exchanges raises yet another motivation. "Rookeyper," from Fort Wayne, Indiana, writes, "I personally have no illusions that the Christmas ornament that I have 'painted' by a rhinoceros at the Cincinnati Zoo is a work of art. The novelty of having that on the tree, explaining it to my grandchildren and by the way mentioning the plight of rhinos in the wild makes it valuable. The same goes for most animal art—it's a way to both raise awareness and also raise some cash for conservation or the individual institution."

Such a selection of comments can in no way be considered a scientifically devised representative sample of those who purchase art by animals, because the interlocutors on the ZooBeat forum (later renamed ZooChat) are more informed about issues facing zoos and their animals today than the general zoo-going public is.[18] Yet by virtue of their interest and level of awareness, they may be in a good position to articulate people's motivations for making these purchases.

Several themes are clearly revealed in the exchanges quoted above: the link between animal art and conservation donations; the link between the physicality of the individual animal artist and the work itself; pleasure in the element of novelty or surprise attached to the item and the ability to use that to connect with and/or educate other people; and the ability to bring a sign of the owner's passions for "wild" animals into the home. The purchasers retain a notion of a hierarchy of what they presume to be the capacity for self-reflexive intent possessed by some animals and not others, closely connected to human assumptions about animal "intelligence" as purveyed in public discourse. The comments also reveal both the attachment of ideas about uniqueness and aesthetic pleasure to the art objects in ways that reflect wider assumptions about human art and artists, along with an ability to separate real "art" (which is the product of artistic intent) from nonart that is *called* art (for instance, the rhinoceros's painted ornament) while still embracing the idea of animal-produced visual items as having value in an economy of exchange.

So for these online posters, the idea of "art making" by animals varies depending on the species creating the product. This isn't an aesthetic judgment, with turtles making "bad" paintings and apes being "good" artists. Rather, the calibration has to do with the notion of the animal's *intent* (and perceived possibility of forming intent) to make an aesthetic object, and to make that object through selective aesthetic choices about color, line, shape, and composition. Of the resultant products, 99% would be termed "abstract" (that is, nonrepresentational) art, sweeping strokes of color like 1950s abstract expressionist works, the appeal of which thus depends on an acceptance of nonrepresentational images as "art" by a wider public in the post–World War II era.[19]

Who Doesn't Paint?

Most of the animal artists discussed above are charismatic "wild" animals kept in captivity: elephants, seals, penguins, chimpanzees, even the occasional rhinoceros, who, if not exactly charismatic, is imposing and rare. Others, like the ratistes, ambush and delight us with surprise, given their general status as unwanted pests. Pets sometimes paint, sometimes for philanthropic reasons, as when a local humane society fund-raiser features a "painting station" for dogs, like my local Champaign County Humane Society did, cashing in on the trend. There are even commercial kits, adorned (of course) by photos of a dog in a beret, that let your "poodle [who can] doodle" create canine canvases at home. They come complete with nontoxic paint, paper, and a frame for display.[20] Cats had their own artistic moment a couple of decades ago in the glossy, coffee-table book *Why Cats Paint* by artist Heather Burch and art critic Burton Silver. With its knowing reproduction of the erudite language of art critics ("Bootsie's painting has a refreshing rawness which enables the viewer to experience the physicality of the artist's deep relationship with process"),[21] this tongue-in-cheek book featured lavish color photos of cats in action, scratching paints on canvas. But this too was based on the "wink," the "I know very well and so do you, but . . ." construction of an insider's self-congratulatory text, oscillating between parody and promise (are the cats actually painting, like the action photos imply?). But beyond the "wild" animals in captivity and the Pup-Cassos at home, there are revealing gaps in the market for art by animals.

The dividing line between "wild" and "domesticated" operates here, but is transected by other categories of value. For example, there is a near total absence of paintings by animals raised for food, like cows or chickens.[22] Such a linkage of art makers and foodstuffs would jar, presumably because an individual subject (a he or a she) produces art, while an object (an it) gets eaten. Also, we generally don't find paintings by animals like squirrels, tarantulas, worms, centipedes (lots of footprints possible there), rabbits, kangaroos, sloths, lobsters, slugs, deer, cougars, armadillos, snails, or alligators for sale.

In some cases, size renders such paintings impractical and unsalable. Imagine the size of a scroll of paper needed to catch the footprints of a hopping kangaroo! And perhaps the physical construction of an armadillo shell would cause the paint to be dragged around in an unattractive (unsalable) "messy" blob as the animal ambled across a piece of paper. Or perhaps the charisma factor is low, or the "eeew" factor is high, which could be said about slugs, snails, worms, and centipedes. (Even if a tarantula could be made to collaborate in a "painting," many people don't like arachnids, and their hairy fright factor militates against their fund-raising ability as painters.) The main painters are either pets or charismatic wildlife in captivity, and this indexes a calculus of train-ability, charisma, and, for lack of a better word, charm or appeal in the cultural matrix of desirable-undesirable animals.[23] All these factors make the huge and hugely popular paintings by Koopa the turtle all the more arresting.

Turtle Artist Koopa: A Case Study

On the human-calibrated intelligence scale, turtles generally rank quite low. Their slow, awkward gait on land gives them a prehistoric, soporific look that contrasts with our human notions of quick-witted intelligence and creativity. In addition, their charisma factor is modest, for unlike mammals, they can't change facial expressions in a way hu-mans recognize as meaningful, their hard shells aren't warm and cud-dly, and they do not appear, to most humans at least, to be very inter-active either with their environment or with people. Nor have I ever seen a "trained" turtle. They seem stolid, solid, and merely reactive, able, as a last resort, to totally withdraw from the world into the protec-tion of their hard carapaces, the ultimate refuge of disengagement.

But Koopa, the twenty-five-year-old Gulf Coast box turtle named for a character in the Super Mario Bros. video game, defies these presump-tions.[24] With his bright-red eyes, inquisitive head movements, interac-tive responses to his owner's physical and vocal communications, and a swift almost jaunty style of chugging across the carpet—revealed in his videos on YouTube—Koopa projects a very distinctive persona. He is a big turtle, almost a foot long and standing six inches high, has a tawny shell, and produces big paintings—up to three feet long and two feet high—that fit well over a sofa, and are so pictured on his Turtle-Kiss-Designs website that sells them. Also available on eBay, most of Koopa's paintings have sold in the $100 to $150 range, but several are priced much higher, including an asking price of $1,200 for one piece.

Koopa has quite an international public, generated by extensive me-dia coverage. He has been featured in the 2006 and 2013 editions of *Ripley's Believe It or Not*, and news stories have appeared domestically and abroad—for instance, on BBC World News, CBS News, and Uni-vision and in the *Taipei Times*, the *Miami Herald*, and the *Age* (Mel-bourne), increasing the market for his work.[25] Today, his works hang on walls in all fifty US states and in Canada, the Netherlands, Italy, Bahrain, and the United Kingdom. And they aren't just hidden away in homes; Koopa's work is on public display in schools, libraries, galleries, government buildings, and offices.

Part of Koopa's celebrity is based on his uniqueness: a Google search turned up no other painting turtles. His anthropomorphized public persona, artfully crafted through visuals and text posted on websites ranging from YouTube to Myspace, is also part of his appeal. His interests include mirrors, things shaped like turtles, hats, painting, long baths, helping in the vegetable garden, and starring in films made by his human keeper. Although he is "not sure" about his sexual orientation, Koopa describes himself on his Myspace page as a "swinger." He lists his occupation as both "professional artist" and "box turtle."[26]

But the ultimate reason for his popularity is the collision of our incommensurate expectations: the stunning painterly sophistication of his artworks collides with the fact that a turtle created them. Add to this astonishment the highly individuated, charming persona so carefully created by his keeper and you have a star worthy of international media attention. However, as the eBay website observes in offering *Hullabaloo*, Koopa's 765th canvas, painted in November 2007: "Don't let the cuteness of the artist fool you—this is an investment-quality original painting complete with photo documentation, articles, and a Certificate of Authenticity." These accompanying materials attest to fine-art uniqueness. They guarantee that the piece is an original, not a copy; document its provenance and ensure that it is not a fake sneakily attributed to the artist; and assert its worth as a financial investment, a commodity with a changing value in the art world. Indeed, underlining the commodity nature of the paintings, Koopa's TurtleKiss website FAQs state, "Buyers of Koopa's art can expect [its value] to rise as he gradually receives recognition as a collectible artist. His artworks currently sell for over 400% more than they did his first year." Authentication is required because, without it, no one would believe that a turtle had painted the pieces.

Koopa has created hundreds of paintings, but of course he doesn't accomplish this alone.[27] While it's true that Koopa is the one to physically spread paint on the canvas, and that the resultant multihued mixes of color could, perhaps, only be achieved through his unique bodily build and gait, the role of his artist-keeper Kira Ayn Varszegi is crucial. Her actions and choices are central to the striking visual results, even if she never physically touches the paint on the canvas. These are truly collaborative works, although probably only Kira regards them as such. She chooses the colors, primes the canvas with a background color, decides where on the canvas to pour blobs of color for Koopa to walk through, positions and repositions the turtle so that his paths result in pleasing blends that cover the entire canvas, and decides when the painting is finished.

According to an apocryphal story, Koopa's art career started one day in 2003, when Kira left her canvas and oil paints on the floor while she took a break. Koopa, free to wander at will around the apartment, scuttled across her palette. As Kira notes, "After returning to my *palette*, I noticed that Koopa had produced a near perfect gradient [of colors] and added some nifty claw marks. I knew I had to find a safe way for him to paint after that."[28] Soon after, she found some nontoxic, water-based paints and acclimated Koopa to being rinsed off in the shower so that he could remain calm and unstressed throughout the process.[29]

As Kira explains, "I openly admit that all our paintings are collaborations. Without my knowledge of color blending and composition the paintings would turn out awful. Koopa does all of the actual 'painting,' but it's also because of how the canvas is prepared for him that the paintings end up looking nice."[30] As the painting unfolds and Kira documents the process for potential buyers with her digital camera, she is constantly making judgments about which parts of the canvas would benefit (aesthetically) from more color blending and which are best left alone. In a sense, Koopa becomes her paintbrush, but one that she does not fully control, since she only decides the direction in which Koopa will head when he is on the canvas.

But keeping the color mixing from becoming muddy requires a human artist's eye as well as careful placement of the blobs of pigment on the canvas. For example, placing red and green blobs side by side and allowing Koopa to walk through them, thus mixing them together, would result in a muddy brown color. Kira also monitors Koopa's movements so he doesn't spend too much time "overblending" one part of the canvas to the neglect of others, picking him up and placing him at the other side of the canvas, then letting him walk freely across its surface again and again until the entire canvas shows blended strokes of pigment.

The results are truly striking. Koopa's works tend toward the bright primary colors of red, yellow, and blue, blended into long swirls reminiscent of van Gogh's skies. The completed canvas is totally covered with layers of paint all the way to the edges, with no raw canvas showing through. Unlike the individual sweeping strokes on a white background typical of so many animal paintings, Koopa's paintings offer a densely worked, multilayered surface thick with pigments. For example, his five hundredth painting, *Celebration #5*, thirty-six inches long and eighteen inches tall, features a basic palette of turquoise, sea green, and ochre, with highlights of bright pink, brick red, and white, especially in the central area of the canvas. The resultant effect is of a fire set amid the ocean.[31]

This piece typifies Koopa's style.[32] Unlike human artists, who mix two colors to yield a third, Koopa produces innumerable miniblends. Thick variations of texture are distributed across the surface, and the dragging marks, accented by a pause and shift of weight with each new footfall, yield a complex series of pulses interrupting longer sweeps of motion. These works invite the viewer to look closely and gaze at length to uncover their secrets.

Buyers' testimonies posted on Koopa's website consistently praise the surprising vividness and depth of the colors as well as the distinctive marks of tiny turtle claws sliding through the paint, details which are lost in the electronic images of the artwork. Judging from my (admittedly unscientific) sample of testimonials, a majority of Koopa's purchasers are female, and many buy a painting as a present for a family member: husband, mother, or child. Many are repeat customers who indicate they are saving up for another purchase. Broadly speaking, this might place a majority of the customers in the vast range of the middle class—having expendable income for luxury purchases, but not so much income that spending a couple of hundred dollars on a luxury item doesn't require being attentive to a budget.

Like the more general comments on animal paintings found on the ZooBeat forum, Koopa's clients echo those posters' values of uniqueness, contribution to conservation, and owning a conversation piece. But what's different is the enthusiasm they express for the aesthetics of the product as a painting. Koopa's works occupy honored places in his clients' homes, with many purchasers even specifying where they will hang their painting: in the bedroom, in the entryway, in the living room, integrated into their lives and their home decor. Many also stress a desire to share the painting with their friends and to experience their friends' amazement that it was created by a nonhuman artist.

Felicia from Iowa captures many of these sentiments about the aesthetic appeal of the work and the function of disbelief in producing desire and wonder. She writes:

All I can say is Oh My God!!! I can't believe the creative genius of Koopa. I simply must have more. It is amazing how the camera doesn't capture the full beauty of these paintings. I knew they would be nice but I honestly didn't expect the colors to jump out at me the way they did. My husband was impressed and couldn't believe that a turtle did such amazing work. I'm glad I had my cd to prove it to him. He thought I was nuts but now he wants one (or two) for his office. Keep up the good work Kira and Koopa. Smiles, hugs and kisses to you both![33]

Koopa's works appeal to both artists and those with little experience of "fine art," as the following testimonials reveal. Laura from Connecticut writes:

I have never purchased a piece of art in my life and couldn't tell the difference between a Picasso and Monet. However, I purchased a Koopa painting and have to say that it is amazing. the way the colors blend and create these peaks and then disappear into another blending of different colors is breathtaking. What I'm trying to say is that unless you are visually challenged, anyone can appreciate the beauty in these paintings.

Kelly from Georgia purchased a painting (*Untitled, #4*) for her grandmother in North Carolina. She described the result, which demonstrates that both artists and art lovers react positively too: "This past weekend [my grandmother] had a party at her house with several of her artist friends. . . . She said that they all raved about the painting—one compared it to Gaugin, another to Monet! I think you've got a hit on your hands!"

In their enthusiasm for the visual aesthetics of his painting, Koopa's fans are exceptionally vocal. They *love* the paintings—the actual visual result—not just the idea of the painting. They find it "amazing" that a turtle did it. I think it is the richness of mark making and the complexity of color and stroke on the surface that make Koopa's work "painterly" in a way that most other animal art, usually composed of a minimal number of strokes, is not. If Koopa could make these paintings on his own, Jackson Pollock would be in trouble. The turtle would *be* a creative, aesthetic being. That he is not, to our knowledge, is the prerequisite for the amazement greeting his products.

But Koopa the international celebrity artist is just one among many painting animals, most much less well known than he and less avidly collected internationally. Most animal art is produced and consumed locally. It's made in zoos and sanctuaries that use art making as an enrichment activity to relieve boredom for captive animals and then sell the results to help fund animal care. But it is one thing to place a turtle on a canvas and encourage him to walk, and quite another to convince an elephant, seal, or rhinoceros to paint. How does this happen?

Teaching a Seal to Paint

Up to this point, except in my discussion of Koopa, I have made only passing references to the processes involved in creating paintings by wildlife, processes that vary somewhat by species. In this section, I describe the art making in detail based on my in-person observations, supplemented by descriptions found in the press and videos. Although animals can't paint without human assistance (they can't go to the store and purchase a canvas or get the paints out of a storeroom), the degree and mode of collaboration clearly vary widely, not only from species to species but also from individual animal to individual animal.

Every aspect of the art-making process presents a moment for decision making. To understand the artwork as a product of the animal-human interaction, I break down those moments into their component parts—a sort of microanalysis of production usually invisible to the public. Among my questions are the following: Who decides to paint in the first place? How does the animal "know" how to paint? What role does the animal play in producing the work? What role does the human play? When, where, and why does the painting activity take place? Is food always involved? Who selects the colors? The brushes? The paper or canvas? The painting's size and spatial orientation? Who decides when a painting is "done"? Who controls where the paint goes on the canvas? Who decides which paintings are "successful" enough to sell? On what basis? How are the paintings priced? By whom and why? Does the genre of "animal painting" have its own aesthetic? I take the case of Midge, a sea lion living at the Oklahoma City Zoo and Botanical Garden, as an example to explore these issues.[34]

Training a sea lion to paint is based on the same type of operant conditioning training techniques used to train him or her for other behaviors, like clapping flippers on cue or balancing a ball on the nose. As operant conditioning is used to train a variety of species to paint, I describe the process briefly here.

Based on the work of B. F. Skinner in the early part of the twentieth century, operant conditioning pairs a stimulus (given by the trainer) with a response (an action by the animal) by tying them together with a reward. For most animals, that reward is a bit of food, but it may also be a back scratch, a belly rub, or even just hearing someone say "Good." Operant conditioning may employ a "negative stimulus" (something that hurts or distresses the animal) to help shape behavior, but this is discouraged and is used as a last resort.[35] (While I have never heard of abusive techniques being used in the United States to get animals to paint, there have been some reports of maltreatment of elephants who paint in tourist camps in Thailand.)[36]

The ultimate goal is to train animal actions (termed "behaviors") to occur reliably on cue. But no sea lion is going to just pick up a brush one day and paint on a canvas to receive a wonderfully smelly fish reward. Training also involves "shaping" behaviors—that is, reinforcing, slowly and over time, behaviors that move the animal closer and closer to the desired one. For example, training a sea lion to paint involves teaching the animal to hold a brush in her mouth for a specified length of time without dropping it. To begin this sequence, the trainer would reinforce even the briefest inquisitive picking up of an object, gradually rewarding only the times the sea lion held on to the object for longer and longer periods.

Next, the trainer would work toward establishing reliable "give" and "take" cues so that the sea lion would take the brush when offered and give it back when commanded to do so. She would then be trained to "target" the canvas (that is, touch a specific spot on command) with the brush in her mouth, and, finally, to shake her head back and forth while holding the brush against the canvas. At some point, the brush would be loaded with paint, and the sea lion would begin to make marks on the canvas.

Once this whole cycle was under stimulus-response control, a painting could be produced through the substantial repetition of the take, target, headshake, and give-back-the-brush sequence of actions, with a different color of paint added to the brush at each sequence repetition to build up a multicolored abstract composition. While all the training for art making sounds tedious, it can provide stimulation and interspecies contact for the animals, that is, behavioral and environmental enrichment, while also building on previously trained behaviors.[37]

Midge, the California sea lion at the Oklahoma City Zoo and Botanical Garden, is a willing and enthusiastic artist, and her experience provides a good case study. Her companion sea lion doesn't particularly like to paint with a brush and so is rarely asked to do so, indicating the role of the animal's choice making in participating in this activity. For him, paint is simply smeared on his flippers, and he then wiggles across paper, leaving his "prints." These talismans of physical uniqueness and species identification can also be sold as art prints to raise money, but it is only Midge who produces actual "paintings" for sale. She is an engaged and energetic (sometimes too energetic) brush painter who often paints in educational shows for the public. I was fortunate to attend a "private" session with her trainers, and describe that experience as follows.[38]

I watch as Midge swims over and slides out onto the concrete apron surrounding her pool while her trainers ready her paints and canvas. Sleek and wet, her dark-brown, short, dense fur rippling across her muscular torpedo shape, her round black eyes glistening, and her nose snorting, she quickly waddles over to one of her trainers. If this eagerness is telling, she seems anxious to paint.

Taking the brush in the side of her mouth, she really gets into the head-shaking part of the behavior, aggressively rubbing the bristles against the canvas, which a trainer strains to hold steadily perpendicular to the floor at Midge's head height. The paintings Midge produces have a great sense of energy, since this "whiskering" is translated into dynamic sweeps of color, with brushstrokes clearly scored into the paint and short jabbing strokes layering on top of wider beds of color. Flecks of flying paint add a final tracery to the surface.

The painting Midge is making for me on a piece of white stretched canvas measures eight inches by twelve inches. Its first layer of color is a vivid turquoise that she thickly applies in broad, fat brushstrokes as she goes at the canvas, pushing her brush into it with short, side-to-side head shakes while the brush protrudes from one side of her mouth. Each such attack on the canvas is greeted ("reinforced," in the stimulus-response vocabulary) with verbal encouragement—squeals of delight from the trainers. A second layer of bright purple is applied in longer sweeping strokes, with bristle lines carving across the surface in upward curves. Finally, a bright rosy pink accents the middle of the painting, with thick matte color sparingly applied. The colors mix a little but mostly read as discrete layers, giving the canvas a sense of depth and vibrancy as the tones of the stacked hues bounce against one another, resulting in a composition of surprising complexity and vigor.

This is truly "action painting" in the Jackson Pollock style of abstract expressionism. The drips, splashes, and sweeping skeins of Midge's brushstrokes record the physical actions that produced them, just as the paint on Pollock's canvases does. For instance, the sweeping motion of the brush results in strokes that begin as dense marks but taper to thin trails of pigment. The animal trainers say that people like these paintings because they have a lot of "energy" in them, but these aren't merely aesthetic judgments: more than energy is written on the canvas. It matters too *whose* energy it is. Midge's paintings render her energetic and unique presence in a tangible way.

Like most artists, Midge "signs" her work after completing it. In this case, the "signature" is a purple nose print on the back of the canvas, the smudge resembling a little heart. On the wooden stretcher across the back, the trainer writes "Midge's nose print" in ballpoint pen, and then draws a heart, directing our reading of the smudge as loving signature. She then dates the piece (9/6/07) and writes "Midge, 22 yr. old female California Sea Lion." Whereas in a humanly produced work, a name and date usually suffice to identify the artist, at least in the European American fine-art tradition, here the individual must be identified by species, age, and sex as well.

For most of the lay public, this information carries little meaning—is a twenty-two-year-old sea lion old or young? Do females paint differently than males? How are California sea lions different from other types of sea lions? But these appended facts serve to further individuate the animal artist while simultaneously genericizing it ("a" California sea lion). The signing process represents a translation of the European fine-art tradition into animal terms, with a resultant taxonomic "signature" combining name and physical status.

As I noted earlier, animal paintings are really human-animal collaborations, and in this case Midge doesn't choose the canvas, the colors, or the brushes. While the trainer holding the canvas tries to move it so that Midge's brushstrokes don't all end up in the same spot, Midge's energy and attack are what drive the process. Her humans make no effort to derive symmetry, a representational sense, or full spatial coverage of the canvas.

The colors are chosen by the trainers, but with an interesting intervention from the zoo's marketing department. A member of the public relations staff had suggested using colors that "go together, sort of like a color wheel," and so the nontoxic tempera paints are numbered and color coordinated to let the trainers know what "goes with" what. My painting uses turquoise, purple, and fuchsia, all combinations of blues and reds. Sea lions are color blind, so we can assume that the color choices provide no particular meaning or pleasures for them, but they certainly do for the viewing public. Note, though, that the notion of which colors "go together" and which do not is a historically and culturally specific valuation of aesthetic relationships. We can assume that the bright colors of my painting are deemed "attractive" in part because they echo current color aesthetics in US visual culture. Midge's paintings are thus structured to read as attractive "paintings," both through format (canvas, paint, brushes) and through color and design aesthetics.

The moment of completion is a negotiation between trainer and animal. While the trainer has complete control over the color choices, the animal has a say in when the painting is finished, mostly by indicating her disinterest in continuing to paint. When the trainer sees Midge's energy or attention beginning to flag, she will ask, "Are you done?" If the answer is a honking "yes," the painting session is over, and Midge trundles over for a big reward of fish.

At the end of the session I observed, I got my own reward when the trainers asked me if I would like a hug from Midge. While she balanced on her tail on the edge of the pool, she wrapped her two flippers around my body, and I then wrapped my arms around her. She punctuated the embrace with a fishy-breathed "kiss"—complete with a blast of warm air from puckered lips—on my cheek. Sucker that I am, I thought that the long duration of the hug indicated Midge's intense fascination with me, but I later learned that the timing was based on her trainer's subtle cue, which I could not see. Still, receiving a dripping hug from Midge fulfilled my desires for cross-species communication, even though the implied affection I associate with "hugging" was (merely) a demonstration of operant conditioning.

The Eye of the Beholder

Somewhat chagrined at my own fantasies of cross-species embrace, I nonetheless think my own desires are symptomatic of what the public goes for when purchasing "artworks" produced by animals. The commodity—a product of the animal's embodied actions—becomes the stand-in for that desired physical touch and psychic meeting. To be in such close physical proximity with a nondomestic animal would require (we assume) some sort of "meeting of the minds"—a permission granted by the animal to enter its world in some minimal way, at least. Captivity, of course, is the unstated and masked prerequisite for such meetings of the mind where the art product is concerned. The symbolic transfer of a painting from animal "artist" to human owner indexes the desired free-will communion between species with the bridging of commodity exchange. We may not be able to embrace Midge, but we can own the talismanic trace of her physical self by purchasing one of her energetic brush paintings. The painting becomes the magical bridge between two physical and emotional entities, human and nonhuman, that otherwise could never meet.

In the foregoing discussion of turtle art celebrity and zoo art production, we discovered the ebullient engagement of the purchasing public that generates this transnational market for "art" by animals. The democratization of philanthropy, that is, the ability of people of relatively modest means to contribute to conservation or to the betterment of animal welfare for captive animals and their cousins in "the wild" through the purchase of such "art," is a strong driving force for this art market. You may need millions to buy a van Gogh, but you only need one hundred or two hundred dollars or pounds to purchase an animal-made masterpiece. And with that purchase, you get not only the material product itself, the "artwork," but also the psychic reward of contributing to animal welfare and the possibility of educating and impressing your friends ("Yes! A turtle made that!").

Finally, and perhaps most important, the purchase activates the sense of contact with a "wild" or unusual animal, even if that animal lives in captivity, through the commodity-mediated connection with that animal's mind and body. The painting, after all, is the result of the (somehow) willing participation of the nonhuman animal in the process of daubing paint on a canvas. The sale—the commodity exchange in a capitalist system—formats this object as "art" and recuperates that animal embodiment into a commodity exchange of object for physical and psychological trace. The commodity for sale captures and records the material rendering of a specific animal's action in space and time and thus serves as both deed and talisman of authentic presence. Its purchase completes the circuit, uniting human and nonhuman animal in an idealized world of mutuality.

The fantasy that such connections could occur outside capitalism's embrace is enhanced by the role that "art" plays in them. "Art," as the material result of creativity, oscillates between the market and the intangible realm. Although embedded in the market, "art" purports to be above utility and beyond commodification, that is, priceless. As such, it promises the primed currency of human and animal connection, offering the imaginary ideal of transspecies connection outside commodified exchange. At the same time, however, it firmly anchors its products, and their sale, in the capitalization of wild animal captivity, no matter how benignly intended, that is the legacy of two centuries of scientism and colonial booty.

But the real stakes in animal-produced art emerge when the species involved shift from turtles and sea lions to apes. The audience for "art" made by animals of all sorts may exceed our expectations in both monetary and geographic dimensions, as I have argued here, positioning sales of this art not only as local events but also as part of a transnational art market. I have uncovered varied human motivations in helping to produce, purchase, and display artwork by seals, turtles, horses, dogs, cats, and even rhinoceroses, among other animals. But this emergent art market has a pinnacle too, at which we encounter works produced by animals in whom we humans recognize an "intelligence" akin to our own. They include elephants and, most especially, nonhuman primates. In considering these animals, the real crux of the matter shifts from conservation support to academic research and the resulting potential for moral and ethical obligation.

In the following chapter on "art" produced by nonhuman primates and its transnational market, I explore the issues of representational art and how that categorization is used to raise the bar in our evaluation of nonhuman animals' intellectual capacities and our resultant moral obligations to them. Only elephants and some primates have produced "artworks" that are representational, that is, works explicitly referring to the world, articulated through a symbolic system of communication that humans understand to be meaningful.

I move, then, from the broader contexts of the transnational market for art by animals like Koopa and Midge to representational works by primates. What happens when the use of quotation marks, the "wink," attached to the category of animal "art" disappears? As we will see, the stakes here—and the potential influence on the lives of animals involved—are much different when the artist is a turtle or a sea lion than when the artist is a human-language-enabled ape like Michael the gorilla.

"Art" by Animals, Part 2: When the Artist Is an Ape—Popular and Scientific Discourse and Paintings by Primates

In May of 2005, three paintings by a very special artist were sold by Bonham's Auction House in London for approximately thirty thousand dollars.[1] This transaction is not so unusual perhaps, except that the artist was an ape, and the sum was the highest ever paid for works of art created by a nonhuman animal.

How could this happen, and what does it mean? This chapter, a companion to the preceding one, builds on that chapter's detailed analysis of the growing global trade in art by nonhuman animals, including paintings produced by rats, dogs, and sea lions, among others. In this chapter, primates are my focus, and as before, I take up key questions animating this market, extending them now in light of primates, who up the ante. Does this art market function as a contestation of humanism? How does the culturally specific category of "art" change when the species producing it changes? What is at stake in naming animal creations "art," and for whom? For scientists? For the lay public? Why do some of these works, especially those by primates, command relatively high prices? What aspect of "the human" and of "mind" does art stand for in related debates about animal capacities? How do such artworks relate to no-tions of "the primitive"? And ultimately, what does this challenge to the humans-only category of art making mean for a posthumanist vi-sion of beings in the world? If the artist is an ape, or the ape is an artist, does that designation have potential political implications for the status of apes—indeed, for their representation, literally and figura-tively—as political subjects?

To consider these larger questions, we must also ask the following, which underpin the art-making phenomenon: What role do notions of intentionality, aesthetic pleasure, design capability, and cultural knowledge of representational conventions play in our understanding of art making by animals? Ultimately, how do we situate these actions and products, and the beliefs they activate and depend on, within the wider, historically specific context of the European-derived notion of "art" as a distinctive realm of expressive individuality? This realm, while supposedly promoting transcendent truths that exceed the val-ues of a market economy, has, for the last several hundred years, been deeply embedded in that economy.

In the preceding chapter, I sketched the transnational contours of this art market, its link to philanthropic support for zoos and sanc-tuaries, and the implied continuum that positions the value of art-works along a scale of increasing capacity for "intent" demonstrated by the species producing the works. As I noted, the toe prints unwit-tingly left by the pigment-dipped feet of the "ratistes" as they stroll across a canvas are valued less than the abstract expressionist–style brush-wielding pictures produced by Midge, the energetic sea lion at the Oklahoma City Zoo and Botanical Garden. And the painterly color mixing of Koopa the turtle gains value precisely because of the con-trast between his assumed lack of ability to generate aesthetic intent and the exceptional aesthetic subtlety of his oeuvre.

Such products, I argued, serve as talismans connecting a desiring public to the imagined touch of the (wild/captive) animal's body—to the foot, trunk, flipper, lip, or feathers that literally traced marks on paper. Impossible in real life, such a touch is rendered in a bodily trace, captured and framed for an aesthetic experience and hung on the wall as a painting, integrated into the space of daily life.

Here, while shifting the species focus, I retain my emphasis on un-derstanding the creation, reception, and circulation of these art prod-ucts within the context of a specifically European-derived notion of art making and its contemporary linkage of individual creativity, sub-jectivity, and visual skill. The conditions of possibility for recognizing these products as art were multiple. Especially important was the post–World War II rise of abstract art, particularly abstract expressionism, which prepared the cultural ground for the public acceptance of animal-produced paintings (99% of which are abstract) as art, and which has been a key prerequisite for the expansion of the animal art market overall.

In addition, the earlier European modernist encounter with, and passion for, so-called primitive art produced by individuals in African and Oceanic societies, for example, helped expand the visual range of European artists like Pablo Picasso and enlarged, for Europeans and those they influenced, the concept of what "art" could look like and who could create it. Primitivizing and orientalist ideologies of the time underwrote the ascription of a lower evolutionary status to non-Europeans vis-à-vis Europeans and fostered a notion that their art was a contemporary representative of earlier evolutionary stages.[2] It's a short leap within this Darwinian ideological landscape to casting primate art as that of the uber-"primitive." And finally, the post–World War II rise of a category of "outsider art"—especially since the 1970s—which recognized works produced by untrained individuals as exhibiting complex, often unique, and even obsessive design qualities, offered another broadening of the concept of "art."[3]

Thus, since the latter half of the nineteenth century, the category of visual art in the European and European-influenced world has been expanding in terms of both who is to be granted the status of "artist" and what their work can look like and still fall within the socially designated realm of "art." The notion of and market for "art" by animals is both part of and simultaneously dependent on this historical expansion.

But even if "abstract art" by animals has gained value within this expanding matrix and market of products, producers, and categorization, the holy grail in animal art making remains purposeful, expressive, aesthetic creation by nonhuman animals who have chosen to engage in this activity. For some humans, even more sought after and more elusive is evidence of the desire for transspecies communication through the creation of representational paintings.

I analyze this aspect of the art market, and its overlap with scientific desires to uncover the human origins of aesthetic expressivity, to argue that in the case of those few apes who live in "bicultural" ape-human communities, such an expressivity may exist. If it does, its greatest value is not in the art market, or in its ability to shine a light down the long history of human evolution, as is often claimed. Rather, its power lies in the pressure it can bring on us to recalibrate our relations with such nonhuman beings. This is the danger, the allure, and the promise of art when the artist is an ape.

As we will see, although the market for art by animals is relatively new, the human search for artistry in nonhuman animal lives, and especially among primates, is not. That history sets the stage for our current understandings.

Evolutionary Stakes and Political Subjectivity:
The Question of Aesthetic "Intent"

For some contemporary scientists of human evolution, an important question is whether an "aesthetic sense" is a transspecies phenomenon, detectable in birds and apes, for example, but most highly developed among humans. Those in this camp care about art by animals because they see animals as human prehistory.[4] Theirs is a search for origins. For example, as Frans de Waal notes,[5] many biologists regard the New Guinea bowerbird's hutlike nests as evidence of protoaesthetic expression.

Male bowerbirds build elaborate nests, decorating the entries with colorful objects like berries and flowers that they arrange and rearrange, analyzing the patterns from a distance and then flying in again to move a petal until the composition is just right, with an eye to attracting a female mate. For de Waal, this activity may not be art making, but it raises the question of whether human aesthetic urges, or—more accurately, I would argue—actions and desires expressed in the realm that has historically come to be called the artistic, may "go deeper than culture" and may relate to basic features of our perceptual systems, like our eyes and ears.[6] As additional evidence, he notes that many birds must learn the songs they sing, that they aren't born with this knowledge, and that many bird populations have different "dialects" reflecting regional variations, just as landscape paintings of the Rhone and the Rhine vary in style even during the same historical periods. Some birds are even apparently more creative singers than others, pioneers in the development of new songs.[7]

While these notions of an aesthetic genealogy appear to connect some evolutionary dots, the real stakes lie in debates about art by primates, the taxonomic group that includes humans and our closest relatives. There are two realms in which debates about "art making" by animals operate: that of science—including especially the work of comparative psychologists and primatologists working on ape cognition and language capabilities—and that of the layperson.

For comparative psychologists and primatologists, ape paintings have served as data for investigations of eye-hand coordination and tool use and for cognitive studies of symbol making.[8] For instance, Sarah T. Boysen and colleagues, on the basis of a coding of 618 drawings by three chimpanzees, conclude that chimps will engage in drawing activities without training or reinforcement, and that "this behavior may reflect their intrinsic interest in exploratory and manipulative play."[9]

In more recent investigations, biological anthropologist Anne Zeller provides additional evidence of deliberate choice making in the production of abstract paintings by captive primates. Between 1993 and 2004, Zeller gathered more than three hundred pictures made by apes and more than fifty by human children and compared them. After an extensive analysis of color preferences, the use of space on the paper, and so on, she concludes that far from being unintentional "scribbles," the mark making by both apes and human children is highly intentional. Zeller argues that

humans can adapt to a wider range of choices than other primates, mainly in numbers of colours and numbers of patterns utilized, but tend to be quite conservative and rule bound when placing their expression centered on the paper and generally within the boundaries. Females seem more constrained by these rules than do males. Chimpanzees, like the other apes, tend towards a preferred number of colours to manipulate but are quite exuberant in expression, breaching the page edges more frequently than remaining inside. However, they exerted control over the location of their colours (rule of thirds) and used complex patterns, such as the cross. This differs from gorillas who tended to use colour masses (smears) more than other species, although they were capable of deft movements with their large fingers.[10]

Zeller concludes that these results point us toward a better understanding of how primates respond to visual stimuli, and that we can understand their pictures in terms of a metacommunicative function.

These findings build on other experiments, like those conducted in the 1950s by Desmond Morris showing that rather than making marks randomly on a page, apes make considered choices about where to make marks in relation to what is already there, apparently seeking a sense of balance. Anecdotal evidence also indicates that apes appear to have a sense of when a painting is "finished." Congo the chimpanzee became agitated if Morris tried to remove a painting before Congo wanted him to. Nor could he be implored to paint more on an image once he stopped.[11] So it appears that nonhuman primates make marks on a surface that reflect choice involving careful consideration of location, relation, color, mass, and even style, and that they can decide what a "completed" item should look like.

Primate specialist de Waal goes further: "Apes can deliberately make what looks like art to humans," he says. While apes don't seem to strive to create enduring works of visual art that will "please, inspire, provoke shock, or produce whatever effect a human painter strives to achieve," they do seem to enjoy the visual and kinesthetic act of making the drawing or painting.[12]

Additional recent work by Boysen, de Waal, Morris, and Masayuki Tanaka (who is using touch screens in Japan to trace scribbling patterns by young chimps)[13] back up these findings, suggesting the possibility of what might be called a "protoaesthetic," components of manual and visual choice making that are necessary to but not sufficient for the development of what humans consider "art making." This interpretation would be important for those concerned with evolutionary issues and human development.[14]

This search for or desire for a protoaesthetic impulse also underlies, I believe, both the public's passion for paintings by apes and the widespread use of painting as an enrichment activity by primate keepers in zoos and sanctuaries. The broad contours of assumptions about art making sketched above are operative in both the scientific and the popular discourse realms, although the scientific realm may parse these concepts more complexly and with greater precision. But in both realms, there is a huge "wow" factor—the sense of a frontier being crossed, a limit being broken. If an ape can make art, then . . . what? What is the passion to know what follows that ellipsis?

Although early isolated case studies of primates showed that some of them like to draw or paint, chimp art really broke through to the popular consciousness in the 1950s. This postwar period coincided with a widening acceptance of abstract art as "legitimate" artistry. That shift in art history prepared the ground for laypeople to see ape art—primarily based on gestural marks, not representational strategies—as "art." This period saw ethologist Desmond Morris, trained at Oxford and a surrealist painter himself, featuring a young chimpanzee named Congo on his popular London television show *Zoo Time*. It was Congo's abstract paintings that were recently put up for auction at Bonham's in London alongside works by Warhol and Renoir. Although the Warhol and the Renoir failed to sell, Congo's paintings did, and for far more than the anticipated equivalent of $1,000–$1,500 each.

As CBS News reported, American Howard Hong, a self-described contemporary painting enthusiast, paid $26,352 for three brightly colored abstract tempera paintings by Congo.[15] This marketability took the Bonham's curator of modern and contemporary art, Howard Rutkowski, by surprise. "We had no idea what these things were worth," he said. "We just put them [on sale] for our own amusement."[16] The unexpected sale was reported in both mainstream and arts-specific media, including National Public Radio, CBS News, the London-based *Guardian*, and *Science* magazine online, demonstrating the artworks' status as entertainment news, science, art, and oddity.[17] Perhaps, as is the case for so many artists, Congo's prices climbed because the artist is dead, having succumbed in 1964 to tuberculosis at the age of ten.[18] At his most prolific in his youth, he produced about four hundred drawings and paintings between the ages of two and four.[19] For Desmond Morris, works like these, and not those of early humans, "represent the birth of art."[20]

Reports of the sale lent additional newsworthiness to a retrospective of Congo's work titled *Ape Artists of the 1950s* at the Mayor Gallery in London in July of 2005. The art critic of the *Sunday Times* in London, Waldemar Januszczak, found that the exhibit challenged his beliefs that only humans can truly paint with intentional rather than accidental aesthetics. He admits, "I like Congo's paintings. A couple of them I love." Calling the retrospective "fascinating and slightly worrying," he describes Congo as a "talented" painter who made active color and compositional choices, threw a tantrum if a human tried to take a picture away from him before he was finished, and refused to add to any painting he regarded as completed, despite entreaties to do so. Each of these actions serves as evidence of intentional aesthetic production. Qualities of unmuddied color, symmetrical balance, and, at times, a "mood [that is] pure Kandinsky" make Congo's best works demonstrations of profound achievement, in Januszczak's words.[21]

But even in this article, we see the smirk, the longtime view of the artist as monkey, as fop, and as self-important boor traced by scholar Thierry Lenain.[22] The title of Januszczak's article, "Monkey Master," and the resounding absence of the question mark are impossible to miss. Even the cavalier repetition of *m*'s in *monkey master* depends on a disregard for the particularity of the painter—for Congo is a chimpanzee, not a monkey. But the word *monkey*, aside from its alliterative use, also conjures up images of an organ grinder's monkey, a trickster, and a miniature and comic humanoid. The fear that we might be monkeys after all erupts through the tongue-in-cheek titling.

But there is another side to this coin: Morris is concerned with tracing the origins of human abilities to their nonhuman primate past (thus assuming, of course, that apes don't have cultural history but rather live in the present as mere exemplars of our long-distant evolutionary cousins). But these discussions rarely recognize what sociologists and theorists of art know—that representational systems aren't simply the results of inherent human eye-hand coordination and perceptual abilities but are historically distinctive symbolic systems, and are learned both actively and passively by members of specific human communities. Just think of the difference between the visually flat medieval paintings of saints and the lush three-dimensional images of Michelangelo, to draw just one example from well-known western European traditions. When some laypersons and even some scientists refer to ape drawings as a mode of protoaesthetics, or representational art, they ignore the fact that "art" is a category of social activity that is historically specific, differing according to time, place, and community.

To better understand art practices and their linkages to what human primates do, we must frame art making as a cultural activity, and this doesn't necessarily mean that apes don't paint but that maybe some do. This is especially resonant when we consider the cases of individual apes like Washoe, Koko, Michael, Kanzi, and Panbanisha, all stars in long-term communication research who have been trained to "speak" with humans through sign language or the use of lexigrams.

After all, Koko and her now-deceased companion, Michael, for example, were raised as members of a bispecies community full of symbolic visual images (they looked through store catalogues and books and watched videos). And they learned to perceive and to name at least some objects, and perhaps even concepts, which is a culturally specific representational act in itself. Perhaps this naming lies at the origin of their art making if, in fact, we are to accept that characterization. At the very least, they complicate the question of meaning and suggest the need to consider seriously what might be happening when the artist is an ape.

But there are other reasons why a documentable artistic ability among nonhuman primates, and even among other animals, might be discomfiting. If animals do produce works of art, might they not be more like us—expressive, self-aware, reflective—than we would like to admit? And if so, might their already contested status—as property, as commodity, as "animal," and hence without rights and with few legal protections—be harder and harder to maintain?

How Do You Teach an Ape to Paint?

For the next part of this discussion, I momentarily leave aside painting by Washoe, Kanzi, and Koko and these apes' symbolic interactions with humans, but I will return to them later. Washoe, for example, was involved in studies on representation and schemata. My understanding is that she hadn't been "taught" to paint in any formal way.[23] By contrast, most of the paintings I describe below are produced through operant conditioning and target training by apes who don't have access to sign or symbolic language.

In the primate painting sessions I observed at the Oklahoma City Zoo and Botanical Garden, painting was usually taught through operant conditioning, just as any other activity might be: for instance, training a primate to present his or her chest close to the bars of the cage so a stethoscope could be used during medical procedures. I had the opportunity to watch primate keeper Jennifer Davis on two different days as she painted with Toba, a forty-year-old female orangutan; Gracie, an eight-year-old female gorilla; and Tatu, Gracie's father and a silverback. Toba is unusual in being self-taught, while Gracie and Tatu are more typical, having learned to paint through specific instructional techniques.

Toba sports a reddish-gold comb-over look and long tangles of fur. She has been painting for a couple of years. Although Jennifer was not the one to introduce her to painting, it appears that upon being presented with the materials, Toba took to it right away without formal instruction. The first day I spend with her, she isn't in the mood to paint, even though Jennifer and I are painting on the other side of her bars, hoping to entice her to join us. But on the second day, she's is ready to go. She loads the brush with paint herself, choosing from among several colors, and then paints on the paper we have put inside her cage. She does two things while painting that she's never done before. First, she shakes the brush when it's loaded with paint to get dribs and drabs spraying onto the page instead of just strokes, and second, she holds the paper upright in one hand while making strokes with the paintbrush in the other. This new behavior indicates she's actively problem solving and choosing how to conduct this activity on this particular day. As a reward at the end of the ten-minute session, I get to feed her some yummy Yoplait yogurt, a treat for both of us.

Toba, as I have noted, is unusual—most primates have to be taught to paint. This is done through operant conditioning, as described in the preceding chapter. To recap briefly: in operant conditioning, a stimulus, like a verbal command, is paired with a reward when the proper response is performed by the animal. Painting involves multiple steps—holding a brush, touching the brush to paper or canvas, and returning the brush to the keeper. Commands like "take" and "give" can prepare the animal to take a brush loaded with paint and then to give the brush back to the keeper. The animal is trained to touch the brush to the paper when the keeper holds the canvas up to the bars of the cage and asks him or her to "target" the brush onto the spot—in this case, to make contact with the paper.

Jennifer has reached the targeting stage with Gracie, who has been training for a couple of months. Gracie received both verbal praise and a few tasty grapes as reinforcement for touching the paintbrush to the canvas. During her father's very first painting lesson, the goal was to get him to return a loaded paintbrush to the keeper through the bars of his cage, whereupon the keeper introduced paper between them, so that the brush left a mark on it. The question of creativity is not being explored here, although keepers I've talked to often try to give the animal options so that part of the enrichment activity is the opportunity to exert control over one's environment by choice making: Which brush? Which color? Nevertheless, keepers intervene in all sorts of ways to heighten the odds that a painting will be salable—aesthetically pleasing—ensuring that the colors won't be muddy and the paint will cover more than one spot on the paper. They turn the paper, remove it at a certain point, offer a limited pallet of colors that "go together," and so on.

But my concern with this process is as an enrichment exercise. One of the primary aspects of the enrichment is its one-on-one activity, which gives the ape attention from the keeper, most often undivided attention. Erica Thiele, chimp enrichment coordinator at the M. D. Anderson Research Center in Bastrop, Texas, calls this shared activity "an intimate behavior." Thiele makes painting available to her captive charge Joey the chimpanzee as an enrichment activity. Joey, she says, appears to love painting, as evidenced by his "uh uh uh" vocalizations in response to praise at the end of a session. And while the painting exercise itself is a positive experience for him, in her estimation, he also likes the tasty reward of a Coke after each session.[24] Moreover, apes have been known to paint other things, including their cages, so the act of mark making may be enriching, engaging, or entertaining in itself.

But while the apes may produce items that can be sold as "paintings" and may engage to some degree with the issues of "expressivity" and aesthetic choice making, the emphasis here is on art making as "enrichment" for the animals. The creation of moneymaking items is merely a byproduct that can help support the primate program. (Joey's canvases sell for varying amounts, depending on size: $250 for a five-by-seven-inch minimasterpiece and twice that for an eight-by-eleven-inch canvas.)

But—when the Artist Is an Elephant? Representational Drawings

Congo, Gracie, Jimmy, Toba, and many other primates produce works of varying aesthetic complexity and attraction for potential buyers. Some, like Congo, become celebrities and are the subjects of scientific studies. For others, painting offers "enrichment," a diversion, a way of engaging with their keepers one on one and doing something different in the potentially undifferentiated daily routine of captivity, thus supporting their psychological health. However, no matter how diverse their motivations, their degree of training or lack thereof, or their amount of active aesthetic choice making in color and design, none of these primates has produced artworks that appear to be representational. In contrast to "abstract art," which is focused on creating relationships between line, color, and a surface as an end in itself, "representational art" is (to put it very simply) art that depicts, through culturally specific symbolic systems recognizable to humans, something in, or knowable about, the world—like a picture of a banana. Only a very few primates and some elephants have produced such work, and I turn to them now, starting with a pachydermic detour to Thailand.

About five years ago, tourist videos of elephants painting in Thailand began to surface on YouTube. Astoundingly, the resulting paintings were unmistakable depictions of elephants, their shapes gracefully outlined in bold black lines and accented in red. Not only were the elephants painting but they also were painting self-portraits, or so it appeared.

These elephant artworks were produced under the auspices of Komar and Melamid's Asian Elephant Art and Conservation Center, which fosters painting at three elephant campuses in Thailand, most notably the Thai Elephant Conservation Center in Lampang. The latter is a government-supported elephant conservation and retirement center in the northern tip of the country near Chiang Mai. The sanctuary supplements its government funding by offering daily educational shows, attended by Thai and foreign tourists.

Ever since logging was banned in Thailand in 1989, elephants, once movers of giant teak logs, have been out of work and lacking in care, reduced, in many cases, to begging in cities with their mahouts (caretakers) or performing circuslike tricks for cash. Moved by the elephants' plight, artists Komar and Melamid introduced painting to them and their keepers.[25] These Soviet émigrés to the United States have been known since the mid-1980s for their catholic tastes in art making as well as their avant-garde interventions in conceptual art. They made a painting session a regular part of the tourist shows at the Asian Elephant Art and Conservation Center. The artworks are sold both onsite and internationally, thanks to Komar and Melamid's artworld connections.[26]

However, unlike so many of the other "painting" schemes used in zoos and sanctuaries as fund-raisers, which result in a colorful smearing of paint in a sort of abstract-expressionist mode (discussed in the previous chapter), the Komar and Melamid elephants produce something different. In addition to that type of colorful, squiggle-lined "expressionist" picture on a white background, they also create ostensibly self-representative images. Crafted in an Asian brush-painting style, these images consist of simple, flowing black lines, unadorned by extensive three-dimensional shading or perspectival renditions of landscape for context.

YouTube videos show the elephants approaching the paper with careful deliberateness as they hold the ink-loaded brushes in their trunks. These videos continue to be popular today, with new ones continually posted, expanding the public for elephant art; "Elephant Painting an Elephant," for instance, attracted 154,300 views in four months.[27] The videos help disseminate the images of elephants actually painting, and generate discussion in posted viewer comments. Generally, commentators are split into two camps: those who find elephant artists amazing but recognize that the elephants have been trained (sometimes noting that human artists are trained too), and those who proclaim that surely the elephants were abused in the training process to get them to paint. While there is no evidence to connect the Thai Elephant Conservation Center with such maltreatment, Thailand has many elephant tourist camps, especially in the Chiang Mai region, and many activists have criticized the traditional method used for "breaking" an elephant. This technique, *phajaan*, is used throughout Asia and involves starving, beating, burning, and severely confining young elephants after separating them from their mothers. By the time the elephants learn how to paint as a performance skill, they may already have been "trained" by the traditional abusive *phajaan* technique, which is kept invisible from the camps' visitors, most of whom are tourists from the United States, western Europe, and Australia.[28]

The YouTube videos themselves show no incidents of abuse, only intensely concentrating elephants, each in front of an easel and grasping a brush in his or her trunk. Deftly, an elephant touches the tip of the brush to the rectangular sheet of paper, draws a specific line, and then deliberately lifts the brush, only to touch its tip to a different part of the paper. Each line, done in sequence, inscribes a different component of the outline of an elephant: the curve of the back, the lilting lift of a tail, the shell shape of a giant ear, the upraised arc of a trunk, until the strokes merge, one connected to the other, and the whole body suddenly appears on the page, perhaps with the added accent of a red poppy held in the trunk.

It's easy to mistake the intense effort of the brush placement and marking on the page for artistic intuition. But as the painting unfolds, we see the trained components fall into place. Even if we know the painting is a "trick," rotely learned by the elephant, the technical accomplishment is astounding—no smudges, each line perfectly connecting with the next, and the resultant image imparting a sense of movement, with front legs sweeping forward in front of hind limbs. The voiceover on the YouTube video cited above captures the viewer's emotions as the painting unfolds:

The elephant (perhaps named Suda, but the audio of the local announcer is unclear), stands in front of the slanted easel and very, very, very carefully reaches his (or her?) trunk toward the unblemished white expanse of the page. Touching the surface, the brush tip traces a strong black line over the paper, curving in a gentle arc. Eventually, we will find that this represents the elephant's huge backbone. "Look at this! Look at the calm face! It's an elephant, ya'll, painting an elephant!" enthuses the commentator on the video. The 1970s tune "Sounds of Silence," by the folk duo Simon and Garfunkel, begins to play during the elephant show performance, underlining the soft, sustained movements. A swelling chorus of appreciative murmurs rises from the crowd onsite watching the demonstration.

The video voice continues to enthusiastically relate the commentator's reactions as the action unfolds. "That is a real elephant, not a person dressed up in an elephant costume! How does this happen? Maybe the elephant is training? Some grown folks can't even draw that right there." (The drawing has now progressed to the point that the body and striding legs of its elephant figure are clearly visible.) Repeatedly, the elephant gives used brushes to and takes fresh brushes from his mahout, returning to the canvas after each exchange for another intensely careful stroke. The contrast between the animal's huge size and the small controlled movements of its trunk is stunning.

In between brushstrokes, in a release of tension, the elephant swishes its tail and bobs its head. "He's dancing!" says the voiceover on the video. "This is amazing! This elephant is a true artist!" (The elephant then draws two oblong lines behind the main body outline, inking back legs in motion.) "The elephant ain't even messin' up at all!" And indeed, it's true. The back-leg lines don't run into the front-leg lines, preserving the sense of bodily volume emerging on the page. "All right! Wasn't that amazing!? It's [drawing a picture of] a happy elephant! Unbelievable!"

Operant conditioning—the training of small behaviors through positive rewards and the linking of those behaviors into a series of multiple actions in a designated sequence—has excelled here. The announcer at the tourist show tells the crowd that it takes three to four months for an elephant to learn how to paint like this. Each rendition of an elephant by a specific elephant is just like the one before it . . . a copy of a copy of an original that was designed by the (human) brush-painting artist, now a teacher of elephant painting, hired by Komar and Melamid to head up this project.

The situation is reminiscent of Chinese factory workers today who paint flower after flower on wineglasses destined to be sold cheaply as "hand-painted" luxuries at US dollar stores. The individual in each case creates the same thing slightly differently, over and over again, according to a formula of strokes and colors. Each glass will have a slightly larger or smaller flower petal than the others, just as each elephant ear is a slightly different outline. Technically, the product will be unique and hand- (or trunk-) made, thus retaining what Walter Benjamin called the "aura" of the original in a time of rampant reproductive copies.[29] The overall production schema, capitalizing on the uniqueness associated with the idea of "handmade" as opposed to machine manufactured, is nevertheless set up to work precisely *against* the individuality associated with the term *artistry*—that notion of individually expressive subjectivity that has been such a defining characteristic of the European-derived art-making process in the past few centuries.

The truth here is that the elephant is not just "naturally" rendering a linear drawing of an elephant because he or she wished to create a self-portrait. This is the fantasy: that the elephant, known to both scientists and the lay public for its intelligence and its ability to recognize itself as a unique being—a subject—could communicate that subjectivity to us by using a symbolic system that we both (elephant and human) could grasp as meaningful and referential.[30] Komar and Melamid know this very well, and video watchers comment on it too; but the accomplishment, its "elephant drawing an elephant" attraction, and the performative rendition of elite skill and focused intent by the elephants all oscillate in the equation of action, product, process, and perception, both for the elephant artists and for their audience. We *wish* the elephant could paint us a picture of herself, even though we know she was probably trained to do what she does. With their signature lack of obeisance to the idea of artistic genius, Komar and Melamid would surely embrace not only this human desire but also the trumping of it by the trained elephant! As Melamid has said, "People can laugh at us. They can dismiss it all as a stupid joke, a travesty, a hoax. But let's not forget that art is not a tragedy, not a drama—it's a circus. And what is a circus without animals and clowns?"[31]

When the Artist Is a ("Bicultural") Ape

In the end, the possibility of representational art making by elephants remains just that—a possibility yet to be ascertained. But there is a frontier of human-animal communication where the ideas of "art," "expressivity," and "representation" come together in what is for some a tantalizing way, and for others a wholly convincing way. A different level of representational intent seems to emerge among those few apes who are "bicultural," in that they have been raised in human-generated visual and material worlds replete with conventions of human aesthetic design. Let me turn now to the small but crucial category of (human-) "language-enabled" apes.

Koko the gorilla, Panbanisha and Kanzi the bonobos, and Chantek the orangutan have all regularly participated in art making. Koko has her own website displaying prints of her paintings for sale (http://www .Koko.org), and many of her pieces are self-titled, like the poetic *Pink Pink Stink Nice Drink*—an acrylic of sweeping blues, greens, and pinks all rushing upward from the bottom-right to the upper-left part of the canvas. Hovering on the brink of representation, this piece, according to the website of the sponsoring organization, the Gorilla Foundation of Woodside, California, is "inspired by a nearby flowering meadow with a stream running through it." Its title is explained thusly: "Koko's word for flower is 'stink' even though she admits that she loves their smell." "Drink" is her sign for water.[32] So the title references a very pink flowering area by a stream—a representation that translates a sense of the sight, smell, and taste of the three-dimensional world onto a two-dimensional canvas.

Koko and her now-deceased companion Michael have also produced images of other beings, often from memory. These portraits of animals, like that of Michael's dog Apple, or Koko's picture of her pet fledgling blue jay, while rarely unambiguously representational, do give a new meaning to the category of portraiture. For example, Michael's painting *Apple Chase* consists of whites and grays sweeping across the paper. Although he had a large selection of colors to choose from, Michael used the black and whites that match the colors of Apple's coat. The title of his painting seems to combine a memory of a being with that of an event, recalling his favorite running game of "chase" with Apple.[33]

In addition, upon request, both gorillas have produced paintings expressing their interpretations of specific emotions—the meanings of which they have come to understand through sign language—including "love," "hate," and "anger." This level of interspecies communication was unavailable to the 1950s ape artists represented in the recent retrospective including Congo's work. None possessed the linguistic knowledge to communicate in a way humans could understand, and so they couldn't be asked to paint certain things or ideas or emotions. Granted, in the case of Koko and Michael, the paintings and their titles, and the interpretations of the titles and of their referential meanings, are all products of bispecies collaboration. Gorilla knowledge is filtered through the medium of human concept-based communication in the English language, as transposed into American Sign Language.[34] In other words, the gorillas speak and understand a form of English, but the humans don't speak Gorilla.

The challenges in and potential for exploring paintings by apes are both enormous. The most extensive investigation so far of apes' pictorial possibilities comes in Tomas Persson's study of how apes interact with pictures.[35] Building on earlier studies but designing his own, Persson brings sophisticated semiotic analysis to bear on primates' engagements with visual images, in an approach that carefully parses the number of abilities and skills needed to see a picture *as* a picture. For example, a photograph, with its historical conventions of realism, is both a thing (a piece of paper with ink on it) and a depiction (an image). We must then relate that surface image to something else, somewhere else in the world that it refers to.[36] And we must not confuse the "realism" of the image with the thing it is an image of.[37] From this perspective, Persson analyzes apes' perceptions of photographs and of line drawings of objects in his attempts to understand how they respond to such complex representational images. Some apes, he proposes, perhaps especially those introduced to human language, seem able to respond to such representations *as* representations.

Reading his work, we can bring the necessary, but often lacking, social and historical dimensions of pictorial understanding to discussions of art by animals. "Bicultural" apes like Kanzi and Koko, who have lived for decades in human-centric worlds full of human words and images, can be, in Persson's term, "inspiring co-workers" in this regard.[38] Humans, after all, learn interpretive strategies for pictorial representations through social interactions and verbal "scaffolding" in their communities, and by a certain age can understand that some drawings "stand for" something else. Culturally specific visual conventions, having to do with strategies for depicting time and space (for instance, three-dimensionality, depth, a moment captured in time, and so on), are, as cross-cultural studies of humans have shown, quite complex, and they too are learned. Various mediums—paper, touch screens, color markers, paint—also impart their own complexities to the representational process. Beyond these considerations, we must remember that not all images are "art." "Art" is a historically contingent and culturally variable category of visual production and reception underwritten by institutional and social formations.

The whole concept of artwork and art making is thus always already constructed through human categories of meaning. But even allowing for that, these primate-produced paintings come strikingly close to the status of "artwork" as a visual representation produced for the pleasure of looking at it or of making it, but not for a utilitarian reason. These works seem to combine a sense of mark making with imagination, resulting in a product that is then perceived as "art" by someone else, thus completing the hermeneutic circle uniting perception with interpretation.

Persson, unlike cognitive scientists who investigate primate pictures in search of origins of human abilities, poses different, less anthropocentric, questions: "Can pictures help us understand them [primates] better? Can we ask them questions through pictures that we cannot do through language? Or rather, through their language, can they tell us things about pictures that reflect their inner worlds in new ways?"[39]

If some apes *are*, or could be, artists, what does that imply about humans' obligations to them? Already, there have been moves afoot in the European Union to grant special status to great apes—a sort of in-between animal and human status garnering legal protections.[40] Recent court cases in the United States are also pushing this boundary, trying to assert that apes should be "legal persons."[41] And even dogs and cats will soon have legally mandated "freedoms" in some European countries—freedom from hunger, from the elements, from isolation. If more studies and more popular reports describe animals, and especially apes, as artists, it becomes politically harder and harder to deny their sentient and intelligent status.

In a liberal humanist social orientation, where individual rights, the rule of law, and a belief in the importance of individual subjectivity are crucial underpinnings of social formations, the line between human and nonhuman primate becomes ever more indistinct. Even in a poststructuralist, posthumanist vision, with decentered subjectivity, and an emphasis on a socially constructed "I" as a position to be occupied, not an essence to be expressed, the social construction of the category "animal" as that which is not human is increasingly exposed as an epistemology with a specific history, not as a "fact" naming an already extant reality. In either case, animal artists subvert the presumed privilege of the human. And this, perhaps, is the utopian ideal (or fantasy?) that people purchase when they buy a painting by Koko to put on their wall.

18. Mama the wire-haired fox terrier made this painting at a Champaign County (Illinois) Humane Society fund-raising event in 2011. Note the imprint of her paw pads, marking the physical trace of the individual animal, as distinctive as a human fingerprint. Water-based paints on paper, 8½ × 11″. Collection of the author.

19. This painting in blues and greens was made by a snake being treated by the University of Illinois Veterinary Teaching Hospital Wildlife Clinic, Champaign, and was used to raise money for the operation of the nonprofit facility. Note the sinewy traces of the snake's body and movement inscribed on the canvas board. Water-based, nontoxic paints on canvas board, 9 × 12". Collection of the author.

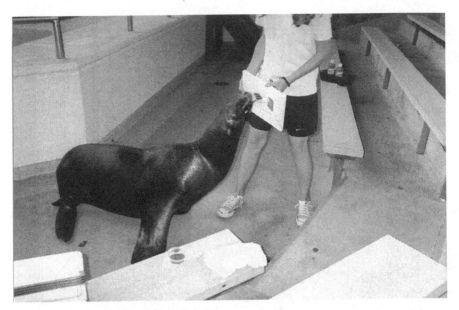

20. Midge the sea lion paints with one of her zookeepers poolside on September 6, 2007, at the Oklahoma City Zoo and Botanical Garden. Holding a modified brush in her mouth, she shakes her head vigorously back and forth, making swift bright-blue and purple strokes on an eight-by-twelve-inch canvas board. Photo by the author.

21. Painting by Midge the sea lion, Oklahoma City Zoo and Botanical Garden, produced September 6, 2007. Water-based paints on canvas board, 8 × 12″. Collection of the author.

22. Koopa the turtle begins a painting within a circle of paint. In this photo, we see the importance of human artist-owner Kira Ayn Varszegi in placing the colors that Koopa will mix into the final image. Photo by Kira Ayn Varszegi, used with permission.

23. Koopa the turtle completes a painting. He and his caretaker-artist, Kira Ayn Varszegi, together create the conditions for him to complete this painting, blending a myriad of colors together. Photo by Kira Ayn Varszegi, used with permission.

24. Chandra the elephant, painting on September 6, 2007, at the Oklahoma City Zoo and Botanical Garden with one of the staff. She is making a painting by blowing and smearing water based paints in golds and greens on a 16 by 20 inches stretched canvas. The painting is signed by her unique "nose print" . . . a smooch from the tip of her trunk in the corner of the painting. Photo by the author.

25. This painting, *Stink Gorilla More* by Michael the gorilla, then in residence at the Gorilla Foundation, Woodside, California, used nontoxic paints to depict a plenitude of multicolored flowers in pastel colors. According to the Gorilla Foundation, the word *stink* in the title of this painting, supplied by Michael, refers to the gorilla's word for "flower," referencing its intense smell. Michael, now deceased, produced many paintings, like his companion Koko, and both titled their paintings in their own words, which were then interpreted by their caretakers. Photo courtesy of Dr. Ronald Cohn/the Gorilla Foundation/Koko.org.

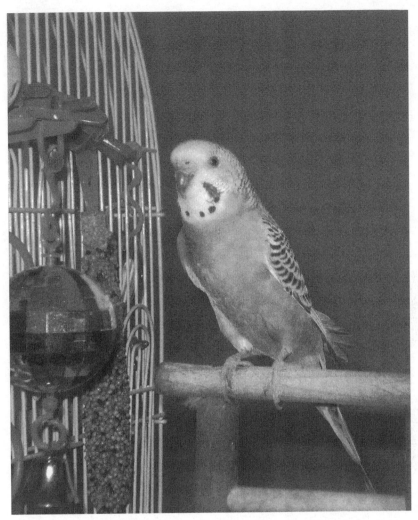

26. Photo of Blueboy the parakeet in the author's living room, 2011. Photo by Michele Hanks, used with permission.

TEN

Conclusion: "Every Bird a 'Blueboy'" and Why It Matters for "Animal Studies"

In September of 2002, a small blue parakeet was spotted walking down a sidewalk in Iowa City, Iowa. This is all I know about Blueboy and his life before I adopted him from the Iowa City Animal Care and Adoption Center. Parakeets don't belong on sidewalks, so someone had scooped him up and taken him into the shelter. I never thought about how he had come to be ambling down the sidewalk when I adopted him. Now I realize that his wings must have been clipped, or he would have flown away. What had he been doing? Foraging for insects? Going for a stroll? And how had he gotten there in the first place? Had he succumbed to the allure of an open window in the crisp fall weather? Perhaps his owner had to move and, unable to keep him, let him loose, figuring that birds can live on their own, since so many millions do. But Iowa City isn't San Francisco or Adelaide, and there was no wild flock of parakeets there to welcome him in. Blueboy, however he ended up on that sidewalk, was on his own, and with clipped wings was easy prey for the first hungry hawk or cat that spied him. On that day, in that city, and in the gentle hands of whoever cupped their fingers around him, he was lucky and he lived.

A dozen years have passed since that day, and I have

gotten to know Blueboy well, or as well as possible across the species barrier and within the limitations of the human-centric home that he shares with me—our mutual habitat. Don't worry, this concluding chapter won't simply be an essay about "me and my pet" and our "special" bond. Those narratives, however, are full of meaningful evidence of intertwined lives, even when dismissed as nonscientific, sentimental, and ("excessively"?) feminized, a dismissal of both animals and women. As valuable as such biographical accounts can be in helping us understand how people live with animals, my goal here is less autobiographical. Blueboy has trained me as a scholar to look carefully at copresence, acknowledging the co-constitution of intertwined lives, while acknowledging the conditions of possibility and the power dynamics that underlie that mingling.

Without the "pet industry," that capitalistic selling of animals to live with humans as pets, Blueboy wouldn't have come to live with me. His very existence, probably the result of breeding for the parakeet (mini-parrot) pet industry, exemplifies the psychological and material stakes of a socially acceptable, culturally and geographically specific practice of "keeping" birds. This practice, like other human-animal interfaces, has a social, political, and economic history—what I referred to in preceding chapters as "the conditions of possibility"—that we must excavate.

Pet keeping, like other modes of human-animal interaction, is not only a social fact with a social history, as Kathleen Grier[1] reminds us, but a political act, with an ethics and ties to epistemologies. These dominant epistemologies, at least as they are played out in the United States, reach back hundreds of years through (predominantly) European-derived frameworks that tether intellectual and religious histories to notions of "the great chain of being," which posited a set of hierarchical relations among humans (above) and animals (below) in conjunction with a conception of a "god," or some other ultimate arbiter and exemplar of an ideal.[2]

I know all that, and recognize the tensions in my "keeping" Blueboy as my "pet."[3] I assuage my feelings of domination by telling myself that Blueboy was already (bred and sold as) a pet, and so my particular relation with him (as his "adopter" from an animal shelter) does not in itself perpetuate this industry of breeding for profit and for human-crafted notions of "companionship." Nonetheless, recognizing the *longue durée* of this history of human relations with animals, there we are with Blueboy walking down the sidewalk. What to do? Adopting him, I tell myself, simply saves a life.

But of course, this isn't the whole story. It never is. Previously, during an extended time abroad, I succumbed to the desire to share my home with nonhuman animals and *purchased* two parakeets (whom I named ZsuZsa and Mister Miklos) in a Budapest pet store. Returning to the States in 2001, after rehoming the Hungarian parakeets with Magyar friends, I knew I wanted more birds in my life. And after eighteen years with me, my cat, Mocha, had died, and the house felt empty with only human inhabitants. So, I purchased two pet store parakeets, ignorant at the time of the transnational industry and the breeders' world that supplies them. Despite our best efforts at care, they did not live long. When Blueboy joined us, he was to be a companion to the remaining yellow-green parakeet, Pesto, whose companion, Sydney, had just died. Unfortunately, Pesto lived only a few more months, but Blueboy has flourished.[4]

Blueboy is still in our home, having far outlived his predecessors.[5] He has been with me for almost a dozen years now, and looks at me as I write this, reminding me that part of my ethical obligation as a scholar is to better understand the forces and possibilities that have brought our lives to this moment of (literal) mutual regard.[6]

But Blueboy is not the first bird to spend many years in my household. Looking back, I see that my cohabitation with "rescued" birds was something I learned and learned to value in childhood from my mother, Dorothy Desmond.

One day while I was in junior high school, my mother discovered a young robin that had fallen from his nest. She cradled the little bird protectively in her hands and brought him into our home. Now I wonder if he was a fledgling learning to fly and not an orphan at all, but at the time, such distinctions were little known by anyone other than specialists. In suburban Washington, DC, avian knowledge was nil, and in my mother's eyes, this little bird needed help. She brought him in from our backyard, an expanse of post–World War II new-home turf and trees, and placed him gently in a tall, turquoise plastic wastebasket upon a padding of paper towels. The container's steep sides meant he couldn't hop out, and covered with a towel, provided some privacy and gave this lone fluffy-feathered being some sense of safety. To this day, the sight of a particular shade of turquoise transports me, like Proust with his madeleines, back to that first encounter with the baby bird, and reminds me how emotionally charged the experience was of bringing a "wild" being into our home.

For days, my mother fed this bird, and I vividly remember her pretending to be the parent bird, swooping down from above with a bit of fatty hamburger on a toothpick, urging the baby bird to eat every two hours. She made this up as she went along, as there were no "how to" videos on YouTube in those days, and no avian or wildlife veterinarians a phone call away. Those information-sharing technologies and medical specialties had yet to be developed when my mother was in her early forties.

But the bird thrived, living with us for several years, and I named him "Robbie." This small being became a big presence in our household, and to some extent, we modified our routines and our household space to accommodate what we imagined to be his needs. There was no question of releasing him back into the "wild" of suburbia. He had bonded with my mother and spent hours on her shoulder, nestled in the strands of her light-brown hair as she read at the kitchen table. He never developed the same physical closeness with me, but he was comfortable enough with my presence to get on my hand and allow me to observe him closely. In my teens, I drew him often, obsessed with the complex patterns of his feathering, the dark and light and in-between of his throat feathers as they shifted from grays to russet, the "robin red breast" of poems. With pen and ink, I inscribed each feather, trying to capture their different shapes and textures, and Robbie's dark-eyed gaze. He was my privileged "window onto the wild." Robbie, I see now, must have been a male, for his bright plumage was striking.

In this bispecies household, Robbie had his own space, let's call it a "bedroom," a place where he slept. This was a tall, gold-colored cage with a rounded top, placed in one of the bathrooms that we then gave over to him. Its door was usually open, so the notion of "cage" as imprisonment was replaced with a more benign sense of "home"—although we, not Robbie, controlled the door, access and egress. Looking back now, I see that we adjusted our physical space to accommodate what we understood to be Robbie's needs, even giving up one of the two bathrooms in the house for his use. That my father, Alton Desmond, was a biologist and had considered being a veterinarian probably played a role in these arrangements. He too endorsed this yielding of domestic space to Robbie, a generosity partly dependent on our class status, which had provided a bathroom to spare.

In addition, we adjusted our *attentiveness* to the domestic space, for in my house, because of Robbie's presence, we couldn't simply bound down the stairs or leave the back door open. Robbie flew freely (no vet for wing clipping in those days) from his home (cage) on the upper floor of our split-level brick house to the lower floor, just a few steps down, where we were likely to be in the living room. Sometimes, instead of flying, Robbie walked, and one of my most indelible memories is of him hopping down the shiny blond wooden surface of the bedroom hallway, coming to see us. (You can see now the connection I make to Blueboy walking down a sidewalk.)

Further evidence of Robbie's integration into our lives appears in old photographs. One day, after my mother's death, as I went through her photos, I found one of myself on the night of my senior prom. As silly as that bright-hued Kodachrome print now seems, I couldn't help pausing over it. There I am, in a long, silky white dress with a pink, empire-waist bodice and a green velveteen ribbon accentuating it, posing next to my escort, David, in front of the fireplace before leaving for the dance. Looking closely, I notice that we aren't alone: off to the side, at the far edge of the frame, perched on top of a brass fireplace poker that leaned against the wall, is Robbie.

This wasn't a staged photo, a sort of "here we are with the BIRD" selfie, posted on Facebook. This posed moment, captured by my father, no doubt, with the Kodak Instamatic of the late 1960s, was meant to document a rite of passage, the heterosexual dating ritual of the high school prom. Robbie was there incidentally, not as the subject of the photo. But his presence tells us that if the photo hadn't been staged to feature Robbie, it was also not posed to avoid recording his presence. There, as a part of daily life in our household, was Robbie, even on prom night.

Remember—Robbie was not a dog. Family photos with the dog posing alongside humans are a genre unto themselves. But Robbie was not "posed" with us as part of this picture; he was simply posing with us of his own accord, to the extent that he had the freedom to choose where to be in the home.

Robbie's presence in that prom-night photo was a moment of bi-species negotiation that echoes today in my relationship with Blueboy. In both cases, there's no doubt about which species holds most of the cards. Both birds, one bred for the pet trade, the other born "wild," were "saved" and brought into my households. I am aware of the ironies and the acts of commodification that crosscut these stories. I don't intend to describe a sort of utopian parity, with the avian and human cohabitants having "equal say" in the spatial usage and activity list of the domestic life in my home. But within these limitations, something has happened as a result of these experiences that has changed the way I move through the world, and it is to that that I now turn.

Over the past dozen years, Blueboy and I have developed a rhythm of activities that constitute the bulk of our interactions in the daily dance of our lives together. First, when I adopted him, we had to find him a cage. Remembering my experience with Robbie, I thought of a cage as a safe haven for him, a place into which we (the humans in the house) could enclose him—for his own safety, as we understood that from our point of view. For instance, when visitors came to the house, we could make sure that their interest in Blueboy did not extend to trying to handle him. He could be safely shut away from their fingers in his cage in the living room, but still see what was going on in the household. Not being avian, I have no exact understanding of how Blueboy interpreted these events. I have only my observations, and interpretations of those observations, of Blueboy's sounds and movements, which seemed to telegraph his combination of interest in and comfort with this arrangement. Some visitors he came out to greet, others he shied away from, hiding away in the towel-covered privacy of his refuge.

Within our multispecies household (also in residence: a terrier and, in their own miniroom in another part of the house, two rabbits), we placed Blueboy's cage in the living room, usually with the door propped open. It had, as its "patio," a colorful wooden playground purchased with some hesitation from the pet store. Was this "playground" just commodified hype? Thirty dollars for a clutch of swings, perches, and ladders on a base? As it turned out, the "playground" was one of our best purchases ever, and Blueboy claimed the patio of his cage area as his own, climbing, eating, bathing, and tossing plastic balls from their baskets in his arena.

The playground became a site of interactive play—humans placing plastic balls on ladders or posts, and Blueboy tossing them halfway across the living room, eyeing us then for a timely pickup and replacement to start the basketball game all over again. Soon the patio became more extended, with a second-level platform for wicker baskets that invited taking apart, as our avian friend became his own Derrida in this academic household, actively practicing "deconstruction" on a daily basis.

As Blueboy elicited actions from us ("training" us) to provide activities for him or engage in games with him, like the plastic ball toss and retrieval, we also tried to interpret his needs, which led to the development of the "going up to bed" scenario that ended each day. Not wanting to leave Blueboy alone at night, we continued to integrate him into what we came to see as the life of his (multispecies) "flock." When we went upstairs to sleep, so did Blueboy, just as in the "wild," birds we had read about might flock to the top of a tree for safety at night. We carried his cage up the stairs to its nighttime location on a side table and "tucked him in" by covering his cage and turning out the lights.

Yes, we were making this up from shards of information, but the bottom line is that our attempts were framed as efforts to understand how we might modulate our behavior (up to a point) to best meet his needs. We can't possibly know, but we can reasonably assume, that Blueboy in turn has accommodated our behaviors as well. Small, quiet chirps seem to say "good night," to check in that we are there too in the darkened bedroom, and of course we reply in our fashion, before we all sink into sleep.

So, what is the point of all this tale telling and narrating of the individual human-animal relations from my past? I don't offer these stories as ideals or as models. What they can do, instead, is remind us that our relations with animals (even as extensively mediated as they often are) are very highly individuated, and from that individuation we can take our cue.

As it turns out, so much of the discussion in this book has focused on how some humans, within the constructs of contemporary social and political frameworks, ideologies, and social conventions, find ways to relate to animals that highlight their (the animals') individuation and their subjectivities. We acknowledge that this notion of "subjectivity" is rendered both in relation to human philosophies, cosmologies, and political frameworks and to the extent that our limited understandings of animals can prevail. This isn't necessarily a limitation but rather a condition of possibility.

I realized this in a realm of my daily, not scholarly, life when I began to see every bird as a "Blueboy." Parakeets, I learned, are part of the parrot family, accorded human valuation for a type of exemplary cognition that we can recognize as such and that we value. Parrots can understand, it seems, numeracy, some human speech, categorical differentiation, and so on.[7] The shorthand for this anthropocentric evaluation of avian life in public discourse is that parrots "are smart."

Since parakeets are the smallest members of the phylogenic parrot "family," we can assume that they too exhibit cognitive abilities that we as humans have come to value and to denote as "intelligence." Blueboy is thus perhaps exceptional in such cognitive abilities in comparison with some other bird species less highly regarded by humans, such as the common house sparrow. For me, however, a transformation has occurred. Now, every time I see a sparrow lined up with a dozen of his or her mates on a telephone wire, I see Blueboy—with his head tilted to get a better look at me, with his ball-tossing invitations to play, with his range of vocalizations tailored to the recipient.

Whereas before I saw a single representative of a type of bird, now I see an individual with a life, with a perceiving eye eyeing me back, and with a home to go to, an intimate avian community to engage. A singular being who just might, in fact, be as interactive, as "smart," as playful, and, yes, as "articulate" or expressive in his or her vocalizations as Blueboy. Fine so far as individual narrations go, but what difference does this make on a broader scale?

If every bird is a "Blueboy," he or she might notice me, might remember me (there is new compelling research on crows' ability to discriminate among and remember different human faces),[8] and might even be part of an out-of-sight social grouping of avians that communicate in sounds and postures I am not privy to. Every bird goes "home" at night to the top of a flocking tree, and every bird communicates with others of its kind and even across avian species to other types of birds and, perhaps, beyond to nonavian species. Every bird is a "Blueboy," an individual being in cohabitaton with others. Consider our easily dismissive regard for masses of birds, for flocks, for the hundred on the wire as dusk approaches, each equidistant from the other. With the "Blueboy" perspective, these masses become individuals in relation to one other and to nonavians.

Looking even at the ubiquitous, brown, drab, and oh-so-everyday sparrow in my backyard, flitting from fencepost to tree, I am reminded that while parrots, and even their smallest rendition, parakeets, have exceptional cognitive powers, every avian has more abilities and relations than I can be aware of.[9] Every bird is not simply "a bird" but rather "that bird," and in that shift from indefinite article to demonstrative pronoun lies the map forward for reconceptualizing our relations with nonhuman animals—from the general to the specific, from the generic to the unique, from the type to the individual among that type, and from "bird" to "Blueboy."

For me now, every bird I see—a hawk hovering over a cornfield in Illinois, a magpie on the grass in Honolulu, a hooded crow foraging for tourist leftovers in Rome—is a potential "Blueboy," a being with a complex set of social, cognitive, and material needs and practices that I, that we, can barely assume to understand. The individuation accorded the "pet" is conceptually extended to the "wild," the "feral," and the "commodified," not only in the abstract but also with the (political) force of trained imagination. There is a before and an after of a particular bird's momentary encounter on the lawn with me, a feathered life history unfolding in time, unbeknownst to me, and with that, a set of relationships, an avian subjectivity.

A Bird's-Eye View of Derrida's Cat

For some readers, this engagement with my pet as a spur to wider theorizing might recall Jacques Derrida's now-famous nude encounter with his cat (it was Derrida who was nude—the cat was not and never could be). As I allude to above, Derrida does make an appearance in this context but not in the ways we might assume, given his centrality to so many discussions of how "animal studies" might develop in the humanities. Derridean deconstruction in my household does not have as its primary referent literary texts with their complex oscillations of referents and their unstated opposites jostling for prominence in the polysemy of language. Rather, in our academic home's parlance, "deconstruction" refers, with a knowing wink, to Blueboy's tearing apart of willow baskets into their component materials, their repurposing from human artifact to avian play.

I don't know what Derrida might have made of our mobilizing of his term in this way, but its playful reorientation might have appealed to him, especially since the identity of a basket depends on its enclosure of a void, which, if filled, obviates the identity of the item—rendering it a container of opposites, as it were. The primary shift here, though, is in the identity of the "deconstructionist"—an avian fellow on the scene.

So nonplussed was Derrida at seeing his cat seeing him naked in his bathroom—his momentary experience of being the object of another (species') gaze, that he had to include the moment in his exceptionally well-cited essay translated into English under the title "The Animal That Therefore I Am (More to Follow)," which has generated significant discussion among animal studies scholars. Should he feel "shame" at his own male nakedness, he wondered, as he stepped out of the shower into his cat's ophthalmic purview, taking us with that word all the way back to the Garden of Eden and inviting us to ponder the ascription of human-generated categories to a nonhuman world.

A different set of questions can surely be generated: how, we might ask, could this moment of mutual regard have been news? While his cat had always looked at him, only late in life was Derrida able to see himself as the object of her vision or to understand that exchange of glances as theoretically significant. What were the conditions of possibility (epistemologically? socially?) that so delayed Derrida's noticing, and taking as worthy of intellectual speculation, that his cat too was a subject, capable of generating "the gaze"? Derrida's careful tracing of western European philosophies engaging the role of "otherness" in constructing an "I" or "we" provides his answer to this question. His gaze turns from the cat, and the cat's looking at him, back to his own looking toward the intellectual work of his predecessors in the continental European philosophical tradition. Here he is highly critical of a pantheon of male philosophers (Descartes, Kant, Heidegger, Lacan, and Levinas), saying that "their discourses are sound and profound, but everything in them goes on as if they themselves had never been looked at, and especially not naked, by an animal that addressed them."[10] Putting aside for a moment that conjured image of a gaggle of naked philosophers, we find a genealogical rendering that even in its critique pushes the moment of actual locked gazes to the side. As Louise Westling argues, scholars engaging with Derrida must take steps he calls for but does not take himself, returning "serious consideration of other animals as sentient agents who share our world and much of our biological lineage."[11]

To be clear, Derrida himself emphasizes that he is writing about a *real* specific cat, not the intellectual, or imaginary, or figurative, or literary *idea* of a cat. "The cat I am talking about is a real cat, truly, believe me, a *little cat*."[12] That he must protest so strongly to his readers ("truly, believe me"), assuring them that he is thinking with and through this *actual* moment of cross-species encounter, signals that this material specificity is not the usual stuff of his strand of philosophy. He goes on to underline the "unsubstitutable singularity" of his (this) cat, its individuated subjectivity.[13]

We can feel Derrida straining here to find a way to theorize this subjectivity yet being limited by his philosophical traditions and their emphasis on language, including, as he notes, the important role that the attribution of linguistic abilities to humans and the denial of such to animals has played in framing ideas of species difference. Yet this type of cross-species, feline-to-human, subject-recognizing, individuated encounter (and the belief systems that support it) is a phenomenon well known outside academic philosophy and embedded in the practices of daily life. It has always been acknowledged, for example, by "crazy cat ladies." Of course, "crazy cat ladies" lack the gendered and credentialed respect that "philosophy" and "philosophers" generate. Yet, unpacking the three words *crazy cat ladies* yields references to cognitive clarity/impairment, felinophilia, and gendered (older, aging) positioning. If the cat is already feminized in relation to the canine companion, then felinophilia by older females is easy to push over the edge into excessive attachment, that is, "craziness," a thrice-feminized refusal of knowledge. I come back to this gendering in a moment.

Donna Haraway is right on target when she notes that at the end of the day, and at the end of his long essay, Derrida, for all his obviously deeply engaged ruminations on animals,[14] "knows nothing *more from, about, and with* the cat at the end of the morning than he knew at the beginning. . . . Actually to respond to the cat's response to his presence would have required his . . . asking what this cat on this morning cared about, what these bodily postures and visual entanglements might mean and might invite, as well as reading what people who study cats have to say and delving into the developing knowledges of both cat–cat and cat–human behavioral semiotics when species meet."[15]

"Thinking perhaps begins there," writes Derrida at the end of his essay, having considered his "shame" at being seen naked by his cat. But for Haraway, the true shame lies elsewhere: "Even if the cat did not become a symbol of all cats, the naked man's shame quickly became a figure for the shame of philosophy before all of the animals."[16] Other scholars are more generous in their assessments of this work. Kari Weil suggests that while the cat fades away, Derrida can still lead us to what Matthew Calarco identified as a "proto-ethics" that focuses more on pushing against the pernicious legacies of speciesism which affect not only animals but also human hierarchies. Weil writes, "Letting animals be in their being, outside our projects and outside our will for knowledge, would, Derrida seems to suggest, constitute the ultimate ethical stance."[17] And yet, I would argue, such an "outside" does not lead us toward the "contact zone" of interactive and mutually constitutive embodied relations, a crucial arena from my point of view. Ethics are articulated in enactment, and the production of knowledge depends on engagement.

Struggling with the complex questions of how we can approach such overlapping multispecies worldings, yet arguing for the scholarly importance and urgency of doing so, some of us come to other answers. Haraway, for example, urges us toward "respect" for other species: "Consider 'regard' and 'respect' a bit longer," she writes. This is not to be a simple notion of politeness but a complex undertaking. "I am drawn," she says, "by the tones of this kind of active looking at / regard (both as verb, *respecere*, and as *respectus*) . . . to have regard for, to see differently, to esteem, to look back, to hold in regard, to hold in seeing, to be touched by another's regard, to heed, to take care of. This kind of regard aims to release and be released in oxymoronic, neces-sary, autonomy-in-relation."[18]

This respect, the basis for an ethical interrelationality, seems miss-ing in another important theoretical text widely cited among animal studies scholars, which Haraway rejects for what she sees as its myopic misogyny. French theorists Gilles Deleuze and Félix Guattari's work in *A Thousand Plateaus* posits linkages with the exceptional as the only way to go: "wherever there is multiplicity, you will find also an excep-tional individual, and with it an alliance must be made in order to become-animal."[19] This search for the worthy individual abjures, and abjects, the quotidian, the female, the domestic, despite its emphasis on unseating the Oedipal. Haraway, while appreciative of much of their previous work, castigates Deleuze and Guattari for their "disdain for the daily, the ordinary, the affectional rather than the sublime,"[20] as they express "horror at the 'individuated animals, family pets, sen-timental Oedipal animals each with its own petty history."[21] Deleuze and Guattari's rejection of the domestic, here figured as the feminine and the feminized, as the emotive ordinary, is chilling in its dismissal. If Haraway's reading is correct, in this particular realm their writings about humans and animals in relation could be regarded as not only ethically troubling but intellectually impoverished.[22] "Thinking per-haps begins" elsewhere.

Contra Deleuze and Guattari, we can find innovative, not simply reductive, and certainly not disdainful, enactments of multispecies, mutually co-constituted "worldings" in the quotidian experiences, and enactments, of daily life. Such practices, like those I have examined in this book, necessarily embrace and articulate the messy push me–pull you two-step[23] of orienteering through the matrices of human-animal relationality. They are worthy of a much greater portion of our effort than they currently receive.

Beyond reporting "how things are or were," beyond a sociological sampling of attitudes toward animals or a few interviews, we need to excavate the historical, social, and epistemological underpinnings of community-specific ways of knowing, of valuing, and of articulating and enacting human relations with nonhuman animals. Archival, ethnographic, discursive, and textual analyses all have a part to play here, in conjunction with institutional, ideological, and material evalu-ations. But this work, even when looking backward, necessarily draws our eyes to a farther horizon—to the future, a time when change is possible. Knowledge, as necessarily profoundly political, is produced in, or adopted for, the service of something and someone. As animal studies scholars coming from multiple disciplinary locations, we can embrace this fact and ask, in whose service, and how do we labor?

Performative Futures

My concerns here are with social practice and social phenomena that unite the human and nonhuman animal realms. Like Haraway, I acknowledge that those working "in the field," literally and figuratively, like primatologist Barbara Smuts, can offer special insights. So too can those who work on issues of companion-animal relations with their humans, as Haraway's own analyses drawing on her canine-centric agility world can do. These works offer us new windows onto the messy intersection between enactment and conception, between practice and law, philosophy, and ideologies. But I would cast a much wider net here and take us beyond laboratories, rain forests, and agility meets.

I take as a given that these realms (and so many others), these relations (and so many others), and the significance we ascribe to them have historically specific, incredibly complex, and at times contradictory structures of meaning that shape how we live and interact with nonhuman animals, how we talk about it, how we represent it, how we inject those relations into our legal systems, our TV shows, our burial practices, and our sciences. Representational practices are an integral part of these phenomena, but in themselves they don't constitute the focal point of my analysis; rather, they construct the productive context of it. I am more interested in what people do, how they interpret what they do, and the conditions—ideological, material, political, cultural, and economical—of generating such interpretations: a performative approach to relationality.

In the chapters of this book, I have been drawn to especially pungent realms of these relations—the world of museums, of cemeteries, of writing the public record through obituaries, of mourning and not mourning; of the categories that such practices articulate and challenge; and finally, of a philanthropic and investment art market that yet again articulates a relationship of value, understanding, and commodity circulation exceeding any one-dimensional understanding of human-animal relations. Sometimes these realms erupt into wider public discourse ("Chimp Paintings Sell for $33,000!"; "Man Buried with Dog!"), sometimes they proceed in a quieter semipublic sphere, revealed in the creative, improvisatory, decorative practices at pet cemeteries or the display of a painting done by an elephant on our living-room wall. At still other times, they give rise to whole communities of practitioners (the World Taxidermy Championships) or invite massive publics (von Hagens's Body Worlds shows, the most popular museum exhibits of all time).

In each realm—taxidermy, cemeteries, museum exhibits, ape painting—the practice is seen as somewhat marginal, unusual, or unimportant compared to the driving political concerns of the day, and hence exploits the freedom of the marginalized to explore unscripted relations and to offer improvisatory and creative responses. Sometimes these responses reinscribe long-dominant hierarchies and tired ideologies of knowledge, as in von Hagens's Animal Inside Out exhibit. But sometimes they point to new nodes of knowledge, new assertions of value and desire, like the emergent human and nonhuman burial practices I analyzed in chapter 6. We should take them—the stuff of the quotidian enactment, the feminized, the marginalized—seriously, not only as focal points for analysis but also as starting points for theorizations. Derrida's cat will thank us.

Excavating the Past and Present to Imagine New Futures

The purpose of this work, and so much work in the humanities and social sciences, is to help us understand how our daily lives—actions, expenditures, behaviors—articulate a complex web of beliefs, economic possibilities, philosophies, and social conventions within our communities during specific historical moments. What are we doing? Why? What effects does it have? On whom? Above all, is this the way we wish the world to be?

Humanities and humanistic social inquiry strive for an understanding of the conditions of possibility and of probability; they are intellectual practices of explication and excavation. They dig deep to reveal the conditions of possibility of a belief, of its (Gramscian) position as hegemonic ideology (that set of beliefs so entrenched as to appear invisible, or as "just the way things are" or "the way things should be"). They strive to shine a light on what we do and to hold it up to analysis, to ask: Why this? Why now? (Or, why then?) Who cares?

And above all, at least implicitly, they ask us to imagine differently. They ask: is this state of affairs, or convention, or socially sanctioned practice what we wish our lives and the lives of others, ultimately, to be? In this way, the humanities are always future oriented even when examining the past.

Few of us have the opportunity to build a work life around the process of bringing such presumptions (philosophies, ideologies, conventional "wisdom") to light, to stopping its productive power for a moment to say—look at this in action, look at the process! This is the privilege and obligation of scholarly investigation.

In this book, I have focused on several arenas of social practice that arrested my attention. In each case the practice under investigation, whether of the killing and stuffing of a taxidermied fawn for public display or the purchasing of a painting by a gorilla, has struck me as "odd." It has elicited the ultimate query—what is going on here? (What is going on here that this seems "normal" or "good" or that it seems "true" or "appropriate" to a group of people?) What are the conditions of possibility that yield that practice (that is, what is the institutional framework of beliefs and organizations that facilitates it)? What difference does it make, and to whom?

Cemeteries are a case in point. When the dead being is a nonhuman animal, the question of burial becomes just that, a question. How do we dispose of the body? What do we do? With human dead, there is always a pregiven answer to that question, for every community encodes a set of beliefs about the relations of the living to the dead and the practices that are deemed "appropriate" to bring to successful conclusion that now-ended life. There are variances in abundance, according to religion, geography, historical era, and even historical circumstance . . . how do we bury the dead of an unimaginable natural or human-made catastrophe, like a tsunami that kills a hundred thousand people? But whether or not conventions are followed or are adequate for addressing the challenge of unimaginable catastrophe, such conventions exist within a framework of social validation.

For animal deaths grieved by humans, there are no such widely acknowledged conventions to be followed or contravened. Creative adaptation and critical innovation must take place, and they offer us, as scholars, a window onto the politics of remaking meaning in human-animal relations.

By taking as the object of my investigations a range of emergent or newly visible practices, from taxidermy to cemetery design, roadkill, obituaries, museum exhibits, and a transnational art market for works by nonhuman animals, I have striven to articulate a set of arenas wherein human and nonhuman animals engage with intimacy, stretch convention, and at times challenge dominant ideologies in the communities in which such practices are embedded. I have focused largely on the nonverbal, visual, and embodied realm, except when the issue of unique "human-language-enabled" and "bicultural" apes and their artistic productions comes into play; but even then the link between physical doing, being, and saying remains paramount.

Embodiment, kinesthetic action, and physical materiality have anchored my investigations. This capacious framework has allowed me to search out connections, contradictions, and productive frictions between realms otherwise seen as unrelated: museum displays of dead animal bodies, cemetery burials of animals and improvisatory mourning practices, and the transmutation of items literally marked by animal bodies, in paint and imprint, into a human art market. I see each of these arenas as a specific type of performative practice, different from textual productions in that they require, and acknowledge, the physical copresence of human and nonhuman animals engaged in doing.

My research seeks to uncover, like a surgeon with a scalpel, the deeply embedded nodes of meaning making that render something possible, probable, or even desirable to and for specific groups of people. The ultimate goal of this type of work, and my specific pursuit of it in embodied, kinesthetic, and largely nonverbal realms, is not simply to reveal the philosophical, ideological, and political workings of a sphere of daily life. The ultimate goal is to provide that rendering, that interpretation, that will help us ask one crucial question: is this as we wish it to be?

Shouldn't our ultimate goal—whether we investigate the animal trials of the Middle Ages, or the production methods of US hog farms, or the textual antecedents of the popular film *Babe*, or the contemporary shifts in Chinese cuisine toward a more animal-meat-centric cooking—be to improve, by offering a clarified understanding of, the intertwined lives of human and nonhuman animals? In the last forty years or so, as the perspectival nature of knowledge production has become a more widely accepted concept in the US academy and elsewhere, we have come to realize that our interpretations are not only always already produced "from somewhere" but that they are also always already enmeshed in webs of social and political practice and valuation from which scholarly investigation is in no way separate. As scholars of animals and human-animal relations, we can not only embrace this enmeshed status but also activate it for change.

So, does it matter that someone pays two hundred dollars to buy a print of a painting by Koko the gorilla and then puts it on the wall? Well, it matters to the buyer, who most probably embraces the notion that Koko is an individual acting on her world, that is, a subject in the philosophical sense—the author of this artwork. But this action takes place in a wider discursive frame. When we consider the larger question of "ensubjectification" (which I have defined as the granting of subjectivity to an individual or category of beings), we see that it underlies numerous realms of belief. These realms shape, enable, or constrain how we produce relationships in individual, community, financial, and cross-species realms.

"Subjectivity"—as the category of being implying individuation, having a life and a life history of social value and an ability to act on the world and to exist in relationship—is a designation that is given in some instances (of historical, philosophical, and legally framed belief) to some beings, under some conditions, with some effects. Obversely, it is a designation withheld from others, or categories of others, also with effects. As such, it emerges as a key node of belief and action in our relations with animals. Giorgio Agamben's distinction between "zoe" as "bare life," which is easily killable, and "bios," or life with a biography and political purchase, is relevant here.[24] But other theorists are also working to redefine this boundary, and to do so on the basis of observations of everyday interspecies interactions.

The innovative work of sociologist Leslie Irvine is a case in point here.[25] Like other ethnographers, Irvine draws on intensive immersion in particular settings as the basis for her theorizations, which she then tests in relation to her discipline's conventions. Using a symbolic interactionist frame, she explores the possibilities for articulating subjectivity, and its cross-species recognition, by focusing not on what most animals lack (a language understandable by humans and recognizable by human standards) but on what animals, like preverbal human infants, have: complex abilities to communicate pleasure, displeasure, desire, and connection and agency through nonverbal signifying systems—movement, sound, touch, relational placement in space, and so on.

Irvine argues persuasively, on the basis of extensive fieldwork in animal shelters, that at least some nonhuman animals have the same core competencies that her discipline of sociology specifies as necessary for demonstrating subjectivity. These include a sense of agency, of acting on the world, of self-coherence, of being a self in relation to other selves, of affectivity (that is, having qualitatively patterned feelings and the ability to communicate them), and finally, of self-history: a notion of a life experience that carries over from one day to the next and enables memory to shape current behavior.[26]

By freeing ourselves from the limiting framework of verbal communication as a prerequisite for articulating a "self," she argues, we are much better positioned not only to ascertain a sense of subjectivity in other species besides our own but also to grasp what I would term the "performative dimensions" of mutually constitutive cross-species crafting of intersubjectivity across species lines. Irvine calls for making the nonverbal, visual, embodied, and kinesthetic realms of life more central to our investigations, as I have tried to do throughout this book.

The greater our collective capacity for granting subjectivity to others (other people, other nonhuman beings), the more possible is the transformation of future relations. If we seek to develop this capacity, if we decide that for us, the current set of relations is lacking, that it is in need of change, then the productive articulation of nonhuman animals' subjectivity, our casting animals as subjects in our philosophical and political formations, is a crucial place to start. "Every bird a 'Blueboy'" is my shorthand for this process.

As my case studies have shown, that start can take place anywhere . . . in a museum exhibit, in the newspaper, at the zoo, or even on eBay. Wherever it is for you, my readers, critics, and interlocutors, I hope these studies will urge you to start or continue that enlarging process, so that each "it" ultimately becomes a "who," with all the repercussions that such a shift requires.

Notes

1. Erica Fudge, *Animal* (London: Reaktion Books, 2002), and Hal Herzog, *Some We Love, Some We Hate, Some We Eat: Why It's So Hard to Think Straight about Animals* (New York: Harper Perennial, reprint edition, 2011).

2. I recognize that the notion of what is "better" is part of the debates surrounding human interactions with animals, and that animal scientists, cultural studies scholars, and the lay public may have radically different views of what "better" constitutes. Still, a progressive goal of changing what exists today to achieve an improved multispecies tomorrow is part of the legacy of animal studies, just as earlier poststructural waves not only strove to articulate visions of how the world works in complex ways, uniting representation, history, and politics, but also assumed that intellectual work that revealed those workings could lead to social change.

3. As Donna Haraway and others have pointed out, the term *nonhuman* sets up the human as the norm. We might try experimenting otherwise: *nonanimal humans*? In the meantime, the use of the term, when held in conceptual abeyance, reminds us of the human-centric force field of linguistics. See S. Eben Kirksey and Stefan Helmreich, "The Emergence of Multispecies Ethnography," *Cultural Anthropology* 25 (2010): 555.

4. The phrase "critical animal studies" has been adopted by a subset of researchers who explicitly link their work to philosophies of animal liberation. Because of this, it isn't used widely among researchers developing "animal studies" in the academy.

5. The term *social formations*, although used differently in various disciplines, means for me here the always-in-flux ways that communities, from neighborhood to nation, organize their modes of interaction; articulate shared or contested values, beliefs, and ideologies; articulate them through social and institutional structures; and regulate, or subject to criticism, the legacies of the past that shape the present.

6. My use of quotation marks here, and at times throughout the book, attempts to mark certain terms as "concept," not transparent referent.

7. Diana Taylor, *The Archive and the Repertoire: Performing Cultural Memory in the Americas* (Durham, NC: Duke University Press, 2003). In addition, I am interested in contemporary written and visual records, and in how they are embedded in public discourse through the media. Chapter 6, devoted to writing animal lives into history through the contemporary newspaper pet obituary form, exemplifies the latter. I then frame these written texts in a larger performative context of public mourning.

8. Among these initiatives, philosophical and literary works have gained special visibility in "animal studies." There are two possible reasons for this: first, the enormous power of English studies in the US academy, still ascendant although under duress, and second, the cultural capital that an engagement with Continental philosophy can provide to emergent scholarly conversations, in addition, of course, to the intellectual purchase it provides.

9. While it is impossible to map all the work involved, key authors in different disciplinary locations whose publications provide a good avenue into these debates include the following: Nigel Rothfels, Steve Baker, Anthony Calarco, Ralph Acampora, Linda Kalof, Margo DeMello, Susan McHugh, Gary Marvin, Erica Fudge, Randy Malamud, Ron Broglio, Giovanni Aloi, Paola Cavalieri and Peter Singer, Marc Bekoff, Cary Wolfe, Rebecca Cassidy, Molly Mullin, Sarah Franklin, Carol Adams, Tim Ingold, Donna Haraway, Gary Francione, Annie Potts, Jennifer Wolch and Jody Emel, Lori Gruen, Harriett Ritvo, Ken Shapiro, Kathy Rudy, Timothy Patchirat, Jennifer Ham and Matthew Senior, Holly Hughes and Una Chaudhuri, Claire Jean Kim, and many others. The names of additional authors appear in endnotes throughout this book.

10. Kari Weil is exceptionally eloquent and astute in tracing these intellectual and philosophical debts and their continuing influence today. The essays in her book, *Thinking Animals: Why Animal Studies Now?* (New York: Columbia University Press, 2012), are very effective in positioning the burgeoning academic work on animals in the trajectory of modernism, postmodernism, poststructuralism, and the "linguistic turn."

11. See, for example, Kari Weil, *Thinking Animals*; Linda Kalof, *Looking at Animals in Human History* (London: Reaktion Books, 2007); Linda Kalof and Amy Fitzgerald, eds., *The Animals Reader: Essential Classic and Contemporary Writings* (London: Berg, 2007); Arnold Arluke and Clinton Sanders,

Between the Species: Readings in Human-Animal Relations (Boston: Pearson Education, 2009); Margo DeMello, *Animals and Society: An Introduction to Human-Animal Studies* (New York: Columbia University Press, 2012); and Susan McHugh and Gary Marvin, *The Routledge Reader in Animal Studies* (London: Routledge, 2014). Herzog (*Some We Love*) and Barbara J. King (*Living with Animals: Why We Are Obsessed with the Furry, Scaly, Feathered Creatures Who Populate Our World* (New York: Doubleday, 2010) are both academics whose writings bring these larger issues to a wider than academic public. The bibliographies of the books noted above also provide a more in-depth view of developments in these conversations.

12. Claude Lévi-Strauss, *Totemism*, trans. Rodney Needham (Boston: Beacon Press, 1963).

13. For an example of new work in this vein, see Claire Jean Kim, *Dangerous Crossings: Race, Species, and Nature in a Multicultural Age* (New York: Cambridge University Press, 2015).

14. Aviva Rutkin, "Monkey Mathematicians Hint at Brain's Number Perception," *New Scientist*, April 21, 2014, accessed October 26, 2015, http://www.newscientist.com/article/dn25447-monkey-mathematicians. Rutkin describes the work of neurobiologist Margaret Livingstone at the Harvard University Medical School, reported in the *Proceedings of the National Academy of Sciences*. See also Katherine Harmon Courage, "Octopuses Gain Consciousness (according to Scientists' Declaration)," *Scientific American*, August 21, 2012, accessed October 26, 2015, http://blogs.scientificamerican.com/octopus-chronicles/2012/08/21/octopuses-gain-consciousness. This article references the inclusion of octopuses in the Cambridge Declaration on Consciousness, signed in July 2012 by a group of neuroscientists who met at Cambridge University in the United Kingdom. The declaration stressed that the absence of a neocortex does not prevent animals from experiencing affective states or exhibiting intentional behaviors.

15. Legal moves to have primates recognized as "nonhuman persons" are not only heating up in the courtroom but are also generating a lot of press, moving these issues into public discourse. The Nonhuman Rights Project, led by Steven M. Wise, filed writs of habeas corpus in New York in the winter of 2013 on behalf of four captive chimpanzees, including "Tommy." Although the lawsuits were dismissed, they may eventually make some legal headway and, in the meantime, bring the moral, ethical, and legal standing of primates into public discourse. See James Gorman, "Considering the Humanity of Nonhumans," *New York Times*, December 9, 2013, accessed October 26, 2015, http://www.nytimes.com/2013/12/10/science/considering-the-humanity-of-nonhumans.html. The lawsuit generated considerable additional reporting. In May 2013, the government of India's Ministry of Environment and Forests issued an order affecting all Indian states that banned captive dolphin amusement parks, citing the

cetaceans' high intelligence and emotional sensitivity. The order declared that "dolphins should be seen as 'non-human persons' and as such should have their own specific rights." Reported by Robert Krulwich, "Why Dolphins Make Us Nervous," National Public Radio blog, June 13, 2013, accessed October 26, 2015, http://www.npr.org/sections/krulwich/2013/06/13/191286344/why-dolphins-make-us-nervous.

16. Michigan State University currently offers the only graduate-level concentration in animal studies, offered as a supplement to the student's degree in her or his home department. The program is affiliated with the Department of Sociology, under the direction of Linda Kalof. New York University recently began developing a minor and funding a faculty line. Tufts University in Boston offers a master's degree in public policy with a focus on animals. Building for the future, the Social Science Research Council offered a competitive dissertation proposal development workshop in 2008 with a focus on animals, with codirectors Harriet Ritvo and Janet Brown at the helm. Individual faculty members at many institutions have developed new courses, with titles ranging from "Prospects for Sustainable Relations with Animals" to "Animals in Literature." A summer institute held at Wesleyan University, under the sponsorship of the nonprofit Society and Animals Institute and directed by Lori Gruen and Kari Weil, brings together a new cohort of postdoctoral fellows for several weeks every summer to develop new work. The *Chronicle for Higher Education*, the leading newspaper of academia, reported on the boom in animal studies scholarship and its growing institutionalization in a series of four articles in the October 23, 2009, issue of its weekly magazine, the *Chronicle Review*, with a cover feature titled "Confronting the Animal." Jennifer Howard's lead article, "Creature Consciousness," tracks the emergence of animal studies in the academy. A full-page close-up of a sheep's woolly face fronts the issue and serves notice that changes are afoot.

17. My book *Staging Tourism: Bodies on Display from Waikiki to Sea World* (Chicago: University of Chicago Press, 1999) compared the historical legacies and contemporary practices of cultural tourism with those focused on what I termed "animal tourism," the display of animals in zoos, ecological tourism sites, and marine mammal parks.

18. International Society of Anthrozoology annual conference, "The Social Lives of Animals: Human/Non-Human Cognition, Interactions, Relationships," held at Kent State University, Canton, Ohio, August 15–16, 2003.

19. While this caveat leads us toward reimagined conferences or collaborative research projects, virtual "gatherings" are already available. One mark of the growing instantiation of animal studies is the emergence of "readers," or textbooks providing introductions to key debates in the field. In recent years, we have seen several of these (see note 9). In addition to providing overviews of a field in formation, and to making those issues more widely available to students and nonspecialists, these books also make visible to

scholars something of the wider range of concerns and investigations in neighboring disciplines. They create virtual conferences, at least for the student and potentially for scholars as well, making easily accessible new avenues leading into subgroups such as geographers who work on the intersection of human and animal lives or literary scholars who query nineteenth-century novels like *Moby Dick* to understand the centrality of animals to human narrations.

A second virtual coming together that promotes this interdisciplinarity is the new phenomenon of "living books," or virtual edited collections that draw on already published material from multiple disciplines that is centered on a specific topic and then open them to commentary, creating evolving, "organic" books. See, for example, Erica Fudge and Claire Palmer, eds., *Veterinary Science: Animals, Humans and Health* (Open Humanities Press, 2012), accessed October 26, 2015 (ISBN: 978-1-60785-273-5), http://www.livingbooksaboutlife.org/books/ Veterinary_science. And although I do not concentrate specifically in this book on the potential for linkages with the visual and performing arts, this too is proving to be a particularly stimulating interface. See, for example, the UK online journal *Antennae: The Journal of Nature in Visual Culture*, and Holly Hughes and Una Chaudhuri, eds., *Animal Acts: Performing Species Today* (Ann Arbor: University of Michigan Press, 2014). Steve Baker's work on animals and contemporary art, *The Postmodern Animal* (London: Reaktion Books, 2000), is essential for these debates.

20. Joan W. Scott, "The Evidence of Experience," *Critical Inquiry* 17 (1991): 773–97.
21. Jacques Derrida, "The Animal That Therefore I Am (More to Follow)," in *The Animal That Therefore I Am*, ed. Marie-Louise Mallet, trans. David Wills (New York: Fordham University Press, 2008).
22. Jorge Luis Borges, *Other Inquisitions* (Austin: University of Texas Press, 1964), cited in DeMello, *Animals and Society*, 10.
23. Gene Tempest, "The Long Face of War: Horses and the Nature of Warfare in the French and British Armies on the Western Front" (PhD diss., Yale University, 2013); Alex Blanchette, "Conceiving Porkopolis: The Production of Life on the American 'Factory' Farm" (PhD diss., University of Chicago, 2013); Susan McHugh, *Animal Stories: Narrating across Species Lines* (Minneapolis: University of Minnesota Press, 2011); Kimberly Marra, "Riding, Scarring, Knowing: A Queerly Embodied Performance Historiography," *Theatre Journal* 64 (2012): 489–511.
24. Molly Mullin, "Mirrors and Windows: Sociocultural Studies of Human-Animal Relationships," *Annual Review of Anthropology* 28 (1999): 201–24, and "Animals in Anthropology," *Society and Animals* 10 (2002): 378–93.
25. These authors "are studying the host of organisms whose lives and deaths are linked to human social worlds." They link Giorgio Agamben's notion of "zoe," or "bare life"—that which is killable—with "bios"—lives that

are legibly biographical and political. Previously separated components of these realms are merging. This complexity, Kirksey and Helmreich argue, requires "a multisensory approach—grappling with unfamiliar sensoriums, with different kinds of touch, smell, taste, and vision" ("The Emergence of Multispecies Ethnography," 565). Eva Hayward's evocative term "fingeryeyes," melding the optic and the haptic in her descriptions of working with corals in a lab, is one example of such grappling with unfamiliar sensoriums; see "Fingeryeyes: Impressions of Cup Corals," *Cultural Anthropology* 25 (2010): 577–89.

26. Kirksey and Helmreich, "The Emergence of Multispecies Ethnography," 545, 546. For another trenchant extended consideration of these issues, see anthropologist Samantha Hurn's closing chapter "From Anthropocentricity to Multi-Species Ethnography," in her book *Humans and Other Animals: Cross-Cultural Perspectives on Human-Animal Interactions* (London: Pluto Press, 2012), 202–20.

27. Agustín Fuentes, "Naturalcultural Encounters in Bali: Monkeys, Temples, Tourists, and Ethnoprimatology," *Cultural Anthropology* 25 (2010): 600–624.

28. Ibid., 601.

29. Ibid., 603.

30. Ibid., 600.

31. Jake Kosek, "Ecologies of Empire: On the New Uses of the Honeybee," *Cultural Anthropology* 25 (2010): 650–78.

32. James Gorman, "Animal Studies Cross Campus to Lecture Hall," *New York Times*, January 3, 2012, accessed October 26, 2015, http://www .nytimes.com/2012/01/03/science/animal-studies-move-from-the-lab-to -the-lecture-hall.html?. Gorman tracks the inroads already being made by animal studies in the academy, and in doing so moves that initiative further into public discourse.

CHAPTER TWO

1. I thank Sharon Lakes for research assistance relating to von Hagens. For more information on Body Worlds, visit its official website at http://www .bodyworlds.com.

2. Figures from the official Body Worlds website, http://www.bodyworlds .com, accessed October 26, 2015.

3. There are a few exceptions to this rule, of course. Generally, these apply to animals who are themselves famous before their death or who are associated with famous humans. The taxidermied remains of cowboy actor Roy Rogers's horse, Trigger, provide one example in which the subjectivity of the animal as an individual with a life history is necessarily acknowledged. And as scholars have shown, individual animals who have been taxidermied then have continuing life histories (or afterlife histories) as

their skin continues to circulate in contexts like museums and private collections. Usually, however, the individual who was killed to provide the skin is not recognized in taxidermy collections. See Samuel J. M. M. Alberti, ed., *The Afterlives of Animals: A Museum Menagerie* (Charlottesville: University of Virginia Press, 2011), which traces the histories of individual taxidermied animals in life and through their museum "afterlives."

4. Ward's Natural Science Establishment continued to be an important institution until the early decades of the twentieth century, when museums started adding taxidermists to their staffs, thereby reducing the need for already prepared specimens. In the late 1920s, the Ward family donated the institution to the University of Rochester, but it returned to the family during the 1940s and transformed itself into a leading supplier of biological materials for the educational market. For more on this history, see "University of Rochester Library Bulletin: Henry Augustus Ward and American Museum Development," vol. 38 (1985), on the University of Rochester's website at http://www.library.rochester.edu/rbscp/4582, accessed October 26, 2015.

5. George Shrosbree, "The Scientific Development of Taxidermy and Its Effect upon Museums," *Wisconsin Academy of Sciences, Arts, and Letters Transactions* 16 (1908–9): 344.

6. For an overview of Muybridge's contribution to photography and our understandings of the biomechanics of movement, see the National Museum of American History's online exhibition *Freeze Frame: Capturing the Moment*, accessed October 26, 2015, (www.americanhistory.si.edu/muybridge). Leading taxidermist Carl Akeley himself also worked in film, inventing a portable motion-picture camera specifically designed to be used in fieldwork; see Mark Alvey, "The Cinema as Taxidermy: Carl Akeley and the Preservative Obsession," *Framework: The Journal of Cinema and Media* 48 (2007): 23–45. For a full consideration of film and animal watching, see Cynthia Chris, *Watching Wildlife* (Minneapolis: University of Minnesota Press, 2006).

7. Donna Haraway, "Teddy Bear Patriarchy: Taxidermy in the Garden of Eden, New York City, 1908–1936," *Social Text* 11 (1984–85): 20–64.

8. See Rachel Poliquin, "The Matter and Meaning of Museum Taxidermy," *Museum and Society* 6 (2008): 123–34, especially 127.

9. Rachel Poliquin, *The Breathless Zoo: Taxidermy and the Cultures of Longing* (University Park: Pennsylvania State University Press, 2012), 39. Poliquin's argument is based on a broad historical trajectory, so it does not solely concentrate on natural history museum dioramas; her overall assertion about taxidermied animals as bodily objects on which human desires and longings are cast is broadly applicable to many types of taxidermy displays.

10. Haraway, "Teddy Bear Patriarchy."

11. Sam Curtis, Elizabeth Majthenyl, and Lionel Atwill, "Whatever Happened to Taxidermy?," *Field and Stream*, August 1994, 62.

12. Still active today, the National Taxidermy Association sponsors seminars, competitions, and publications. It unites a network of professionals, part-timers, and hobbyists while disseminating information about taxidermy schools, suppliers, and legal regulations regarding hunting, importing, and mounting endangered species. In fact, several years ago, an officer from the Iowa Department of Natural Resources appeared at my door to check my freezer for illegal animal corpses. Having recently obtained a taxidermy license (which, like a fishing license, gives the right to practice but does not certify competence), I was subject to inspection. Although I was not then practicing taxidermy (nor have I since), I needed the license to attend the Iowa Taxidermy Association's annual meeting and seminars.

13. Some artists like Damien Hirst and Annette Messager use taxidermy in their art installations as well. See Steve Baker's *The Postmodern Animal* (London: Reaktion Press, 2000) for a discussion of animals in these artists' work.

14. Similar practices were popular in some Victorian taxidermy, playing on the potential for humor and satire by substituting animals for human actors in vignettes. Mr. Potter's Museum of Curiosities in England, featuring hundreds of taxidermied animals in humanlike scenes prepared by taxidermist Walter Potter, was one of the most famous venues to capitalize on this trend. Scenes included rabbits attending school and kittens playing croquet. The collection was sold twelve years ago by Bonham's Auction House in London at a record price of more than £500,000, as reported by BBC News, "Curiosity Auction Makes 500,000 Pounds," September 24, 2003, accessed October 26, 2015, http://www.news.bbc.co.uk/2/hi/uk_news/england/cornwall/3131144.stm.

15. The recent popularity of fish replicas—fiberglass bodies painted to look like a particular fish but containing no fish parts whatsoever—also begins to challenge taxidermy's reliance on the masking of death and the display of skin, but this replication accounts for a very small part of the market and lacks the status of large mammal taxidermy.

16. Baker, *The Postmodern Animal*, 54.

17. See, for example, works by the artists of the Minnesota Association of Rogue Taxidermists. Recent newspaper articles have brought this work to a wider public. See Jessica Contrera, "Taxidermy Moves from Hunting Lodges to Hipster Havens," *Washington Post*, September 8, 2014, accessed October 26, 2015, www.Washingtonpost.com/lifestyle/style/taxidermy-moves-from-hunting-lodges-to-hipster-havens. Sarina J. Brewer, Nate Hall, and Scott Bibus are three of the artists involved. Mounts include a two-headed baby chick, a griffin combining a bird head and wings with half a cat body, and a bloody-mouthed beaver chewing on a (fake) human finger.

Displayed in art galleries and art museums, work like this foregrounds and simultaneously contravenes the notions of realism I am investigating in current practice by taxidermists working outside this avant-garde artworld. Art taxidermy provides an implicit commentary on that work while being dependent on it for its referent. For a good discussion of this work by visual artists and photographers, see Stephanie S. Turner, "Relocating 'Stuffed' Animals: Photographic Remediation of Natural History Taxidermy," *Humanimalia* 4 (2013), accessed October 26, 2015, http://www .depauw.edu/humanimalia/issue 08/turner.html. Steve Baker's *The Postmodern Animal* remains foundational for these discussions. See also Baker, "You Kill Them to Look at Them: Animal Death in Contemporary Art," in *Killing Animals*, ed. the Animal Studies Group (Urbana: University of Illinois Press, 2006), 69–98; Baker, "What Can Dead Bodies Do?," in *Nanoq: Flat Out and Bluesome; A Cultural Life of Polar Bears*, ed. Bryndís Snaebjörnsdóttir and Mark Wilson (London: Black Dog Press, 2006), 148–55; Ron Broglio, *Surface Encounters: Thinking with Animals and Art* (Minneapolis: University of Minnesota Press, 2011); and Giovanni Aloi, *Art and Animals* (London: I. B. Tauris, 2012).

18. Jane Desmond, "Displaying Death/Animating Life: Changing Fictions of 'Liveness' from Taxidermy to Animatronics," in *Representing Animals*, ed. Nigel Rothfells (Bloomington: Indiana University Press, 2002), 159–79. Since this work appeared, a number of other authors have taken up these issues, and taxidermy has generated an increasing amount of attention in both the academic and the trade press and from journalists (likely kick-started by Susan Orlean's *New Yorker* essay about the 2003 World Taxidermy Championships: "Lifelike," *New Yorker*, June 9, 2003, accessed October 26, 2015, http://www.susanorlean.com/articles/lifelike.php). While I cannot cite all relevant works here, the following are among the most visible: Joan B. Landes, Paula Young Lee, and Paul Youngquist, eds., *Gorgeous Beasts: Animal Bodies in Historical Perspective* (University Park: Penn State University Press, 2012), which includes an article by Nigel Rothfels, "Trophies and Taxidermy" (pertaining to elephants); Melissa Milgrom, *Still Life: Adventures in Taxidermy* (Boston: Houghton Mifflin Harcourt, 2010); and Dave Madden, *The Authentic Animal: Inside the Odd and Obsessive World of Taxidermy* (New York: St. Martin's Press, 2011). Stephen Christopher Quinn's *Windows on Nature: The Great Habitat Dioramas of the American Museum of Natural History* (New York: Harry N. Abrams and American Museum of Natural History, 2006) and Alexis Turner's *Taxidermy* (New York: Rizzoli, 2013) are short on text but long on stunning illustrations. For a slightly earlier take on related issues, including art and science in dioramas, taxidermy, and the display of human body parts, see Stephen T. Asma's *Stuffed Animals and Pickled Heads: The Culture and Evolution of Natural History Museums* (New York: Oxford University Press, 2001).

19. Awards banquet, Iowa Taxidermists Association, April 23, 2005, Des Moines (emphasis added).

20. Information obtained at the "Strutting Turkey" workshop I attended at the 2005 World Taxidermy Championships. This event was held March 29–

April 2, 2005, at the Crowne Plaza Hotel and Convention Center, Springfield, Illinois. Website available at http: www.taxidermy.net./wtc05/wtc
.html, accessed October 26, 2015.

21. Comment by expert taxidermist Jason Snowberger during his presentation
in the "Super Seminar" at the 2005 World Taxidermy Championships.

22. Overheard at the 2005 World Taxidermy Championships.

23. One expert I observed leading a squirrel-mounting seminar at the 2005
championships advises blowing a squirrel with an air compressor to get
that "alive fluffy look" and then using a clean mascara brush to comb the
delicate hairs around the eyes. The final coiffure is held in place with hair-
spray. These techniques were demonstrated in the seminar by Amy Ritchie.

24. Judge's comment at the Iowa Taxidermists Association's twenty-first annual competition, April 2005, Des Moines.

25. *The Random House College Dictionary*, unabridged, rev. ed., 1980, s.v.
"taxis."

26. Marcus Zimmerman, leading the "Super Seminar" at the 2005 World Taxidermy Championships, held in Springfield, Illinois.

27. Ibid.

28. I discuss this aspect of zoos in chapter 4 of my book *Staging Tourism: Bodies on Display from Waikiki to Sea World* (Chicago: University of Chicago
Press, 1999).

29. References to the 2015 event, the most recent one as of this writing, are
based on reporting in the *New York Times*. See Brent McDonald, "Masters
of Taxidermy Seek to Replicate More Than an Animal's Appearance," *New
York Times*, June 2, 2015, accessed October 26, 2015, http://www.nytimes
.com/2015/06/02/us/taxidermy_championship_springfield.html. The
article was linked to a seven-image slide show and to a six-minute video,
indicating the level of interest the *Times* editors expected their largely
urban, East Coast readership to show in the report.

30. Categories for "reproductions" and "re-creations" also exist but draw
few entrants, indicating their minor standing and marginal status in a
field that depends on the authenticating presence of the animal body.
Reproductions must be originally molded by the entrant; re-creations
can use some natural materials but not those of the species portrayed.
For instance, a re-creation of an eagle could be constructed using turkey
feathers, or a cowhide could be used to portray a zebra. These exceptions,
like the popular fish-carving championships, emphasize the artistry of
the competitor over the authenticity of the skin. Their marginality in the
event underscores the continuing centrality of the animal skin.

31. The 2005 World Taxidermy Championships program, "Rules and Regulations," p. 15. The championships were held that year in Springfield,
Illinois.

32. One 2005 winning entry, "Best in World Large Gamehead," goes counter
to this assertion: a massive elk head is supported on a bronze arrow that,

if the mount were full body, would pierce its heart. But the specifics of the mount make this arrow metaphorical, marking the act of hunting though still distanced from an actual kill scene.

33. Some taxidermists do offer commercial freeze-drying services for dead pets. See, for example, the website for Mac's Taxidermy and Freeze Dry business (http://www.macstaxidermyandfreezedry.com/, accessed October 26, 2015), which tells customers that the business has been featured on the television newsmagazine *20/20* and includes photos of preserved pets. Freeze-dried pets, like conventionally taxidermied animals, can be posed in reclining or seated postures, even holding a toy, ready to play again.

34. Competitors at the World Taxidermy Championships are allowed to include "reference photos" of living animals or of the animal just after death to justify the specific choices they have made, such as the placement of ear-butt attachments. And criteria are stricter for competition entries than for commercial work. Seminars instruct taxidermists in two different approaches: how to do acceptable commercial work and how to prepare acceptable competition entries. For example, one instructor explained that she doesn't sew up all the buckshot holes in a duck torso if the wings will cover them, but such a method would be inappropriate for competitions. Another commented that some taxidermists purposely use incorrect eye sizes to obtain an effect they want for their customers, which also would be inappropriate for competitions.

35. Information from the judging criteria for the Collective Artists Division in the 2005 World Taxidermy Championships program, "Rules and Regulations," p. 17.

36. Ibid., p. 16.

37. Taxidermy melds craftsmanship and manual skills with artistic expression, and most often, for commercial taxidermists, is based on the mounting of trophies—trophies procured mainly through hunting by men. To the extent that emotional expressivity is associated with the arts and disassociated from manliness in lower-middle-class communities in the United States, taxidermy may provide a more acceptable artistic outlet than, say, painting. That it is a potential profession as well as a part-time hobby and could bring money into the household adds to this allure and legitimizes it as a way for men to spend their time. Such practicality can also trump any notions of artistic expression as self-indulgent feminized behavior.

38. Personal observation and information from McDonald, "Masters of Taxidermy" and linked video. Some of the newer urban participants would likely describe themselves as "hipsters," and their blue-accented hair and tattoos bring a new mode of self-presentation to the event. See also Stuart Miller, "Morbid Anatomy Museum's Taxidermy Classes Offer a Slice of Life (and Death)," *New York Times*, April 12, 2015, accessed October 26, 2015, http://www.nytimes.com/2015/04/13/nyregion/morbid-anatomy

-museums-taxidermy-classes-offer-a-slice-of-life-and-death.html. Miller notes that in classes held at a Brooklyn museum, a majority of students are women, and many are artists. Demand for taxidermy classes is apparently high—there are often hundreds of people on waiting lists. Museums and urban taxidermy artists' studios may be seen as "safe spaces" for women to try taxidermy, obviating the need for them to venture into hunting or to travel to rural areas far from home to learn the craft. Previously, few such arenas were available to urban-based women. These new taxidermists may represent a shift in the nature of cultural capital among practitioners, although additional research would be required to test this assumption.

39. A call for donations to fight antihunting organizations like PETA and the Humane Society was made during the 2005 awards banquet at the Iowa State Taxidermy Championships by a speaker from the Iowa Trappers League, but his vehemence seemed out of tune with the more relaxed tenor of the event and did not generate a vociferous response. The only defensiveness associated with the practice of taxidermy, when it appears, is in the assertion that taxidermy is an art and should be accorded the respect that such a category garners. Although the notion of a "championship" casts the work as more of a sporting event than an art show, the major taxidermy magazine, the glossy *Breakthrough: The Magazine for the Serious Wildlife Artist*—one of the main sponsors of the championships—highlights this viewpoint. The potentially feminizing idea of "art" and the perceived dangers or discomfort this association might suggest to the predominantly male practitioners are negated through an association with the wild—the "wild" in wildlife.

40. This trend has continued to the present. The *New York Times* coverage of the 2015 championships, in print, photo montage, and video formats, did not raise ethical questions about killing and the display of death, and no protests were reported.

41. At the 2005 World Taxidermy Championships held in Springfield, Illinois, competitors are allowed to submit photographs of the dead animal they have mounted and also pictures documenting an animal's live poses.

42. In discussions at the 2005 World Taxidermy Championships, however, some confessed that they would exaggerate in this way in commercial work if a client insisted on it, but never in professional exhibition taxidermy for competitions.

43. Colonial relations played out in nineteenth-century world's fairs placed some colonized peoples alongside animals in the same category of "available to be looked at" exhibits. While prohibitions against or demands for looking at someone or something are historically, culturally, and context specific, it is safe to assume that hierarchical distinctions play a complex role in these visual economies.

44. See the Native Graves Repatriation Act for details. Available online at www .nps.gov/archaeology/tools/laws/nagpra.htm, accessed October 26, 2015.

45. Adam Tanner, "Lucky Stiff," *National Review* 7 (1994): 33–34. Lenin was looking watery though still intact when I saw him in January 2001. For the latest on Lenin's preservation, see Jeremy Hsu, "Lenin's Body Improves with Age," April 22, 2015, accessed October 26, 2015, www .scientificamerican.com/article/Lenin-s-body-improves-with-age1/.

46. "Black Man Who Died 66 Years Ago Is Finally Buried," *Jet*, August 1994, 56–59.

47. Diane Haithman, "Exhibition on the Human Body Gets under People's Skin," *Los Angeles Times*, June 26, 2004.

48. Laura Casey, "'Body Worlds' Exhibit Looks Inside Human Body," *Alameda (CA) Times-Star*, July 27, 2004.

49. Diane Haithman, "Arts Notes: Hey Mister, Do You Want My Body?," *Los Angeles Times*, July 25, 2004.

50. In the spring of 2005, Body Worlds moved to the Museum of Science and Industry in Chicago, where it ran through September 5 of that year. A second exhibit, Body Worlds II, with different plastinates, returned to that site in 2007 for another successful engagement.

51. John Bohannon, Ding Yimin, and Xiong Lei, "Anatomy's Full Monty," *Science* 301 (2003): 1172.

52. Haithman, "Exhibition on the Human Body."

53. By far, a majority of these plastinates are male. While I have not determined the reasons for this yet, one of the effects may be to subtly insist that the human scientific norm remains male. I thank Susan McHugh for raising this point. In addition, the exhibit features a few animals, such as a rabbit, in an acetate-filled case, stripped of their skin and injected with red dye so that we can see the complicated brachiation of their nervous system. Another animal exhibit features a horse and rider, both plastinated. The horse body is impressive, in part because of the sheer size of its muscles, which dwarf ours. But the animals aren't the draw; they are subsidiary. In conversations I had with exhibitgoers, all said that if the displays had been of animals and not humans, they would have been less likely to attend. The acts of looking at something we see as the "same" as us and something we regard as fundamentally "different" yield two distinct types of reactions.

    Von Hagens later mounted an animal-focused exhibit, Animal Inside Out, which I discuss in the next chapter.

54. One dramatic exception is a man holding his entire skin, which dangles from his upraised fist. This pose is a copy of a Renaissance anatomy illustration, also included in the exhibit.

55. I thank Kristine Stiles for raising the issue of the fetus's skin.

56. There are other limits too to what can successfully be staged. For example, none of the Body World's US exhibits has, to my knowledge, shown staged sexual poses between two individuals. However, in May of 2009, a plastination exhibit by von Hagens—his Body Works and the Cycle of

Life project—opened in Berlin and contained two bodies arranged as if making love, with a female lying atop a supine male. The exhibit immediately drew censure. To my knowledge, this depiction has never toured to the United States. See "Gunther von Hagens Exhibition Criticised over Corpse Sex Display," *Daily Telegraph* (London), May 7, 2009, accessed October 26, 2015, http://www.telegraph.co.uk/news/newstopics/howaboutthat/5289311/Gunther-von-Hagens-exhibition-criticised-over-corpse-sex-display.html. See also "Controversial Doctor Unveils Corpse Sex Exhibition," CNN.com, May 7, 2009, accessed October 26, 2015, http://edition.cnn.com/2009/WORLD/europe/05/07/germany.vonhagens.dead.bodies/.

57. For three considerations of von Hagens's exhibits specifically in terms of the history of anatomy, anatomical knowledge, and the legal status of human remains, see Petra Kuppers, "Visions of Anatomy: Exhibitions and Dense Bodies," *Differences: A Journal of Feminist Cultural Studies* 15 (2004): 123–56; Marett Leiboff, "A Beautiful Corpse," *Continuum: Journal of Media and Cultural Studies* 19 (2005): 221–37; and Megan Stern, "Dystopian Anxieties versus Utopian Ideals: Medicine from *Frankenstein* to *The Visible Human Project* and *Body Worlds*," *Science as Culture* 15 (2006): 61–84. The first full-length edited book of essays on the von Hagens exhibits appeared in 2009. See T. Christine Jespersen, Alicita Rodriguez, and Joseph Starr, eds., *The Anatomy of Body Worlds: Critical Essays on the Plastinated Cadavers of Gunther von Hagens* (Jefferson, NC: McFarland, 2009). These essays examine the exhibits from a number of perspectives, including the legal, the religious, and the aesthetic. My concerns here are more specifically with the status of presence and social identity when von Hagens's antitaxidermic technique (display with skin removed) is employed.

In a recent article about tourism, I discuss von Hagens's exhibits in terms of audience engagement, specifically in terms of imagination, and draw on both reports of audience reactions by other scholars and some of my own research. For more on von Hagens's audiences, see Jane C. Desmond, "Touring the Dead: Imagination, Embodiment and Affect in Gunther von Hagens' *Body Worlds* Exhibitions," in *Great Expectations: Imagination and Anticipation in Tourism*, ed. Jonathan Skinner and Dimitrios Theodossopoulos (New York: Berghahn Books, 2011), 174–95.

58. In the United States, Body Worlds has been hosted only by science museums, not art spaces. This choice, given the respect and seriousness with which science is regarded, may be one reason why the exhibition has drawn relatively little complaint in this country.

59. There is no implication or guarantee that the bodies on display ever actually took part in the activities or professions referenced by their arrested motions, like playing soccer, running, or ballet dancing. Instead, we are invited to examine how muscles, tendons, and bones shift in relation to one another to enable complex movements through space. The bodies aren't presented as a way to help us understand how specific use shapes

them, as in the movements that produce the long muscles of a professional dancer as opposed to those yielding the bulky ones of a weight lifter, or how bone thickens in response to the pull of muscles on it, as it does in professional athletes. Motion is depicted, then, not to produce a sense of particularity but to demonstrate general human biomechanics.

60. Broglio, *Surface Encounters*, cited in S. Turner, "Relocating 'Stuffed' Animals."

61. Comments taken verbatim from the audience comment book that was available on the days I visited the Chicago show in 2007. Although instructions suggested that people include their name, age, hometown, and occupation, relatively few supplied all this information.

CHAPTER THREE

1. Steve Johnson, "'Animal Inside Out' Is Body Worlds' Take on Beasts and Birds," *Chicago Tribune*, March 13, 2013, accessed October 26, 2015, http://articles.chicagotribune.com/2013-03-13/entertainment/chi-animal-inside-out-smi-20130313_1_show-benefits-hagens-body-worlds.

2. I discussed the plastination process in detail in chapter 2.

3. Quoted in Jeanna Bryner, "Beauty in the Beast: Exhibit Shows Off Animal Insides," LiveScience, April 5, 2012, accessed October 26, 2015, http://livescience.com/19514-animal-corpses-plastination-von hagens.html.

4. An elephant and a gorilla were highlights of the British version of the show, just before it traveled to Chicago; but those specimens were held up in customs and, to my knowledge, never made it to the Chicago show, attenuating somewhat the colossal scale of the animals promised.

5. Erica Fudge, in her book *Animal* (London: Reaktion Books, 2002), grapples with the linguistic issue of using *a, an, the,* or no article in her volume title, ultimately opting for the latter. She quotes Jacques Derrida, in his influential essay "The Animal That Therefore I Am (More to Follow)," who asserts, "Whenever 'one' says, 'The Animal,' each time a philosopher or anyone else says 'The Animal' in the singular and without further ado claiming thus to designate every living being that is held not to be man, . . . should confirm not only the animality that he is disavowing but his complicit, continued and organized involvement in a veritable war of the species" (in *The Animal That Therefore I Am*, ed. Marie-Louise Mallet, trans. David Wills [New York: Fordham University Press, 2008], 161). Von Hagens's choice of exhibit title, Animal Inside Out: The Beauty in the Beast, reproduces this taxonomic division between "all" animals and all not-animals, here not meaning rocks and trees but humans. However, the lack of an article in the title ("The" Animal) shies away from a uniform similarity while pointing to a fundamental sameness, "animality," perhaps, that could potentially include humans while not making them the focus of the show. It also allows somewhat for the extraordinary differences among

animals, the scallop compared to the gorilla, for example, each of which is "an" animal in contemporary human typologies but neither of which could ever adequately stand in for the range of beings designated by the all-inclusive "the" animal. See Fudge, *Animal*, 160–65.

6. Fragonard was renowned for his creation of "écorchés" in France during the latter quarter of the 1700s, and his work, which included some human flayed specimens as well, became an important basis for the development of comparative anatomy and of veterinary training. See Christophe Degueurce, *Fragonard Museum: The Ecorchés—the Anatomical Masterworks of Honoré Fragonard* (New York: Blast Books, 2011).

7. The MSI's Animal Inside Out website's Exhibit Guide reported that as of September 2013, more than 36 million people worldwide had visited a Body Worlds exhibition, and 1.44 million guests had visited the three Body Worlds exhibitions appearing at the museum in 2005, 2007, and 2011. See Museum of Science and Industry, Chicago, Animal Inside Out, accessed October 26, 2015, http://www.msichicago.org/whats-here/exhibits/animal-inside-out.

8. Of course, we don't even use the same term, *cadaver*, to refer to both dead animals and dead humans. This differential nomenclature after death is yet another way of drawing a line between the human and nonhuman animal worlds.

9. Michel Foucault, *Birth of the Clinic: An Archaeology of Medical Perception* (New York: Vintage, 1994).

10. See Barbara Kirshenblatt-Gimblet's notion of the "ethnographic fragment" in the essay "Objects of Ethnography," in her *Destination Culture: Tourism, Museums and Heritage* (Berkeley: University of California Press, 1998), 17–78.

11. For two recent considerations of gender in Body Worlds and feminist analyses of them, see the following: Joyce Davidson et al., "'Doing Gender' at *Body Worlds*: Embodying Field Trips as Affective Educational Experience," *Journal of Geography in Higher Education* 33 (2009): 303–14; and Rebecca Scott, "Body Worlds' Plastinates, the Human/Nonhuman Interface, and Feminism," *Feminist Theory* 12 (2011): 165–81. As Davidson et al. put it, discussing gendered stereotyping in the displays in Body Worlds II, the exhibit "reflects and reinforces social constructions of gender, where women are alternatively sexualized or maternalized, or seen as passive objects in demure or graceful display. While men are subject to 'equally' stereotypical treatment, they seem *enabled* as athletic or intellectual and never sexualized or *simply* objectified for another" (308).

In the animal exhibit, sexual difference plays a muted role, except when animals in the small "reproduction" section of body parts are referred to in wall text as "mothers and fathers" or when the female camel is shown with her calf, that is, as a "mother." Generally, body parts are not labeled with the sex of the animal they come from. And with few exceptions, as in the powerful posing of the bull, most animals are not posed in ways to evoke their cultural stereotypes of power, delicacy, neoteny, and so on, as so little context, even in posed movement, is provided.

12. Erica Fudge (*Animal*, 100) notes the linkage of Rene Descartes's philosophical formulation of "animal as machine" devoid of "mind" to the development of scientific uses of animals, emphasizing the presumed similarities of human and nonhuman animal bodies as a basis for using animals in laboratory science. I don't mean to imply that von Hagens simply reinscribes the "machine without mind" model, but we can place his exhibit within this long arc of emphasis on animals as material bodies. This near-total excision of discussion of new knowledge about animal sociality, cognition, and even, some argue, emotions and emergent "ethics" runs counter to the trends pushing the envelope in these debates and is certainly reductivist.

13. Such a framework draws implicitly on a Christian vision of human "dominion," or God-given dominance, over animals tied to an ethical obligation to care for them while putting them to our use. See Erica Fudge's discussion in *Animal* (especially 92–104) on the link between dominion and the history of animals in science. See Mathew Scully, *Dominion: The Power of Man, the Suffering of Animals, and the Call to Mercy* (New York: St. Martin's Press, 2002), for a contemporary interpretation of the Christian concept as the grounds for a more "merciful" relation with animals, especially in terms of our use of them for food.

   Of course, the entire exhibit emerges from and makes sense within a belief in a realm of human thought and knowledge production that has historically come to be called "scientific," based on observation, notions of "objectivity" (the ability to observe without interfering or interpreting), and Darwinism, that places humans within the "natural" world.

14. While none of the audience studies I read (see chapter 2) foregrounded this interpretation, and nothing in the exhibits themselves rhetorically urges the viewer toward this response, opting instead to urge the reform of individual health habits, it is possible that some visitors, upon later reflection, came to this type of conclusion. Further in-depth interviews would be needed to probe this possibility.

15. This and subsequent visitor comments given in the text and notes were overhead at the Chicago MSI, August 22–23, 2013.

16. See Stanley Fish, *Is There a Text in This Class? The Authority of Interpretive Communities* (Cambridge, MA: Harvard University Press, 1982), for just one such formulation. Literary formulations of "ideal," "negotiated," and "oppositional" readers combined with reception studies from museums help us theorize these frameworks.

17. I noticed a great deal of interaction among those who arrived together as they reacted to the exhibit. They discussed the objects described in the text in terms of their own bodies, pointing from animal features to their

own, and conferred about the exhibit ("Did you see that???"). They corrected their interpretation of a human lung containing gray spots, which they often thought were the result of smoking, after reading the accompanying text: it was a nonsmoker's lung, and all lungs collect pollution over the years, which is what the spots show. Parents and grandparents also pointed things out to the children in their midst.

Especially poignant was a glass case of fetuses (of humans and of a giraffe), located toward the end of the exhibit and with none of the expected "warning" text so that adults could redirect their children elsewhere, as was the case in earlier Body Worlds shows. One group of adults told their elementary-school-age child, "See . . . this is what you looked like at three months," a concept that a young child was unlikely to really grasp, as she would have had to acknowledge that the fetus on display, unlike herself, did not get born. Here the copresence of human and animal fetuses may have facilitated a conversation that might have been too challenging were the specimens human-only. In addition, even visitors who were strangers to each other could interact over the specimens. A couple of times, I shared observations with people I didn't know while leaning over a vitrine: "Wow, is that really a nonsmoker's lung?" I didn't necessarily see other people interacting this way except among groups that arrived together, but it was possible for strangers to create, for that millisecond, a broader sense of shared community.

18. Museum exhibit designers generally try to limit the number of words in signage and the degree of reading skills required to engage in an exhibit, as articles in museum studies show. See, for example, Fiona McLean, *Marketing the Museum* (London: Routledge, 1997), for a discussion of reading as it relates to extant and potentially expanded audiences.

19. As a majority of the visitors are from the United States, and as a majority of the US-educated population would have encountered some form of animal dissection in high school biology class, we can assume that one of the dominant frames of reference visitors bring for engaging with the animal exhibits will be that of science as a mode of knowledge learned in the lab—a framework easily transferred from one authoritative public institution, public schools, to another, the science museum.

20. F. B. Orlans, cited in Garcia Barr and Harold Herzog, "Fetal Pig: The High School Dissection Experience," *Society and Animals* 8 (2000): 53. In the past fifteen years, the number of students agitating for and receiving access to nondissection alternatives, such as 3-D models or computer texts, has increased. Still, they form a minority, and we can safely assume that most visitors to Animal Inside Out have experienced taking apart some sort of animal body in a scientific lab context.

21. A recent article examining how high school students in Sweden make sense of their biological training provides some useful findings that may also obtain in the US situation. This research argues that to truly under-

stand how students make sense of lab-based biology training, we must grapple with their sense of their own bodily experience. See Auli Arvola Orlander and Per-Olof Wickman, "Bodily Experiences in Secondary School Biology," *Cultural Studies of Science Education* 6 (2011): 569–94.

22. The role of teachers is discussed in ibid., 591. An anecdote from my research shows that the role of docents as guides to embracing scientism sometimes fails dramatically, and without warning, showing the limits to the exhibit's power to direct interpretations. When I asked one of the Animal Inside Out docents about any protests to the exhibit, she mentioned that a few people objected to its references to evolution. She recounted how another docent had engaged a child who was looking at the exhibit's one human skeleton by asking, "Can you tell if this is a female or male skeleton?" The child's mother replied (I paraphrase here), "Just count the ribs. Men have one less rib than women, since God took a rib from Adam to make Eve." The docent replied, "Well . . . actually . . . if you count them you will see that they are the same number"—a conclusion based on physical not theological evidence, and rejected by the mother. To smooth things over, the docent then directed the mother's attention to the beauty of the bodily design (intelligent design?). Commenting on this incident, the docent I spoke with said, "We don't try to tell people what to believe, we just present the best science we can," a position reiterated to me by another docent almost verbatim.

    Although this example involved the human rather than an animal display, the docent's role is the same throughout the exhibit—guiding viewers toward a "just the facts" approach to the organic material and former beings exhibited, and leading them away from any deeper engagement with the lives of those beings; their own viscerality, even when the (literal) viscera are shown in vitrines; and certainly from any sense of cohabitation (the dog by your side, the scallop on your plate, the camel in the zoo).

23. As mentioned in the main text, it is important to note that this accepted mode of learning through dissection and reductionist specimenization has a countermovement too, a growing emphasis on alternative ways of learning biology through computer-generated and 3-D models that don't require the killing of animals for the lab. There are many references. For information on alternatives, two well-regarded sources are the University of California at Davis Veterinary College (http://www.lib.ucdavis.edu/dept/animalalternatives, accessed October 27, 2015) and the Physicians Committee for Responsible Medicine (http://www.dissectionalternatives.org, , accessed October 27, 2015).

24. In *Animal*, Erica Fudge briefly summarizes alternative religious traditions that certainly frame the exhibit experience for some MSI attendees (including Islam and Buddhism), but even for nonpracticing Christians in the United States, the ideologies of Christianity exert enormous influence

on public discourse. Note simply the US president's invocation of "God bless America" at the end of State of the Union addresses to Congress, a secular, democratically elected body. As Fudge notes, "Dominion cannot exist comfortably with the idea of sameness, but somehow, in contemporary culture, we manage—to have an understanding of a shared origin, and shared capacity, but also, and simultaneously, to believe in the human right to domination" (21).

25. Such documentation would probably make von Hagens's human Body Worlds exhibits untenable, but it would be a similarly radical, yet possibly acceptable move for the animal exhibit.

26. I am not able to specify the name of the docent with whom I spoke on August 22, 2013, while touring the exhibition, as I couldn't obtain official approval to interview docents away from the exhibit floor. Presumably, any interested attendee could engage these guides in this type of discussion, although I haven't heard of anyone who did. Without official permission, I choose not to identify the workers with whom I spoke during the exhibit while they were on duty. The exhibit designer, however, was willing to meet with me, but we weren't able to arrange a time before the end of the show.

27. Contrast this absence, and its ideological impact, with another current exhibit, the ongoing Think Tank at the Smithsonian's National Zoological Park in Washington, DC. Describing the Think Tank as "a place to think about thinking," the zoo helps researchers and the visiting public understand animals "as complex cognitive beings" through the hosting of research (visible to the public) and opportunities to interact with the orangutans and other primates who live there. Sections of the exhibit focus on language/communication, tool use, and social organization as "evidence of thinking." See http://www.nationalzoo.si.edu/Animals/ThinkTank/Exhibit, accessed October 27, 2015, for more about the exhibit, which includes opportunities for the resident orangutans to enter and leave the space at will, further enforcing visitors' perception of them as sentient, cognitively aware, self-directing individuals. I thank Barbara J. King for bringing this exhibit to my attention.

28. The extent that animals are granted a history is now dependent on human recordings of breedings, life stories of celebrity animals, or, for entire species, histories of extinction, near extinction, or recovery of populations. Some new studies challenge that limited realm. See, for example, Barbara J. King, *How Animals Grieve* (Chicago: University of Chicago Press, 2013); Frans de Waal, *The Ape and the Sushi Master: Reflections of a Primatologist* (New York: Basic Books, 2001); and Charles Siebert, "Should a Chimp Be Able to Sue Its Owner?," *New York Times Magazine*, April 23, 2014, accessed October 27, 2015, http://www.nytimes.com//2014/04/27/magazine/the-rights-of-man_and_beast.html. See Irene Maxine Pepperberg, *The Alex

Studies: Cognitive and Communicative Abilities of Grey Parrots (Cambridge, MA: Harvard University Press, 2002), for work on parrot cognition.

CHAPTER FOUR

1. For further information on the industry abroad, one place to begin is the Association of Private Pet Cemeteries and Crematoria in the United Kingdom, currently the only organization in Europe setting standards for pet cemeteries and crematoria.

2. For recent work on Japanese mourning for pets, see Richard Chalfen, "Celebrating Life after Death: The Appearance of Snapshots in Japanese Pet Gravesites," *Visual Studies* 18 (2003): 144–46. Chalfen suggests that the inclusion of pet photographs at pet gravesites is an outgrowth of the Japanese custom of keeping portrait photographs of deceased human family members on a family altar. His conclusion is also based on surveys showing that a majority of pet keepers in Japan regard pets as "part of the family." Since mourning practices, everyday practices of visual representation, and notions of the "family" and its related obligations are by no means universal, detailed site-specific studies such as Chalfen's are necessary. See Barbara Ambros, "The Necrogeography of Pet Memorial Spaces: Pets as Liminal Family Members in Contemporary Japan," *Material Religion* 6 (2010): 304–35. Ambros, a scholar of religion at the University of North Carolina at Chapel Hill, bases her research on thirty pet cemeteries in Japan, and discusses shifting legal restrictions and everyday practices regarding pet burials, cremations, and mourning. See also Elmer Veldkamp, "The Emergence of 'Pets as Family' and the Socio-Historical Development of Pet Funerals in Japan," *Anthrozoos* 22 (2009): 333–46. We need many more similar studies of the United States as well as cross-national and cross-cultural studies.

    A forthcoming book, edited by Margo DeMello, will help expand these discussions of mourning for animals.

3. In the late 1990s, the International Pet Cemetery Association listed between six hundred and seven hundred members, the majority in the United States, where this association was and is still located. Today, under new leadership, it lists constituent contact information for a couple hundred members. Membership in the association is not required for a pet cemetery business to be legally sanctioned. On the basis of my research, I think that the number of pet cemetery and pet crematory services in the United States is growing, not declining, but there is no national requirement that such businesses be legally registered. They are, rather, regulated by state and municipal ordinances, so it is impossible to know their total numbers. I think it is safe to say that there are hundreds of such sites in the United States.

4. Hal Herzog, *Some We Love, Some We Hate, Some We Eat: Why It's So Hard to Think Straight about Animals* (New York: Harper Perennial, reprint edition, 2011).

5. Sociologist Clinton R. Sanders elaborates on this concept of the in-between in his excellent article "Killing with Kindness: Veterinary Euthanasia and the Social Construction of Personhood," *Sociological Forum* 10 (1995): "The central differences between human and animal medical death work interactions revolve around differences in conventional understandings of the distinctions among persons, nonpersons, and those beings residing in the definitional space between these two constructed categories. . . . In contemporary society, companion animals exist in the liminal position between the socially constructed categories of person/being and that of nonperson/object" (208–9). While the very important topic of animal euthanasia is related to my concerns in this chapter, a full discussion exceeds the boundaries of my investigations here. However, the status of the pet as "in between" is crucial to my arguments about cemeteries. For excellent discussions of the rise of pet keeping in Europe, see Kathleen Kete, *The Beast in the Boudoir: Pet Keeping in Nineteenth-Century Paris* (Berkeley: University of California Press, 1995). For the United States, see Katherine Grier, *Pets in America: A History* (New York: Harcourt, 2006), and Herzog, *Some We Love.*

6. Norwegian scholar Liv Emma Thorsen, in her book *Hund! Fornuft og folelelser* (Oslo: Pax Forlag A/S, 2001), discusses pet cemeteries in Norway and in the United States (213–45). I thank Dr. Kristin Solli for translating sections of this book for me from the original Norwegian into English. Thorsen draws a distinction between the decorative practices allowed at some pet cemeteries, like Bubbling Well in California, and the restrictions at some others, like the pet cemetery in Hartsdale, New York, which she describes as "the most prestigious of the animal burial grounds in the U.S." She continues, "The prestige is established by a well-thought-out aesthetic and ceremonial self-presentation. At the celebration of the cemetery's 100th anniversary on September 29, 1996, all the graves were decorated with pink flowers. . . . There were no artificial flowers, whirligigs, angels, or toys to give away the fact that the costly granite monuments mark the graves of dogs and cats. The cemetery's location . . . along with the flowers on the graves, make this animal burial ground remarkably similar to Vestre Aker Cemetery in Oslo" (239).

   While my remarks in this chapter are substantiated by observations at Bubbling Well, that site alone, of course, does not define the only genre of animal cemetery mourning, and different animal cemeteries may have variable requirements limiting freedom of expression, as Thorsen notes. Even at Hartsdale, though grave decoration is more restrained, it provides a number of memorial options for particularizing the gravestone or mausoleum. The Hartsdale Pet Cemetery website states, "Memorial planning is a celebration of life. A personalized memorial for your beloved pet(s) is a wonderful way to commemorate the lives of those who gave us so much love and companionship. Using the finest granite available, we offer a wide variety of choices to meet all budgets. Memorial portraits, religious symbols, floral carvings and etchings are all additional items that can be selected to customize your pets' monument" (accessed October 29, 2015, http://www.petcem.com/assets/pdf/MONUMENTS.pdf). Cemeteries that restrict exuberant memorialization strive to echo the dignity of some human cemeteries, "elevating" the status of the animal through parallelism of commemorative practices. However, the practices I analyze in this chapter, those that are more exuberant, more intimate, and more creative, acknowledge the pet as both part of the family and uniquely connected to it. The end of that relationship takes advantage of the less-regulated status of pet cemeteries to celebrate the unique status of that transspecies bond.

7.   Susan McHugh, *Dog* (London: Reaktion Books, 2004), 18.

8.   For additional resources on animal burials in prehistory and history, see Steven Mithen, *After the Ice: A Global Human History, 20,000–5,000 B.C.* (Cambridge, MA: Harvard University Press, 2004), and Aleksander Pluskowski, ed., *The Ritual Killing and Burial of Animals: European Perspectives* (Oxford: Oxbow Books, 2011). I thank one of the anonymous manuscript reviewers for bringing these works to my attention.

9.   See Charlotte Price Persson, "Unique Find at Viking Burial Place," January 22, 2012, accessed October 29, 2015, http://sciencenordic.com/unique-find-viking-burial-place. The report describes the burial site unearthed at Naesby in the peninsula of Jutland, Denmark, in 1951.

10.   Barbara J. King, *Being with Animals: Why We Are Obsessed with the Furry, Scaly, Feathered Creatures Who Populate Our World* (New York: Doubleday, 2010), 51–53.

11.   J. Bryan III, "Paris: Visit to a Cat-and-Dog Cemetery," *Holiday Magazine* 25 (1959): 42–44.

12.   For a brief history of pet burial, including references to Egyptian practices, see Mary Elizabeth Thurston, "Friends to the End: The History of Pet Burial," in *Dr. Johnson's Apple Orchard: The Story of America's First Pet Cemetery* (Hartsdale, NY: Hartsdale Canine Cemetery, 1997), 102–15. Victorian practices associated with animal death must be seen in relation to the status of pets at the time and to Victorian attitudes toward death and mourning more generally. See Harriet Ritvo, *The Animal Estate: The English and Other Creatures in the Victorian Age* (Cambridge, MA: Harvard University Press, 1987). Katherine Grier also discusses Victorian practices in chapter 2 of *Pets in America*.

13.   Thomas Hardy, "Last Words to a Dumb Friend," in *Funeral and Memorial Service Readings, Poems, and Tributes*, ed. Rachel R. Baum (New York: McFarland, 1999), 89–90. Chapter 8 of that book, "Tributes to Companion Animals and Pets," includes works by several other Victorians and earlier

nineteenth-century figures, including Rudyard Kipling, Warren G. Harding, and Lord George Gordon Byron. See also Phyllis Theroux, ed., *The Book of Eulogies* (New York: Scribner, 1997), chapter 13, "Animal Loves."

14. As the number of household pets increases, the pet cemetery industry is also expanding. The pet burial trend is definitely upward. A 1990 survey found that nearly 43% of all US households have a pet, including approximately 58 million dogs and 49 million to 60 million cats (Blayne Cutler, "A Spot in the Country," *American Demographics*, May 1991, 42). Later surveys, reported by the American Humane Association, state that approximately 65% of US households currently own at least one pet (defined as a bird, cat, dog, horse, fish, reptile, or small animal), including approximately 70 million to 78 million dogs. See American Humane Association, "Pets by the Numbers," accessed October 29, 2015, http://www.americanhumane.org/issues/pet_overpopulation/facts/pet_ownership_statistics.html. Pet cemetery owner Bill Remkus estimates that currently only 1%–2% of the nation's pets end up in pet cemeteries. See Linda Young, "Pet Cemeteries Giving Owners Peace of Mind," *Chicago Tribune*, February 4, 1993. I have no further related figures. The growth in the number of pet cemeteries suggests that this figure will rise in the future, whether for full-body burials or the burials of cremated remains.

15. Unlike the case for human remains, a cheaper option, involving cremation of several animals at once, may be offered.

16. Sarah Lyall, "Pet Burials Rivaling Some for People," *New York Times*, July 1, 1991.

17. Dennis Hevesi, "A Singer Joins Pet Owners in a Fury over Fake Graves," *New York Times*, July 13, 1991.

18. Press release by the Office of New York State Attorney General Eliot Spitzer, April 22, 1999, accessed October 29, 2015, http://www.ag.ny.gov/press-release/ag-issues-checks-saratoga-county-pet-cemetery-case.

19. Lisa Hoffman, "Pet Cremation Industry Rife with Fraud," Stories in the News, Ketchikan, Alaska, July 11, 2005, accessed October 29, 2015, http://www.sitnews.us/0705news/071105/071105_shns_petcrematory.html, or see www.sitnews.us/sitnewsarchives/0705/071105_sitnews.html. Not only individual pet owners but also veterinarians who contract with crematories have been victims.

20. An advice line for veterinarians suggested offering pet owners a chance to see, in advance, what the "cremains" (the cremated remains) of their pet will look like, by showing them the cremains of some other pet. "Be sure to explain whose cremains they are," advised the website, so that individuality is retained. Colorado State College of Veterinary Medicine, "Resources for Veterinarians," accessed June 20, 2000, but no longer available, http://www.cvmbs.colostate.edu.

21. Fears still linger, however, and websites for pet cremation take pains to explain their processes for tracking individual animals. One service that

does so is Faithful Companions Pet Remembrance Services of Coralville, Iowa. Run by the same family that owns a leading human funeral service in nearby Iowa City, this newer venture highlights consummate professionalism. See the Faithful Companions Pet Remembrance Services website, accessed October 29, 2015, http://faithfulcompanionsia.com.

22. This figure was available on the International Association of Pet Cemeteries and Crematories website in 2008, but the configuration of that organization has since changed, and no total figures are now available. See Stanley Brandes, "The Meaning of American Pet Cemetery Gravestones," *Ethnology* 48 (2009): 100, which cites the 2008 association figure.

23. Linda Young, "Pet Cemeteries Giving Owners Peace of Mind," *Chicago Tribune*, February 4, 1993.

24. Vivian Spiegelman and Robert Kastenbaum, "Pet Rest Memorial: Is Eternity Running Out of Time?," *Omega* 21 (1990): 5.

25. Special small caskets are available for hamsters, birds, gerbils, and small puppies and kittens; larger ones accommodate cats and dogs. These are made of high-impact plastic with interior resting pads of satin and lace or even camouflage material. See the supply list of the Hoegh Pet Casket Factory in Gladstone, Michigan, which even offers tours of its production facility and a product display room: www.hoeghpetcaskets.com, accessed October 29, 2015.

26. Liturgical prayers for memorializing animals are available, and article 3.3 of the 1978 Universal Declaration of Animal Rights (Paris) states, "A dead animal must be treated with decency" (p. 80); cited in Andrew Linzey, *Animal Rites: Liturgies of Animal Care* (London: SCM Press, 1999), 158.

27. Conversation with Dan Harberts, November 2000, Bubbling Well Cemetery, Napa, California.

28. Ibid.

29. Young, "Pet Cemeteries Giving Owners Peace of Mind."

30. Conversation with Dan Harberts, November 2000, Bubbling Well Cemetery, Napa, California.

31. A dog must be certified as a coon dog by the owner, a witness, and a member of the local coon hunters' organization, who must be allowed to view the dog, states the Key Underwood (Alabama) Coon Dog Memorial Graveyard's website, accessed October 29, 2015, http://www.coondogcemetery.com.

32. Gregory Jaynes, "In Alabama: 'A Coon Dog Indeed,'" *Time*, September 30, 1985, 12.

33. See "Funeral for a Friend," Key Underwood (Alabama) Coon Dog Memorial Graveyard website, accessed October 29, 2015, http://www.coondogcemetery.com/merch/html.

34. Lynn Gosnell and Suzanne Gott, "San Fernando Cemetery: Decorations of Love and Loss in a Mexican-American Community," in *Cemeteries and Grave Markers: Voices of American Culture*, ed. Richard E. Meyer (Logan: Utah State University Press, 1992), 217–36; quotation is from page 217.

35. This type of cemetery arose in the mid-twentieth century in the United States as distinct from the parklike or "garden" cemeteries on urban peripheries, which had appeared in the early 1800s and had themselves replaced earlier urban burial grounds. Typically, these new memorial-park-style cemeteries have strict regulations and limitations on grave decoration, the planting of flowers, and the erection of fences around individual graves, limiting expressivity. They do, however, often offer trees and shrubs and decorative ponds and fountains in their landscape. See Marilyn Yalom, *The American Resting Place: Four Hundred Years of History through Our Cemeteries and Burial Grounds* (Boston: Houghton Mifflin, 2008), 46–48. For two examples of rural cemetery traditions, see Beverly Kremenak-Pecotte, "Folk Art in Texas Cemeteries," in *Folk Art in Texas*, ed. Francis Edward Abernethy, Publications of the Texas Folklore Society, 45 (Dallas: Southern Methodist University Press, 1985), 53–63, and John A. Milbauer, "Southern Folk Trains in the Cemeteries of Northeastern Oklahoma," *Southern Folklore* 46 (1989): 175–85.

36. Yalom, *The American Resting Place*, 47–48.

37. Future research by scholars of mourning must address more fully this range of material culture and performative practices associated with mourning, and how it does or does not align with specific ethnic, religious, and class divisions. So far, extensive comparative studies have not been published.

38. This practice, especially when it involves toys the deceased pet played with, recalls the African American tradition, especially in the South, of leaving a personal object on a grave, often the last object the deceased touched. African-legacy practices of grave decoration include leaving items associated with water, like cups or vases, on graves to assist the deceased in crossing a body of water on the way to the afterlife. See Yalom, *The American Resting Place*, 35. While the traditions may differ, and the creative impulse draw, knowingly or not, on a variety of ethnically or religiously associated practices, the end result for pet cemetery decoration is that pet mourning uses available discourses and available practices to creatively address new needs.

39. Gosnell and Gott, "San Fernando Cemetery," 234.

40. For example, Gosnell and Gott found that the socially valued practices of adorning graves in the mainly working-class Mexican American section of the cemetery they studied also began to show up in other ethnically marked sections of the same cemetery, including graves in older Polish, German, Belgian, and Lebanese sections. "We believe that the similarities between the decorations of the relatively small percentage of these gravesites with the Mexican-American family graves can be understood as a pleasing and powerful community aesthetic structuring the practice of other Catholic families" ("San Fernando Cemetery," 221). In addition, the authors suggest that although they have their origins in the Mexican

American working class, these decorative practices continue to influence the practices of Mexican American children in the community who have moved into the middle class and out of the neighborhood but who continue to return to decorate graves. Thus, we can see a dominant aesthetic in a particular community (working-class Mexican Americans in that geographic location) spreading its aesthetic and performative influence (what people do to commemorate death and decorate graves) beyond the class and ethnic specifics of the originary community.

41. Erika Doss, *Memorial Mania: Public Feeling in America* (Chicago: University of Chicago Press, 2010), 19.

42. Ibid.

43. Ibid., 37.

44. Pet cemeteries are technically public (no admission is charged and no membership is required to visit), but in fact they, like many nonnational cemeteries, function more as semipublic spaces, attracting those who already see themselves as part of the community of mourners, rather than a general public or an oppositional public who might see such mourning as, at best, silly and, at worst, worthy of ridicule. I take up this question of degree of publicness in chapter 6, in my consideration of pet obituaries in newspapers.

45. "Pet lovers" is the social group implicitly constructed through the presence of a pet cemetery. This "interest group" is one that not only pumps a lot of money into the economy through the purchase of pet-specific supplies but also could potentially influence the structure of public space (e.g., through support for the building of municipal dog parks), changes in federal policy (federal evacuation procedures post–Hurricane Katrina now require attention to the evacuation of pets), and legal systems that challenge the "property" status of pets in courts when emotional damages are requested in cases of abuse. Like other interest groups that work across demographic groupings of age, region, ethnic origin, gender, socioeconomic class, and religious affiliation, this group could be considered a political "bloc" in the Gramscian sense, and deserves increased scholarly attention in the future. It holds and exercises significant economic power and potentially includes, according to pet-keeping data, a majority of US households.

46. See Doss, *Memorial Mania*, chapter 2, for an overview. Doss's discussion of the temporary memorial phenomenon as part of wider practices of memorialization is especially good. The irony, as she notes, is that some spontaneous shrines are now deemed so important to the healing of the nation or as historical traces of the emotive dimensions of nationalism, as is the case in the 9/11 Twin Towers site, that museums and other municipal organizations, like the National Park Service, are now charged with saving and archiving the massive tonnage of material associated with them as a part of national history. The ephemeral now becomes the archived histori-

cal document awaiting future resurrection and interpretation. Marita Sturken offers a compelling discussion of temporary memorials at sites of public devastation, like New York City after the 9/11 attacks, in her book *Tourists of History: Memory, Kitsch, and Consumerism from Oklahoma City to Ground Zero* (Durham, NC: Duke University Press, 2007).

47. Doss, *Memorial Mania*, 71.

48. Ibid., 75.

49. The phrase "semantically dense" was coined by C. Nadia Serematakis. It is especially appropriate in the context of the material culture of mourning, given its associated heightened affect and the ability of specific objects to trigger feelings of grief.

50. Diana Taylor, *The Archive and the Repertoire: Performing Cultural Memory in the Americas* (Durham, NC: Duke University Press, 2003).

51. There is a growing discussion of these memorials among scholars of death and mourning and among communication studies scholars. In addition to Doss, *Memorial Mania*, see Jack Santino, ed., *Spontaneous Shrines and the Public Memorialization of Death* (New York: Palgrave Macmillan, 2005); Jennifer Clark and Majella Franzmann, "Authority from Grief, Presence and Place in the Making of Roadside Memorials," *Death Studies* 30 (2006): 579–99; Una MacConville, "Roadside Memorials: Making Grief Visible," *Bereavement Care* 29 (2010): 34–36; Rebecca M. Kennedy, "Getting Messy: In the Field and at the Crossroads with Roadside Shrines," *Text and Performance Quarterly* 22 (2002): 229–60; and Jon K. Reid and Cynthia L. Reid, "A Cross Marks the Spot: A Study of Roadside Death Memorials in Texas and Oklahoma," *Death Studies* 25 (2001): 241–56.

52. See Doss, *Memorial Mania*, 84–87, for a discussion of roadside memorials. Public discourse is also increasingly referencing this phenomenon, and newspaper reports are numerous. Among many specific reports appearing in public newspapers, see, for example, Peter Maller, "I-43 Memorials Restored Again: Rift over Crosses for Crash Victims Continues," *Milwaukee Journal Sentinel* On Line, April 24, 2003, accessed October 29, 20015, http://www.jsonline.com/nl-search/we/archives.document #OFAA6113D82CC67C. See also Ian Urbina, "As Roadside Memorials Multiply, a Second Look," *New York Times*, February 6, 2006, accessed October 29, 20015, http://www.nytimes.com/2006/02/06/national/06shrine .html. Websites like RoadsideAmerica.com, which offers information and photographs as available discourse, position the *descansos* as roadside attractions, even if respectfully doing so. On its "Descansos: Highway Fatality Memorials" pages, RoadsideAmerica.com argues that the particularity of the informal *descansos*, with their photographs and offerings to dead individuals, is being overtaken by state-sponsored responses to the clutter and chaos that some see in these memorials. Florida, for example, marks the spot of a highway fatality with a round sign that reads "Drive Safely"; the name of the deceased appears in smaller print below. State author-

ity trumps individual improvisatory creativity in this case. Meanwhile, new businesses offer premade roadside crosses, providing a standardizing template for limited individual adornment. Erecting roadside memorials can be viewed as an act of civil disobedience in some states. See www .roadsideamerica.com/story/33006, accessed October 29, 2015.

53. So far, with one exception that I know of, these roadside memorials commemorate human deaths. People for the Ethical Treatment of Animals has been campaigning to erect signs marking the sites of accidents involving animals on the way to slaughter. Its efforts have been denied in all cases except one, in Mount Horeb, Wisconsin, which has no laws prohibiting the posting of memorial signs. There a simple blue sign with black lettering reads, "In memory of the cows who were crushed to death in a truck accident at this spot. Try vegan." Like the Drive Safely memorial markers that some states erect, this transgressive marker combines mourning with a proposed solution.

54. Richard E. Meyer and David M. Gradwohl, "'Best Damn Dog We Ever Had': Some Folkloristic and Anthropological Observations on San Francisco's Presidio Pet Cemetery," *Markers: Journal of the Association for Gravestone Studies* 12 (1995): 161–205. The cemetery is now closed to new burials but is maintained by a nonprofit organization.

55. Nikki Tundel, "Tracking the Tombstone Trends," Minnesota Public Radio News, May 8, 2009, accessed October 29, 2015, http://minnesota .publicradio.org/display/web/2009/05/08/gravestones. Even if displaying unusual etchings, the tombstones usually (but not always) have conventional shapes, retaining a visual solemnity out of sync with the engraved decoration. These tombstone design trends echo changes in funeral customs too, which now often feature casket linings printed with images recalling the deceased's favorite pastimes, like a camouflage interior for one who loved hunting. Caskets are even made in unique shapes, one built like a golf bag. Nikki Tundel, "Death: Have It Your Way," Minnesota Public Radio News, May 21, 2007, accessed October 29, 2015, http://minnesota .publicradio.org/display/web/2007/05/18/personalization.

56. Pamela Brown and Holly Yan, "Cemetery Denies SpongeBob Monuments for Slain Army Sergeant," CNN, October 22, 2013, accessed October 29, 2015, http://www.cnn.com/2013/10/22/us/spongebob-gravestone -controversy.

57. The Internet offers another space for the semipublic expression of ambivalence, with many individuals commemorating dead pets on their blogs or posting memorials online. Here is one such blog entry, from a colleague describing her dead, six-year-old tortoiseshell tabby cat. The post is titled "RIP XXX 2007–2013." After describing the cat's life and death, the writer concludes with these lines: "I loved that damn cat. And that sentence sums it up. He was a good buddy, but he was still a cat, and I've never been that in to cats. That turd drove me nuts, but he was also one-of-a-

kind. So here's to XXX: As much as he was an asshole, he was also my friend and an amazing cat. The world is a less mellow place without him." Photos of the writer, the cat, and a surviving dog follow the post, and comments express condolences—some addressed not only to the writer but to her dog as well. It's hard to imagine inscribing the words "He was an asshole, but he was also my friend" on a tombstone, even one for a pet cemetery, where there is greater range for the expression of ambivalence and regret; but this freedom of expression is granted in a blog, especially one with access (theoretically) restricted to family and friends. We can see these various modalities of expression (cyberspace, pet cemetery, graveside service, human cemeteries) as falling along a continuum of formality, with the pet cemetery, by definition, combining some of the formality of a physical and enduring space with the freedom accorded the second-ary status of both the real estate and those buried there, and the gravity granted (or not) to those who mourn for them.

58. Even those participating in the burial may have differing opinions of its appropriateness. In a study of pet burial in the United States, David Witt notes that the range of motivations for such burial is quite large. He heard the following during his fieldwork: "I hated that bird, we did it for the children"; "My wife wanted to bury the damned cat, and I felt obliged"; "That dog treated me better than my old lady ever did." See David Witt, "Pet Burial in the United States," in *The Handbook of Death and Dying*, vol. 2, ed. C. D. Bryant (New York: Sage, 2003), 757–66.

59. Websites like PetLoss.com provide a safe space for the posting of reminis-cences and descriptions of loss and are actively used by tens of thousands. These sites function somewhat differently from physical memorial locales. Although they attract a virtual community of presumably like-minded individuals, they lack the copresence that a physical cemetery provides for the mourner and the physical remains of the mourned animal, brought together in a secular/sacralized space. Other mediated resources include pet-loss phone helplines that are run by many veterinary colleges. Staffed by volunteers and veterinary students, they provide a sympathetic ear for callers who are receiving insufficient support from family, friends, and co-workers, and can help validate the mourner's right to grieve. Volunteering on one of these helplines one night, I was struck by callers' descriptions of how dismissive some families can be, how they seem to expect instant recovery from the pet's death, regarding it as an inconvenience to be recti-fied rather than an emotional loss.

60. Phillip Bachelor, "Practical Bereavement," *Health Sociology Review* 16 (2007): 405–14. Bachelor employs on-site observation, a small number of in-depth interviews, and a large survey of mourners at several Australian cemeteries in his research.

61. This is one reason why backyard burials, denied humans, can be comfort-ing in the case of animal deaths, although this practice has its own prob-

NOTES TO PAGE 99

lems in a mobile society in which moving to a new house means leaving the remains behind. That most pets live far shorter lives than humans exacerbates this problem, because a mobile family may experience pet deaths in many different states. A 2005 column by the widely syndicated advice columnist "Dear Abby" addresses this issue. See "Readers Offer Advice on Dealing with Departed Pets," *Iowa City (IA) Press-Citizen*, June 28, 2005. In this column, readers recount their trauma at seeing pet graves destroyed by new owners of their former homes, to make way for home improvements. Some commentators urge cremation, with its promise of portability, precisely to avoid that problem. That one of the most widely syndicated advice columnists in the United States devoted a whole column to this issue marks it as one of widespread concern. The portability of cremains for pets addresses the need to remain close to the remains of the deceased while accommodating contemporary familial mobility, but it also reflects the sparsity of local pet cemeteries. If every community had a repository for pet cremains, I suspect that, as they do for human cremains, many families would choose a designated site in perpetuity for the deposition or scattering of animal cremains, a physical site providing them with a focus for mourning.

62. Bachelor, "Practical Bereavement," 413.
63. Ibid., 60. While simply generalizing from one national study to other nations would be foolhardy, I think it is reasonable to assume that significant parallels between the Australian and US cases may exist. Both countries were European settler colonies with imperial histories as far as indigenous populations are concerned. Today, both have ethnically complex populations, although this is more recent in Australia's case and is markedly shaped by a history of enslaved African workers in the case of the United States. In both nations, Christianity is a dominant religious force.

    Cemetery behavior may be shaped by social and religious conventions, but it is further defined by age and gender. Middle-aged and older and female visitors predominate in Bachelor's extensive Australian study, and females tend both to visit more often and to stay longer at the graves of loved ones. There could be many reasons for this: perhaps women are enacting the fact that, overall, they are granted greater permission to express sorrow and to cry in public, or maybe they are accepting their conventional role of caretaker, doing most of the emotional "care work" for a family.

64. See, for example, the Facebook page of Faithful Companions Pet Remembrance Services in Coralville, Iowa, accessed October 29, 2015, https://www.facebook.com/Faithful-Companions-Pet-Remembrance-Services-/250983288316057.
65. On gender difference, see the Associated Press 2009 poll of one thousand pet owners by Roper Public Affairs and Media, which reported that

women more than men, and single women more than married women, were more likely to regard their pet as "a full member of the family." See NBCNEWS.com, "Poll: Americans Consider Pets Part of Family," June 23, 2009, accessed October 29, 2015, http://www.nbcnews.com/id/31505216/ ns/health-pet_health/t/poll-americans-consider-pets-part-of-family/# .AoDPZN1JO.

66. I discussed aspects of online mourning, especially gender, in a presentation at the 2003 International Society for Anthrozoology meetings held at Kent State University, Canton, Ohio, August 15–16, in an unpublished paper titled "Relating to Animals after Death: Virtual Pet Cemeteries and the Public Act of Grieving Online."

67. Bachelor, "Practical Bereavement," 413.

68. Errol Morris, dir., *Gates of Heaven* (Gates of Heaven Production Company, USA, 1978). The horror film *Pet Sematary* (1989), based on Stephen King's novel, also provides negative images.

69. Kari Weil bridges the gap we often see in "animal studies" between approaches that examine contemporary issues, like sociological approaches, and those that focus on grasping epistemologies and ontologies, developed in philosophical studies, for example. She does so not only through her approach to literary and visual artworks but also in her insertion of self-reflexive commentary into her readings of those texts. In her decision to cremate Peanut's body, rather than have it disposed of by, say, a rendering plant, which is often the case for horses, she thought Peanut "deserved a better afterlife," and that a testament to Peanut's life "depended on 'proper treatment' of the body—one that did not grind it up for the market." Still, she struggled with the question "for whom am I doing this?" See Kari Weil, *Thinking Animals: Why Animal Studies Now?* (New York: Columbia University Press, 2012), 103.

CHAPTER FIVE

1. William Wordsworth, "Tribute—to the Memory of the Same Dog," in *Funeral and Memorial Service Readings, Poems, and Tributes*, ed. Rachel R. Brown (Jefferson, NC: McFarland, 1999), 95. Wordsworth lived from 1770 to 1850.

2. Some pet cemeteries have formal sections dedicated to "working dogs" such as police dogs, who are saluted as heroes. While police dogs may live with the families of their human police partners, they do not fall simply into the pet category. The cemeteries, however, give them an honored status—a sort of superpet whose value extended beyond the family of her or his "owner" to the wider public the dog protected.

3. Katherine Grier, *Pets in America: A History* (New York: Harcourt, 2006), 11.

4. The US legal status of animals currently codes pets as "property," but this classification is under pressure from within the US juridical system, with

some legal scholars proposing the new category of "sentient property." The status is also being contested by pet owners who believe their pets are not simply property but affective beings, and who file legal claims for emotional damages as well as replacement "costs" for a lost pet. We are also seeing worldwide shifts in legal protections for selected species like apes and cetaceans, including legislation in the European Union and in India, which recently passed legislation protecting cetaceans as "nonhuman persons." See Robert Krulwich, "Why Dolphins Make Us Nervous," NPR blogs, June 13, 2013, accessed October 31, 2015, http://www.npr.org/blogs/krulwish/2013/06/13/191286344/why-dolphins-make-us-nervous. See also Government of India Ministry of Environment and Forests, Central Zoo Authority, Circular, May 17, 2013, F. No. 20-1/2010-CZA(M)/2840, "Sub:—Policy on establishment of dolphinarium—Regarding."

5. See especially chapter 2, "At Home with Animals," and chapter 3, "A Domestic Ethic of Kindness to Animals," in Grier, *Pets in America*. Books like Anna Sewell's *Black Beauty* (1877) contributed significantly to popularizing this call for kindness.

6. Although, presumably, most pet owners who mourn at pet cemeteries think of their practice of pet keeping in positive terms, Yi-Fu Tuan takes a different approach in his book *Dominance and Affection: The Making of Pets* (New Haven, CT: Yale University Press, 1984), in which he composes an analysis from a mélange of elements, from garden keeping to fish husbandry, skidding wildly across time and geography, to make broad associations and assertions about human interactions with a "natural" world. "Human relation with nature is seldom pure," he writes. "Whether we use plants and animals for economic or playful and aesthetic ends, we *use* them; we do not attend to them for their own good except in fables" (176). The pet relation, like other human relations between dominant classes and subordinates, may combine curious renditions of dominance and affection, with domestication of pets dependent on developing manageability and control or on the exhibition of the pet, like a goldfish, as an art object, not as a subject in its own right. Certainly, pet keeping is a complex ideological, social, and material practice that does combine elements of care and domination. Its dynamics often follow a family model of adult supervision and care for a childlike pet dependent on the human for the very basics of survival: food, water, and shelter. But such a model ignores the multitude of ways in which animals as "pets" contravene the assumptions and household "rules" that are meant to structure these exchanges. Anyone who has lived with a dog knows that canine desires assert themselves vocally, physically, and psychically within the framework of a "home." Except in extreme cases, negotiation, rather than domination, would seem to be the norm. See Donna J. Haraway, *When Species Meet* (Minneapolis: University of Minnesota Press, 2007). *Domestication* is a freighted term that applies to some pets as well as to noncompanion

animals used for food. For an extensive consideration, see Molly Mullin and Rebecca Cassidy, eds., *Where the Wild Things Are Now: Domestication Reconsidered* (New York: Bloomsbury Academic, 2007).

7. Grier, *Pets in America*, 198–99.

8. This trend was consistent with the founding of similar social-improvement organizations, like the New York Society for the Prevention of Cruelty to Children (NYSPCC), the first child protective agency in the world, founded in 1875 (see its website, accessed October 29, 2015, http://www.nyspcc.org). Both reflect a historically specific notion of a wider concern for and sense of moral obligation to "vulnerable" populations incumbent on the majority population as part of the social contract of a nation.

9. Grier, *Pets in America*, 142–46.

10. These statistics are taken from the American Pet Products Association (APPA) website ("Pet Industry Market Size and Ownership Statistics," accessed October 29, 2015, http://www.americanpetproducts.org/press_industrytrends.asp). Other sources provide slightly different figures, probably relating to differing definitions and research designs. The American Humane Association website, for example, as noted in chapter 4, note 14, gives figures from both the American Veterinary Medical Association and the APPA, and gives estimates for underserved communities, too. Despite variations, all figures show that more than half of all US households have a pet. See www.humanesociety.org/issues/pet_overpopulation/facts/pet_ownership_statistics.html, accessed October 29, 2015.

The APPA's figures on pet ownership and expenditures are fully accessible only by paying a fee of more than three thousand dollars to purchase a membership, but some basic statistics are made available for free. It is clear that despite the impact of the economic downturn in the United States in recent years, the overall pet-keeping trend is upward, with increasing numbers of households having at least one pet. It may be that recent economic pressures have shown up in decreased expenditures on veterinary services, grooming, or pet toy purchases, as well as, to a smaller extent, the number of pets relinquished to humane societies if a family feels it can no longer afford to pay for its pet's needs. Given the trends, and barring some unanticipated limit, we can reasonably assume that awareness of "pets" in US culture will only continue to grow, and that pet keeping will demand increased recognition in the public sphere, reflected in news reports, TV programs, legislative initiatives, and so on.

11. The American Veterinary Medical Association (AVMA) estimates that the recent recession in the United States resulted in a drop in the number of pets between 2006 and 2011, with households owning dogs declining nearly 2% and those owning cats decreasing just over 6% during that time. Against an overall growth trend in pet keeping in the last quarter century, the figures reflect that pet keeping costs money and that, when money is tight, the pet may be discarded or rehomed. Thus, although a

majority of households regard the pet as "part of the family," the pet's *status in the family is often a fluid and more marginal one than for human family members.* AVMA figures are reported in the American Humane Association's fact sheet at http://www.americanhumane.org/assets/pdfs/pets-fact -sheet.pdf, which also notes that the top three reasons for relinquishing a dog were moving, landlord issues, and cost of pet maintenance, but that the top three for cats were "too many in house," allergies, and moving. These differences indicate that species difference is another factor that needs to be assessed when making generalizations about pet keeping and human bonds with their pets.

12. GDP figures from the World Bank website (accessed October 31, 2015, http://www.worldbank.org).

13. In 2011, six out of ten pet owners, or 63.2%, considered their pets to be family members. See American Veterinary Medical Association, *U.S. Pet Ownership and Demographics Sourcebook* (Schaumburg, IL: AVMA, 2012). A 2009 Associated Press poll of eleven hundred pet owners, conducted by by GfK Roper Public Affairs and Media, found that half of all pet owners say their pet is as "much a part of the family as any other person in the household," while another 36% say their pet is not as full a member of the household as humans. Gender, marital status, and childbearing appear to shape this response: "Singles are more likely to say a pet was a full member of the family than married people—66 percent of single women versus 46 percent of married women, for example. And men were less likely to call their pet a full member of the household." Taken together, these figures, while necessarily imprecise, are suggestive. They imply that 86% of US pet-keeping households today regard their pet as integral if not core to their conception of their family. Therefore, a "familial" or kinship relation is the primary lens through which human-pet relations are perceived or at least talked about. See NBCNEWS.com, "Poll: Americans Consider Pets Part of Family," accessed October 31, 2015, http://www.nbcnews.com/ id/31505216/ns/health-pet_health/t/poll-americans-consider-pets-part -family/.

14. Christina Risley-Curtiss et al., "She Was Family: Women of Color and Animal-Human Connections," in *Between the Species: Readings in Human-Animal Relations*, ed. Arnold Arluke and Clinton Sanders (Boston: Pearson Education, 2009), 61–69.

15. Ibid.

16. Gregory Berns, "Dogs Are People Too," *New York Times*, October 5, 2013, accessed October 31, 2015, http://www.nytimes.com/2013/10/06/opinion/ sunday/dogs-are-people-too.html.

17. Stanley Brandes, "The Meaning of American Pet Cemetery Gravestones," *Ethnology* 48, no. 2 (2009): 99–118. It should be noted, although Brandes does not make this connection, that the inclusion of such photos has also

become more common for human gravestones, and the practice may be an aesthetic bleed-over from human cemetery designs.

18. Ibid., 109. At Hartsdale, other mourners have adopted and changed this custom, leaving commercially manufactured shiny stones as a sign of their visit. This practice indicates a transreligious community of pet lovers whose deceased beloveds are not separated into religiously segregated burial grounds as their human dead might be, thus allowing for more hybrid spillover of customs. Hartsdale even offers the services of a minister if pet owners request that burial be accompanied by a religious ceremony (see ibid., 110).

19. Ibid., 113. While I appreciate and find persuasive Brandes's historical tracking of increasing individuation and familialization over time based on a reading of material culture, the notion that pets are "children" needs further investigation. Although human mourners often use that term (e.g., "My Baby"), other actions, such as making sharp distinctions between what sort of expenditures on medical care are appropriate for animals versus human members of a family, indicate that the rhetorical adoption of the kinship term is not unproblematic and may indicate in part a use of available discourse adapted to a new conception of the familial.

20. Larry S. McGrath, review of *Frames of War: When Is Life Grievable?* by Judith Butler, *MLN: Modern Language Notes* 124 (2009): 1232.

21. Judith Butler, *Frames of War: When Is Life Grievable?* (New York: Verso, 2009), 38.

22. Ibid.

23. Ibid., 39.

24. Kari Weil notes this limitation of Butler's conception of the "grievable life": "Of course, for Butler, death of an animal is by definition not grievable—grief being reserved for and constitutive of what is human." See Kari Weil, *Thinking Animals: Why Animal Studies Now?* (New York: Columbia University Press, 2012), 113. See also Chloe Taylor, "The Precarious Lives of Animals: Butler, Coetzee, and Animal Ethics," *Philosophy Today* 52 (2008): 60–72.

25. James Stanescu, "Judith Butler, Mourning, and the Precarious Lives of Animals," *Hypatia* 27 (2012): 580.

26. Ibid., 579.

27. Ibid.

28. Despite my emphasis on lived experience, I certainly do not mean to suggest that as scholars, we merely take our respondents' interpretations of their actions as dogma. Their interpretations exist and come to active fruition only in a larger and often contradictory context (as do ours, of course). It is the scholar's obligation and privilege, as both "inside" and "outside" the meaning systems of a particular community, to endeavor to articulate this complex terrain through which meaning making happens, is claimed, or is ascribed, and to articulate and understand the mecha-

nisms involved while investigating their effects in multiple realms such as law, ethics, social formations, and so on. See Joan W. Scott, "The Evidence of Experience," *Critical Inquiry* 17 (1991): 773–97.

29. Explorations of the legacy of western European philosophical traditions and their relation to the constitution of the political are highly developed and increasingly drawn on in animal studies. However, in the work of political theorists, and in Stanescu's development of Butler's ideas, the leap from ontology to history is often made with a single word: *thus.* One can bridge the gap between the ancient Greeks and the US bombing in Afghanistan with this simple word. Although politics and ethics are often invoked, the actual structures of social formations over time and place—that is, history—get short shrift. This is understandable perhaps, as philosophers aren't required to be historians or anthropologists. But the scope of claims made sometimes belies the fact that such historical specificity could, in fact, generate more subtle philosophical claims and render their purchase on present political actions more profound. For example, Stanescu bases part of his argument on the presumption that mourning is often relegated to the realm of the private, but in many cases this is not true, and the hiring of public "mourners" may even be necessary to enact the embodied signs of grief for a specific public.

30. Statements heard in the clinical rotation "Exotic Pet Management" offered at the University of Illinois College of Veterinary Medicine, December 2014, directed by Mark Mitchell, DVM.

31. Erin Alberty (*Salt Lake [UT] Tribune*), "Roadside Memorial for 'Terrified Turkeys' Killed in Crash Pushed by PETA," *San Jose (CA) Mercury News,* May 7, 2014, accessed October 30, 2015, http://www.mercurynews.com/ pets-animals/ci_25712006/roadside-memorial-terrified-turkeys-killed -crash-is-pushed#. I thank Gabrielle Basile for bringing this incident to my attention. PETA has previously attempted to memorialize other animals and has succeeded in doing so for cattle killed in a road accident in Wisconsin, where the legal restrictions on such memorials are loose.

32. Municipal regulations requiring minimal standards of care for domestic animals, including the provision of food, water, shelter, and medical care, vary substantially from community to community but are encoded in animal cruelty statutes. A new professional specialty in forensic animal law is enabling the legal prosecution of those who deliberately inflict pain on such animals or who fail to provide these minimal requirements.

33. Adam Cole, "A Musical Memorial for the Face of Extinction," National Public Radio, January 11, 2015, 5:43 a.m. E.T. accessed October 31, 2015, http://www.npr.org/2015/01/06/375481820/a-musical-memorial-for-the -face-of-extinction. I thank Barbara J. King for bringing this story to my attention.

34. This seems to be the case, for example, in the shifting landscape of gay and lesbian relationships, which are increasingly receiving recognition

from the states and the federal government as they are more broadly deemed "worthy" of social support and recognition. There are not only political and affective results from this shift (e.g., access to the bedside of a dying partner) but also, in the case of same-sex marriage, significant monetary ones in terms of inheritance and other matters.

35. Lisa Marie Cacho, "'You Just Don't Know How Much He Meant': Deviancy, Death, and Devaluation," *Latino Studies* 5 (2007): 182–208.

36. Ibid.

37. I thank Jennifer Baldwin for bringing this issue to my attention. See, for example, John Van Aerde, "Guidelines for Health Care Professionals Supporting Families Experiencing a Perinatal Loss," *Pediatric Child Health* 6 (2001): 469–77.

38. Recently, in a contestatory move in Florence, Italy, the mayor announced that city hall would dedicate a section of the municipal cemetery of Trespiano to "babies who died 'before birth,' including by abortion." This move angered some feminists and some on the Far Left, including the Radical Party, who have denounced the move as "macabre" and an attack on the country's liberal abortion law. See Hilary White, "City of Florence Approves Cemetery for Unborn Victims of Abortion, Attacked by Leftists," *LifeSiteNews*, November 11, 2013, accessed February 2, 2014, but no longer available, http://www.lifesitenews.com/news/city-of-florence-approves -cemetery-for-unborn-victims-. I thank Giorgio Mariani for bringing this cemetery to my attention.

In the United States, some Catholic cemeteries provide burials for fetuses and stillborns. While most babies who die in utero do not make it out of the hospital to a formal burial, the Rachel Mourning and Holy Innocents sections at Holy Cross Cemetery in Avondale, Arizona, provide burial services for fetuses who do not survive outside the womb, and the Queen of Heaven Cemetery and Mortuary, a Catholic facility in the Phoenix, Arizona, Diocese, also provides a section for the "unborn." These burial and funeral practices can be seen not only as establishing the important religious context for the mourners but also as part of the larger context of asserting the importance of a "grievable life." In this case, the emphasis is on "a life beginning at the moment of conception," since these practices link also to the Catholic Church's opposition to abortion. See "Catholic Cemeteries Provide for Unborn," *Catholic Sun*, October 18, 2012, accessed October 31, 2015, http//www.catholicsun.org/so12/10/18/ catholic-cemeteries-provide-for-unborn.

These particular cases help us see the sociopolitical stakes in public mourning that are part of all mourning, whether or not that aspect is recognized. At the basis of some of these debates lies the lineage from fetus to personhood, a politically fraught traverse for feminists and others who support abortion rights. More broadly in the case of animals, there is no such presumption of a line toward personhood, whether an animal dies in the womb or on the road. Only very slowly is this categorical designation of ultimate social value being reconfigured to potentially include, in the legal realm at least, some types of animals, like primates. A recent Argentine court, for example, ruled that a captive orangutan, Sandra, must be moved to a sanctuary from a Buenos Aires zoo because her cognitive capacity makes her a "non-human person" who has some basic (human) rights. See Marc Bekoff, "Sandra Orangutan Declared a Person with a Right to Freedom," *Psychology Today,* December 22, 2014, accessed October 31, 2015, http://www.psychologytoday.com/blog/animal-emotions/201412/sandra.

39. Mathew Scully, surprisingly, unpacks this notion of Christian dominion over animals to argue not simply for responsible "use" of nonhuman animals by humans but also for a more dynamic notion that underlines a position of human *responsibility* toward nonhuman animals, and the necessity of human intervention in assuring their welfare. See Matthew Scully, *Dominion: The Power of Man, the Suffering of Animals, and the Call to Mercy* (New York: St. Martin's Press, 2003).

40. Unitarian Universalist Association, "Ethical Eating: Food and Environmental Justice, 2011 Statement of Conscience," accessed October 31, 2015, http://www.uua.org/statements/statements/ethical-eating-food -environmental-justice.

41. Take, for example, the report that 98% of sexually active Catholic women in the United States say they use contraception forms other than the church-approved "rhythm method" for avoiding pregnancy. See "Most Catholic Women in U.S. Use Birth Control Banned by Church," Reuters Edition.com, April 13, 2011, accessed October 31, 2015, http://www .reuters.com/article/2011/04/14/us-most-catholic-women-use-birth-cont -idUSTRE73D4522.

42. Kay Cozad, "Honoring the Dead Awakens New Trends," *Today's Catholic News*, October 26, 2011, accessed October 31, 2015, http://www .todayscatholicnews.org/2011/10/honoring-the-dead-awakens-new-trends.

43. August 13, 2013, Facebook postings, accessed January 27, 2014, but no longer available, https://www.facebook.com/msn/posts/101515911536966409. The comments responded to "Plan for Pet Cemetery in SF Spurs Religious Argument," msn.com, August 12, 2013, accessed January 27, 2014, but no longer available, http://news.msn.com/pop-culture/plan-for-pet-cemetery -in-sf-spurs-religious-argument. The news item, posted on Facebook on August 13, 2013, was framed by the question, "Is it inappropriate to have beloved pets' ashes laid to rest at a shrine to St. Francis? Francis is, after all, the patron saint of animals." See also Chris Roberts, "Plan for North Beach Church Pet Cemetery Laid to Rest," *San Francisco Examiner*, March 8, 2014, accessed October 31, 2015, www.archives/sfexaminer/ sanfrancisco/plans-for-north-beach-church-pet-cemetery-laid-to-rest.

44. It is possible that with the papacy of Francis, the Catholic Church is itself moving toward a more liberal view on the status of animals. A widely

reported remark made by Pope Francis in a general audience at the Vatican in November 2014, indicating that "God's wonderful design affects everything around us," was taken to mean that it included animals too. Some have interpreted it to mean that the pope believes that animals go to heaven. The remark generated wide discussion, especially as it came after earlier papal remarks by Francis that seemed to indicate a softening of the church's stance on gays and lesbians and on unmarried couples. Pope John Paul II had seemed to reverse earlier church doctrine when he proclaimed that animals do have souls and are "as near to God as men are," but this assertion wasn't publicized widely by the Vatican. Reported in Rick Gladstone, "Dogs in Heaven? Pope Francis Leaves Pearly Gates Open," *New York Times*, December 11, 2014, accessed October 31, 2015, http://www.nytimes.com/2014/12/12/world/europe/dogs-in-heaven-pope -leaves-pearly-gate-open.html.

45. Although most will use this template for *pet* burials, the format also allows for variations to be used at the burial of a *farm animal*, upon the disappearance of a pet, and at the burial of a *wild animal*. See "At the Loss of a Pet or Other Animal: A Service of Grieving and Thanksgiving," accessed October 31, 2015, http://www.philosophy-religion.org/dogs/pet-funeral .htm, or contact the Reverend Robert E. Stiefel at RENStiefel@aol.com.

46. A panel participant in a discussion of grieving for pets held at the University of Illinois in 2013 related a personal anecdote about such a mass. The speaker reported that she was, at the time of her dog's death, a practicing Catholic and wanted a memorial mass said for him, just as she had when her mother passed away. Rather than listing the dog's full name, which would have been a giveaway, she simply converted his name to initials followed by her own family name. The priest was none the wiser, and the mass was said. Through this subterfuge, the woman found a creative way to meld her own religious practice with her desire to mourn formally for her dog.

47. As a result of the tension between states and the federal government and between local communities and a state government, many cemetery regulations come down to the municipal level. See, for example, Florida Department of Financial Services: Division of Funeral, Cemetery, and Consumer Services, accessed October 31, 2015, http://www.myfloridacfo .com/Division/funeralcemetery/.

Even the practice of interring pet remains with human ones varies by community ordinance. Florida, for example, states that "pets can be buried with their owners, if the animal pre-deceased the owner. Their ashes may be placed in the grave or crypt. The licensed cemetery by-laws will determine if they allow this practice." In this case, the pet must have died prior to, not subsequent to, the human, and her/his body must have been cremated. Such burials cannot be added to a human cemetery plot after the fact, so to speak, of the relevant human burial.

In addition, many types of cemeteries in the state of Florida are "exempt cemeteries," falling outside state mandates. They include small-scale family cemeteries of less than two acres, cemeteries owned and operated since 1915 by a fraternal organization, cemeteries owned and operated by a religious institution before 1976, and community and nonprofit association cemeteries, as well as county and municipal cemeteries. While religious cemeteries may separate the graves of individuals along religious lines, no cemetery, exempt or not, may refuse burial based on race or color, according to Florida law. Pet cemeteries have no statewide regulation but may be regulated by municipal ordinance. Similarly, the state of Florida does not prohibit scattering of cremated ashes in backyards or on any state lands; it prohibits disposal in freshwater bodies because of environmental or health concerns. Landlords or condominium associations may have restrictions. As just this sample of Florida state laws reveals, local restrictions and permissions can vary, not only at the state level but also at the municipal level, and even, where condominium associations are concerned, at the level of the apartment complex!

48. State of Florida website for Cemetery and Consumer Services: http://www
.myfloridacfo.com/Division/funeralcemetery/Consumers/ConsumerFAQ
.htm, accessed October 31, 2015.

49. See "Alabama Man Loses Battle to Keep His Wife Buried in His Front
Yard," Reuters, November 15, 2013, accessed October 31, 2015,
http://www.reuters.com/article/2013/11/15/us-usa-alabama-burial
-idUSBRE9AE17020131115. The removal of the body was undertaken based
on claims that groundwater could be contaminated otherwise, since the
site was not approved as a public or family cemetery.

50. And this change is newsworthy. A Cleveland, Ohio, TV newscast, for
instance, covered the launch by the family-run DeJohn Funeral Homes
of the DeJohn Pet Service, to "provide cremations or burials, memorial
products and pet loss support." "We understand the love our clients have
for their pets and the pain of losing a member of the family. That empathy helps us provide the highest quality care to each of the families that
we serve," stated Ross DeJohn Jr., owner and founder, in a news release
quoted in the news story. See Elizabeth Misson, "Family-Owned Funeral
Home to Start Pet Cremation and Grief Support Center," newsnet5.com,
October 6, 2011, accessed October 31, 2015, http://www.newsnet5.com/
news/local-news/family-owned-funeral-home-to-start-pet-cremation-and
-grief-support-center.

51. This potential growth would respond to the need I have articulated of
bringing the remains of the deceased into the physical copresence of
those who are mourning, to facilitate grieving and the ultimate psychological integration of the loss into the ongoing life of the survivor.

52. In 2004, I attended the association's national convention in Las Vegas and
gave an invited talk on how people mourn for their pets. Seminars for

the participants focused on how to develop a pet cemetery business, and highlighted the growth of this industry as it arose from human death-care professions. I thank the association for inviting me to speak and for enabling me to attend these meetings, which informed my research. The association, founded in 1971 in Chicago, now has members in fifteen countries. For further information, see its website: http://www.iaopc.com, accessed October 31, 2015.

53. See, for example, the July/August 2004 issue of *Mortuary Management*, a funeral industry publication. I thank Michael Lensing for sending me a copy of this issue. It features two news items about pet funerals; one reported on All Pets Crematory and Remembrances, a business in Stamford, Connecticut, that provides pet funeral services, with an interfaith minister and a Catholic priest on call for "for families who want to hold a memorial service for their pet" (27). In the same publication, the Clock Funeral Home, which handles human funerals in Muskegon, Michigan, was recognized for offering a pet memorial service for Charlie, a twelve-and-a-half-year-old Labrador retriever belonging to Diane Conklin. The service included a minister, guest speakers, and a "tribute" video presentation on the dog's life, all practices that typify human memorial services. A reception at the funeral home's family center followed the service, which was deemed a "first" for Muskegon (23). That this event was considered newsworthy and even highlighted in a trade publication for the human funeral industry indicates its status as a harbinger of things to come while underscoring how unusual it still was in 2004.

54. "Pet Services: Innovation in Tough Times," *Mortuary Management*, March 2009, accessed October 31, 2015, http://www.abbottandhast.com/mm09 .html#March. See also the "Pet Passages" portion of the Anderson-McQueen website (http://petpassagespinellas.com/GriefSupport.aspx, accessed October 31, 2015), which emphasizes the normalcy of feeling grief for a lost pet.

55. See the website of Faithful Companions Pet Remembrance Services, Coralville, Iowa, accessed October 30, 2015, http://faithfulcompanionsia .com. Even before this formalization of pet-loss services, Lensing Funeral Services endeavored to serve those mourning the loss of their companion animals, even if the solution was unconventional. As director Michael Lensing noted at a pet-loss support information session I attended on September 26, 2002, in Iowa City, Iowa (cosponsored with local veterinarian Denis Cowles, the Friends of the Animal Center Foundation, also in Iowa City, and the local humane society), he had accommodated family wishes that month when a woman and her pet died at about the same time. The pet was placed in the casket with the woman for the formal viewing, per the family's request.

56. Donnelle Eller, "Horse Burial Rules Debated in Iowa," *Des Moines (IA) Register*, January 15, 2014, accessed October 31, 2015, http://www.usatoday

.com/story/news/nation/2014/01/15/horse-burial-rules-questioned-in
-Iowa/449945.I thank Kim Marra for bringing this issue to my attention.

57. See Yvonne J. Milspaw, "Segregation in Life, Segregation in Death: Landscape of an Ethnic Cemetery," *Pennsylvania Folklife* 30 (1980): 36–40, and
James C. Garman, "Viewing the Color Line through the Material Culture
of Death," *Historical Archaeology* 28 (1994): 74–93.

58. Marilyn Yalom, *The American Resting Place: Four Hundred Years of History
through Our Cemeteries and Burial Grounds* (Boston: Houghton Mifflin,
2008), 41.

59. Ibid., 28.

60. The proposed columbarium in San Francisco at the St. Francis of Assisi
Shrine would have been the first pet cemetery installed at a religious site.
However, as noted earlier, it has generated significant controversy pre-
cisely because of this fact, and in 2014 plans for it were abandoned.

61. I thank my colleague Dr. Rui Kohiyama for finding this site, the Enmeijizo-
son Animals Memorial Park, and taking me there. The grounds included
aboveground vaults and numerous burial sites marked by ceremonial Buddhist posts with pet names inscribed on them; in a columbarium space,
many types of niches were offered in different sizes. Visiting families supplied water and rice offerings in the individual niches, which they could
open, and which also included photos of their deceased pets. The whole
atmosphere was one of formality and dignity. A glossy brochure advertised
the multiple services available at the cemetery, and featured a photograph
of a well-attended religious service. A pet cemetery located several miles
outside Rio de Janeiro that I visited several years ago also offered individual burial sites but differed in many respects from the Yokohama site. The
grounds were only moderately maintained, and the site was far outside
the urban center and hard to get to. Nonetheless, many people had chosen
to bury their pets there. In both of these instances, my inability to speak
the local language limited my chances of gathering information, but even
so, the sites provide evidence that the contemporary formal pet cemetery
phenomenon isn't limited to Europe and the United States.

62. Keith Cunningham, "Navajo, Mormon, Zuni Graves: Navajo, Mormon,
Zuni Ways," in *Cemeteries and Gravemarkers: Voices of American Culture*, ed.
Richard E. Meyer (Ann Arbor: UMI Research Press, 1989), 197–215.

63. Recently, the debates about abortion and when a fetus gains viability and
even "personhood" have erupted in Italy in a controversy over burial.
A cemetery in Florence has recently formalized a section devoted to the
remains of aborted pregnancies, to the dismay of some liberals and the joy
of some conservatives. See White, "City of Florence Approves Cemetery."
This example demonstrates that the category of the "grievable life" is
constantly in flux, and is a question not only of ethical or religious significance but of political import as well. I thank Giorgio Mariani for bringing
this example to my attention.

64. I use the term *apartheid* here, drawing on the legally enforced system of racial segregation and denigration in place in South Africa during the latter half of the twentieth century and most intensively from 1970 to 1990. "Species" and "race" are different historical hierarchical systems of supposedly scientific distinction, and the parallel I draw here is not to equate the two or to imply that the conditions in pet cemeteries somehow approach the misery the apartheid system caused for black South Africans. Instead, I am referencing the parallels in bodily categorization and legal geographic separation, a separation based in both cases on presumptions of difference and fear of potential for mixing or "pollution." Similarly, in the United States, separate graveyards for "blacks" and "whites" as well as for members of distinct religious groups historically manifested a social belief that "mixing" should not occur after death. Even "family graveyards" were intended only for members of a family, excluding outsiders. Each of these social divisions is different in scale and convention or legal enforcement, and none is the same as the animal-human divide per se. But both the function of social division and, in some cases, the denigration of those not allowed inside served to maintain through material means the social formations that shaped interactions in life.

65. See, for example, Barbara J. King's account of the man interred with a lamb in his family burial site in the Turkish village of Catalhöyük eight thousand to nine thousand years ago: *Being with Animals: Why We Are Obsessed with the Furry, Scaly, Feathered Creatures Who Populate Our World* (New York: Doubleday, 2010), 51.

66. Lucy Howard and Carla Koehl, "Stay with Me," *Newsweek*, September 30, 1996, 8.

67. See Alison Smith Squire, "Man's Best Friend Forever: Why We Buried Our Husbands with Their Pets," *Daily Mail* (United Kingdom), February 3, 2010, accessed October 31, 2015, http://www.dailymail.co.uk/femail/article-1248104/Mans-best-friend-forever-Why-buried-husbands-pets.html. Squire estimates that only a small number of pets in the United Kingdom are currently being buried in cemeteries, but I suggest that this number will increase, as it will in the United States, when more burial options become available. The UK Association of Private Pet Cemeteries and Crematoria estimates that of the 1.5 million cats and dogs that die each year, about 300,000 are buried in owners' gardens, 100,000 are individually cremated, and only about 1,000 are buried in pet cemeteries, with the rest, the vast majority, merely being incinerated as clinical waste. For a nation that regards itself as "a nation of pet lovers," as the article puts it, this is an odd calculus that probably reflects a lack of viable options more than the individual pet owners' desires.

68. Tom Suk, "Handler, Dog Are Together Forever," *Des Moines (IA) Register*, July 7, 2002, B1–2.

69. Nathan Place and Glenn Blain, "Pet Cemeteries Will Now Accept Human Remains for Burial alongside Beloved Family Pets," *New York Daily News*, September 14, 2013, accessed October 31, 2015, http://www.nydailynews .com/new-york/pets-pet-owners-allowed-buried-article-1.1455809.

70. "Spending More Time—Say, Forever—with Your Pet," CBS News/AP, February 5, 2011, accessed November 16, 2015, http://www.cbsnews.com/news/ spending-more-time-say-forever-with-your-pet. In 1925, this article reports, a woman had her ashes scattered over her dogs' grave at Hartsdale. In 1995, Arthur Link had his ashes interred there, joining those of his wife, Marjory, and sixteen "Longtime Friends," their cats (Aspen, Fritzie, Ginger, Gidget, Muffin, Bambi, Cricket, Snoopy, Gina, Patches, Foxy, Buttons, Dudley, Omar, Khayyam, and Valentino), whose names are engraved on a black granite monument. Just this collective listing of names, playful, historical, descriptive as they are, gives a sense of the humans who cared for all these pets.

71. After a strong campaign by Hartsdale patrons, the state approved the interment of Officer Ryan's cremated remains there in 2011—but at that time, a news story related, the six other pet cemeteries in the state "were still prohibited from putting Granny in the ground next to Fluffy or Fido . . . this [2013] rule change will allow New York pet owners from every corner of the state to play fetch for eternity with loved ones of any species or breed . . . as long as pet cemeteries don't charge a fee for a human burial and don't advertise their human burial services" (Place and Blain, "Pet Cemeteries Will Now Accept Human Remains"). Several things are of note in this news story. The tongue-in-cheek tone reminds us, first, that this practice is still open to censure as weird or lacking seriousness, and second, that the state has an interest in supporting the human burial industry, preventing "unfair" competition between animal burial organizations and the human funeral industry. Note too that these cases refer only to cremated remains—sterile and, in a sense, disembodied.

72. Burial plots on family-owned land could enable both human and pet burials. In addition, I have seen one brief news item reporting that apparently, "people will be allowed to be buried with their dogs at their feet at a remembrance park in Whalley, Lancashire," but I haven't been able to find any further information on this park. See "Lie Doggo," *Guardian* (Manchester), August 21, 2002.

73. Joe Schoenmann, "Legislation Would Allow Pets, Humans at Same Crematory," *Las Vegas Sun*, May 26, 2011, accessed October 31, 2015, http://www .lasvegassun.com/news/2011/may/26/owner-fears-proposed-legislation -will-hurt-his-pet/. Note that Mastny invokes the (aged, female) grandmother as representative of the most-beloved human deceased in need of protection, even if he references the potential polluter as the seemingly childlike and innocuous "Fluffy" rather than, say, "Butch."

74. Torri Akman, "Owners Being Buried with Pets, Sometimes in Pet Cemeteries," Philly.com, June 6, 2013, accessed October 31, 2015, http://articles .philly.com/2013-06-06/entertainment/39766798-1-pet-cemeteries-human -cemeteries-pet-remains.

75. Ibid.

76. Website of Hillcrest-Flynn Pet Funeral Home and Crematory and Hillcrest Memorial Park People and Pet Gardens, accessed October 31, 2015, http:// www.hillcrestflynn.com/code/default.asp.

77. Individuals who feel so strongly about their pets that they choose to be buried with them may face a dilemma, though. Given that so many pets (dogs, cats, most birds, rabbits, etc.) have much shorter life spans than most humans, pet lovers may have many pets over the course of their lives, perhaps retaining ashes from successive cremations. How would they buy a plot big enough to have room for all the pets they have cared for if that was their goal? Implicitly, in this arrangement, the size of the plot is built around human conventions.

78. Website of Hillcrest-Flynn Pet Funeral Home and Crematory and Hillcrest Memorial Park People and Pet Gardens.

79. Akman, "Owners Being Buried with Pets."

80. Recent scholarly work on what appears to be "mourning" by animals for other animals is also relevant here, broadening the notion of mourner, as does the recent trend in the writing of obituaries, which now sometimes include a listing of pets among those left behind by the deceased. See, from among many examples, the obituary for Anthony Hardman, age fifteen, published in the *Iowa City (IA) Press-Citizen*, June 2, 2005. It lists among his survivors not only family and friends but also "his best friend of all 'Annie Bell,' his rat terrier." For an extended discussion on what appear to be mourning behaviors by animals, see Barbara J. King, *How Animals Grieve* (Chicago: University of Chicago Press, 2013).

CHAPTER SIX

1. Bear's obituary appeared in the regular obituary section of the Tuesday, April 15, 2003, edition of the *Iowa City (IA) Press-Citizen*. Like all the other obituaries, it was titled simply by name and age, in this case, "Bear, 13," and was accompanied, like many of the others, by a black-and-white photo of the deceased (showing Bear outdoors, lying in the grass and staring into the camera). On May 8, 2003, Georgi Addis's sister-in-law, Sue Dayton of Iowa City, published a letter to the editor in the same paper (in the opinion section), with the title "Apology Owed for Dog Obituary." Other follow-up discussion included an April 21, 2003, letter to the editor (in the opinion section) from Tami Bryk, titled "Have the Editors Lost Their Minds?" This letter included, in its list of several complaints about the newspaper's choice of news stories, the following statement: "As a pet owner myself,

I understand completely the loss of a beloved pet. However, including it with the loss of a 91-year-old woman and her extensive contributions to humanity or the tragic loss of an infant son is simply appalling." Bryk called for a separate section for pets if the paper wishes to publish pet obituaries.

On May 10, 2003, *Press-Citizen* managing editor Jim Lewers apologized in his column "Meet Your Managing Editor" for not having considered an appropriate way to handle pet obituaries when the paper shifted to paid obituaries in 2002. "I apologize for that mistake, particularly to those whose loved ones' obituaries appeared on the same page as Bear . . . we've [now] decided to run all other pet obituaries in the classified section." The final act in this public debate in print occurred in another letter to the editor on May 16, 2003, titled "Pet Obituaries Belong in Paper" and signed by several members of the board of directors of the Friends of the Animal Center Foundation, Iowa City (supporting the work of the local animal shelter), including myself. This letter suggested that a weekly "pet memorials" section be established in the paper, because placing such announcements in the classified section, as the managing editor proposed, "reinforces the perception that pets are property." After writing this chapter, I see this as a useful compromise position at the present historical moment, but not as a final solution to the question of how to facilitate public mourning for animals.

2. Lewis Grossberger, "Spot Dead! City Mourns," *MediaWeek*, June 5, 2002, accessed November 4, 2015, http://www.ebscohost.com.

3. American Pet Products Association figures taken from the Humane Society of the United States website, accessed October 29, 2015, http://www.americanhumane.org/issues/pet_overpopulation/facts/pet_ownership_statistics.html, which reports statistics from the association's 2015 National Pet Owners Survey. For a report on the AP poll, see http://www.surveys.ap.org, accessed November 4, 2015.

4. The 2009 Associated Press poll gives some indication of a range of actions that the notion of "full part of the family" can elicit in individual humans, including buying gifts for the animal, giving the animal a human-like name, letting the animal sleep on the bed, and so on. This accounting, however, does not give us a sense of the hierarchy between human and nonhuman animal members of the family.

5. Throughout this chapter, I use the term *pet* instead of *companion animal*, because it is more widely used in the discourse I am analyzing. I also use the terms *animal* and *human* instead of *nonhuman animal* and *human animal* to emphasize the conceptual distinction repeatedly drawn in these debates about categories of beings that are deemed worthy of obituaries and those that are not.

6. Pulitzer Prize–winning obituary writer Jim Sheeler makes the point about obituaries as models for living in his book *Obit: Inspiring Stories of Ordinary People Who Led Extraordinary Lives* (New York: Penguin Books, 2007), ix.

7. Janice Hume, *Obituaries in American Culture* (Jackson: University Press of Mississippi, 2000).

8. Nigel Stark, *Life after Death: The Art of the Obituary* (Victoria, Australia: Melbourne University Press, 2006), 46. This is a wonderful comparative study of the histories of English-language obituary writing in England, the United States, and Australia.

9. Karol K. Maybury, "Invisible Lives: Women, Men, and Obituaries," *Omega* 32 (1995–96): 27–37; Robin D. Moremem and Cathy Cradduck, "'How Will You Be Remembered after You Die?' Gender Discrimination after Death Twenty Years Later," *Omega* 38 (1998–99): 241–54.

10. Alan Marks and Tommy Piggee, "Obituary Analysis and Describing a Life Lived: The Impact of Race, Gender, Age, and Economic Status," *Omega* 38 (1998–99): 37–57. New studies calculating the effect of the family-written paid obituary will be needed to determine if "cash, not cachet" will have an effect on these social differentials in the number and comprehensiveness of obituaries.

11. A year later, in 1932, the death of another canine, movie star Rin Tin Tin, received *New York Times* coverage. The photogenic German shepherd had starred in a series of popular adventure movies in the late 1920s and early 1930s. See "Rin Tin Tin Dies at 14 on Eve of 'Comeback,'" *New York Times*, August 11, 1932.

12. "Igloo, Byrd's Dog, Polar Hero, Is Dead," *New York Times*, April 22, 1931.

13. "Igloo, Byrd's Dog, Buried," *New York Times*, June 1, 1931.

14. E. A. Torriero, "Kabul Zoo's Shell-Shocked Lion Dies," *Chicago Tribune*, January 27, 2002, accessed November 2, 2015, http://www.chicago.tribune.com.

15. See, for example, "Denver Post, Rocky Mountain News to Charge for Obituary Notices," *Denver Post*, March, 24, 2002, accessed November 2, 2015, http://www.ebsco.com.

16. Cara DeGette, "Public Eye: Free Obituaries; A Dying Breed," *Colorado Springs (CO) Independent*, April 10, 2002, accessed November 2, 2015, http://www.csindy.com.

17. Michael Roberts, "Dead Lines: The Denver Dailies Change the Way They Handle Obituaries—for Better and for Worse," Denver *Westword*, April 18, 2002, accessed November 4, 2015, www.westword.com/news/dead_lines_5070282.

18. Paraphrase of Tom Peterson, "Media: Your Fame, Their Fortune; C-J Moves to Paid Obituaries," *LEO: Louisville (KY) Eccentric Observer*, July 25, 2001, accessed June 10, 2003.

19. Ibid.

20. Deborah Hastings, "Antonia 'Toni' Larroux's Hilarious Obit Goes from Inside Joke to Viral Internet Sensation," *New York Daily News*, May 6, 2013, accessed November 4, 2015, http://www.nydailynews.com/news/national/

hilarious-obit-viral-article. I thank Susan Balee for bringing this obituary to my attention.

21. As of early 2000–2001, the *Sun* (Bremerton, WA) ran pet obits with human ones as a matter of policy. At that time, the paper had run only four pet obits, but expressed its intention to continue to do so. It inaugurated this policy right around the time that contestations of the practice erupted nationally. I am not aware if the paper has followed through on its stated policy.

22. Debra McKinney, "Newspaper Obituaries Pay Tribute to Pets," *Anchorage Daily News*, April 7, 2002, accessed November 4, 2015, http://www .newsbank.com/resources/doc/nb/news/OF81CCAOCD2DSE6D. Also, the fourth-largest daily newspaper in Texas, the *San Antonio Express News*, started to include pet obits in 2015, but in a special section of its classifieds notices. This is not simply a domestic phenomenon. In 2014, the *Straits Times* of Singapore began a similar service. See Jeff Winkler, "Fido is Survived by His Water Bowl and Chew Toys," *Daily Post* (Texas), February 18, 2015, www.texasmonthly/com/the-daily-post, accessed November 3, 2015. Winkler cites my earlier work on this topic but without, he confesses, actually having read it in full (!). He ultimately falls into the snide sniggering of Lewis Grossberger of the *Washington Post*.

23. Jenny Walker, retired obit writer for the *Durham (NC) Morning Herald*, communicated this story to me at the 2008 International Association of Obituarists conference in New Mexico and provided details in a follow-up e-mail on June 20, 2008, but she could not remember the deceased's name or the date of the obituary. Interestingly, her mother had also improvised a way to publicize an animal's death, taking out a classified ad in the local Chapel Hill, North Carolina, paper, "announcing (the dog's) death to all of his friends" in town. This wording positions the people of the local community as mourners, assumes they have both a desire and right to know of the animal's passing, and manipulates the categories of the newspaper to achieve the otherwise prohibited goal of providing a dog's obituary for the public record. This act of resistance or creative improvisation is echoed in pet cemeteries and in some pet burial practices, as when a pet is surreptitiously included in the casket of a person who died at the same time (personal communication, Michael Lensing, funeral director, Lensing Funeral Home, Iowa City, Iowa, 2006).

24. "Tracking Bad Guys in Heaven," *News Tribune* (Tacoma, WA), April 25, 2001, B5.

25. Joann Loviglio, "*Philadelphia Daily News* Adding Pet Death Notices," Associated Press, March 5, 2002; reprinted in the *Fredericksburg (VA) Free Lance–Star*, www.fredericksburg.com/wire/newspaper_accepts_pet_death _notices/article_34b7cfd-36bl-58c4-9b66-e3e6baof2932.html, accessed November 4, 2015.

26. Kathryn S. Wenner, "Dog Gone, Not Forgotten," *American Journalism Review* 24 (2002): 14–15.

27. Bob Levey, "Latest in Questionable Taste: Pet Obituaries," *Washington Post*, May 1, 2002, accessed November 4, 2015, https://www.washingtonpost.com/archive/lifestyle/2002/05/01/latest_in_questionable_taste_pet_obituaries.

28. Lewis Grossberger, "Spot Dead! City Mourns," *MediaWeek*, June 5, 2002, accessed November 4, 2015, http://www.ebscohost.com.

29. Levey, "Latest in Questionable Taste."

30. Among the serious issues this response raises is what constitutes a "grievable life." As I discussed in the preceding chapter, I expand on Judith Butler's formulation, extending it to animals and ultimately recasting it in terms of a "politically grievable life," to emphasize the role of social recognition of a "right to mourn publicly," granted in some situations and withheld in others. Charges of mawkishness or sentimentality are discursive ways of denying the legitimacy of another's grief, and the term in each case carries a gendered overtone of excessive and misplaced emotionality associated with females. When applied to male mourners, it can imply a failed masculinity. For columnist Bob Levey, mourning animals by adapting formal strategies conventionally reserved for humans—like writing an obituary—is apparently inappropriate to the level of absurdity, whether the life being mourned is that of an attack dog or a goldfish. But he reserves the worst of his vitriol for the smallest pet—the goldfish, which he depicts, with wicked delight, as having his funeral in the toilet bowl.

    Here Levey raises the specter of species-based differential valuation, with fish among the lowest of the low, disposable, as goldfish so often are, carried home by children in tiny plastic bags from carnivals or pet stores as "starter pets"; they often fail to survive, only to be flushed down the drain. Part of the devaluation presumes that unlike mammals or some birds, fish lack the ability to relate to humans, cannot be differentiated, and are thought to have a mental ability just above that of a cockroach. Of course, some fish, like carp, can be highly valued for their symbolic or ornamental value, but they are rarely appreciated for their petlike interactive qualities. As fish veterinarian Dr. Mark Mitchell has remarked, though (see the previous chapter), the type of pet one has is no marker of the level of attachment that one feels for it. When emotive attachment is directed toward an animal presumed to be unable to return it (e.g., a snake vs. a dog or a fish vs. a cat), grief upon that animal's death is subject to ridicule as excessive and inappropriate.

31. Quoted in Levey, "Latest in Questionable Taste."

32. "Are Americans Too Attached to Their Pets?," CNN *Talkback Live*, March 6, 2002, accessed November 4, 2015, http://www.cnn.com/TRANSCRIPTS/0203/06/tl.00.html.

33. For two research-based discussions of this lack of public support and the mourning and burial rituals that people develop to combat it, see the following studies: Tami Lynne Harbolt, "Too Loved to Be Forgotten: Pet Loss and Ritual Bereavement" (master's thesis, Western Kentucky University, 1993), and Elizabeth Van Loo, "A Study of Pet Loss and Its Relationship to Human Loss and the Valuation of Animals" (PhD diss., Troy State University, 1996). Loo writes, "Often their [pet lovers'] grief goes unrecognized and proper support for their bereavement is unwittingly denied them by society. As a result, their grief becomes disenfranchised" (12).

34. I explore these issues of online mourning further in "Relating to Animals after Death: Virtual Pet Cemeteries and the Public Act of Grieving Online" (paper presented at the annual meetings of the International Anthrozoology Association at Kent State University, Canton, Ohio, August 15–16, 2003). Numerous contemporary popular books exist on coping with pet loss, many written by psychologists and counselors for the lay public. Among the best academic examinations of historical practices of pet mourning and its representation is Teresa Mangum's "Animal Angst: Victorians Memorialize Their Pets," in *Victorian Animal Dreams: Representations of Animals in Victorian Literature*, ed. Deborah Denenholz Morse and Martin A. Danahay (Aldershot, UK: Ashgate, 2007), 15–34.

35. Natalie Pompilio, "The Brides Wore White," *American Journalism Review*, October 2002, 12. By the time the *New York Times* made its announcement, thirty-six of the top one hundred papers in the United States were already accepting notices of same-sex ceremonies, at least in theory, reports Carl Sullivan, "Same-Sex Unions Gain Notice; but Papers Not Wedded to Policies," *Editor and Publisher*, September 2, 2002, 6.

36. I thank Jean Olsen of Santa Barbara, California, for sending me this clipping.

37. Remarks by Kay Powell at the annual meeting of the International Association of Obituarists, June 12–14, 2008, in Las Vegas, New Mexico.

38. Marilyn Johnson, *The Dead Beat: Lost Souls, Lucky Stiffs, and the Perverse Pleasures of Obituaries* (New York: Harper Perennial, 2007), 31.

39. Ibid., 35.

40. *News-Gazette* Staff, "Honoring Your Loved One in Print: Your Guide for Writing and Submitting a Personalized Obituary" (Champaign, IL: *News-Gazette*, 2010), 3. See also http://www.news-gazette.com/sites/all/files/pages/2010/09/30/obit_manual.pdf, accessed November 4, 2015.

41. *News-Gazette* Staff, "Honoring Your Loved One in Print."

CHAPTER SEVEN

1. So far, there has been little ethnographic work on this topic. How people actually think of, feel about, and respond to roadkilled animals is a crucial area for further research. In this chapter, I speculate on responses to

roadkill gleaned from a variety of reports, representations, and observations; where possible, I report preliminary evidence or anecdotal information that should be useful in formulating further research. This future research will benefit from focus groups, surveys, and interviews to uncover attitudes and actions in this underresearched realm. Donna J. Haraway's interventions in proposing a less anthropocentric mode of research focused on *relations* among different species may provide a particularly fruitful framework of investigation. See her *When Species Meet* (Minneapolis: University of Minnesota Press, 2007).

2.   Alexandra Koelle, "Rights of Way: Race, Place, and Nation in the Northern Rockies" (PhD diss., University of California, Santa Cruz, 2010); Mike Michael, "Roadkill: Between Humans, Nonhuman Animals, and Technologies," *Society and Animals* 12 (2004): 277–98; Dennis Soron, "Road Kill: Commodity Fetishism and Structural Violence," *Topia* 18 (2007): 107–25; David Lulka, "The Intimate Hybridity of Roadkill: A Brechtian View of Dismay in Persistence," *Emotion, Space and Society* 1 (2008): 38–47; Susan McHugh, "Stains, Drains, and Automobiles: A Conversation with Steve Baker about Norfolk Roadkill, Mainly," *Art and Research: A Journal of Ideas, Contexts, and Methods* 4 (2011): 1–14; Helen Molesworth, "This Car Stops for Roadkill," in *Concrete Jungle: A Pop Media Investigation of Death and Survival in Urban Ecosystems*, ed. Mark Dion and Alexis Rockman (New York: Juno Books, 1996), 170–80; Julia Schlosser, "Bodies of Roadkilled Animals in the Work of Steve Baker and Craig Stecyk," paper presented at "Living with Animals," the conference she co-organized with Robert Mitchell, held at Eastern Kentucky University, Richmond, March 21–23, 2013.

3.   Peter Chilson, "Right of Way," *Audubon Magazine* 6 (2003), accessed November 4, 2015, http://audubonmagazine.org/cuttingedge/cuttingedge0306.html; Alisa Coffin, "From Roadkill to Road Ecology: A Review of the Ecological Effects of Roads," *Journal of Transportation Geography* 15 (2007): 396–206; Stephen C. Trombulak and Christopher A. Frissell, "Review of Ecological Effects of Roads on Terrestrial and Aquatic Communities," *Conservation Biology* 14 (2000): 18–30.

4.   In one instance, the only one I am aware of, an ordinance has been passed to give animals, not humans, right-of-way on a public street. The city of Olney, Illinois, population 8,600, passed an ordinance in 2002 (Section 6.12.020, "Squirrels protected") to protect its population of white squirrels, for which it is known. That ordinance states, "Squirrels are hereby given and granted the right-of-way on all public streets, sidewalks, rights-of-way, and thoroughfares" (Ord. 02-1, Sec. 1), (2002-1, Added, 1/14/2002, New Ordinance). Furthermore, "Whoever violates any provision of this Chapter shall be fined not less than sixty dollars ($60.00), nor more than seven hundred fifty dollars ($750.00) for each offense." Reported in *Wikipedia* entry "Olney, Illinois," when accessed June 7, 2014, http://en.wikipedia.org/wiki/Olney,_Illinois#cite_note-3. Roadkilling of white

squirrels in Olney is thus subject to a substantial fine. Usually, roadkilling is regarded as an unavoidable accident, not a "crime" or infraction subject to fine. In this case, the white squirrels have value to the community, helping make it unique, so a potential loss of that value can be seen as an infringement on the well-being of the human community and hence worthy of censure. Note that brown squirrels can apparently be run over without sanction.

5. See, for example, Ben Martin, "Roadkill: Sickening or Sustainable," *Ecologist*, February 20, 2012, accessed November 4, 2015, http://www.theecologist.org/green_green_living/food_and_drink/1249525/roadkill_sickening_or_sustainable.html.

6. McHugh, "Stains, Drains, and Automobiles," 6. Some figures are also available for the numbers of animals killed on roadways in national parks. See Janet Loehrke and Anne R. Carey's presentation "Roadkill along National Park Roadways," *USA Today*, July 27, 2013, accessed November 4, 2015, http://www.usatoday.com/story/news/nation/2013/07/26/interative-national-parks-road-kill/2590739. The graphic notes that road collisions with animals vary from park to park, from year to year, and from species to species.

7. Richard T. T. Forman et al., *Road Ecology: Science and Solutions* (Washington, DC: Island Press, 2003), 118.

8. Koelle, "Rights of Way," 230 (emphasis added). Some groups in specific states are trying to gather more accurate information. See, for example, the California Roadkill Observation System, started in 2009. It publishes a newsletter, *Road Apple: A Collection of Road Ecology Related News, Scientific Papers, Observations, and Anecdotes*. The July 2011 issue provides an example of an intervention into these policy discussions and encourages "citizen scientists" to add to the tally and discussion.

9. "Given the more than 258 million vehicles on the country's four million miles of public roads, it is little wonder that cars regularly strike animals. Estimates for just how many run-ins occur each year vary widely. The Humane Society of the United States also estimates that a million animals are killed by vehicles every day, while a 2008 Federal Highway Administration report puts the number of accidents with large animals between one million and two million a year. The agency estimates such accidents result in over $8 billion in damages annually. In addition, about 200 people die each year in accidents with deer and other animals, according to the Insurance Institute for Highway Safety." Quoted from Malia Wollan, "Mapping Traffic's Toll on Wildlife," *New York Times*, September 12, 2010, accessed November 4, 2015, http://www.nytimes.com/2010.09.13/techology/13roadkill.html?_r=0.

10. Koelle, "Rights of Way."

11. As Barbara J. King notes (personal communication, 2014), however, there can be significant cultural differences in this dismissal of responsibility.

She relates that in rural Kenya, great anger might be directed toward a driver, especially if the dead animal is livestock. This situation raises the question of cultural variability in attitudes toward roadkill and roadkilling, which could be researched further. The cases I discuss in this chapter are set in the contemporary United States, where generally, legal and moral strictures assume that such killing is the result of an unavoidable accident. I thank Barbara J. King for raising this issue.

12. Personal communication, Teresa Mangum, 2011.

13. I thank my colleague Amy Fischer for inviting me to lecture to her Animals and Society class in the College of Agricultural, Consumer, and Environmental Sciences at the University of Illinois at Urbana-Champaign, where this discussion took place on November 8, 2011. Anonymous responses to my questions about roadkill were gathered electronically, with the aggregate results projected on a screen and followed by discussion. While the course topic implies that those with an interest in animals would be overrepresented in the class in terms of the general student population at my institution, the course counts toward fulfillment of a general education requirement, and so draws relatively broadly from the total undergraduate population. It requires no prerequisites.

In addition to these student responses, which represent a diverse population in terms of gender and ethnic/racial groups, but which cluster in the under-thirty-years-of-age category, some of my colleagues have discussed their personal rituals of mourning with me, including Teresa Mangum and Michele Hanks. These rituals, usually a hushed version of "Sorry, animal," echo the students' responses. That these acts, no matter how brief, rarely emerge in public discussion strongly supports the need to conduct further inquiry into how widespread such emotive responses are. These responses all come from college-educated individuals in the middle of the country. Are they shaped by social class and region? By national origin? Would further research reveal quite different attitudes?

14. Gary Snyder, "The Dead by the Side of the Road," in *Turtle Island* (New York: New Directions, 1974), 7.

15. Ibid.

16. Barry Lopez, "Apologia," in *A Road Runs Through It: Reviving Wild Places*, ed. Thomas Reed Peterson (Boulder, CO: Johnson Books 2006), 49. I thank artist Deke Weaver for bringing this work to my attention.

17. Carolyn Duckworth, "From a Wonderland Road," in *A Road Runs Through It: Reviving Wild Places*, ed. Thomas Reed Peterson (Boulder, CO: Johnson Books, 2006), 46.

18. Barbara J. King, *How Animals Grieve* (Chicago: University of Chicago Press, 2013). While King focuses mainly on how animals seem to grieve for their own, numerous reports also detail how animals appear to mourn for humans. For one example, consider the fact that when South African conservationist and renowned "elephant whisperer" Lawrence Anthony

died suddenly in early 2012 of a heart attack, the elephants resident on his sanctuary, Thula Thula, somehow "knew" of his death. On their own impetus, they arrived at his household compound, walking together in a long procession, some for more than twelve hours from the far reaches of the reserve, to converge there for the first time in a year and a half. They remained there for more than a day on their own volition, perhaps in solidarity with Anthony's grieving humans. See Mark Beckoff, "Elephants Mourn Loss of 'Elephant Whisperer' Lawrence Anthony," *Psychology Today*, March 7, 2012, accessed November 4, 2015, http://www .psychologytoday.com/blog/animal-emotions/201203/elephants_mourn _loss_elephant_whisperer_lawrence_anthony, and George Stroumboulo- poulos, "UPDATE: Elephants Who Appear to Mourn Their Human Friend Remain Protected," on the Stroumboulopoulos Tonight website, accessed November 4, 2015, http://www.cbc.ca/strombo/news/saying-goodbye -elephants-hold-apparent-vigil-to-mourn-their-human-friend.ht. For more on Anthony and his history with those elephants, see Lawrence Anthony, with Graham Spence, *The Elephant Whisperer: My Life with the Herd in the African Wild* (New York: Thomas Dunne Books, St. Martin's Press, 2009), which recounts the elephants' relation to their advocate on his reserve in South Africa.

19. King, *How Animals Grieve*, 14. King emphasizes that it's not only the "big-brained" animals like chimpanzees and elephants who appear to grieve. She recounts instances of rabbits and ducks responding with what appear to be depressive signs of mourning after the loss of a companion. The latter species may end up being killed on roads, and while we can't know the response of any companions in the wild, we can at least speculate that the loss, the waiting for the companion to return, may also be marked by behaviors we might associate with mourning.

20. In addition, I know of one other artist who has approached the issue of mourning for roadkill. West Coast artist and anthropologist Margaret Mackenzie-Hooson, professor emerita of the California College of the Arts, created a series of coffins for roadkilled animals and presented them in gallery shows prior to 2000. I haven't been able to get any images of this work, but Mackenzie-Hooson does note (by e-mail, April 22, 2014) that the coffins caused quite a stir when they were exhibited. The response indicated, perhaps, not only the uniqueness of the subject matter but also the power exerted by an invitation to mourn for the usually unmourned, a category shift. I thank Kari Weil for bringing Mackenzie-Hooson's work to my attention.

21. Schlosser, "Bodies of Roadkilled Animals."

22. Ibid., quoting Bolton T. Colburn, *Papa Moana: Craig Stecyk* (Laguna Beach, CA: Laguna Art Museum, 1989), 11.

23. A few filmic images of Stecyk's actions and sculptures are included in "Luxuria" (2011), a montage of film and photographic images taken from

the artist's archive dating to 1965, posted on the Museum of Contemporary Art website courtesy of the artist and accessed February 18, 2014, http://sites.moca.org/thecurve/category/c-r-stecyk-iii.

24. In "Bodies of Roadkilled Animals," Schlosser connects Stecyk's actions to commemorative ritual by drawing on the writings of Kirk Savage, whom she quotes: "Commemoration as a practice . . . involves ritual acts in and occupations of public space as well as other kinds of performance and consumption that may leave no lasting trace on the landscape." Kirk Savage, "History, Memory, and Monuments: An Overview of the Scholarly Literature on Commemoration," http://www.cr.nps.gov/history/resedu/savage.htm (no longer available).

25. Schlosser ("Bodies of Roadkilled Animals") is quoting here from an interview with Baker. See Gregory Williams, "Where the Wild Things Are: An Interview with Steve Baker," *Cabinet Magazine Online* 4 (2001), accessed by Schlosser July 11, 2012, http://www.cabinetmagazine.org/issues/4/SteveBaker.php.

26. Other artists have used and continue to use roadkilled animals in their art, but not with the goal of drawing attention to the death of those animals on the road. "Rogue Taxidermist" Beth Beverly, part of the art taxidermy minimovement that for the last decade has abjured the imperative to "liveness" that undergirds taxidermy for trophy displays and museum dioramas, sources some of her animals from roadkilled specimens. She and other artists dissemble and reassemble animal body parts with abandon to comment on death, species, and human conventions of display. See, for example, Tara Murtha, "Rogue Taxidermist Beth Beverly: Fox Scrotums, Animal Ethics, and AMC's Reality Show 'Immortalized,'" *Philadelphia Weekly*, February 12, 2013, accessed November 4, 2015, http://www.philadelphiaweekly.com/arts-and-culture/cover-story/190905781.html.

27. I am grateful to art historian Julia Schlosser for generously sharing with me her unpublished work on artist Craig Stecyk, originally presented at "Living with Animals," the conference she co-organized with Robert Mitchell, held at Eastern Kentucky University, Richmond, March 21–23, 2013, which we both attended. Her presentation was titled "Bodies of Roadkilled Animals in the Work of Steve Baker and Craig Stecyk." Although I had already written about the work of Brian Collier, I was unaware of Stecyk's memorials until Schlosser spoke about them.

28. Erin Alberty, "Roadside Memorial for 'Terrified Turkeys' Killed in Crash Is Pushed by PETA," *Salt Lake (UT) Tribune*, May 7, 2014, accessed November 4, 2015, http://www.mercurynews.com/pets-animals/ci_25712006/roadside-memorial-terrified-turkeys-killed-crash-is-pushed#. See also "PETA Seeks Roadside Memorial for Turkey Deaths," May 4, 2014, Foxnews.com., accessed November 4, 2015, www.foxnews.com/us/2014/05/04/peta-seeks-roadside-memorial-for turkey-deaths.

29. McHugh, "Stains, Drains, and Automobiles." Norfolk is a county in the east of England, lying on the North Sea; the city of Norwich is its county seat.

30. Julia Schlosser, "Stopping, Seeing: Bodies of Roadkilled Animals in the Work of Steve Baker," original English version supplied by the author. This piece appeared in German as "Anhalten, sehen: Die Körper Überfahrener Tiere in de Arbeit Steve Bakers," *Tierstudien* (Animal Studies), Fall 2012. In it, Schlosser also discusses Baker's 2011 photo series *Roadside* and considers his artwork in terms of the ethics of documentary photography, trauma, and the taboo against showing the killing of animals, issues that exceed my focus on memorialization here. I thank Julia Schlosser for generously sharing this English version with me.

31. McHugh, "Stains, Drains, and Automobiles," 12.

32. Ibid., 6.

33. Ibid., 9.

34. Ibid., 11.

35. Michele Hanks, personal communication, 2011, and discussion with University of Illinois students in the Animals and Society course, fall 2011. Of 162 students responding anonymously during the discussion, 60% said that they think roadkilling is "sometimes intentional." One young man spoke of a friend who hunts squirrels with a gun and sometimes purposefully runs over them with his car. Another reported he has seen cars swerve to hit skunks, and a third mentioned the same for a coyote. This intentional killing action could correlate with the type of animal: for example, a snake perceived as deadly or the stink associated with a skunk may elicit a deadly driving response.

    Certainly, these data should be taken only as suggestive and not conclusive. But especially when the behavior discussed could be controversial or invoke censure, it's important to note that the student responses I report here were gathered via electronic push-button "clickers" and thus were anonymous. In addition, they were used to gather aggregate data, which were then immediately displayed on a screen to the class to foster discussion. This doesn't guarantee the reliability of the data per se, just that the method of gathering it allowed for anonymity, which could have increased the likelihood of a truthful response if the students were engaged enough in the discussion to take the questions seriously. My assessment of their attentiveness that day suggests that that was the case.

    See also Barbara J. King's interchange with country music star Blake Shelton on Twitter, summer 2012, regarding a joke he made about roadkilling on purpose. When King objected to it, he implied she just needed to get a sense of humor. See Barbara J. King, "Why Blake Shelton's Animal-Cruelty Tweet Matters," NPR Cosmos and Culture, July 28, 2012, accessed November 4, 2015, http://www.npr.org/blogs/13.7/2012/07/28/157528291/why-blake-sheltons-animal-cruelty-tweet-matters.

36. B. R. "Buck" Peterson, *Original Road Kill Cookbook* (Berkeley, CA: Ten Speed Press, 1987).

37. There are exceptions, of course, in which animal lives are granted standing in the debates about human mobility needs and are brought into community-based public discourse. Alexandra Koelle's discussion ("Rights of Way," 109–267) of recently constructed ecopassages, tunnels, and bridges for animals to safely cross roads on the Flathead Indian Reservation in western Montana well exemplifies how animal lives can be factored into human design if such lives are valued.

38. Claire Palmer, "Killing Animals in Animal Shelters," in *Killing Animals*, ed. Animal Studies Group (Urbana: University of Illinois Press, 2006), 170–87.

39. Animal Studies Group, *Killing Animals*, 4.

40. Ibid.

41. Elaine Scarry, *The Body in Pain: The Making and Unmaking of the World* (New York: Oxford University Press, 1985), 126, cited in Steve Baker, "Animal Death in Contemporary Art," in *Killing Animals*, ed. the Animal Studies Group (Urbana: University of Illinois Press, 2006), 83.

42. Unlike the rationale behind the creation of the animal passages that Koelle ("Rights of Way") discusses—that animal deaths on roadways result from competing claims to use of shared space—this presumption, which renders roadkill unrecognizable as a social problem, chalks them up to "bad luck": wrong place, wrong time; cause for "regret" but not for change.

43. I am grateful to PhD candidate Stephen Vrla, who is completing an animal studies concentration in sociology at Michigan State University, for sharing some of his preliminary, unpublished research on roadkill with me. Following up on his own experiences and my previously published call for research on the phenomena, Vrla has used multiple regression analyses on survey data, supplemented by Personal Meaning Mapping, to help pinpoint the relationships among attitudes toward animals in general, sensitivity toward animals, and reactions to the encounter of roadkilled wild or domestic animals in daily life, and to correlate those issues with demographic factors such as age, region, religion, gender, and political orientation.

    Vrla's preliminary findings, reported in his unpublished 2013 paper "'Something to See Here': Looking at Road-Killing and Road-Killed Animals," indicate that repeated exposure to roadkilled animals can have a desensitizing effect on an individual's concern for those animals, but can also generate increased concern for roadkilling as a larger problem. Also, perhaps not surprisingly, he found that people were more bothered by the sight of dead dogs and cats on the highway than by the bodies of wild animals, as they perhaps intuited that someone at home was missing those pets. Hence, the impact of seeing roadkill varied with the species killed.

    I look forward to Vrla's published reporting of this first stage of his research and to his longer-term development of this research initiative.

Ultimately, his research and that of others may reveal strategies to lessen roadkill that will complement the geographic initiatives behind the construction of animal passages and the reorientation toward space as a multispecies habitat that includes humans. Until we know what people actually think and feel about their personal encounters with roadkill and about their conceptions of it as a social phenomenon, we aren't likely to be able to make significant inroads in decreasing it.

CHAPTER EIGHT

1. See discussion on ZooBeat, 2008. Now renamed ZooChat: Zoo and Animal Conservation Community, the online forum is searchable at http://www.zoochat.com, accessed November 4, 2015.
2. Among the many critical writings since the 1970s that strive to situate the European-derived categories of "art," "art making," and the "art world," along with the latter's producers and consumers, in a culturally specific historical narrative, John Berger's *Ways of Seeing* (New York: Penguin, 1990 [1972]) and Howard Becker's *Art Worlds* (Berkeley: University of California Press, 2008) remain lucid and influential.
3. Megan Levy, "Tony Blair, the Rat, Launches Artistic Career," *Daily Telegraph* (London), March 1, 2008, accessed November 4, 2015, http://www.telegraph.co.uk/news/uknews/1580403/Tony-Blair-the-rat-launches-artistic-career.html.
4. See the "Events/Exhibits" page on the Scamperat website, accessed November 4, 2015, http://www.scamperats.com. For an elite take by a British artist, see the work of Lucy Kimbell and her performance-lecture "One Night with Rats in the Service of Art," discussed in Steve Baker, *Animal/Artist* (Minneapolis: University of Minnesota Press, 2013), 41–63.
5. See the "Welcome to ScamperART!" page on the Scamperat website, accessed November 4, 2015, http://www.scamperats.com.
6. Thierry Lenain, *Monkey Painting* (London: Reaktion Books, 1997), 21.
7. Ron Broglio, "Contact Zones and Living Flesh: Touch after Olly and Suzi," in *Surface Encounters: Thinking with Animals and Art* (Minneapolis: University of Minnesota Press, 2011), 82. In this chapter, Broglio asks "how the surface as a theoretical space occupied by the animal has a productivity and meaning different from the privileged self-reflection of the human subject; in other words, how does the animal and its noninteriority produce thought differently?" (81).
8. Baker, *Artist/Animal*, 24. Baker's work is similarly an indispensable analytical guide to a landscape of experimental artists investigating the interface of humans and animals: Sue Coe, Sophie Utting, Eduardo Kac, and Angela Singer, among others. Some of these artists use living or dead animal bodies in their art making, which includes live performance, photography, and film.

9. Nor is the process usually documented in film or photographs that then become artworks in themselves. The exchange of money, in the majority of cases I discuss, goes mostly to support the animals themselves (e.g., supplementing nonprofit budgets at animal sanctuaries). And finally, for the majority of both the consumers and the scientists I discuss, the goal in engaging with these artworks is not to deconstruct the notion of a surface as the ground for shared action or to self-reflexively take apart the conventions of art making to see it as a historically constituted zone of visual conventions and social relations. Although it exceeds the parameters of this chapter, further comparison of audiences, consumers, and the market for these two related categories of art by and with animals would be illuminating.

10. Michael Kilian, "Trunk Show: Asia's Out-of-Work Elephants Find a New Career in Art—and Now Their Work Is On the Block at Christie's," *Chicago Tribune*, March 13, 2000, accessed November 16, 2015, http://articles .chicagotribune.com/2000-03-13/features/0005180027.

11. Elizabeth Bukowski, "Why Do Elephants Paint?," March 12, 2000, accessed November 16, 2015, http://www.salon.com/2000/03/23/ elephantart.

12. Graciela Flores, "When I See an Elephant . . . Paint?," *Scientist*, June 1, 2007, accessed November 16, 2015, http://www.the-scientist.com/?articles .view/articleNo/25148. The children's book *Ruby the Painting Pachyderm of the Phoenix Zoo*, by Dick George (New York: Delacorte Press, 1995), goes into surprising detail about Ruby's painting experiences, describing her beginnings, color choices, and rendering of the colors she saw around her.

13. Teresa Annas, "Animals Earn Their Keep in Hampton Roads and Abroad with Art," *Virginian-Pilot* (Hampton Roads, VA), August 11, 2007, accessed November 16, 2015, http://hamptonroads.com/node/309221. I thank Mary Bennett for bringing this article to my attention.

14. Ibid.

15. Ibid.

16. ZooBeat.com, accessed February 18, 2008, http://www.zoobeat.com/2/ paintings-animals. ZooBeat has since been relaunched as Zoochat.com.

17. All comments from the ZooBeat forum presented here preserve the writers' original spelling and punctuation.

18. Now searchable under http://www.zoochat.com, ZooBeat was launched by an administrator in Australia in 2003. The first of its kind to focus on an English-speaking community of posters, it is still going strong. Other sites bring together users in other communities, and attitudes obviously may differ across the globe. "ZooChat started life using the name ZooBeat and was hosted on a server in Australia. The first post was made on October 19, 2003 and gradually grew over the following 5 years. Early members were primarily from Australia and New Zealand, but over time more and more international members joined, with the majority of the

traffic now coming from the UK, US and other parts of Europe. . . . As part
of a rebranding exercise and a move to a more international focus, the
site was renamed to ZooChat on October 19, 2008 (exactly 5 years after
the site was launched). The site was relocated to a U.S.-based server at the
same time" ("About ZooChat," accessed November 16, 2015, http://www
.zoochat.com). Today, most members are in the United Kingdom, Australia and New Zealand, the United States, several European countries, and
Singapore.

19. Lenain (*Monkey Painting*, 27) emphasizes the historical congruity of a public interest in painting by apes, especially the celebrity ape Congo, with a
growth in the 1950s in the science of primatology and a broadening passion among European artists and collectors for what they termed "primitive art," which had influenced artists like Picasso earlier in the century.
My emphasis here is on the expansion of an acceptance of human abstract
expressionist painting into the wider public realm after World War II.
Without this public acceptance, a market for art by animals would never
have developed to the extent it has today, because such markings couldn't
have been aesthetically framed as "art."

20. My kit is called "A Paint Kit for Dogs," by Pup-Casso (manufactured by
Art-Casso, LLC, Saratoga Springs, NY). It "makes a great gift," is "recom-
mended for dogs ages 1–154 (in dog years of course)" and is "the World's
first No Mess, non-Toxic paint kit for dogs!" as the white boxer in the red
beret proclaims on the front of the box. Not surprisingly, a portion of the
proceeds goes to animal protection causes. Helpful hints in the instructions urge the owner to avoid dropping too much paint in just one or two
spots, which can cause smearing. Even here, a specific aesthetic is advised.
The results can also be transformed into mugs and T-shirts, extending the public for the creations of your pet, who just might be the next
"Mutt-isse."

21. Heather Burch and Burton Silver, *Why Cats Paint* (Berkeley, CA: Ten Speed
Press, 1994), 75.

22. The dimension of philanthropy that undergirds this market does not
extend to the rare sanctuary for farmed animals whose lives are, for most
people, destined for the dinner plate and hence not in need of "saving." A
pig—when raised as a pet and noted for intelligence—can be an exception, as it has changed categories, going from "food" to "pet."

23. This charisma correlates with the fund-raising strategies of animal welfare
groups who use ahh-inspiring photos of baby seals or of mother polar
bears and their young. Research by Dr. Bob Smith of the Durrell Institute
at the University of Kent in the United Kingdom has shown that most
nongovernmental organizations raise money for species that they can
"sell." Especially popular are large animals with forward-facing eyes.
These species get the most conservation dollars from these campaigns,
whether or not they are the closest to extinction. See "Study Highlights

New Mammal Species for Promoting Conservation Fundraising," Phys.org, May 17, 2012, accessed November 16, 2015, http://phys.org/news/2012 -05-highlights-mammal-species-fundraising.html. By contrast, groups fighting animal cruelty picture abused, starved animals in their materials, representing a situation that demands correction and calls forth empathy, not through charisma but through pity.

24. Koopa was originally taken from the wild more than twenty-five years ago. Box turtles aren't endangered but are included on a CITES (Convention on the International Trade in Endangered Species) watch list. They can live to be several decades old. Koopa is raised in a tank-free environment and receives veterinary care. No adverse effects from the painting have been documented by the veterinarian. Despite this, Kira, his collaborator-guardian (Kira Ayn Varszegi, who, like Koopa, also goes by a one-name appellation), warns other turtle owners not to let their pets paint. "Koopa has been acclimated to being rinsed off in the shower, and he is fully trusting of me. Precautions are taken to make sure he doesn't prolapse in the paint." A statement on eBay offers this caveat: "Koopa . . . paints under the close supervision of a turtle expert. We do not condone anyone attempt [sic] to use their turtles to paint. What is safe for Koopa is not necessarily safe for other turtles or tortoises. We consider all copycat attempts to be unsafe as well as disrespectful to us as established individual artists" (eBay listing for item 360006925995, accessed February 25, 2008, cgi.ebay.com/ws/eBaylSAPI). I'm not sure who the "we" is who considers turtle painting unsafe, but clearly the individual artists here are Kira and Koopa. This defense of artistic property rights is another way that Kira situates Koopa's products as fine art.

25. eBay listing for item number 360006925995. "Turtle with Talent," Ripley's Believe It or Not! September 5, 2013, accessed May 30, 2014, but no longer available, http://www.ripleys.com/weird/inside-ripleys-world.

26. See Koopa's MySpace page, accessed November 16, 2015, http://www .myspace.com/koopatheturtle.

27. Koopa has made more than eight hundred paintings, each taking only a few minutes to complete. Now retired, he paints only twice a week, completing about three paintings in each session. A portion of the proceeds from sales goes to support Kira, but a portion has also been donated to turtle rescue work, with more than $12,000 going to that cause as of 2008.

28. Kira Ayn Varszegi, e-mail communication with the author, March 5, 2008.

29. In the case of other celebrity animal artists who aren't primates (like Tillie the Dog and Komar and Melamid's painting Thai elephants), the profession of the guardian as an artist him- or herself was crucial in envisioning the animal's potential to paint and in creating the conditions for the result to be recognizable to humans as "artistic." Tony Blair the rat's chewed items became "art" when so declared by his artist-owner, who photographed them for the Saatchi gallery's website. Her actions in turn

depended on the transformed category of art since the early decades of the twentieth century, when Marcel Duchamp's signed urinal and other works successfully challenged the category of what, in the European realm, might be considered "art."

30. Kira Ayn Varszegi, e-mail communication with the author, March 5, 2008.

31. http://www.turtlekiss.com, accessed February 25, 2008. Now defunct.

32. A sample of more than two hundred pieces, available under the "Galleries" section of Koopa's website, gives a sense of the complexity, differences, and similarities among the works. A "Koopa" is immediately recognizable, based on his technique and Kira's choices for color combinations and color designs as well as her judgment about when the painting is "done." Overall, bright hues dominate, especially blues and reds. Although Koopa's painting technique has remained the same over the years, the color palette has changed somewhat as new colors became available and old ones disappeared.

33. http://www.turtlekiss.com/testimonials.htm, accessed February 25, 2008. Now defunct.

34. I am very grateful to the staff at the Oklahoma City Zoo and Botanical Garden, who assisted my research so generously. On my visit in 2007, they welcomed me "backstage" into the aquarium, elephant, and primate regions of their institution, introduced me to many special animals, and demonstrated painting techniques as they are done with sea lions, elephants, and apes.

35. For example, to train a monkey to move from one cage to another, the trainer may entice him to move toward the door by using the positive reinforcement of a grape as a reward for that action—or she may, if all else fails, squirt water at the monkey (a negative reinforcement) until he moves out of his cage and into the new one. The monkey is then rewarded with a grape for complying; the next time he sees the open door, it's hoped that he'll move from the first cage to the second to receive that reward without the use of the squirting hose.

   While operant conditioning thus does not rule out causing distress to the animal as a mode of teaching, this option is regarded as the last resort. I'm not saying here that coercive techniques aren't still used in certain captive settings, like some circuses, or that operant conditioning never involves coercion.

   Karen Pryor, animal behavioral specialist and former trainer of marine mammals at Sea World, has written what some regard as a classic book on the subject of animal training and positive behavioral modification: *Don't Shoot the Dog: The New Art of Teaching and Training* (New York: Bantam Books, rev. ed., 1999). It features an introduction by B. F. Skinner and explains the operant conditioning method.

36. I take up this issue further in the next chapter, when I discuss elephants. In the United States, most progressive, accredited zoos now practice

"protected-contact" management techniques with their elephants, which protect both the animals and their keepers. Keepers and elephants may touch each other through strong metal bars but never directly side by side. While I am not endorsing keeping elephants in captivity and recognize that for many captive elephants, conditions are intolerable, significant advances in addressing their physical and psychological welfare are under way in at least some US zoos. For some of those elephants, painting may be one enrichment activity among others.

When I visited the Oklahoma City Zoo and Botanical Garden in 2007, in addition to seeing Midge the sea lion create a painting, I also had the opportunity to accompany keepers to the elephant enclosure. There, through stout metal fencing, the keepers interacted with Chandra, an elephant who had been trained to present her trunk for procedures like taking medicine. Painting was presented to Chandra as an enrichment or play activity in her interaction with the keepers, and it used some of the same medical training techniques, like "blowing out." The keeper held a sixteen-by-twenty-inch canvas up to Chandra along with some preselected pots of nontoxic paint in golds and metallic greens. Chandra touched her trunk to the canvas, making swooshes with the paint, and sometimes blew the paint out in splotches and drops. She "signed" the painting by making an imprint in gold paint of the distinctive tip of her trunk. The canvas surface bears traces of the encounter's context, as bits of hay are stuck on the surface too. No representational drawing was involved, and Chandra was never touched during the ten-minute interaction. A treat at the end of the art-making session was an additional reward beyond the fun. In the Thai situation, the elephants are working elephants, performing the painting routines in exactly prescribed sequences of motions several times a day.

For information on the controversy surrounding some Thai elephant painting and allegations of abuse, see, for example, Kate Good, "Elephant Artists? Here's Why Making an Elephant Paint Is Cruel, Not Cute," October 7, 2014, accessed November 4, 2015, One Green Planet, http://onegreenplanet.org/animalsandnature/why-making-an-elephant-paint-is-cruel-not-cute. Images on this website show how elephant keepers (mahouts) can subtly use bullhooks and nails secreted in their hands as they tug on elephants' ears to give directions, even in front of tourist audiences during art-making shows. In addition, traditional training methods can be abusive in themselves. I thank Barbara J. King for bringing this source to my attention.

37. Behavioral and environmental "enrichment" is increasingly considered important, not only in zoos and sanctuaries but also in laboratory settings, where animals may live in captivity for long periods of time. Nonharmful ways to increase mental and physical stimulation for captive animals include hiding food in "puzzle feeders" that require the success-

ful manipulation of objects to retrieve it; designing a more interesting visual and audio environment, such as including the movement and the sound of a waterfall; and providing "artistic" opportunities. For example, part of the "enrichment program" for animals at the National Zoo in Washington, DC, involves apes playing with apps on iPads and pandas painting.

Even otters get a chance to participate. See, for example, Joel Landau, "Otters at Smithsonian Zoo Play Music on Keyboard," *New York Daily News*, May 28, 2014, accessed November 4, 2015, http://www.nydailynews .com/news/national/otters-smithsonian-zoo-play-keyboard-article-1 .1808851#ixzz33Iq3SM00. Whether or not we think the otters enjoy an arrangement of sounds that humans would call "music," providing them with a way of producing novel effects through the manipulation of their environment appears to enhance their well-being. Many of the captive painting programs have yielded the same results. Some participants (human and nonhuman) may primarily enjoy the human-animal interaction necessitated by painting, and others—for example, some primates—may actually enjoy the act of painting itself, as I describe in the next chapter.

38. With the generous help of the staff in 2007, I was able to watch several species of animals paint, including Midge. She painted for me during a quiet time between public shows in the zoo's outdoor amphitheater.

CHAPTER NINE

1. Lloyd Vries, "Dead Chimp's Art Sells Big: Three Works by the Late Chimpanzee 'Congo' Sell for $25,620," CBS News, June 20, 2005, accessed November 16, 2015, http://www.cbsnews.com/stories/2005/06/20/ entertainment/main703057.shtml.
2. Key works on the development of these ideologies include Edward Said, *Orientalism* (New York: Vintage Books, 1979), and Johannes Fabian, *Time and the Other: How Anthropology Makes Its Object* (New York: Columbia University Press, 2014).
3. See Lyle Rexer, *How to Look at Outsider Art* (New York: Harry N. Abrams, 2005), for one discussion of this category.
4. The philosopher of art Denis Dutton summarizes a narrative of evolutionary origins for artistic "instinct" in his book *The Art Instinct: Beauty, Pleasure, and Human Evolution* (New York: Bloomsbury Press, 2009). Deeply knowledgeable about artistic trends and practices, he searches for their evolutionary origins by turning back to prehistory. "Preoccupied as we are with the flashy media and buzzing gizmos of daily experience, we forget how close we remain to the prehistoric women and men who first found beauty in the world. Their blood runs in our veins. Our art instinct is theirs" (243). Evolutionary biologists look even further back, to prehominid times.

5. Frans de Waal, *The Ape and the Sushi Master: Cultural Reflections of a Prima-tologist* (New York: Basic Books, 2001).

6. Ibid., 151–52.

7. Ibid., 155.

8. K. Beach, R. S. Fouts, and D. H. Fouts, "Representational Art in Chim-panzees," *Friends of Washoe Newsletter* 3–4 (1984): 1–4; Sarah T. Boysen, Gary G. Berenson, and James Prentice, "Simian Scribbles: A Reap-praisal of Drawing in the Chimpanzee (*Pan troglodytes*)," *Journal of Comparative Psychology* 101 (1987), accessed November 16, 2015, doi: 10.1037/0735-7036.101.1.82; Frans de Waal, "Apes with an Oeuvre," *Chron-icle of Higher Education*, November 19, 1999, B6; Masayuki Tanaka, Masaki Tomonaga, and Tetsuro Matsuzawa, "Finger Drawing by Infant Chimpan-zees (*Pan troglodytes*)," *Animal Cognition* 6 (2003), accessed November 16, 2015, doi: 10.1007/s10071-003-0198-3; John Mathews, *Starting from Scratch: The Origins and Development of Expression, Representation and Symbolism in Human and Non-Human Primates* (London: Psychology Press, 2011).

9. Boysen, Berenson, and Prentice, "Simian Scribbles," 82.

10. Anne Zeller, "What's in a Picture? A Comparison of Drawings by Apes and Children," *Semiotica* 166 (January 2007): 181–214; quotation is from pp. 210–11. Zeller concludes that apes may produce ideational and pos-sibly representational images, even if those modes of representation are more understandable by apes than humans.

11. While these incidents could certainly be attributed to factors such as boredom or distraction from the task at hand, the multiplicity of such anecdotes in reports of ape painting indicates they deserve further inves-tigation, as they point to a human-associated trait of deciding when an artwork is "finished."

12. De Waal, "Apes with an Oeuvre," B6. Of course, not all communities value enduring material artistic representations. The implicit reference here is to a European-derived value system for painting, sculpture, and so on. In addition, although undocumented, I know of one instance (relayed informally to me by a primate scientist) in which a primate painted on a material surface and then hung that surface on the wall of his cage for a day. Anecdotally, captive apes have also been known to paint on the walls and floors of their enclosures when pigments were supplied for painting on paper. If this mark making serves communicative purposes beyond the kinesthetic pleasures of producing it, we do not know.

13. Boysen, Berenson, and Prentice, "Simian Scribbles." See also Eveline Seghers, "Cross-Species Comparison in the Evolutionary Study of Art: A Cognitive Approach to the Ape Art Debate," *Review of General Psychology* 18 (2014): 263–72; de Waal, "Apes with an Oeuvre"; Desmond Morris, "Ape Artists of the 1950s," artnet.com 2005, accessed November 5, 2015, www.mayorgallery.com/exhibitions/117/works/; and Tanaka, Tomonaga, and Matsuzawa, "Finger Drawing by Infant Chimpanzees."

14. Not all cognitive scientists are interested mainly in what apes can tell us about ourselves. Some psychologists, ethologists, and primatologists are engaged in understanding primate "theory of mind," or the attribution of thought by one individual to another, or in learning more about communicative systems based on sound, gesture, posture, and marking, as these have an impact on primates' communication among themselves and with humans. The full extent of this work exceeds the bounds of this chapter. For a sample of such works by leading scholars, see the following: Barbara J. King, *The Dynamic Dance: Nonvocal Communication in African Great Apes* (Cambridge, MA: Harvard University Press, 2004); Sue Savage-Rumbaugh and Roger Lewin, *Kanzi: The Ape at the Brink of the Human Mind* (New York: John Wiley and Sons, 1994); Sue Savage-Rumbaugh, Stuart G. Shanker, and Talbot J. Taylor, *Apes, Language, and the Human Mind* (New York: Oxford University Press, 1998); Francine Patterson and Eugene Linden, *The Education of Koko* (New York: Holt, Rinehart and Winston, 1981); and Roger Fouts with Stephen Tukel Mills, *Next of Kin: My Conversations with Chimpanzees* (New York: William Morrow, 1997). Even John Mathews, a child psychology specialist, concludes his largely comparative study with extremely detailed observations of primate explorations of drawing materials, arguing ultimately that all expressive behavior is developed through full-body expressivity and playful exploration, and that these activities are similar for human and nonhuman primates. For Mathews, nonhuman primates' abilities aren't simply a potential source of evolutionary information about humans but have become the impetus for a better understanding by humans of these nonhumans.

These debates take place in the wider context of comparative cognition studies. Donald R. Griffin's *Animal Minds* (Chicago: University of Chicago Press, 1992) not only summarizes many studies of cognition and communication across species, ranging from snakes to birds to primates, but also argues that the results must influence human beliefs (philosophy), ethics, and resulting actions. Critics often argue that influential studies, like those by Savage-Rumbaugh on the communicative and learned-language abilities of bonobos, are not replicable and are too dependent on the human and ape context in which they are conducted. Proponents, with whom I agree, say that such transspecies social context is integral to the communication being assessed.

15. Vries, "Dead Chimp's Art Sells Big."

16. Ibid.

17. Sam Jones, "Chimp's Art Fetches £14,000," *Guardian* (Manchester), June 21, 2005, accessed November 5, 2015, http://www.theguardian.com/uk/2005/jun/21/arts.artsnews; "No Chump Change for Chimp Art," National Public Radio, *All Things Considered*, June 21, 2005, accessed November 5, 2015, http://www.npr.org/templates/story/story.php?storyId=4712948.

18. Vries, "Dead Chimp's Art Sells Big."

19. Ibid.
20. Morris made this comment in connection with the Mayor Gallery ape art retrospective discussed subsequently in the text. See Andrew Dodds, "Ape Artists of the 1950s," *Frieze* 99 (2006), accessed November 5, 2015, http://www.frieze.com/issue/review/ape_artists_of_the_1950s/.
21. Waldemar Januszczak, "Monkey Master," *Artists Ezine* 1 (2006), accessed November 5, 2015, http://www.artistsezine.com/WhyChimp .htm. Januszczak's comments were published in the *London Sunday Times* ("Art: Congo the Chimpanzee," September 25, 2005, http://www .thesundaytimes.co.uk/sto/culture/article149103.ece) and in the *Australian* ("This Is a Masterpiece . . . and This Is the Artist—monkey Master," October 8, 2005, http://www.theaustralian.com.au/).
22. Thierry Lenain, *Monkey Painting* (London: Reaktion Books, 1997).
23. Beach, Fouts, and Fouts, "Representational Art in Chimpanzees," part 2, *Friends of Washoe Newsletter* 4, no. 1 (Fall [no year given]): 1. Washoe initiated drawing sessions when presented with an array of possible activities. She apparently developed representational schema, but these were not always the same as human ones for images like "dog" (pp. 1–3). I thank Roger Fouts for supplying this newsletter. Undated but, based on content, probably ca. 1985.
24. Erica Thiele, interview by the author in Bastrop, Texas, February 7, 2008.
25. In addition, mahouts have trained elephants to play percussion instruments on cue, resulting in CDs by the Thai Elephant Orchestra that are sold along with the elephant paintings to support the conservation site. Like the trained linear renditions that allow an elephant to paint a picture of an elephant, these trained actions result not in responsive improvisation with sound-making instruments but rather in the cued rendition of strikes in time with a human-composed script. Of course, we could say that this simply duplicates how a (human) orchestra normally plays—producing predetermined, prerehearsed sounds on cue—but we assume that with humans, an individual expressivity leaks out even within the most highly regimented musical scripts, and we reward that with accolades and positive critical reviews.

    Some human musicians seek a more collaborative engagement, and so bring their music to the elephants without training a response in advance. Electronic cellist Jamie Sieber recounts her experience in that regard at the Thai Elephant Conservation Center in a 2011 YouTube video. Invited to play music for a film being made there about the elephants, she instead plays with the elephant orchestra, but not in their pretrained way. She sits surrounded by them and plays *for* them, until they coalesce in a semicircle, physically enclosing her and responding to her sonic rhythms with high-pitched cries and untrained dancing motions of their heads, trunks swinging to the beat. See "Elephants Accompany Cellist Jamie Siever/ Part 2/Living Yoga," YouTube, accessed November 5, 2015, https://www

.youtube.com/watch?v=duSgIcEqUzQ&feature=youtube. I thank Mary Bennett for directing me to this video. We have yet to explore elephants' potential interest in sonic design and its use to communicate with humans, nor have we ascertained whether they have an interest in communicating with us through a visual medium of gestural mark making, or "art."

26. Now a regular part of the conservation site's activities and fund-raising sales, these artworks are promoted in the United States and elsewhere through auctions that Komar and Melamid, trading on their own somewhat outré reputations, help to get staged. One such auction, in March 2000 through Christie's in New York City, raised $75,000 in one evening, with all paintings by the elephants selling out, at prices ranging from $350 to $2,200. See Komar and Melamid, *When Elephants Paint: The Quest of Two Russian Artists to Save the Elephants of Thailand* (New York: Perennial Books, 2000), 75. For more on the Asian Elephant Art and Conservation Project, visit their website at http://www.asianelephantart.com, accessed November 5, 2015.

27. "Elephant Painting an Elephant," video posted January 23, 2014, on YouTube by "TeamWakeUp," accessed November 5, 2015, https://www.youtube.com/watch?v=yQv5mE42Yos. The linked Facebook page identifies a young African American man as the commentator.

28. See Nick Kontogeorgopoulos, "Wildlife Tourism in Semi-Captive Settings: A Case Study of Elephant Camps in Northern Thailand," *Current Issues in Tourism* 12 (2009): 429–49. See also my discussion of elephant painting in US zoos in the previous chapter, note 35.

29. Walter Benjamin, "The Work of Art in the Age of Mechanical Reproduction," in *Illuminations: Essays and Reflections*, ed. Hannah Arendt (New York: Schocken Books, 1969), 217–52.

30. As Benjamin L. Hart and Lynette A. Hart note, elephants excel at long-term spatial memory. See Benjamin L. Hart and Lynette A. Hart, "Unique Attributes of the Elephant Mind: Perspectives on the Human Mind," in *Experiencing Animal Minds: An Anthology of Animal-Human Encounters*, ed. Julie A. Smith and Robert W. Mitchell (New York: Columbia University Press, 2012), 186–200. This ability may help them to execute complicated, discrete, and spatially meaningful motions that result in the paintings I am discussing. As for the attribution of subjectivity, Hart and Hart note the importance of social empathy in elephant social bonds, including mourning of group members who die. The "mirror test," in which elephants are seen to recognize themselves in a mirror, is regarded as a prime measure of individuated subjectivity. The popular press has reported these findings, making them available in public discourse and influencing the popular perception that elephants are "intelligent" according to human standards. See, for example, John Roach, "Elephants Recognize Selves in Mirror, Study Says," *National Geographic News*, October 30, 2006, accessed

November 5, 2015, http://news.nationalgeographic.com/news/2006/10/
061030-asian-elephants.html. Humans and "higher" primates like chimpanzees also pass the mirror test.

31. Komar and Melamid, *When Elephants Paint*, 99.

32. See Gorilla Foundation, "Gorilla Art," accessed November 5, 2015, http://
www.koko.org/gorilla-art-0.

33. Copies of Michael's paintings may also be purchased at the Gorilla
Foundation's website, http://www.koko.org. Some critics feel that the
representational claims made for this painting are exaggerated. Indeed,
the studies with Koko have garnered significant academic skepticism from
some primate experts, and some have even expressed concerns about
the way that Koko is cared for. The larger world of ape language studies,
and of "bicultural" apes—like the bonobo Kanzi, who paints, and the
orangutan Chantek, who makes necklaces as well as drawings—forms
the background for this discussion of Koko, on whom I focus because of
what appears to be her explicit naming of some of her paintings, suggesting a link between verbal and visual representational techniques. While
scientists may debate the clarity of this linkage, the lay public embraces it
enthusiastically through the purchase of Koko's paintings.

34. It should be noted that American Sign Language is a full, complex language, and that Koko uses a form of ASL, not ASL per se.

35. Tomas Persson, *Pictorial Primates: A Search for Iconic Abilities in Great Apes*,
Lund University Cognitive Studies 136 (Lund, Sweden: Lund University,
2008). I thank Dr. Benjamin Beck for giving me a copy from his personal
library.

36. Ibid., 280.

37. Persson (ibid., chapter 2) discusses various experiments with young children that try to chart their developing competencies in iconic pictorial
representation, and he notes that while these capacities seem to develop
at a very young age, around two years, according to some studies, they
are developed in a constant context of naming, pointing, and behavioral
modeling by adults and of language directing attention and interpretation
(just think of the reading of bedtime stories). During the learning process,
children sometimes react to images as if they were the real thing, confus-
ing representation and material reality. "Realism" is a historically shifting
aesthetic. Compare early photography from the nineteenth century with
the three-dimensional movies in IMAX format today.

38. Ibid., 284.

39. Ibid., 276.

40. Lee Glendinning, "Spanish Parliament Approves 'Human Rights' for
Apes," *Guardian* (Manchester), June 26, 2008, accessed November 5,
2015, http://www.theguardian.com/world/2008/jun/26/humanrights
.animalwelfare.

41. Steven Wise is among those leading this legal battle. See Charles Siebert, "Should a Chimp Be Able to Sue Its Owner?," *New York Times Magazine*, April 23, 2014, accessed November 5, 2015, http://www.nytimes.com/ 2014/04/27/magazine/the-rights-of-man-and-beast.html.

CHAPTER TEN

1. Katherine Grier, *Pets in America: A History* (New York: Harcourt, 2007).
2. See George W. Stocking Jr., *Race, Culture, and Evolution: Essays in the History of Anthropology* (Chicago: University of Chicago Press, 1982). Encoded in laws, literature, belief systems, scientific practice, popular culture, and the actions of everyday life, the legacies of these historical "grand narratives," to use Jean-François Lyotard's term (see his *The Postmodern Condition: A Report on Knowledge* [Minneapolis: University of Minnesota Press, 1984]), remain with us still, even as we attempt to disrupt them and even as they are interrupted too by emergent beliefs and new practices, and by episte-mologies drawn from non-European-derived legacies.
3. Pet keeping as a social practice should also be seen in relation to larger projects of domestication of certain animals and not others, a relationship in which the animals historically codetermine part of that relationship. See Molly Mullin and Rebecca Cassidy, eds., *Where the Wild Things Are Now: Domestication Reconsidered* (New York: Bloomsbury Academic, 2007).
4. Now, knowing more about the breeding industry, I would not purchase a bird from a pet store. A dozen-plus years ago, however, I was ignorant of how my purchase supported this industry.
5. In late December 2014, after I had originally crafted this chapter, Blueboy died of a cancerous leg tumor. He had received outstanding care from his avian veterinarian, Dr. Ken Welle, and had lived with us for more than a dozen years. We had no idea how old he was when we adopted him, but he was surely at the high end of a parakeet's life span. I like to think of him as the oldest parakeet on record, even if this isn't true. Up to a day and a half before his death, Blueboy continued to clamber energetically on his playground and toss balls for interactive games, a true gift to our household. In his final hours, he made an active choice to be held in our hands rather than to rest in his compound.
6. Blueboy has unusual coloring, with a sky-blue breast and turquoise back accentuated by black-and-white feathers. He has a cere, or area above the nostrils, whose coloring in some species can indicate the sex as male or female. Using the normal markers, I'd assumed for a decade that Blue-boy was a boy. A few years ago, however, Dr. Welle, an avian specialist, revealed that Blueboy is not a "boy" at all but really is "Bluegirl": his pastel-blue coloring had confused his sexual designation. By the time I found out, it was too late for me to change his name and to reorient my

positioning of him as a male in the household . . . a bit of "gender trouble" in Judith Butler's sense, to be sure, but one I accepted with its own irony.

7. Irene Pepperberg's scientific experiments with her African grey parrot, Alex, have become widely known beyond scholars working on comparative cognition. See Irene Maxine Pepperberg, *The Alex Studies: Cognitive and Communicative Abilities of Grey Parrots* (Cambridge, MA: Harvard University Press, 2002). Alex died unexpectedly on September 6, 2007, at age thirty-one, and his death was mourned in private and in public through web-based communication by many bird lovers outside the scientific community. He had become a celebrity. "Brainy Parrot Dies, Emotive to the End" headlines the article about him in the science section of the *New York Times*. The article itself followed some of the conventional tropes of the obituary, as I discussed in chapter 6, although it appeared not in the obituary pages but in another part of the paper. See Benedict Carey, "Brainy Parrot Dies, Emotive to the End," *New York Times*, September 7, 2011, accessed November 5, 2015, http://www.nytimes.com/2007/09/11/science/11parrot.html?_r=0.

8. Harvey Black, "Crows Show Off Their Social Skills," *Scientific American Mind* 24, August 8, 2013, accessed November 5, 2015, http://www.scientificamerican.com/article/crows-show-off-social-skills.

9. For a stimulating study of avian ways of experiencing the world and an acknowledgment of our limitations to understanding them, see Tim Birkhead, *Bird Sense: What It's Like to Be a Bird* (New York: Walker, 2012). Other work examines the physiology of being in the world of other species, such as the sonar-echo imaging of bats and the importance of electrosensory capacities for fishes. Howard C. Hughes, in *Sensory Exotica: A World beyond Human Experience* (Cambridge, MA: MIT Press, 1999), offers many case studies of ways of being in the world that depend on sensory apparatuses different from our own. He acknowledges, without irony, that humans' interest in understanding the phenomenology of nonhuman animals is not "value-free" but will most probably be used to develop interventions that will affect, sometimes negatively, the animals studied. These include better "pest control," and will potentially affect humans as well. Studying other species' scent worlds, he suggests, might increase, for example, our understanding of the role of scent in human sexual attraction, a sort of comparative scent-sexology. A 1974 essay by Thomas Nagel is now a classic in this arena. See Nagel, "What Is It Like to Be a Bat?," *Philosophical Review* 83, no. 4 (1974): 435–50.

10. Jacques Derrida, *The Animal That Therefore I Am*, ed. Marie-Louise Mallet, trans. David Wills (New York: Fordham University Press, 2008), 14.

11. Louise Westling, "Still Anthropocentric," *New Formations: A Journal of Culture/Theory/Politics* 78 (2013): 201. She is discussing selections from Anne Emmanuelle Berger and Marta Segarra's edited book *Demenageries: Thinking (of) Animals after Derrida* (Amsterdam: Rodopi, 2011).

12. Derrida, "The Animal That Therefore I Am," in *The Animal That Therefore I Am*, 374; quoted in Donna J. Haraway, *When Species Meet* (Minneapolis: University of Minnesota Press, 2007), 19.

13. As Karl Steel notes, Derrida does not deny the specificity of the feline in front of him. In fact, he insists on it: "Derrida refuses to let his own cat stand in for universal felinity. He writes, 'If I say "it is a real cat" that sees me naked, it is in order to mark its unsubstitutable singularity. When it responds to its name (whatever *respond* means, and that will be our question), it doesn't do so as the exemplar of a species called cat, even less so of an animal genus or realm. It is true that I identify it as a male or female cat. But even before that identification, I see it as *this* irreplaceable living being that one day enters my space, enters this place where it can encounter me, see me, even see me naked. Nothing can ever take away from me the certainty that what we have here is an existence that refuses to be conceptualized.'" See Karl Steel, "How to Make a Human," *Exemplaria* 20 (2008): 21, quoting Derrida, "The Animal That Therefore I Am," 378–79. This language stops short of asking, and answering, how can we know more about "*this* irreplaceable living being"?

14. Haraway notes in *When Species Meet* that Derrida's goals include overturning the legacy of the Cartesian split between mind/body and between animal as body/human as mind that lingers so powerfully still. Yet in attempting to do that, he cannot seem to engage with the specific mind/beings of actual living, individual animals as the ground of philosophical thought, despite his insistence on the specificity of his feline companion and his abhorrence of the ways that legacies of speciesism subject animals to unimaginable violence.

15. Haraway, *When Species Meet*, 22.

16. Ibid., 23. I suspect that part of Haraway's palpable annoyance with this text is less about its pronouncements than about the influence it has among humanities scholars engaged in the emergent field of animal studies, for Derrida does not explicitly model a bringing together of philosophy and its power to help us interpret the actions of everyday life. What engagement with Derrida and other Continental philosophers does for animal studies scholars, in addition to the obvious intellectual grist it can provide, is signal to scholars who do *not* work on animals, and who might dismiss animal studies work on the basis of its object of analysis, that our scholarly work is worthy of respect and serious engagement. Bringing Derrida and others into central debates in animal studies provides evidence of gravitas to a set of emergent conversations in search of respect and institutional support as they develop.

Comparisons to other emerging arenas of scholarly work in the last few decades, and their strategies for developing or commanding respect in the academy, might be illuminating here. These new formations could include not only gender, sexuality, and women's studies, ethnic studies, and comparative studies of racialization but also studies of popular culture, music, dance, and film, each of which has had to, and sometimes still does, fight for recognition and legitimation in the intellectual force fields of the academy and its distribution of resources. Engaging with the work of scholars already widely respected in the US and European communities, including critiquing that work, is one way of claiming a shared legitimacy for emergent fields-in-formation as they wedge themselves into the academy.

17. Weil notes our difficulty in doing so: "As autobiographical animals, however, we may have difficulty, as does Derrida, thinking a principle of life outside of our own projects. What we can do is to track and scrutinize those projects, paying particular attention to how and for what purposes we construct difference." Kari Weil, "Animal Tracks, Review of *The Animal That Therefore I Am*, by Jacques Derrida," H-Net Reviews, H-Animal, October 2008, accessed November 5, 2015, http://www.h-net.org/reviews/showrev.php?id=22808.

18. Haraway, *When Species Meet*, 164. Haraway clarifies that this attitude is not to be classified as "posthumanism": "I see the regard I am trying to think and feel as part of something not proper to either humanism or posthumanism" (ibid.). Her cataloguing of aspects of "respect" draws on her own human family experience of growing up with her father and his legacy in modeling relationships. "Species and respect are in optic/haptic/affective/cognitive touch: they are at table together: they are mess-mates, companions, in company, *cum panis*. . . . 'Species' includes animal and human as categories, and much more besides; and we would be ill advised to assume which categories are in play and shaping one another in flesh and logic in constitutive encounterings" (ibid.).

19. Gilles Deleuze and Félix Guattari, *A Thousand Plateaus: Capitalism and Schizophrenia* (Minneapolis: University of Minnesota Press, 1987), 241–42; quoted in Haraway, *When Species Meet*, 28.

20. Haraway, *When Species Meet*, 29.

21. Deleuze and Guattari, *A Thousand Plateaus*, 240; quoted in Haraway, *When Species Meet*, 29.

22. I recognize that Deleuze's utopian theorization of "becomings" as ways of assembling new identities that exceed the conservative lines of social formations can be seen as a counterweight to this critique, and that some feminist scholars like Patty Sotirin see in the practice of daily life just such a potential for a Deleuzian reading (see her "Becoming Woman," in *Gilles Deleuze: Key Concepts*, ed. Charles J. Stivale [Montreal: McGill-Queens University Press, 2005], especially 105–6). My point here is that the complexities of daily life must be engaged, even in the search for evidence of such liberatory possibilities in action.

23. I use this phrase with a nod to the Dr. Doolittle storybook character, the two-headed camel-like being called the "pushmi-pullyu." This being had one head at each end of the body, and it was difficult to get a clear sense

of the direction in which he/she was moving. My use of the term, though, implies not a potentially paralytic canceling out of directional desires but a more mutually and constantly negotiated set of relations.

24. Giorgio Agamben, *Homo Sacer: Sovereign Power and Bare Life*, trans. Daniel Heller-Roazen (Stanford, CA: Stanford University Press, 1998 [1995]). Referenced in S. Eben Kirksey and Stefan Helmreich, "The Emergence of Multi-Species Ethnography," *Cultural Anthropology* 25, no. 4 (2010): 545–76.

25. See Leslie Irvine, "A Model of Animal Selfhood: Expanding Interactionist Possibilities," *Symbolic Interaction* 7 (2004): 3–21. Irvine's innovative work is another reason to keep the transdisciplinary formulation of "animal studies" alive in the humanities and social sciences, so that conversations cross from literary studies to sociology to anthropology to social history in vigorous and productive ways.

26. Ibid. See also her book *If You Tame Me: Understanding Our Connections with Animals* (Philadelphia: Temple University Press, 2004).

Index

Page numbers followed by the letter *f* refer to illustrations.

Ministry of Environment and Forests
(India), 247–48n15
Minnesota Association of Rogue Taxidermists, 252n17
Mitchell, Mark, 109, 294n30
Molesworth, Helen, 142
Morris, Desmond, 204, 205, 206, 207,
312n20
Mortuary Management, 117, 286n53
mourning: absence of mourning for roadkilled animals, 142, 144–45, 151–52,
157, 158; cemeteries' offering of a public validation of, 99, 275n63; cemeteries' prohibition against individualized
human memorials, 96; concept of a
"grievable life," 107–9, 111–12, 282–
83n38; democratization of death in
obituaries, 127–28; importance of the
physical site of the cemetery, 98–99,
274n63; invoking of rituals of mourning by roadkill observers, 145, 298n13;
material culture of grief and, 93,
272n49; motivation behind erecting
public memorials, 91–92; for pets (*see*
pet mourning); political act of public
mourning, 92, 110–11, 281–82n34,
282n38; possibility that animals
mourn, 147–48, 298–99nn18–19;
provisions for the "unborn" in cemeteries, 282n38, 287n63; responses to
artistic engagements with roadkill,
154–55; roadside memorials and,
93–94, 167f, 272–73n52; spontaneous
practices associated with tragedies,
93–94, 271–72n46, 272–73n52; subjectivity and the act of, 109, 281n31;
tombstone and casket design trends,
96, 273n55
Mr. Potter's Museum of Curiosities, 252n14
Mullin, Molly, 20
"multispecies ethnography," 20, 21,
249–50nn25–26
Munchkin (penguin), 183
museum displays. *See* Animal Inside Out
exhibition; Body Worlds exhibition;
taxidermy
Museum of Natural History, New York, 30
Museum of Science and Industry, Chicago,
Illinois, 53, 257n50, 260n7
Museum of Technology and Work,
Mannheim, Germany, 28

mutual ecologies model, 21–22
Muybridge, Eadweard, 30, 251n6

Nagel, Thomas, 316n9
Names Project Foundation AIDS Memorial
Quilt, 91
National Museum of Health and Medicine,
Washington, DC, 43
National Taxidermy Association, 31,
252n12
National Zoological Park, Washington,
DC, 264n27
Natural Science Establishment, Rochester,
New York, 30, 251n4
News Tribune (newspaper in Tacoma, WA),
130
New York burial laws, 121–22
New York Society for the Prevention of
Cruelty to Children (NYSPCC), 278n8
New York University, 248n16
Nonhuman Rights Project, 247–48n15
Norfolk Roadkill, Mainly (Baker), 152, 169f
Northern California Rat Community, 179

obituaries: cost of a newspaper obit, 129;
democratization of death in, 127–28;
format used, 136; for pets (*see* pet
obituaries); social hierarchies reflected
in, 128, 138–39, 292n10
octopuses and consciousness, 13, 247n14
Odin the Red-Tailed Hawk, 174, 179
Oklahoma City Zoo and Botanical Gardens, 183, 193, 208, 307n34
Olly and Suzi, 180
operant conditioning process: elephant
artists and, 213; teaching an ape to
paint, 208, 209; teaching a seal to
paint, 193–94, 307n35
Original Road Kill Cookbook, 156
otter artists, 309n37

Palgrave Macmillian, 14
Palmer, Claire, 157
parakeets, 233–34. *See also* Blueboy
Penn Forest Natural Burial Park, 123
Penn State University Press, 14
Penwith Pet Cemetery and Memorial
Gardens, 121
People for the Ethical Treatment of Ani-
mals (PETA), 40, 110, 151–52, 256n39,
272n53, 281n31

37866858R00212

Made in the USA
San Bernardino, CA
27 August 2016